T0373324

COMMUNITY-BASED ARCHAEOLOGY

ni kani gana — to all my relations
Looking to the future, and the world
of my sons' great-grandsons. With
hopes that they will consider this the
work of a good ancestor.

CONTENTS

PREFACE

Hundreds of years before European contact, my Ojibwe ancestors were told of future events by their spiritual leaders who warned of unimaginable changes that would take place with the coming of a "light-skinned people." These prophecies described the struggles that Anishinabe[1] people would face to keep our culture and ourselves alive. They foretold that our way of life would be nearly lost but would eventually be regained. Elders today explain that this was a prediction of both European colonization and the Native American cultural resurgence that started in the 1970s. As you will find in reading this book, community-based participatory research (CBPR) has a fundamental role to play in this resurgence.

As both an Anishinabe woman and an archaeologist, I set out to understand how archaeology might benefit from engaging CBPR. I started this research inspired by another central prophecy and teaching from Ojibwe oral history as related by Eddie Benton-Banai (1979), Grand Chief of the Three Fires Midewiwin Society: The teaching tells of a time when the Anishinabek, along with others globally, will face a choice between two paths. One path is made of scorched grass, signifying short-term success but eventual destruction. The other path is a lush trail that leads to a future of lasting peace. The teaching states that the second path is one of

---

1. The Anishinabek are the indigenous people from what is now the midwestern region of the United States and Canada. The Anishinabe peoples include Ojibwe, Odawa, and Potawatomi communities who share a cultural identity and are related through kinship and language.

compassion. Choosing this path involves finding ways to combine our Indigenous systems of knowledge and traditional ways of understanding with those of Western science. Joining these forms of knowledge can increase our strength as a society. Our spiritual leaders tell us we have reached the time to choose paths. The challenge for *our* generation is to work cooperatively—to use the diverse knowledge of all to build strength on the path to mutual success and peace.

This teaching has inspired my research on community-based participatory archaeology. I embarked on this investigation to explore archaeological research practices that allow for the "braiding knowledge" called for in my ancestors' teachings. I hoped to find a research methodology that enabled people with archaeological science and community knowledge to work together and complement one another, using practices that are sustainable long-term. I hoped the process could also benefit communities in their efforts to regain and strengthen their connections to their cultural heritage.

What I found was community-based participatory research—a research methodology that braids together knowledge systems in the very ways that Ojibwe teachings call for. This book outlines the principles and benefits of CBPR and details how community-based archaeology—done with, by, and for communities—is the framework for archaeology's future.

ACKNOWLEDGMENTS

This book exists because of the kind generosity, support, help, and wisdom of so many. I wrote the words (and take responsibility for any errors or shortcomings), but the work belongs to the individuals, families, and communities who partnered with me. I am so grateful for what you've taught me and what we've learned together. Miigwetch—all that you give I hold in the highest regard.

I'll begin by thanking the communities, governments, families, and individuals who worked on and supported the five CBPR projects presented in this book. Miigwetch to the Saginaw Chippewa Indian Tribe of Michigan, the Tribal Council, and the Ziibiwing Center of Anishinabe Culture & Lifeways. Ziibiwing's board of directors has always supported our collaborative endeavors, and the incredibly committed and talented staff made the magic happen. Bonnie Ekdahl had the initial vision for our work together, William Johnson gave such attention to detail with an unending concern for the ancestors, and Judy Pamp provided helpful guidance. Dorothea Botimer organized my travel and ensured all the loose ends (large and small) were resolved. Jennifer Jones assisted with images, Charla Burton's grant writing expertise was invaluable, and Anita Heard and Robin Spencer's research assistance and organization of site visits during the Native American Graves Protection and Repatriation Act (NAGPRA) project was instrumental. Your Ziibiwing team is a model of excellence.

Miigwetch to Charmaine Benz, Saginaw Chippewa Tribal Council member, for her commitment to the ancestors, her support of our research, and her example of encouraging her grandchildren to live and honor their culture. (Baby) Dave Merrill Jr. has been a role model for my sons. I also want to acknowledge the outstanding efforts of Dr. Beverley Smith, Frank Raslich, Nicole Raslich, and Ruby MeShaboose for their work in the field at the Flint Stone Street Ancestral Recovery Project.

I want to acknowledge and thank the elders and leadership of the Three Fires Midewiwin Society. Grand Chief Bawdwaywidun (Eddie Benton-Benaise) and Eastern Doorway Chief Onaubinisay (Jim Dumont) shared spiritual teachings and provided assistance and guidance during repatriation research and ezhi-biighadek asin/Sanilac petroglyph project. Odawa (George Martin), Three Fires Ogichidaw Chief, Ogimaa kwe (Sydney Martin), and Grandmothers' Council and Midewanikwe shared knowledge and guidance during all Ziibiwing partnerships. The Shananaquets provided love, support, and much-needed humor, always in the right balance. All of you live the 7 Grandfather Teachings in your work every day. You each continue to teach and inspire me.

Sincere thanks to the Kültür ve Turizm Bakanlığı (Turkish Ministry of Culture and Tourism) and Çumra Belediye Başkanı Yusuf Erdem for allowing me the pleasure of working in your beautiful homeland. I worked with two muhtars in Kücükköy (Ali Bey and Hasan Husein Bey), two school principals (Murat Bey and Mehmet Ali Bey), and numerous teachers at the Kücükköy-Çatalhöyük Ilk Okülü. Thank you all—for your support, innovative ideas, and assistance with the many projects that have now sprouted from our work together. It's beautiful to see Kücükköy's children and residents as such positive and progressive models for others in Turkey and abroad. Sincere respect and thanks to Çumra's Kaymakam for meeting with me to discuss heritage tourism and for being supportive of village-level inclusion. Ian Hodder and Shahina Farid had the vision, energy, and patience to make the Çatalhöyük project happen. I looked at Çatalhöyük's shelters and buildings from satellite images online today and was moved and overwhelmed, thinking: *Wow—Ian and Shahina—you did this!* A true legacy. Sema Bağcı is an incredible scholar with a heart that matches her intellect. The Çatalhöyük CBPR project thrives because of her. Thanks to the entire Çatalhöyük "family" of team members, past and present.

Many families in Kücükköy, Dedemoğlu, Karkın, Hayıroğlu, Abditolu, and Çumra opened their homes and hearts to me. I am humbled by your generosity and thank you all. I want to particularly acknowledge the partnership, help, and hard work of Çatalhöyük's security team: Mustafa Tokyağsun, Hasan Tokyağsun, and Ibrahim Eken. The kitchen team gave us wonderful meals and warm smiles, with particular thanks to Chef Ismail Salmancı. The project interns—Rahime

Salur, Nesrin Salur, and Ebru Sivas—were fantastic to work with. Levent provided many early-morning rides to and from the bus stop. Yasemin Özarslan and Filiz Toprak both served as translators. Lewis Jones (in 2008) and Burcu Tung (in 2006) also assisted the CBPR work, each for a season: I learned important lessons from each of them. Sheena Ketchum kept the "balls rolling" in the clay lab, allowing me to focus on the CBPR work. Duygu Çamurcuoğlu Serdar Bilis, and Kemal Öruç gave energy, passion, and vision to the Community Theatre project. Gülay Sert offered many helpful insights and suggestions.

Sincere thanks to the fantastic team that worked on the Waapaahsiki Siipiiwi mound project. Our partners at the Sullivan County American Indian Council, particularly SCAIC President Reg Petoskey and Treasurer Susan Petoskey, brought passion and dedication to the project. Indiana Senator John Waterman's support of Native people in Indiana and the Waapaahsiki Siipiiwi project is so appreciated. Susan Alt provided extensive volunteer labor (intellectual and physical) on the SCAIC project. Cheryl Munson generously loaned us equipment. Students in Susan Alt's Cultural Resource Management course at Indiana University volunteered their time doing fieldwork. Maura Hogan volunteered many hours to analyze the artifacts. Zarko Tankosic and Kaeleigh Herstad spent happy hours together writing the final report. Miigwetch to each of you. I hope we can walk together along the Waapaahsiki Siipiiwi trail some day.

I want to thank my colleagues, friends, and students at Indiana University, particularly Anne Pyburn, Beverly Stoeltje, and Beth Buggenhagen. Discussions with IU graduate students in the 2008 and 2009/10 CBPR classes helped me work through some challenging ideas. The administrative staff in IU's anthropology department cannot be topped. Special thanks to Linda Barchet and Jena Hanes for helping me wade through the financials. Denise Breton did a wonderful job assisting me with editing.

Thank you to those who conceived of, work for, and support the Ford Foundation! The Ford Postdoctoral Fellowship gave me quiet time to write this book, and the mentorship of other Ford fellows is priceless. Know that I continue to lift as I climb. The Closet Chickens provide a special kind of support. It's been challenging to blaze a trail with you and I look to the future we are building together for archaeology. Linda Tuhiwai Smith's work has been inspirational—it challenged me to think about how we might decolonize the way research is done in archaeology.

My sincere gratitude to the organizations that funded the research for this book: the Social Science and Humanities Research Council of Canada funded the ezhibiigadek asin/Sanilac Petroglyph project through their support of the Intellectual Property Issues in Cultural Heritage (IPinCH) Project. The National Science Foundation (Proposal # 0512031) provided me two years to get these projects off the ground, and the National NAGPRA Program funded Ziibiwing's repatriation research. Indiana University's Center for Arts and Humanities Institute provided support through a Travel/Research grant.

It has been a pleasure to work with the University of California Press. Thank you to Blake and his team for putting all the pieces together and making this a painless process. Thanks Randy McGuire for walking me over to Blake's Society for American Archaeology booth and for your kind introduction. Five reviewers provided helpful comments and critiques of this work, and the book is stronger as a result. Thank you for your time.

My family is my foundation—they provide laughter, strength, guidance, and a depth of love that can't be measured. They ground me, and that makes everything else possible. My boys never falter—my husband Ted, and my three sons Niigani, Bungishimo neemi, and Kige koons are my light. If there is heart and a spirit in this work, it came from their hugs and "nuggles." I am eternally grateful to Creator for bringing Ted into my life. There is no greater gift. Miigwetch, Ted, for your unending support. I'm so thankful for the trusted caregivers who look after my family when I'm working; they provide such a vital gift: peace of mind and love to our future generation. For that, I want to thank the teachers and staff of both IU's day care facilities as well as Rukiye Salmancı of Çumra and the women of the Tokyağsun family in Küçükköy.

And finally, thank you to Shannon Martin and Amy Lonetree. You are my sisters and my friends. The support and care you provide make the challenges and joys of navigating the academic world one of my life's great adventures. You are both true ogichidaw kwe. It can never be enough, but to you both I give a heartfelt miigwetch/pinigigi.

ONE · A Sustainable Archaeology

Archaeology is at an exciting juncture. As those in the field explore new directions, facets of archaeological research simultaneously evoke tensions, raise ethical dilemmas, and open possibilities. One such area is how archaeologists have engaged with Indigenous, descendant, and local communities. The past two decades have brought important changes to the ways archaeologists see these communities and are shifting their relations with them.

Another area of change is how archaeologists engage the public at large. Public involvement, heritage management, and collaboration with communities are now major concerns, and archaeologists are responding to the public with serious scholarly attention. The public shows a growing interest in archaeology. Beyond reading about archaeology, people are visiting archaeological sites and participating in cultural heritage tourism in higher numbers (Gazin-Schwartz 2004; Holtorf 2007). One recent study (Mandala 2009) found that 78 percent of all U.S. leisure travelers (118.3 million adults each year) now participate in cultural and/or heritage activities.

As archaeology matures as a discipline, archaeologists (and those outside the field) have begun to reflect critically on its current and future directions. The movement toward community engagement and heritage management combined with archaeology's involvement with heritage tourism demand that archaeologists develop new skills, methodologies, and practices. The next generation of archaeologists will be quite different from those of past decades, and as a result, archaeology students must master new types of skills and training.

Pondering the goals and potentials of social science research in the decades to come, Paulo Freire (Couto 1995, 25) argued for the need to "problematize the future." He stated that, "The future depends on what we change or what we preserve." Freire, a Brazilian sociologist, is widely known for developing collaborative research partnerships with community members in his home country. His work focused on solving community-identified problems, most notably, adult illiteracy. His concept is profound: strengthen human agency over the possible futures that people and communities can create (Couto 1995). To meet the needs of the next generation, archaeologists need to actively, intentionally "problematize the future." What does that mean? Among other things, it means thinking hard about involving communities. And it means engaging with archaeological places and landscapes in ways that have long-term sustainability.

If we problematize archaeology's future, three important considerations come to the forefront: the issue of *relevance,* the question of *audience,* and concerns about *benefits.* Archaeological research is not a necessity to most nonarchaeologists; it is a luxury. Moreover, this luxury has real-world economic, social, and political impacts on people's daily lives. These consequences continue long after excavations end. In decades past, archaeologists often did not think about these impacts, nor did they hold themselves as accountable for them. For some time now, however, archaeologists have been grappling with how to define their relationship with the contemporary world. They simply cannot function as they once did.

Notably, archaeologists now struggle with how archaeological research relates to society. They are concerned with questions such as: Who has access to archaeological research? Who benefits? In what ways? Although concerns of relevance are now central, these are not new issues for archaeologists. Fritz and Plog (1970, 412) raised these issues four decades ago, and their words apply today: "We suspect that unless archaeologists find ways to make their research increasingly relevant to the modern world, the modern world will find itself increasingly capable of getting along without archaeologists." Archaeological projects compete for funding dollars and public attention against life-and-death problems: wars, public health issues, human rights concerns, and environmental collapse (Pyburn 2003; Sabloff 2008). Archaeological research may not seem as urgent or important in the minds of taxpayers and citizens. However, the ethical implications of conducting archaeological research are immense. Excavations and cultural tourism have had many negative effects on community members, who have been routinely excluded from heritage management and decision making.

In many communities where archaeologists work, local residents have limited access to the knowledge and other benefits from the research that is taking place in their own backyards. Clearly, archaeologists must become more involved with and must make their work relevant to wider, nonacademic audiences. Some archaeologists now engage communities in the archaeological process to increase archaeology's relevance. "Community archaeology" is growing. Over the past two decades, archaeologists globally are increasingly intersecting in complex and nuanced ways with a range of descendant and nondescendant communities and public audiences (Marshall 2002; Simpson 2010). These developments offer positive directions for archaeology. Elsewhere, I've argued that they constitute a paradigm shift toward collaborative research within the field—a shift that is occurring across the social sciences (Atalay 2008b).

To develop effective methods for collaborating with descendant and local communities, we have to look critically at current archaeological practices with an eye to improving them. Developing collaborative methods and practices for archaeology while creating the theoretical and ethical guidelines that must accompany such practices holds the promise of building a possible future for archaeology. It is an archaeology that is engaged, relevant, ethical, and, as a result, sustainable.

COMMUNITY-BASED PARTICIPATORY RESEARCH

Relevance and audience are not new issues for archaeology. However, the discipline now seems serious about addressing them. Archaeology's future direction appears closely linked with successes in these areas. Already, many archaeologists seem interested in exploring how to involve local communities in research in substantive ways. Most archaeologists today take seriously the need to share knowledge *results* with multiple, diverse publics through archaeological education programs. However, democratizing knowledge *production* now forms a cutting edge of change for archaeologists and how they do their work. The theoretical basis for collaborative practice is firmly established in archaeology. What remains to be established are effective methods for putting collaborative theories and concepts into practice. Problematizing the future of archaeology requires identifying new methodologies. This is what we need to create the future we envision as possible for our discipline.

There are many ways to work collaboratively in archaeology. Community-based participatory research (or CBPR) is one approach. It has remarkable potential for archaeologists who seek to engage with Indigenous groups and a wide range of public audiences and local communities. For example, CBPR brings reciprocal benefits to each partner, and it allows communities to build capacity in many ways. Another central CBPR tenet is to value information and ways of knowing contributed from diverse knowledge systems. This is crucial for archaeology and communities, because Indigenous people and other descendant and local communities have experienced disenfranchisement from their own past and their own ways of understanding, engaging with, and preserving it.

Stoecker (2004) provides an excellent example of the value CBPR places on community knowledge in his discussion of the hantavirus outbreak in the southwestern United States in 1993. Those studying the outbreak were initially unsuccessful at pinpointing the virus killing people on the Navajo reservation. Community members were not comfortable talking about death with outsiders, leaving the U.S. Centers for Disease Control (CDC) with no useful data to solve the health crisis. Relying on Navajo traditional knowledge, a Navajo public health researcher used CBPR principles and practices to identify the virus and its cause. Navajo teachings told of the connection between excess rainfall and increased mouse populations, which would result in bad luck and poor health. This knowledge, combined with what Stoecker terms "scientifically derived knowledge," helped those involved to identify and control the hantavirus outbreak.

This traditional Navajo knowledge is now listed on the CDC website. The experience led the CDC to develop community advisory committees that support further community-based research practices. CBPR played a critical role in solving this health crisis by taking seriously Navajo teachings, which have too often been dismissed as "myth" or "storytelling." Stoecker concludes, "Lives were lost by ignoring community knowledge, and others were saved by treating that knowledge as legitimate."

A CBPR approach combines knowledge that has been arrived at through different traditions and experiences: This is one of its great strengths. CBPR also requires that scholars and community members develop equitable partnerships. Their projects must be community-driven and must address concerns that matter to members of descendant and local groups.

These principles of CBPR set the research compass for this book. My goal has been to explore how the principles and practices of CBPR can apply to archaeology. How would working together within a CBPR framework to create knowledge that is beneficial to both archaeologists and communities look "on the ground"? How might CBPR change day-to-day practice and fieldwork? What challenges might be involved, and are they insurmountable? How might these practices impact, even change, the way the archaeological research of the next century is developed, funded, and carried out?

ARCHAEOLOGY THAT MATTERS

Lives are rarely saved or lost in archaeological research. Archaeologists don't cure epidemics, solve poverty, stop the abuse of battered women, or save our diminishing forests. But the archaeological record is not only a *finite* resource but also a very important one. We can all benefit and learn from it. In his recent book, *Archaeology Matters*, Sabloff (2008) provides examples of how archaeology projects make a difference in the real world. Others demonstrate how archaeology figures prominently in nationalism (Arnold 1992; Kohl and Fawcett 1996; Kohl, Kozelsky, and Ben-Yehuda 2007; Meskell 1998); politics (Kane 2003; Layton 1989; McGuire 2008; Shanks 2004); and in documenting genocide (Komar 2008; Martin 1995; Zimmerer 2008).

Furthermore, many communities care deeply about the sacred areas, cultural places, and archaeological sites that are near them or to which they have a cultural connection. CBPR can help communities solve their problems—real problems in the real world. Multiple knowledge systems and forms of data can contribute immensely to understanding the past and to managing and protecting archaeological sites and materials. The reciprocal nature of CBPR means that, while partnering with communities in ways that benefit communities, archaeologists also research subjects of interest to them. CBPR provides a method for a community and an archaeologist to work together to pursue a research design that benefits them both as equal partners. Both build skills and increase knowledge that can be applied to other areas of research, particularly for how sites can be protected and managed respectfully.

The methodology of community-based research is a crucial step forward for archaeology. It moves concerns about sustainable, reciprocal research with communities from theory to practice. At least, this is what CBPR aims to do. But the inevitable questions follow: How does this goal translate into practice? How does CBPR hold up on the ground in real-life archaeological fieldwork situations with diverse communities across the globe?

THE GLOBAL APPLICABILITY OF CBPR FOR ARCHAEOLOGY

Today, archaeological research and cultural tourism are having major impacts on a diverse range of descendant and local communities globally. Many people, in communities and academia, are concerned about managing and protecting cultural places and materials. As state and national budgets tighten, local communities may continue to find themselves pulled further into heritage management. They may also be the ones expected to care for and protect traditional cultural properties. Although much of the CBPR research has been done with Indigenous communities or with those who are economically disadvantaged, the approach is not limited to them. A growing literature now documents how CBPR is being used outside of poor, "minority," or marginalized communities. All of this makes CBPR equally relevant and timely for archaeological collaborations with a wide range of descendant and local communities. I first experienced the power of the CBPR approach on the ground in an archaeological research partnership with a community in Turkey.

I came to understand the global applicability of CBPR for archaeology through analyzing clay and studying foodways at Çatalhöyük, a 9,000-year-old village site in rural Turkey. After only a short time of doing archaeological research at Çatalhöyük, I realized that I had to draw on different knowledge systems, work in partnership with the community, and create research that was relevant locally. These core values of CBPR are, I learned, as important in rural Turkey as they are among Native Americans or any other descendant community.

In North America and other Indigenous communities, cultural and spiritual beliefs and kinship connection to the places and items of the past are powerful and must factor into the research equation. Not so in rural Turkey. There, other factors held sway. Gender differences, class standing, and other issues of power played central roles in disenfranchising people from their heritage. What I found most surprising is how deeply entwined these issues are with archaeology in Turkey. Even—or perhaps especially—among local residents in the villages surrounding Çatalhöyük, where people espoused no cultural connection to the site where a 100-person team of foreign excavators had come to investigate.

My early convictions about involving local communities in the research process were confirmed once I learned the Turkish language. I spent time living locally and talking in more substantive ways with community members in the region. Local residents regularly spoke to me and others about their involvement with the site as laborers, and they were pleased to have the income that working at the site provided (Bartu 2005). Although locals clearly demonstrated interest in the research being carried out, a level of disenfranchisement had obviously taken place. They were disconnected from the cultural heritage of their country.

The Çatalhöyük project is exceptional for its concern with the social context of archaeology. This is not surprising. The project's director, Ian Hodder, has written extensively about multivocality and has developed a "reflexive methodology" (Hodder 1999). Several social anthropologists have studied the inner workings of the archaeology taking place at Çatalhöyük—and with the full support of Dr. Hodder and the Çatalhöyük project.

Social anthropologist Ayfer Bartu has done some excellent work on the role of communities at the Çatalhöyük site, and her findings are central to the discussion. Bartu's research (1999, 2000, 2005, 2007) focuses on the impact that archaeological excavations at Çatalhöyük have had on local residents. She has documented the economic and social benefits as well as other consequences of the excavations locally. Bartu's work also demonstrates that involving nonarchaeologists in doing archaeology is as relevant and of value among the rural communities in Turkey as it is in Native North America or elsewhere. The local circumstances are different, but the relevance is clear. A methodology that involves communities in the research process (making it participatory) gives communities the power to create and share knowledge that is relevant and of use to them (community-based). Archaeology can only benefit by embracing these values and methods.

ARCHAEOLOGY'S COMPLEX RELATIONSHIPS WITH INDIGENOUS COMMUNITIES

Within many Indigenous communities, the move to make research accessible and relevant involves Indigenous peoples not only as important *audiences* for research but also as partners in planning the research and carrying it out. This shift away from research "on and for" communities toward research "by and with" them is well under way in Native American and Indigenous studies (McNaughton and Rock 2003; Jackson 1993). It is also seen in public health, natural resource management, and sociology.

At this juncture of the discipline, archaeology's sustainability is linked to collaboration. Research endeavors must be relevant to, accessible by, and done for the benefit of local communities. When we consider the future of archaeology, especially in view of what young scholars entering the profession want to do, the direction is unmistakably toward collaboration with communities. For the next generation of archaeology students, these concepts seem to form a fundamental and natural part of their knowledge base. In response, their education and training require effective and rigorous models of collaborative practice.

Yet, negotiating collaborative relationships remains complex, especially between archaeologists and Indigenous peoples. In the United States, consultations between archaeologists, museum professionals, and Native Americans have increased as a result of legal mandates: most notably, the National Historic Preservation Act of 1966 and its amendments; the National Museum of the American Indian Act (NMAI Act) of 1989; and the Native American Graves Protection and Repatriation Act (NAGPRA) of 1990. Some of the consultations initiated under NAGPRA or the NMAI Act developed into collaborations between communities and archaeologists. Positive working relationships grew beyond those required by law. Collaborations also developed between archaeologists and Indigenous communities independent of laws, both in the United States and in other settler countries, including Canada, New Zealand, and Australia.

Archaeologists and communities—Indigenous peoples as well as descendant and nondescendant, local resident groups—are, in fact, improving existing relationships and forming positive new ones. Recent literature gives evidence of this trend. When the will to work together exists, Indigenous people and archaeologists can find ways to partner effectively in conducting archaeological projects that produce rigorous results of interest and use for both partners (for example, Allen et al. 2002; Ardren 2002; Clarke et al. 2002; Crosby 2002; Dongoske 2000; Ferguson and Colwell-Chanthaphonh 2006; Fredericksen 2002; Friesen 2002; Gonzalez et al. 2006; Kerber 2006; Nicholas and Andrews 1997; Rossen 2006, 2008; Swidler 1997; Silliman 2008a; Smith and Jackson 2007; Smith and Wobst 2005; Wilcox 2009). According to this literature, working together in various capacities on archaeological projects can be highly productive and successful.

However, tensions remain. Native Americans and other Indigenous communities do not always see eye to eye with archaeologists. While the number and variety of collaborative projects have increased, archaeologists engage with Indigenous and other descendant communities mostly for public education or in a consultative format. Unfortunately, these relationships still do not involve equal partnerships or substantive power sharing. Yet that is precisely what is required to move toward a decolonized archaeology that can have not just long-term sustainability but also moral integrity as a discipline. Archaeologists, Native American studies scholars, as well as community members and American Indian policy makers have all called for improved relationships, which involves more substantive partnerships with American Indian nations. Amy Lonetree (in press, 2012) has examined museums and their changing relationships with and representations of Native Americans through time. She points out (2008) that archaeologists and museum professionals often subscribe to a "narrative of progress" for archaeology and museology, yet critical imbalances between these professions and Indigenous communities remain unresolved. Similarly, Boast (2011) points to the "fundamental asymmetries, appropriations, and biases" that museums of the twenty-first century must still address.

A major issue in the United States is the struggle of many Native peoples to repatriate nearly 125,000 Native American individuals who have been termed "culturally unidentifiable" and who are held by museums and federal agencies throughout the country. The Native American Rights Fund, the National Congress of American Indians, along with many Native American nations have stated their positions on this issue of culturally unidentifiable human remains, and their positions are markedly different from most professional museum and scientific organizations (Atalay 2008a; Marek-Martinez 2008). Within the area of Indigenous archaeology, a number of scholars (Atalay 2006, 2007, 2008b, 2010; Jackson and Smith 2005; Nicholas 2006; Smith and Jackson 2006; Smith and Wobst 2005) are working to resolve the tensions between Indigenous communities and archaeologists by moving the discipline toward a decolonized practice. Efforts to decolonize archaeology reflect broader critiques of research methods as well as cross-disciplinary calls for decolonizing the way research is planned and conducted on a global scale.

PALPABLE TENSIONS, EXCITING POSSIBILITIES

The research I present in this book moves within a complex position: palpable tensions exist alongside exciting possibilities. CBPR methodologies emerged from critiques of conventional researcher-driven approaches and from scholarship and activism that names and problemitizes the power imbalances in current practices. CBPR strives to conduct research based in communities and founded upon core community values. With these broader critiques in mind, I wanted to consider how archaeology might be practiced if the concepts of decolonization and postcolonial theory were applied to the discipline. How might archaeological research change to create a reciprocal practice that truly benefits communities, at least as much as it benefits the scholarly interests of archaeologists?

DECOLONIZING RESEARCH PRACTICES

Scholars, activists, and community members have raised critiques of current research practices in general (Smith 1999; Wilson 2004; Mihesuah 1998, 2000, 2005; Mihesuah and Wilson 2004; Nahanni 1977) and particularly of anthropological research (Deloria Jr. 1969; Smith 1999; McNaughton and Rock 2003; Sahota 2009). They claim that much of the research process exploits Native Americans and other Indigenous peoples, because these peoples are viewed only as research subjects. Also, the knowledge that such research produces is neither accessible nor of benefit to the community being studied. Joe Garcia, president of the National Congress of American Indians, notes, "Historically, researchers, and anthropologists have visited our communities to extract information from us, frequently misinterpreting and misusing it, and have minimized the validity of our Indigenous knowledge" (Garcia 2009, 1). The recent dispute between Arizona State University (ASU) and the Havasupai tribe over blood samples obtained for diabetes research demonstrates the concerns that Indigenous communities have with research. In the Havasupai case, an anthropologist and a genetic researcher initiated a study of diabetes that involved blood samples. The samples were later used for research not related to understanding and solving the community's diabetes concerns. The community never gave their consent for their blood to be used in additional studies. After nearly a decade of disagreement and investigation, ASU paid the Havasupai tribe a settlement of $700,000 (Harmon 2010). In comments about the case, tribal members made it clear that they were not against research, but simply that it must be done appropriately. They spoke about the ways that the research benefited the scholars who conducted it but did nothing to help the Havasupai community. In fact, as several tribal members noted, it harmed the community. It produced information that was in contradiction to their traditional origin stories. The research may even hurt the tribe's land claims.

To address outcomes such as this, scholars and communities call for research that is community-driven and that produces results relevant for the communities involved. Many scholars go further to argue for a decolonizing approach to research that aims to resolve some of the long-standing tensions between researchers and communities (Bishop 1998; Smith 1999, 2000, 2005, 2006; Denzin, Lincoln, and Smith 2008; Soto 2004; Mutua and Swadener 2004). In her book, *Decolonizing Methodologies: Research and Indigenous Peoples*, Linda Tuhiwai Smith both analyzes the problems with exploitative research practices and outlines the need for developing a set of "decolonizing methodologies." As Smith defines it, decolonizing research does not involve "a total rejection of all theory or research or Western knowledge. Rather, it is about centering our concerns and world views and then coming to know and understand theory and research from our own perspectives and for our own purposes" (1999, 39).

Approaches to decolonizing archaeology and postcolonial critiques have gained momentum in recent years (for example, Atalay 2006; Liebmann and Rizvi 2008; Schmidt 2009; Rizvi and Lydon 2010; Smith and Wobst 2005). Applied to archaeology, decolonizing centers research on Indigenous concerns and concepts about the past (for example, see Atalay 2007, 2008b). It also identifies effective research models for working in partnership with, by, and for Indigenous communities (Atalay 2006). CBPR is a central part of a decolonizing approach to archaeological research, because it provides a methodology that is both rigorous and ethically minded, while also being community-driven and involving community members in a respectful, participatory way that values them as research partners.

The result is that archaeological knowledge is produced in full partnership with communities and aimed at addressing their research concerns and questions. Applying a CBPR model to archaeology resolves some of the tensions between archaeologists and members of Indigenous communities. My comparative analyses of a number of archaeological CBPR projects shows how CBPR is "able to resolve the permanent tension between the process of knowledge generation and the use of that knowledge, between the 'academic' and the real worlds, between intellectuals and workers, between science and life" (Vio Grossi 1980, 70).

Interest in CBPR has come not only from the academic world. Native American communities, many of whom had negative reactions to research of any kind, are involved in creating knowledge that benefits their communities using a CBPR approach. The National Congress of American Indians Policy Research Center provides an excellent example. The Policy Research Center is a tribally driven think tank that supports American Indian self-determination by compiling data, building tribal research capacity, providing research support, and convening forums on critical policy questions. Its website presents a series of modules about the research process written for Native American community use and developed through direct community involvement and feedback. The modules recommend a community-based participatory research model as a way for American Indian people to claim research as a tool for themselves. The modules explain how to conduct research in harmony with core tribal values while building community capacity (National Congress of American Indians Policy Research Center 2009).

FIVE ARCHAEOLOGICAL CBPR PROJECTS

The comparative analysis of archaeological CBPR presented in this book is grounded in theory, but it also stems from something more than abstract concepts or decolonizing theories. It is grounded in practical necessity. I needed to identify a working process for conducting collaborative research in the places where I am from and where I work. Initially, I hoped to develop and create research that could be done with, by, and for the local residents in Turkey. They are the ones most impacted by the excavations and cultural tourism taking place in their communities near the archaeological site of Çatalhöyük.

This research started as a two-year postdoctoral study funded by the National Science Foundation. I aimed to document the collaborative process from the earliest planning stages in very different locations. My hope was to gain a better understanding of the problems and challenges archaeologists and community partners face in conducting community-based research and how these might be minimized or even resolved. I also hoped to understand how CBPR methodologies might allow for more culturally effective means of sharing archaeological knowledge once it was produced.

To move from theory to practice and to address how CBPR can be applied to archaeology on the ground—through fieldwork—I conducted comparative research using CBPR methods in different settings. These comparative projects helped me understand how to use a CBPR methodology within an archaeological context. All five projects have been developed and are being conducted in partnership with communities from the United States and Turkey. Each followed a different path to its development, and each set out to achieve different goals. But all share the common thread of having been developed and conducted in full partnership with a community, using the principles and methodology of community-based participatory research. The projects also share a commitment to reciprocity. That is, each addresses community goals, while at the same time providing information that serves my primary research goal, which is to better understand the potential of CBPR in archaeology.

ÇATALHÖYÜK CBPR PROJECT

The first CBPR project was organized with rural village residents near the archaeological site of Çatalhöyük, Turkey (see Map 1). I had worked at Çatalhöyük as an archaeologist studying clay materials and cooking processes for nearly ten years, and I had developed close connections with local residents who lived nearby and worked on-site. This made Çatalhöyük an ideal choice to begin a research partnership. The project involved working with local educators, community leaders, and village residents to develop research partnerships that make aspects of the research at Çatalhöyük accessible and useful to local communities.

Using long-established contacts from previous ethno-archaeology work in the region, I worked with residents from six nearby towns and villages (Küçükköy, Çumra,

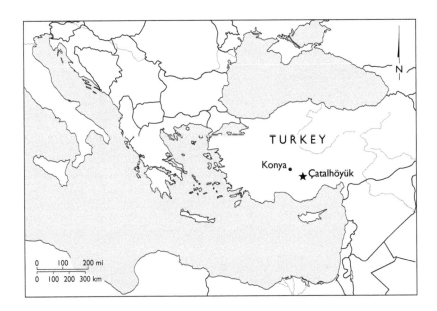

MAP 1.
Eastern Mediterranean region. The Çatalhöyük site, in
south-central Turkey, is marked with a star.

Karkın, Abdıtolu, Dedemoğlu, and Hayıroğlu) (see Map 2) to develop a community based participatory research design. These communities were chosen as potential partners because of their close geographic connection to the Çatalhöyük site.

Building on Bartu's work (1999, 2000, 2006) with the local communities around Çatalhöyük, I originally aimed to put together a team of archaeologists and local community members. Together, we would develop a series of regular community meetings that would create a two-way sharing of information about the research at Çatalhöyük. Local communities would participate in designing some of the research questions that they, in partnership with archaeologists, would investigate. The aim was to expand the concept of "the site"—a method that Bartu advocates (Bartu 2000, Bartu Candan 2006). The idea was to involve local communities in the Çatalhöyük research by working with local residents to develop and answer research questions that meet community needs.

In 2006, I initiated the project by conducting a series of interviews with residents from the six local communities I just named. I had hoped these interviews could identify the level of interest that community members had in archaeology and the roles they might like to have in archaeological research at the site. However, community members

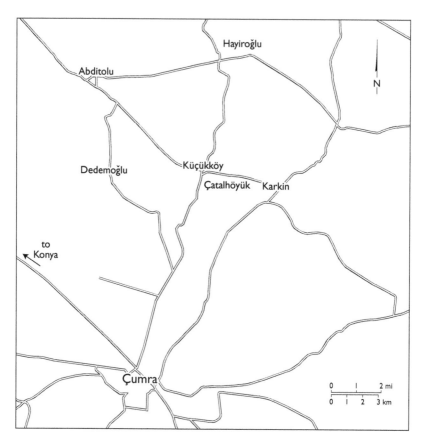

MAP 2.

Çatalhöyük and the surrounding town and villages.

told me that they felt they knew far too little to contribute to a community partnership. Following community needs and suggestions, I continued to talk with local residents about their interest in the research at Çatalhöyük and archaeology generally and about which next-steps might be appropriate for them to partner with archaeologists.

The CBPR project developed from the suggestions and ideas raised during those interviews. The next step focused on creating and distributing archaeological educational materials to local residents: a regular newsletter, informational kiosks, site and lab tours and visits, a comic series for children, and an onsite annual community festival. They served to educate local children and adults in natural and fun ways about the archaeological research taking place and what was involved in managing and protecting the site.

Through regular feedback and input from the local community, the partnership expanded to include a much wider range of projects. Each built community capacity for research and fund-raising, while also increasing local involvement in the management, protection, and heritage tourism at the Çatalhöyük site. And, we have a number of projects currently in development. A traveling archaeological theater troupe is now being trained; a women's craft cooperative is using the dig house buildings (both during and outside of summer field seasons) to create handicrafts with archaeological designs to sell in nearby art and tourist markets; an internship research training program has been created; and a village-based community cultural heritage board is in place to participate in regional site planning and management decision making (Atalay 2010). Although this collaboration did not follow the path I expected and was slow to get started, it has made incredible strides and continues to grow. Community interest and trust in the research process are expanding.

ZIIBIWING REPATRIATION RESEARCH PROJECT

The second CBPR project that informs this analysis of CBPR methodologies involves my working partnership with the Ziibiwing Cultural Center. This is a community-based organization (CBO) that developed and now directs both a tribal museum and the cultural society of the Saginaw Chippewa Indian Tribe of Michigan (see Map 3). Like the Çatalhöyük collaboration, this partnership was also an obvious choice, but for different reasons. I am Ojibwe myself and, as an Indigenous archaeologist, I feel it is important to highlight the perspectives of a Native American community that is partnering productively in archaeological research. I also wanted to understand the ways that being a Native American working in a Native American context might affect the CBPR partnership, possibly in both positive and negative ways.

In stark contrast to the Çatalhöyük community partnership, my research with Ziibiwing got off to a very quick start. Bonnie Ekdahl, Ziibiwing's director at the time the project started, had a very clear idea about the types of research on which the center wanted to partner with me. At the top of the list was repatriation research for the return of Anishinabe ancestors held by the University of Michigan Museum of Anthropology. Ziibiwing's goal was to gather archaeological data about ancestral remains that the university had labeled "culturally unidentifiable" and to work with tribal historians and spiritual advisors to document the tribal perspective on the affiliation of the remains.

Ekdahl and her Ziibiwing team wrote a National Park Service grant that funded the initial research for this project, currently in its seventh year. The research started with meetings between myself, Ekdahl, Shannon Martin (Ziibiwing's cultural education

MAP 3.

Midwestern United States with numbered locations indicating key
places discussed in this book: (1) Ziibiwing Center of Anishinabe
Culture & Lifeways in Mt. Pleasant, MI; (2) Flint Stone Street
Ancestral Recovery Project in Flint, MI; (3) Sanilac Petroglyph
site; and (4) Waapaahsiki Siipiiwi Mound in Fairbanks, IN.

specialist, who is now Ziibiwing's director), and William Johnson (Ziibiwing's curator) to determine the plan for approaching the research. Spiritual leaders and tribal
historians were involved from the outset of the project and provided oral history
teachings about Anishinabe knowledge of kinship, the need for repatriating ancestors, and tribal migrations and occupation of the region where the remains were
found. From the start, we also worked collaboratively with the Michigan Anishinabek
Cultural Preservation and Repatriation Alliance (MACPRA). Formed to address
issues of repatriation, this coalition of Native peoples includes representatives from
state and federally recognized tribes in Michigan.

In conducting research for this project, the group made site visits to three locations from which ancestral remains had been exhumed through archaeological excavations between the 1920s and 1960s. The site visits gave the spiritual leaders and tribal historians the opportunity to assess the site locations for further cultural connections. The project also included a visit to the University of Michigan to view the ancestral remains and the associated funerary objects that the tribe was claiming. In addition, our team collaboratively authored and presented community reports about the research findings and progress. We authored reports and updates for the granting agency. And we made decisions about how the research should proceed. Such decisions were particularly critical for this project because of the high degree of resistance the tribe encountered in their efforts to repatriate these ancestors from the University of Michigan. The tribe is now preparing to repatriate a portion of these remains, but our collaborative work is ongoing.

ZIIBIWING SANILAC PETROGLYPH INTELLECTUAL PROPERTY PROJECT

This book draws from three additional collaborative projects. Two of these grew out of the research partnership with the Ziibiwing Center, and the third involves collaboration with the Sullivan County American Indian Council, a CBO in southern Indiana. These further research collaborations with the Ziibiwing Center are truly a testament to the potential of CBPR methodologies.

The Ziibiwing repatriation research project was well underway when the opportunity arose for a second collaboration around intellectual property issues in cultural heritage. Dr. George Nicholas of Simon Fraser University in British Columbia invited me to participate in a comparative project on intellectual property in archaeology. The $2.5 million grant from the Canadian Social Sciences and Humanities and Research Council (SSHRC) funds the Intellectual Property Issues in Cultural Heritage (IPinCH) project. IPinCH is global in scope and aims to study intellectual property issues related to archaeology (Hollowell and Nicholas 2009; IPinCH 2012).

Ziibiwing provides cultural education for both Native American and nonnative communities. The center hosts an annual summer solstice ceremony and language teaching at the nearby petroglyph site in Sanilac, Michigan (see Map 3). In the Anishinabe language, this site is called *ezhibiigaadek asin*—teachings on stone. In initial discussions with Ziibiwing's former director, Bonnie Ekdahl, about intellectual property issues and Ziibiwing's potential interest in being part of the IPinCH project, the tribe's role in both protecting and sharing the teachings found on the petroglyphs became a central focus of our discussion. Ekdahl had a clear view of the ways we could partner to study how to protect the petroglyph teachings and the intellectual property issues involved. Before the *ezhibi-igaadek asin* research got off the ground, Bonnie Ekdahl stepped down from her role as Ziibiwing's director, but the partnership continued under the guidance of Shannon Martin, Ziibiwing's new director. Martin and I worked together, along with Ziibiwing's curator, William Johnson, to develop a case study for the IPinCH project, focusing on protecting the traditional knowledge and imagery of the Sanilac petroglyphs.

Visitors to this and other rock art sites globally have been known to draw, photograph, or even use the images they see at these sacred places for economic pursuits. They have reproduced the images on T-shirts, coffee mugs, jewelry, and other merchandise. One clear example that we cited in our joint application for grant funds to support the Sanilac case study involved a visitor who attempted to use one particular petroglyph from the *ezhibiigaadek asin* site—the archer—for commercial purposes. If this petroglyph site is further developed, it will draw a greater number of visitors. Protecting the images and the knowledge and cultural teachings associated with them will become all the more critical. Through the collaborative *ezhibiigaadek asin* intellectual property project, we are investigating how cultural knowledge about this place can be shared, as our Anishinabe ancestors instructed, while at the same time ensuring that such information is appropriately protected. A critical component to this research is a tribal management and education plan, which is being developed in consultation with tribal members and spiritual leaders.

The Sanilac petroglyph research is still in the early stages. Together, we have developed a research design, coauthored a successful grant to fund the project, and produced all the documents for tribal council review and approval, and for the university's "human subjects" review process. We have developed a survey to gain input from several Anishinabe communities. We are also planning several workshops with spiritual leaders that will help us consider the most appropriate approach to protecting the teachings and other intellectual property related to the site. Although this project is not complete, the collaboration has already provided both interesting and useful insights about archaeological CBPR: for example, how community partnerships grow; how projects build on one another; how to manage community/university timelines; collaborative grant writing; and the institutional review board (IRB) review.

This book draws on yet another project that grew from the partnership between Ziibiwing and myself. The Flint Stone Street Ancestral Recovery and Site Management Project started in January 2008. During the construction of a new housing development in Flint, Michigan (see Map 3), construction workers inadvertently discovered multiple ancestral remains. The area is part of the traditional territory of the Saginaw Chippewa Indian Tribe of Michigan (SCIT), and Ziibiwing staff members were called in to consult on behalf of the tribe to develop a plan for handling the remains. The situation was dire. The remains of multiple individuals, a mother and baby among them, were unearthed as a backhoe dug multiple seven-foot-deep foundation trenches for houses that were to be built on the property. Houses previously located on the property were originally built in the early 1900s, but they had been abandoned and condemned. To rebuild the financially troubled area, the Genesee County Land Bank reclaimed the land, tore down the dilapidated turn-of-the-century houses, and funded the new construction as part of a plan to build new homes on the same location.

Federal funds were initially part of the housing development project, but once the state archaeologist inspected the site and declared it a major burial ground, construction came to an immediate halt. Federal funding was pulled, and Ziibiwing's staff was left wondering how they could possibly care for their ancestors in the respectful and dignified way they deserved. Martin and Johnson needed to make a decision. They saw the ancestral remains scattered among 75,000 cubic feet of back dirt, mixed in with modern garbage, including diapers, used condoms, and a host of other dirty refuse. They consulted with spiritual leaders, as well as several archaeologists including myself; Dr. Beverly Smith, an archaeologist from the local University of Michigan-Flint Anthropology Department; and two graduate students, Frank Raslich (a Saginaw Chippewa tribal member) and Nicole Raslich. Ziibiwing proposed a plan to the tribal council to conduct a salvage reburial project relying on the work of local volunteers and tribal members. Dr. Smith and I would serve as coprincipal investigators, and Frank and Nicole Raslich would work as field supervisors. Tribal council agreed and funded an initial five-week field season.

Starting in August 2009, the archaeology team trained and led volunteers and a small paid crew of tribal members to recover the remains left exposed in the four massive back dirt piles. My involvement on the ground, in the fieldwork aspect of this project, was comparatively minimal. I was on-site for only one week in early

September 2009. I served as the principal investigator, instructing volunteers on the cultural protocols for handling human remains and overseeing their work as we sieved through the soil to recover ancestral remains. Although my on-site work for this project was limited, I continue to be involved as a research partner during discussions, planning, and decision making about the project. Starting in September 2010, students in a CBPR research methods graduate course that I developed and teach at Indiana University also became involved in the Flint Stone Street project. Course participants gained hands-on experience in CBPR methods by working in partnership with Ziibiwing to develop a site management plan for the Flint Stone Street site. This project is ongoing as the tribe works to develop a management and protection plan for the site in partnership with tribal members and Flint residents and government entities.

WAAPAAHSIIKI SIIPIIWI MOUND PROJECT

The fifth and final CBPR project that informs my research for this book is a partnership with the Sullivan County American Indian Council (the Council), a nonprofit Native American group whose mission includes preserving the Native American past and educating Native Americans and local residents about it. The Council has roughly seventy members, all residents of Sullivan County, Indiana, and surrounding regions (see Map 3). In 2007, the Indiana Michigan Power Company turned over stewardship of five acres of land in Fairbanks, Indiana, to the Council, with the understanding that the Council would develop a plan to care for and protect the mound located on the land. The Council named the site in the Indigenous language of the Miami people, *Waapaahsiiki Siipiiwi*, after the nearby Wabash River. The Miami people had a long-term presence throughout Indiana.

The mound is documented with the state archaeologist's office but has not been scientifically investigated. Although I live nearby, I knew nothing of its existence, and only learned of it after meeting the Council's president, Reg Petoskey. As a new faculty member at Indiana University (IU), I knew it was important to develop connections with the local Native American community and wanted to do so. I arranged to meet with the Council (and other Native American groups in the state) to discuss developing research partnerships of mutual interest and benefit. Council president, Reg Petoskey, informed me of the *Waapaahsiiki Siipiiwi* mound. He expressed interest in conducting research there with the vision of preserving and protecting it. He also shared his idea of eventually developing a public interpretive trail to provide visitors with a place to learn about Indiana's First Peoples. The Council's long-term plans included developing a community museum and youth center on the site to serve both Indiana's greater Native American community and the local residents of the region.

The Council and I have since worked closely to develop a preliminary research design for recording and studying the *Waapaahsiiki Siipiiwi* site. Our initial scope of work includes archaeological fieldwork at the site, an oral history project, a management and protection plan, and several educational components. All are being carried out in direct partnership with the Council. Some of the research is complete, while other aspects are ongoing. We have collaboratively developed an excellent preliminary research design and put together a grant proposal to help fund the research. However, we have not yet obtained funding for developing the interpretive trail and educational components of the project.

As with the Flint Stone Street project, I incorporated the *Waapaahsiiki Siipiiwi* Mound project partnership into my graduate methods course. So, a significant portion of the project has been completed without funding, much of it by student volunteers from a CRM course taught by Dr. Susan Alt, a fellow archaeologist at IU, and graduate students in my CBPR graduate classes. As service-learning courses, the CBPR classes are designed to provide students with hands-on training in CBPR, while also providing needed research benefits to the Council. One team of graduate students focused on the Ziibiwing Flint Stone Street project. A second team worked in partnership with the Council to develop a detailed research design and grant proposal. They also carried out the archaeological fieldwork and worked on components of the oral history and educational portions of the project.

We conducted comparative background research on archaeological site management and protection at heritage sites globally. We are using this comparative knowledge to produce a site management and protection plan specific to *Waapaahsiiki Siipiiwi*. We surveyed and mapped the site and the surrounding area, which enabled us to assess the degree of looting from visible looting pits on the mound. We also developed a photographic, audio, and video archive of the participatory fieldwork process. These data are being shared with the Indiana State Archaeology office as part of the site registration process. Our IU research team also worked with the Council to collect oral histories about Native American life in Indiana and the history of the mound that existed in local memory. We also worked in partnership with local teachers to begin incorporating project results into the fourth grade curriculum.

Although not complete, this project has yielded very useful information about CBPR's application to archaeology, particularly in how to incorporate CBPR into training and the archaeology curriculum.

COMPARATIVE APPROACH TO
STUDYING ARCHAEOLOGICAL CBPR

With these five projects, I have taken a comparative approach to studying how to apply CBPR to archaeology. In one project (Çatalhöyük), I was clearly an outsider; in the others, I have closer cultural connections. Three of the projects (Ziibiwing partnerships) are with a community-based organization that is officially part of a federally recognized Native American tribe, while the Sullivan County partnership involves a small intertribal community. In stark contrast, the Çatalhöyük project took place in an international setting and required a large level of community organizing with rural, nondescendant local residents living near a site. Each is challenging and complex in different ways. All are very interesting for understanding the challenges with CBPR and how it can be applied to archaeology.

I derived the qualitative data I present from multiple sources: my observations and experiences initiating and conducting the five projects; information from interviews I conducted with community members during the planning stages of the Çatalhöyük CBPR project; and one interview with Ziibiwing's director, Shannon Martin. I've also integrated examples of archaeological projects that are collaborative to greater or lesser degrees as well as numerous CBPR examples from outside archaeology. These include CBPR case studies from the fields of conservation, forestry and natural resource management, sociology, education, theater and the arts, and public health.

More input for this research came directly from the classroom. I decided to write a book to fill a need I found while teaching and training archaeology students. Published examples of CBPR from an archaeology context are extremely limited. While teaching my CBPR graduate methods course, I found that the ambitious and bright graduate students I was teaching were repeatedly asking for specific examples of CBPR practices in archaeological fieldwork and research. They wanted to know, for example: How do you start an archaeological CBPR project? How do you work in partnership with a community to develop a research topic of mutual interest? How does a CBPR grant differ from a standard National Science Foundation grant?

Since archaeologists study material culture and remains from the past, they do not typically see themselves as working with "human subjects." Thus, they rarely go through the human subjects protection protocols that are in place in universities. Few receive training or have experience working with the institutional review board (IRB) process, which puts their research proposals through a careful review to make sure that those being studied are duly protected. Archaeology students in the CBPR methods course wanted to know how to navigate this process, particularly because community members were going to be directly involved in the research—not as "subjects" but as *partners*.

As evidence for how to apply CBPR to archaeology, I offered practical examples all through the course, from the fieldwork in the five CBPR projects with which I am involved. I wished countless times for a resource that would show how the principles and benefits of CBPR apply to archaeology. I finally decided that the best way to provide students with such a resource was to create it myself.

ARCHAEOLOGY OF THE
TWENTY-FIRST CENTURY

Throughout this book, I present some successes of conducting archaeological CBPR, yet I also talk about the complexities, messiness, and questions it leaves unanswered. I undoubtedly support the theoretical tenets on which it is based. I also link the approach to a wider paradigm shift in archaeology (and the social sciences more broadly) to democratize knowledge production and decolonize the discipline. However, as Wilmsen (2008) points out, there is no guarantee that these aims will be met. A number of important critiques of CBPR leave lingering questions about its ability to reach its lofty goals. These critiques warrant careful consideration, and I address them throughout the book. Most of the critiques can be overcome. None seem fatal, but they may still be unresolvable. For these reasons, like Wilmsen, I suggest to those who adopt CBPR, do so with great care.

The chapters that follow present a range of complex issues for archaeologists to consider. These are not restricted to the area of "Indigenous archaeology," nor are they significant only for those working in Native American or Indigenous communities. The questions community-based research has prompted have broad, global applicability and are relevant for anyone involved in the practice of archaeology in the twenty-first century. This book doesn't aim to provide all the answers, but it does highlight some of the important questions that we need to ask. It warns of possible challenges and provides ideas for integrating CBPR research into any archaeology project. I do not offer this work as a preset recipe for success but rather as an outline of CBPR's methodology and rationale. I hope it can provide a set of lessons learned from multiple experiences with CBPR. Archaeologists and community members who engage in research partnerships will develop protocols, strategies, and practices that best fit their local context. The chapters that follow are meant as tools to guide that process.

The archaeological literature gives many case studies that are useful for framing any discussion of collaboration and working with communities. I find these examples both inspiring and helpful. Chapter 2 provides a historical overview of the development of collaboration within the field of archaeology. The arc of development moves from legally mandated consultation to archaeological projects that involve communities to varying degrees along a "collaborative continuum." No single "prime mover" is responsible for the development of CBPR in archaeology. Rather, multiple factors played a role—some from within the discipline, some from other disciplines, and many from outside the academic world. From Native American activism and Vine Deloria's critique of anthropology to postmodern movements within the social sciences more broadly, I outline the major factors and influences of this development. I talk about global activism by Indigenous communities; archaeologists' interests in heritage management and cultural tourism; theoretical concerns with postcolonial and decolonizing methods; and collaborative practices in other disciplines. All these are linked to the move toward collaboration that we see in contemporary archaeology.

Chapter 3 details the principles and benefits of a CBPR approach. I examine five primary concepts: (1) what it means to pursue a fully collaborative process, (2) community participation in research, (3) how to build community capacity, (4) how to achieve reciprocity in beneficial outcomes, and (5) how to use multiple knowledge systems.

CBPR has a diverse history that can be traced to the 1940s. I present the roots and development of CBPR, including Paolo Freire's work in adult literacy education in Brazil and Myles Horton's involvement in the labor and civil rights movements in the United States. Some question the ability of practitioners of CBPR and other forms of what has been termed "activist scholarship" (Hale 2008) to maintain objectivity and produce rigorous results. This chapter discusses the action aspects of CBPR and the value it places on social change and democratizing knowledge. These values are, it turns out, fully supportive of research rigor and objectivity. The chapter closes by raising some of the primary critiques of CBPR: How do we define and represent "the community"? How much time will it take to carry out the research this way? How much *authentic* power can communities take on in research partnerships?

For archaeologists and communities who want to develop a community-based project, one of the most important concerns is practical: How are CBPR projects started? How do archaeologists initiate collaborative relationships with communities? And how can communities find suitable academic partners? Chapter 4 provides tangible approaches for establishing and sustaining community research partnerships. I detail some key elements for creating positive connections within a community. The chapter also discusses how to broaden participation to include a wide spectrum of community members.

CBPR projects are not started or built in the same way or with the same goals in mind. The CBPR projects I conducted in Turkey and North America followed quite different paths. In North America, both communities had a clear vision of the questions and topics they wanted to investigate. In Turkey, members of local villages seriously undervalued their own knowledge and felt they had nothing to contribute to a community research project. These different experiences provide useful guidance on how to establish a partnership—from the ground up; with community-based organizations; in large, diverse communities; and with multiple stakeholders. Very often, archaeologists may wish to integrate a CBPR component into a current field project, yet this can entail a complex process of shifting priorities and adjusting established relationship dynamics.

The concrete examples of the chapter are juxtaposed with a theoretical discussion about how to define communities: who forms them, how they are defined, who defines them, and who has the right to speak on behalf of the group. Politics, factions, and community divisions are inevitable and can have detrimental effects on a CBPR project. These topics are addressed in this chapter as well. To deal with these challenges, I emphasize building cultural competency and understanding the social and political context in which potential community research partners operate.

The early, foundational steps of creating a working relationship with a community partner strongly affect the trajectory and long-term success of the project. Patterns of interaction and daily working practices form during this opening phase of the research, and they can be hard to change later on. Chapter 5 identifies multiple factors important for building a strong foundation for successful archaeological CBPR. Some of these factors include establishing trust and a sense of like-mindedness, clarifying timelines, and understanding each other's goals and expectations. Qualitative methods, including ethnographic skills, play an important role in CBPR. They are particularly useful in assessing a community's interest and level of commitment to a research partnership as well as for identifying topics to investigate. These methods are also valuable for identifying areas of potential conflict—charged topics that require extra awareness and sensitivity. I address each of these subjects and use examples from the Çatalhöyük project.

In short, the bulk of Chapter 5 focuses on the complexities of transitioning from a conventional, researcher-driven approach to more participatory processes—making decisions in partnership with communities. I also carefully consider human-subject protocols and research permission processes, particularly tribal IRBs, governing councils, community consent, and university IRB requirements.

With CBPR, developing an archaeological research design has many steps: determining research questions in participatory ways, finding methods for answering those questions that are participatory as well, formulating an approach to interpreting data, and devising a plan for disseminating results—again, all done in inclusive, participatory, power-balanced ways. These are familiar steps for archaeologists; however, the daily practice of carrying out these steps changes substantially when communities become research partners. Chapter 6 focuses on the themes that emerge in the day-to-day process of identifying research questions and developing community-based research designs.

As shared decision making becomes part of daily practice, archaeologists find that open dialogue and frequent communication figure prominently in their research skill set. Chapter 6 gives examples that demonstrate this point. It also highlights how important it is to build flexibility into community-based research designs, while also remaining flexible throughout the research planning process. In many cases, particularly in working with Indigenous communities, CBPR research designs will include a set of cultural protocols and practices that must be followed during data collection, analysis, or at other points in the research process. Because this is so important, I cover the process of formulating such protocols.

The chapter concludes with an in-depth discussion of what I have termed community-based archaeological education. I detail how to develop educational materials about archaeology using a CBPR approach.

In Chapter 7, the focus turns toward gathering and interpreting data and presenting results to scholarly and public audiences. Archaeologists have been quite successful at involving members of the public in archaeological fieldwork. This chapter provides examples of some of those "best practices." It also shows how to make field and lab processes participatory, so that community members are fully engaged in both data collection and analysis. Community research teams and local internship programs are two approaches that I highlight. Chapter 7 also shows how researchers—archaeologists and community members—can use participatory field and lab experiences to build research capacity within communities.

Some of the most complex issues that archaeologists face in conducting CBPR relate to data interpretation: Do we give primacy to one interpretation over another? How are conflicts between community interpretations and those of the scholar best approached? And how might conflicts of interpretation productively be addressed? These are challenging issues, and the CBPR literature does not provide any easy solutions.

To address this challenge, I present the idea of "braided knowledge." Community knowledge intertwines with archaeological data to create new and richly textured interpretations of the past. The braided knowledge concept poses an alternative to multivocal approaches, adding to the complexities of interpreting and presenting data. Archaeologists and community members often have different goals and desired outcomes for research. These goals and outcomes may even conflict. Even within a community, diverse goals and views surround the types of data that people see as appropriate for publication. Furthermore, participants on all sides may assume different measures of success. Chapter 8 discusses these issues, as well as evaluation methods and measures of success.

The field of archaeology has made great strides in the past century. I am on board in supporting the momentum of change for my field. Frankly, I cannot imagine the archaeology of the next century without envisioning a collaborative aspect to the daily ins and outs of practice. Chapter 8 considers the long-term impact and positive potential of CBPR. Communities, who previously may have had quite negative reactions to research of any kind, have utilized CBPR to create knowledge that benefits their communities. This constitutes a major shift for the discipline.

For Indigenous peoples, I argue that CBPR can provide a mechanism through which communities can claim research as a tool that they can conduct in harmony with core tribal values. This powerful point links CBPR to a broader project of decolonization within Indigenous communities. In Chapter 8, I highlight some of the outcomes and benefits of the five CBPR projects as well as some of the benefits to the discipline of archaeology.

Community benefits vary. They include (re)engaging the community with site management and protection, developing new cultural tourism and heritage management programs, and gaining the right to rebury ancestors. Some added benefits were not as expected, such as creating an archaeological community theater troupe, providing a school for young girls who wouldn't otherwise have access to education, and using archaeology to build a community health clinic. Again, major shifts in archaeological practices.

Chapter 8 also addresses research ethics and student training. I argue that CBPR decenters some of the current archaeological ethics principles and refocuses the ethics discussion through a new lens. Fluehr-Lobban (2003) calls for anthropology to move beyond an ethic of "do no harm" toward one of "doing some good." The chapter highlights the ways that CBPR contributes to a "do some good" ethic. It also considers how archaeology ethical codes and guidelines might be reenvisioned as a result of collaborative practice and CBPR approaches.

In the end, though, the effects and benefits of CBPR can impact archaeology only if students learn the principles and techniques and are trained how to move abstract, theoretical concepts of collaboration and reciprocal community partnership into the work of daily, on-the-ground, dirt archaeology. Chapter 8 aims to open that dialogue. I explore how to integrate CBPR into the archaeology curriculum of the twenty-first century.

TWO · Origins of Community-Based Research in Archaeology

In contemporary archaeology, heritage management, community and joint stewardship, cultural tourism, and accessibility of archaeological knowledge combine with more traditional areas of archaeological excavation and survey work to form new and exciting directions of inquiry. Now pervading archaeological research, collaboration is woven into many theoretical discussions, publications, and on-the-ground practices. This convergence is garnering archaeologists' interest and attention.

Collaborative approaches with descendant and local communities are not limited to newer topics of archaeological inquiry, though, but are also having an impact on more established areas of archaeological research. Not all projects will work effectively as collaborations. In some cases, CBPR may not be appropriate or feasible. Yet the influence and importance that the collaborative concept has for contemporary practice is undeniable. Collaboration is proving to be a critical component for the archaeology of the twenty-first century.

Around the globe, Indigenous peoples are asserting their rights and responsibilities to care for and interpret archaeological places and materials. Indeed, the paradigm shift is already "well underway" toward inclusive and community-based approaches to studying Native American and Indigenous topics. We can expect that collaboration will not only retain a central place in archaeology but will also grow and become further elaborated and nuanced in the years and decades to come.

It is not practical or helpful to develop a single definition of "collaboration" within an archaeological context. Archaeologists currently use the term in different ways, and the practices implied in an archaeological collaboration vary along a wide spectrum. Colwell-Chanthaphonh and Ferguson (2008b) refer to this spectrum as the "collaboration continuum." They note that, "While each project along the 'collaborative continuum' is consequently unique, all move the discipline of archaeology toward a more accurate, inclusive, and ethically sound practice" (2008b, 1–2).

Not only does collaboration mean different things to different people in present day archaeology, but the concepts implied—as well as the on-the-ground practices—have evolved. Both have developed significantly through a history that can be traced as far back as the 1960s, perhaps farther. So, while community-based participatory research is new to archaeology, its incorporation has been a natural progression. The collaborative methodology has developed from various earlier efforts, such as legally mandated consultations, various forms of "working together" with communities, and engaging with numerous archaeological "publics."

INTERNAL AND EXTERNAL INFLUENCES

Historically, both external and internal influences led to community-based participatory approaches in archaeology. In the United States, the primary external influence was Native American activism, notably the Red Power movement of the late 1970s and early 1980s. I would not go so far as to consider this the "prime mover" in the development of collaborative and community forms of archaeology. Multiple factors clearly had an impact. However, Native American activism undoubtedly played a critical role in pushing the discipline toward more community-engaged practices.

Multiple internal influences also drove archaeology toward an increased focus on collaboration. Discussions of self-reflexivity, multivocality, and the role of subjectivity emerged from theoretical developments linked to post-processualism. These and other theoretical dialogues have played key roles. Furthermore, a greater focus on archaeological ethics and a growing concern over responsibilities to public education and "outreach" spurred the move toward collaborative approaches.

Pressures from outside the academic world combined with new intellectual directions within archaeology to move the discipline to our current position. The collaborative continuum now includes community-based participatory research as well as a critical discourse of the CBPR approach (for example, see La Salle 2010). Together, these trends call both archaeologists and communities to further define community-based research and to formulate guideposts for the best practices of a CBPR methodology.

"RED POWER" AND ARCHAEOLOGY

As I've already noted, Native American activism in the United States in the late 1960s and early 1970s was one of the earliest and most influential factors responsible for the movement toward collaborative approaches to archaeology. First published in 1969, Vine Deloria Jr.'s often-cited book, *Custer Died for Your Sins*, certainly played an important role. But neither Deloria nor any other scholar warrants sole credit for the rise of collaborative partnerships in archaeology and anthropology, or for raising the ethical and human rights concerns that led to community-based approaches to research. Elders, activists, and traditional spiritual leadership within Native American communities first voiced these concerns (Hammil and Cruz 1989). Colwell-Chanthaphonh provides extensive examples, dating back as early as 1632, of "Native peoples resisting archaeological inquiry" (2009, 180). Elders, spiritual leaders, and community members hold the traditional knowledge of how to care for sacred sites, traditional landscapes, and ancestral remains. They also maintain the traditional responsibilities of what archaeologists refer to as "steward-ship." Traditional stewardship requires caring for and protecting the knowledge held in such places and materials, so that they are properly passed on to coming generations.

When these traditional caretakers, many of whom view themselves as the most appropriate cultural stewards, spoke out about how archaeological research and excavation were violating their rights and knowledge systems, Native activists and scholars took up the cause (for example, see Hammil and Cruz 1989). They took action within the wider social and political climate of the late 1960s and early 1970s, and their efforts formed an important aspect of the Red Power movement (Fine-Dare 2002; Josephy, Nagel, and Johnson 1999).

Archaeologist Chip Colwell-Chanthaphonh discusses the long history of objections that Native peoples have voiced regarding archaeology and the pivotal role that Deloria and the public protests of the 1970s played within the archaeological world: "Archaeologists in the 1970s and 1980s may have felt as if their work was being threatened for the first time, but the ethical crisis of this period already existed at the very beginning of archaeology's formation as a profession, science, and moral community. The difference was not that earlier Indians failed to protest archaeological practices, but that archaeologists were finally truly forced to listen to these complaints through such powerful voices as Deloria's and through such violent tactics as the invasion of field camps" (2009, 180).

Native American activist groups, such as the American Indian Movement, and activist scholars and public intellectuals, such as Vine Deloria Jr., raised awareness of these issues both within an academic context and in the public eye. With the aim of reaching a very public albeit predominantly male audience outside of the academy, Deloria first published the chapter "Anthropologists and Other Friends" from *Custer Died for Your Sins* in *Playboy Magazine* in 1969 (Deloria Jr. 1969). In both this early piece and in his later work, Deloria's critique of anthropology not only rejected the rights of archaeologists to excavate Native American graves, but also called into question the motivations and benefits of archaeology and anthropology more broadly. He maintained that anthropological studies conducted on Native Americans were done only for the benefit of the researchers and did nothing to address issues of importance to Native communities.

Fine-Dare (2002) details how discussions of research and cultural property took center stage twice at major Native gatherings: for Native American scholars at the "Second Convention of Indian Scholars" held in Aspen, Colorado, in 1971, and for students of the American Indian Student Association at the University of Minnesota in 1970. Activists who participated in "The Longest Walk," from San Francisco, California, to Washington, DC, between March and July 1978, worked on the national scale to bring attention to Native American concerns about archaeological excavations.

Native activists also challenged research and museum practices, forming the American Indians Against Desecration (AIAD) project (Hammil and Cruz 1989). In AIAD's statement before the World Archaeological Congress, Native American activists lambasted those who made a living conducting research on Native Americans' lifeways, bodies, and sacred places, stating, "As the most studied peoples on the face of the earth, the American Indian is well acquainted with the 'Indian Expert' as found in the anthropological, archaeological, paleopathological, physical anthropological associations" (Hammil and Cruz 1989, 196). AIAD members questioned whether archaeologists have "the legal and moral authority" to interfere with the relationship that Indian people have to the Creator. They asked:

> Could it be that the "Indian Experts" didn't care that their acts were interfering and affecting traditional religious practices, or did they justify the genocide of Indian religion by placing a higher priority on their objectives? Just as the

US Government justified wholesale slaughter and extermination of hundreds of thousands of Indian people with noble objectives, had the archaeologist concluded that altering and destroying traditional Indian religious practices was justified by the results of their scholarly studies and research—acceptable casualty rates, so to speak?

(HAMMIL AND CRUZ 1989, 196)

The American Indian Movement (AIM) actively engaged in protests against the excavation and display of Native American human remains. One of the first protests of this sort was carried out by AIM at an archaeological excavation in Minnesota (Thomas 2000, 198–208). Encounters and debates between Native Americans and archaeologists were not limited to excavation protests. Vine Deloria Jr. and other Native Americans participated in sessions at anthropological and archaeological professional conferences (Fine-Dare 2002). They actively engaged in discussions, often heated debates, particularly in relation to reburial and repatriation issues. Through actions and writings, Native American activists and scholars challenged anthropologists and archaeologists to rethink their practices and the ways they had engaged with both Native American communities and their ancestors.

The activism of this period was not limited to Native American intellectuals and activists operating in large, nationwide organizations, such as AIAD and AIM. Members of Native American communities voiced similar critiques. They took proactive steps at the local and regional levels to make sure that they had a primary role in how the remains of their ancestors and important cultural places were treated.

One example is in Michigan. Tribal members began working together to protect Native American graves and to conduct repatriations and reburials of ancestors found on private land long before the national repatriation legislation passed (Sydney Martin, personal communication, October 2009). This statewide activism eventually led to the formation of the Michigan Anishinaabek Cultural Preservation and Repatriation Alliance (MACPRA), an organization founded to facilitate reburial and to protect Native American cultural materials. MACPRA includes members of federally and state recognized tribes in Michigan. The significance of community activism and the critical importance that communities place on repatriation and the work of MACPRA is demonstrated in the Ziibiwing Cultural Center.

The permanent exhibit of the Saginaw Chippewa Indian Tribe's Ziibiwing Cultural Center in Mt. Pleasant, Michigan, features the work of MACPRA. The exhibit gives the organization and the work they have accomplished a prominent place in the tribe's telling of its community's history. In Ziibiwing's permanent exhibit, *Diba Jimuyoung—Telling Our Story*, the museum relates Saginaw Chippewa tribal history through a series of prophecies. Spiritual leaders gave these prophecies to the Anishinabek long before European contact. One of the prophecies in the exhibit talks about a time when the Anishinabe people will become strong once again. It explains that these people will be the *oshki anishinabe* (new Anishinabe), and the period in which the prophecy locates this change coincides with the activism of the late 1960s and early 1970s. To illustrate the kinds of actions of the *oshki anishinabe*, the exhibit directly highlights MACPRA's work to protect sacred sites and to insist on Native American involvement in any research or decision making that involves study and handling of Native American ancestral remains.

THREE IMPACTS OF NATIVE AMERICAN ACTIVISM

LEGISLATIVE CHANGES

Without question, the activism during the Red Power movement and beyond raised dilemmas for those within the fields of anthropology and archaeology (Thomas 2000). Academic practitioners were challenged to rethink what constitutes ethical practices in their disciplines and the obligations that they as anthropologists and archaeologists had when they engaged with Native Americans to conduct research. Did their research benefit the Indigenous peoples being studied and address real-life problems in their communities?

The response from both academics and communities paved the way to today's growing commitment to collaborative archaeology and to using community-based research practices in three ways. First, political, social, and ethical pressures from Native American scholars, activists, and community leaders played direct roles in developing and passing cultural resource protection and repatriation legislation, including the National Museum of the American Indian Act of 1989 and the Native American Graves Protection and Repatriation Act (NAGPRA) of 1990. These two pieces of federal legislation, and the 1992 amendments of the National Historic Preservation Act, mandated that Native Americans be consulted about archaeological sites and materials (Fine-Dare 2002). This legally mandated consultation meant that, by law, Native peoples must be included in discussions about repatriation and what happens at historic places.

As important as this step was, these and other laws had limited impact in promoting the use of collaborative and community-based research practices. The legislation (1) failed to define what is involved in substantive consultation; (2) did not make provisions for nonfederally recognized tribes; (3) did not require that museums, federal agencies, or other entities involved follow the advice obtained through the consultation process; and (4) did not provide for adequate funding to pay for substantive consultation, monitoring compliance with the laws, or their enforcement.

ARCHAEOLOGISTS SEEK ALTERNATIVE
METHODOLOGIES

Native American critiques of archaeological and anthropological research goals and practices had a second important impact. They caused some scholars to consider alternative approaches to research and how archaeological practice might change to become more inclusive. In the late 1980s and early 1990s, disagreements and tensions between archaeologists, museum professionals, and Native Americans ran high. Yet some interactions were positive.

AIAD's statement to the World Archaeological Congress in September 1986 (Hammil and Cruz 1989, 198–99) described positive partnerships between Native American communities and archaeologists. One project increased preservation for the Black Hills region, including the repatriation of 5,000 ancestors; another ensured that significant archaeological sites would not be disturbed during the Peacekeeper MX construction project. The same statement that harshly criticized archaeologists for arrogance and lack of respect highly praised the archaeologists who worked in partnership with Native communities and were willing to share power and decision making.

When equitable partnerships and respectful relationships are forged that give Native Americans power of self-determination over their own spiritual beliefs, ancestral bodies, and the protection of important sites on their traditional homelands, then Native Americans have been willing to work with archaeologists, and often have an interest, even a passion, for conducting archaeological research. Not surprisingly, when Native American input was ignored and their trust and respect violated, the desire to work in partnership quickly dissipated. AIAD's statement to the World Archaeological Congress in 1986 made this point very clear:

> The arrogance of archaeologists was again illustrated in April when the
> Executive Committee of the Society for American Archaeology on behalf of
> all archaeologists in the United States passed a resolution opposing reburial.
> Reburial might be considered, said the SAA, in cases of "known individuals
> from whom specific biological descendants could be traced." Needless to say,
> the merits of any reburial request would be determined by archaeologists based
> on their opinion and judgment of Indian religious values and interests.
>
> (HAMMIL AND CRUZ 1989, 199)

The critical need for Native Americans to have substantive input, decision-making authority, and inclusionary powers appears throughout the statement:

> We suggest it was not the American Indian that chose again to polarize relationships between Indians and archaeologists. We suggest that a handful of individuals have conspired for their own purposes and interest to establish unreasonable procedures and policies with the specific intent of excluding Indian input or consideration. We suggest that if anyone is excluded from input into the disposition of our ancestors' bodies, it will be archaeologists.
>
> (HAMMIL AND CRUZ 1989, 199)

Some archaeologists listened. For many members of the World Archaeological Congress and other archaeologists, the powerful statements Native American activists and scholars gave at the 1986 WAC meetings led them to consider alternative ways of conducting research. These new ways involved varying degrees of collaboration and partnership with Native American communities.

During the same critical period of the late 1980s and early 1990s, the legislation that mandated consultation with Native peoples, although it had undeniable limits to its influence, also resulted in some unexpected positive outcomes that impacted collaborative partnerships. In some cases it allowed archaeologists to grasp that Native people were not simply decrying the theft of their ancestors for political purposes; they truly felt a deep responsibility to care for their ancestors. In other situations, archaeologists and museum professionals found that consultation enhanced their knowledge about sites and/or museum collections and improved their understandings of the past. In some situations, positive working relationships between tribes, archaeologists, and museum staff developed as a result of legally mandated consultations. However, this did not always happen, nor was it the norm.

Silliman and Dring (2008) point out that many interactions traced to NAGPRA activities are not voluntary collaborations, but rather legally mandated consultations. They point to routes other than NAGPRA that have led to successful partnerships between Native Americans and archaeologists: "We need to explore and recognize the possibilities of collaborative efforts built on other foundations, such as cultural and historic preservation or a recognition that multiple histories can be constructed in a political present." They go on to argue that, "these . . . two elements [cultural preservation and recognition of multiple histories], rather than concerns about human remains or NAGPRA, have created a context for truly collaborative educational projects between tribal and archaeological communities" (2008, 67).

Certainly, the museum world has a rich scholarship that documents cases of collaborative curation (Lonetree 2002, 2006; Bowechop and Erikson 2005; Cash 2001). These examples demonstrate that productive partnerships in community curation can be fruitful in contexts other than a NAGPRA framework. Indeed, there are many cases in which future collaborative projects did *not* develop between tribal groups and archaeologists who were involved in NAGPRA-related claims or after engaging in other legally mandated forms of consultation.

So, while NAGPRA and other mandated consultations had some role to play in building collaborative relationships in archaeology, more important was a shift in archaeologists' attitudes toward and approach to Native peoples. A close analysis of the early successful collaborations between archaeologists and Native Americans in the mid-1980s to late 1990s reveals some recurring themes: Building trust and mutual respect are central in nearly all cases. Power sharing, reciprocity, and doing research in ways that are accessible to Native communities and that benefit them are also critical for the collaboration to be successful (Adams 1984; Dowdall and Parrish 2003; Ferguson 1984; Zimmerman 1989; Spector 1993; Anyon et al. 1997; Nicholas and Andrews 1997; Ferguson, Watkins, and Pullar 1997; Kluth and Munnell 1997; Lightfoot et al. 2001; Parrish, Murley, and Lightfoot 2000). Wylie (2000, viii) raises another critical theme: Archaeologists who engage in collaborative research must be willing to accept the validity of other knowledge systems. Dowdall and Parrish (2003) make a strong argument for the impact that a demonstrable respect for Indigenous knowledge has had on collaborations with Native Americans.

BEGINNINGS OF A PARTNERSHIP APPROACH

During the early part of the new millennium, these relationships grew, more collaborations developed, and the literature about these collaborations blossomed. The literature about these projects emphasized a *partnership* approach. Such community-based projects show how to develop substantive research *with* and *for* communities. They also demonstrate the importance of conducting research in this way. Many of these projects include *reciprocity* as a key feature, prioritizing the benefits gained for both academic and community partners (Atalay 2003a, 2003b, 2006, 2007, 2008a, 2008c, 2010; Brady 2009; Budhwa 2005; Chirikure and Pwiti (2008), Chilton and Hart 2009; Harrison 2001; Murray et al. 2009; Silliman 2008a; Bendremer and Richman 2006; Smith 2006; Nicholas 2005, 2006; Robinson 1996).

Mills et al. (2008, 30–31) highlight this point when they discuss the University of Arizona field school and the evolving nature of their relationship with tribal communities in the region. They discuss the need to involve Native communities in the process of archaeology more substantively than as mere guests to tour sites or visitors to the field school. They note that community involvement must also go beyond simply having appropriate tribal representatives review the research proposal, which, they note, is required under federal law: "We felt that more fundamental changes were required to create a field school that offered true benefits to the affected tribal communities."

Trust and mutual respect are the components most commonly reinforced for these collaborative projects, but the literature also cites other key values. For example, in Colwell-Chanthaphonh and Ferguson's edited volume *Collaboration in Archaeological Practice*, Thomas cites the importance of "civility, benevolence, generosity, loyalty, dependability, thoughtfulness, and friendliness" (Thomas 2008, xi–xii). Colwell-Chanthaphonh and Ferguson (2004, 2006) agree, highlighting the need for "virtue ethics."

The type of community-based research that Mills et al. (2008) and others describe during this period moved archaeology well beyond including Native people as site monitors on projects (Lightfoot 2008, 213) or other limited forms of *"working together."* Now, community members not only approve and monitor projects but are actively involved in planning and implementing them as well. Such collaborations are "decidedly different" (Silliman 2008, 7) from the legally mandated consultations, and the two can be clearly delineated. "Consultation involves legal mandates, procedural steps, and compliance, whereas collaboration emphasizes social relationships, joint decision-making, equitable communication, mutual respect, and ethics" (Silliman 2008b, 7). Community collaborations that involve partnerships and aim to provide reciprocal benefits have a broad geographic scope. Archaeologists now engage in projects globally with Indigenous communities and with other descendant and local groups as authentic partners (Atalay 2003a, 2006, 2007; Smith and Wobst 2005; Leone et al. 1987).

McNiven and Russell (2005) and Brady (2009) detail their view of community archaeological partnerships in Australia. Both utilize a "partnership-based approach" that follows a "host–guest" model in which archaeologists are guests in Indigenous communities and are only able to carry out research with the consent of their Indigenous hosts. The host–guest model explicitly shifts research power and ownership to Indigenous communities. McNiven and Russell also problematize the view of Indigenous communities as one of many interested "stakeholders," because it places Indigenous communities external to their own heritage. Although they don't reference CBPR theory or methods, the partnership-based approach they advocate parallels closely with what I've outlined in this book as community-based archaeology that is informed by CBPR.

INDIGENOUS ARCHAEOLOGY

Not coincidentally, the rise of community-based research has occurred alongside the beginning and sharp rise of Indigenous archaeology. George Nicholas has worked extensively in partnership with Aboriginal peoples and co-edited one of the first books about Indigenous archaeology (1997). He defines Indigenous archaeology as "an expression of archaeological theory and practice in which the discipline intersects with Indigenous values, knowledge, practices, ethics, and sensibilities, and through collaborative and community-originated or -directed projects, and related critical perspectives" (2008, 1,660).

"Indigenous archaeology" and "collaboration" are not synonymous. Indigenous archaeology frequently relies on a community-based methodology, but it is also more than that. It involves integrating Indigenous concepts and cultural knowledge to improve how archaeologists interpret archaeological materials (Nicholas 2008; Atalay 2006). Indigenous archaeology examines ways of making archaeological practices more relevant to descendant and local communities (Nicholas 2008; see, for example, Atalay 2007). It also aims to integrate Indigenous forms of producing knowledge with Western approaches to archaeological research to improve research practices (Atalay 2006, 2007, 2008b, 2008c; Silliman 2008b). Silliman (2008b, 3) maps the overlap between the two, noting points of difference:

> At their core, indigenous archaeologies respect openness, multivocality, personal engagement, ethics, sharing of authority and interpretation, local and cultural knowledge, and the fact that history matters to people. . . . These goals are shared by many collaborative archaeologies, . . . but the intersection of colonialism, sovereignty, dispossession, and anthropology's tainted history with indigenous people make collaborative indigenous archaeology a unique enterprise.

In short, the intellectual conversations and on-the-ground practices that have surrounded Indigenous archaeology have had a substantial impact on furthering collaborative practices.

Native American activism influenced the trajectory of research paradigms and led to community-based participatory approaches to archaeology in a third way. A strong Indigenous activist push came from the academic world, but well outside the disciplinary boundaries of archaeology and anthropology. Indigenous communities had been openly critiquing the research practices of academics, and scholars and activists globally soon followed by challenging conventional approaches to research, including its goals and aims. These conflicts had a substantial impact in the social sciences and humanities disciplines. The goals of research, the ethics and methods of their practices, and the benefits to those being studied became central concerns for those working in Native American and Indigenous studies.

Scholars in this interdisciplinary field responded with a plethora of new scholarship in critical Indigenous methodologies and decolonization theory. Linda Tuhiwai Smith's *Decolonizing Methodologies* (1999) is the most well-known and frequently cited example of this growing literature on decolonization, coming from both Indigenous and non-Indigenous scholars. The aim is to interrogate the goals and outcomes of research; consider who benefits from it and why; and, most importantly, examine how research might be done in a way that is not exploitative and that provides benefits to Indigenous and other communities (Denzin, Lincoln, and Smith 2008; Mihesuah and Cavender Wilson 2004; Wilson 2008; Kovach 2009; National Congress of American Indians Policy Research Center 2009; Battiste 2000; Wilson and Yellow Bird 2005; Rains, Archibald, and Deyhle 2000; Smith 2005, 2006; Miller 2008, 2009).

By engaging critically with what it means to decolonize research and to indigenize the academy, these scholars lay out a framework for Native American and Indigenous studies: Research must be done with, by, and for Indigenous communities. Evans et al. 2009 explain that an Indigenous methodology is:

> research by and for indigenous peoples using techniques and methods drawn from the traditions of those peoples. This set of approaches simply rejects research on indigenous communities that uses exclusively positivistic, reductionist, and objectivist research rationales as irrelevant at best, colonialist most of the time, and demonstrably pernicious as a matter of course. Rather than nonindigenous peoples framing indigenous worldview from a distance, IM [Indigenous methodology] situates and is reflected on by research/researchers at the location most relevant to that being gazed on, the indigenous experience.
>
> (2009, 894)

Developed, in part, as a critique of the exploitative research practices within anthropology and archaeology, this scholarship has come full circle, in a sense, to influence the very anthropological and archaeological practices that it set out to critique. Some of the recent research on Indigenous archaeology and collaborative approaches in archaeology—particularly projects utilizing a CBPR paradigm (Atalay 2003a, 2003b, 2003c, 2004, 2006, 2007, 2010; Hollowell and Nicholas 2009; Greer, Harrison, and McIntyre-Tamwoy 2002)—follow or have been heavily influenced by research in critical Indigenous methodologies. These Indigenous currents within the academy, combined with Native activism and Indigenous voices outside of it, have had a direct impact on the methodological discussions leading to community-based research.

INTERNAL INFLUENCES

At the same time that archaeologists were reacting to influences and critiques outside the discipline, archaeology was simultaneously transforming in response to new theories and approaches that were being developed *within* the discipline. In their recent edited volume on contemporary archaeological theory, Preucel and Mrozowski (2010, 6–7) trace how post-processual, feminist, and Marxist approaches gained favor during this time. These theoretical discussions impacted collaborative practice in that each, in different ways, led archaeologists to consider (1) the social impact of archaeological practice on contemporary society, and (2) the value of involving multiple voices when they examine the past and the ethical imperatives to do so.

Because many of the theoretical and philosophical concepts underpinning these approaches were imported from other disciplines, the changes that followed were not entirely *internal* to archaeology. Postmodern concepts, for example, were widely present throughout much of the arts and humanities fields long before they entered archaeology through post-processualism. However, the debates and scholarly wrestlings over post-processual, feminist, and Marxist approaches—their validity and practical implications, for example—were internal. Their integration into archaeological theory and practice was not the result of pressures from outside the academy.

A wide literature (for example, see Funari, Zarankin, and Stovel 2005; Trigger 2006; Johnson 2010; Hodder 2001) documents the debates and theoretical changes that began taking place during this period, and it describes the impact on archaeology. Dowdall and Parrish (2003) link post-processual concerns with multivocality and shared authority to the increase in archaeological collaborations, while Atalay

(2008b) draws connections between multivocality and Indigenous approaches to producing knowledge. These new theoretical arguments complicated the process of archaeological knowledge production. Whether archaeologists subscribed to these arguments or held tightly to the positivist goals of processual archaeology, post-processualism did raise issues about multivocality and the validity of alternative knowledge systems, and it put these issues at the center of debate. This had a positive influence on archaeological collaborations.

IMPACT OF PUBLIC ARCHAEOLOGY

Discussions about archaeologists' engagement with those outside the discipline were not limited to concerns over Indigenous or local community inclusion. Another important aspect of the history of archaeological community-based research involves the working relationships that archaeologists developed with multiple and diverse public audiences. During the 1980s and 1990s, archaeologists were keen to foster these relationships. Commitments to involve the public in archaeology are within the mission statement of the Archaeological Institute of America (AIA), the World Archaeological Congress (WAC), and the Society for American Archaeology (SAA). The SAA's Principles of Archaeological Ethics define working with a range of public audiences as part of ethical practice. Similarly, the AIA Code of Professional Standards defines public involvement as an important part of professional responsibility. Both definitions developed during this period. Today, the SAA and AIA maintain active committees that focus specifically on public engagement and education. Academic and professional archaeologists now sponsor and promote public workshops and activities related to archaeology on a regular basis. And a significant print and Web-based literature has developed related to public archaeology and community outreach that dates to this same period (Jameson 1997; Smardz and Smith 2000; Bender and Smith 2000; Little 2002; Society for American Archaeology 2005).

The SAA most clearly defines the responsibilities that archaeologists hold to the public in its principles of archaeological ethics. The fourth SAA principle reflects concern over the public's rights to and benefits from research. It states:

> Archaeologists should reach out to, and participate in cooperative efforts
> with others interested in the archaeological record with the aim of improving
> the preservation, protection, and interpretation of the record. In particular,
> archaeologists should undertake to: (1) enlist public support for the
> stewardship of the archaeological record; (2) explain and promote the use of

archaeological methods and techniques in understanding human behavior and culture; and (3) communicate archaeological interpretations of the past. Many publics exist for archaeology, including students and teachers; Native Americans and other ethnic, religious, and cultural groups who find in the archaeological record important aspects of their cultural heritage; lawmakers and government officials; reporters, journalists, and others involved in the media; and the general public. Archaeologists who are unable to undertake public education and outreach directly should encourage and support the efforts of others in these activities.

(SOCIETY FOR AMERICAN ARCHAEOLOGY 1996)

In 1991, less than one year after the passage of NAGPRA, which mandated consultation with Native American communities, the SAA convened an ethics committee to address a wide range of issues related to the practice of archaeology. The committee revised the SAA code of ethics and called for more "cooperative efforts" with various public audiences. Adopted by the SAA membership in 1996 and still used today, the "Principles of Archaeological Ethics" affirm not only the significance of educating the public but also the importance of reaching out to Native American tribes and other stakeholders.

MOTIVATIONS FOR ARCHAEOLOGICAL COLLABORATION

We gain some insight into why collaboration gained ground in archaeology during the early to mid-1990s when we consider the reasons given for engaging in cooperative efforts. The emphasis on public interaction and education was driven primarily by two needs: to gain public support for site preservation and to secure funds.

Certainly, looting and destruction of sites were—and continue to be—serious concerns for archaeologists. Furthermore, archaeological research and preservation of cultural resources rely on public funds. It was thus critically important for the future of archaeology that public audiences know about and understand the importance of archaeological research. In such a climate, it makes sense that the SAA placed an emphasis on public education in its ethics principles. Building cooperative relationships that would help educate multiple publics, including Native Americans, became an important motivating factor for "working together." At that time, the focus on building collaborations was not motivated so much by an ethical obligation to partner with descendent and local communities (as we see later), but primarily by the perceived benefits that such relationships would bring to archaeology (continued funding and site preservation).

Since then, though, how archaeologists view collaboration and their motivations for working with Indigenous and local communities have continued to develop. These developments carry concerns over accessibility to research into the realm of ethics. Today, motivations vary for working collaboratively in archaeology. The term *collaboration* can mean many things to different archaeologists—a point I discuss later in this chapter. Many still place high priority on educating those outside the discipline. For others, collaboration remains linked to preservation: both preserving sites and self-preservation, that is, maintaining public interest to gain funds for archaeological research.

Today, archaeologists also acknowledge the connections between the ethical responsibilities stemming from their role as stewards of the archaeological record and the need to work in collaborative partnerships with public audiences. For many, the archaeological record "belongs," for lack of a better term, to the public broadly. Archaeologists view themselves as stewards of the archaeological record *itself*. It follows, then, that ethical practices should include sharing archaeological knowledge through public education and collaboration. Linking community collaboration with archaeologists' stewardship responsibilities was first clearly articulated in the mid- to late 1990s, and continues today. Collaborating with descendant and local communities and other stakeholders and creating diverse public education programs remain important goals for all prominent archaeological organizations—both academic and professional.

ARCHAEOLOGICAL CBPR

Recently, some archaeologists began to question the stewardship-first approach to ethics and the effects that collaboration has had—both on the practice of archaeology and on the ethics principles that guide it (Atalay et al. 2009). Over twenty years, collaborative approaches to archaeology, post-processual critiques, Indigenous archaeology, Native American activism, Indigenous studies scholarship, and participatory action research (PAR) set the stage for CBPR to enter archaeology. CBPR has a much longer history in cultural anthropology, where it is strongly linked to the pioneering work of Sol Tax (1958). In archaeology, CBPR can be traced to at least 1996, in the PAR that Michael P. Robinson advocated. Only much later did Indigenous and collaborative archaeology identify CBPR as an effective methodology (Atalay 2003a, 2003b, 2003c, 2004, 2006, 2007, 2010; Greer, Harrison, and McIntyre-Tamwoy 2002; Hollowell and Nicholas 2009; Pyburn 2009).

The first published reference to CBPR in relation to archaeology of which I am aware appears in Robinson's (1996) article, "Shampoo Archaeology," which appeared in the *Canadian Journal of Native Studies*. The date was surprisingly early, but it was no surprise that it appeared first in a journal devoted to Native studies rather than to archaeology.

Robinson's approach, labeled as "participatory action research," focused on how projects are funded. He advocated for a corporate model of social responsibility, modeled by the work of The Body Shop founder, Anita Roddick. Robinson calls for a "trade-not-aid" approach to archaeology. Drawing on participatory action research examples from several other fields, Robinson highlights a collaborative archaeology in which communities, academics, and corporations form partnerships. Corporations fund research as they work with communities to produce sustainable products. Robinson discusses reciprocity of benefits, community control, participatory practice at all levels, and building community capacity—all central principles of CBPR. Some of these principles are clearly recognizable from the early collaborative archaeology projects that started in the 1990s, and have continued (for example, see Brady 2009; McNiven and Russell 2005; Rossen 2006, 2008; Smith, Morgan, and van der Meer 2003). These authors did not, though, explicitly connect archaeology to the wider literature or to the theoretical underpinnings and methodological practice of CBPR in Indigenous studies, or in the social sciences and medical fields.

For those using a CBPR approach, collaboration is not motivated primarily by the benefits it bestows on archaeology. Rather it advocates a partnership approach that is motivated by the rights communities have to be active participants in the creation of knowledge. Archaeological projects that follow a CBPR methodology take a partnership approach to do research with, by, and for Indigenous, local, and descendant communities. They focus on increasing capacity in communities and involving community members in joint decision making.

Rossen's (2006, 2008) "advocacy research" demonstrates ways that reciprocity and building community capacity can be operationalized, and Silliman's (2008a) important edited volume on collaborative field schools provides examples of how participatory practices can increase archaeological literacy in communities. Archaeological CBPR projects often take these efforts a step further: They aim to extend such capacity building and community education beyond the archaeological project. By participating in archaeological CBPR, community members discover that they gain skills and research literacy that they can use in areas unrelated to archaeology (Atalay 2010; Rossen 2008).

This democratization of archaeology is understood by those following a CBPR approach to be a necessary part of ethical archaeological practice and one of the basic rights held by people in *all* communities. CBPR challenges the assumption that archaeologists are the only—or even the best qualified—stewards of the archaeological record. It asserts instead that both descendant and nondescendant communities have an ethical right to (1) be involved in producing knowledge about the past, and (2) gain benefits from the research.

Calling attention to the role of collaborative partnerships in contemporary archaeology, Preucel and Mrozowski (2010, 8) link archaeology that is done "with, for and by Indigenous communities" (citing Nicholas and Andrews 1997) to postcolonial and Indigenous archaeology. They note that attempts to involve Indigenous people in archaeology as a matter of Indigenous rights have also been made in Australia, New Zealand, Africa, Bolivia, and Canada. As the history I traced shows, collaborative approaches to archaeology now occur on a global scale. In Canada and Australia, the ethics principles that the primary archaeological professional associations in those countries now follow emphasize working collaboratively with Indigenous communities. Some of the earliest and most notable collaborative archaeology took place with First Nations communities in Canada (Nicholas and Andrews 1997).

The approach is not limited to Indigenous communities. More recent literature on collaborative archaeology (sometimes referred to as "community archaeology") describes how archaeologists are working in equitable partnerships—some using a CBPR methodology—with a diverse range of communities globally. Examples exist for Turkey (Atalay 2007), Egypt (Moser et al. 2002), Kyrgyzstan (Pyburn 2009), Central and South America (Heckenberger 2008), in urban settings (Shackel and Gadsby 2008; Mullins 2004; Blakey 2008), and rural communities (McDavid 2002). CBPR has also been used to address issues related to cultural heritage in law (Bell and Napolean 2008; Bell and Paterson 2009) and intellectual property matters (Mortensen and Nicholas 2010).

TRIBALLY DRIVEN RESEARCH WITHIN GOVERNMENT CONSULTATIONS

Tribes in the United States working with archaeologists are doing a significant amount of excellent community-based participatory research in historic preservation projects, primarily in relation to Section 106 of the National Historic Preservation Act (NHPA) and for implementation of the Native American Graves Protection and Repatriation Act (NAGPRA) (Silliman and Ferguson 2010;

Watkins and Ferguson 2005). This research involves archaeologists and anthropologists working with tribal communities and Community Based Organizations (CBOs), often as hired consultants, to create knowledge used for reports within the context of federal laws and regulations.

Archaeologists have been hired as consultants to identify historic properties or determine cultural affiliation for NHPA or NAGPRA claims (see Murray et al. 2009 for several examples). This is similar to the cultural affiliation research project that Ziibiwing and I partnered on. Another example is that of archaeologists working with Native American tribes as they provided testimony during the Indian Claims Commission (Silliman and Ferguson 2010). These types of tribally driven research initiatives undoubtedly hold a wealth of information that would be very helpful for informing a CBPR process in archaeology.

Much could be gleaned from an analysis of these case studies with regard to how tribal members and researchers can best partner together. The problem is that the majority of reports on these research projects are not easily accessible. They are often published outside of academic venues, as a form of "gray literature" with limited distribution, no ISBN numbers, and not available through bookstores, university libraries, or online booksellers. Specialists working in particular geographical areas or those engaged in professional cultural resource management (CRM) networks are often the only ones who are aware of, or have access to, this literature. Much of it is held in report repositories of governmental agencies, or in tribal archives.

While these reports focus on content and not process, they may also provide further details about contemporary community-based participatory research in the United States that could inform "best practices." Yet getting access to them presents a real hurdle. Watkins and Ferguson (2005) do provide a set of twenty habits for researchers who are working with Indigenous communities during formal consultation or otherwise. The authors also provide ten suggestions for Indigenous communities who are involved in consultations with archaeologists.

TERMINOLOGY: DEFINING AND DIFFERENTIATING CBPR

The "collaborative continuum" includes many forms of practice along an ever-changing spectrum (Colwell-Chanthaphonh and Ferguson 2008b). Figure 1 illustrates the way I envision this continuum, as a series of interconnected and overlapping practices, each with its own history and goals. I distinguish "consultation," which includes a variety of legally mandated forms of collaboration, with a rectangular shape. This highlights the fundamental differences of consultation because it

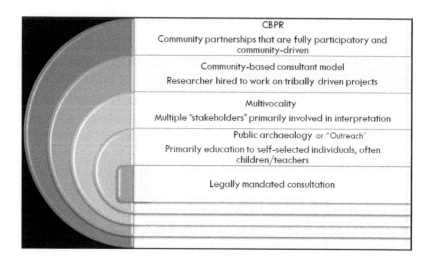

FIGURE I.
Interconnected and overlapping practices within a "collaborative continuum"

is subject to legal requirements in ways that voluntary collaborations are not. This visual of a collaborative continuum is organized around: 1) the level of participation and 2) community decision making within these collaborative practices. These two key principles are important because they signify the level of capacity building and power sharing within a project. CBPR is specifically focused on being community-driven and participatory; however, these two important principles are visible in, or can be infused into, practices along the entire collaborative continuum. With some effort, even legally mandated consultations can become fully participatory, utilize power sharing, and build community capacity.

Differentiating various forms of collaborative practice is challenging. Archaeologists have not always clearly defined the concept or approach they are using. Terminology and associated practices overlap, and the result is that the same word can refer to quite different practices. For example, some use the term *community archaeology* to refer to any form of engagement with any "public" group, whereas others use the term to describe practices quite similar to CBPR. It is not my intent to define the theory and method of each of these practices. For clarity, Table I provides a brief framework that outlines my understanding and use of these approaches.

Archaeological collaborative practice should not be something archaeologists stumble upon or do haphazardly. Certainly, there are archaeologists who have

TABLE I   Approaches to Archaeological Collaboration Highlighting Key
Concepts and Examples

Type of Approach	Emphasis and Key Concepts	Examples and References
Collaboration	Defines a continuum of collaborative approaches. Some have resisted use of the term because of negative connotations in language of war (e.g., "collaborating with the enemy").	Colwell-Chanthaphonh and Ferguson (2008b) discuss and define "collaborative continuum."
Collaborative archaeology	Closely parallels CBPR approach. Emphasis is on the "collaborative inquiry" approach that aims to meld distinct and disparate understandings of the world.	See Colwell-Chanthaphonh and Ferguson (2008b). See Bray et al. (2000) for details of collaborative inquiry.
Cooperative archaeology	Similar to CBPR, but not explicitly community-driven or participatory. Brings together community members and archaeologists for projects that interest communities. Communities are involved, but are not necessarily decision-making partners.	Tesar (1986) discusses an early example at St. Augustine that involved a community advisory board in decision making.
Covenantal archaeology	Native American tribes and archaeologists develop and utilize agreements for archaeological project goals and methods on tribal lands.	Zimmerman (2000) frames the concept. See Bendremer and Thomas (2008) for one example of practice.
Community archaeology	Describes wide range of practices. Engagement of community with the local archaeology is central, primarily at fieldwork stage (not planning and interpretation). Focus is often on education to children/teachers. Others use it in ways similar to CBPR.	Simpson (2010) compares multiple U.S. and UK projects. Marshall's (2002) special edition of *World Archaeology* provides an international set of case studies. Moser et al.'s (2002) use of the term is nearly synonymous with CBPR principles.

(continued)

TABLE I   (continued)

Type of Approach	Emphasis and Key Concepts	Examples and References
Public archaeology	Often termed "public outreach," archaeological interpretations are shared with the public, often in schools or with teachers, but they rarely involve the public in planning and decision making. Participants self-select without explicit effort to engage a wide cross-section of community. Some link the term with "applied anthropology" to describe a practice closely akin to CBPR.	Simpson (2010, 1) defines it as archaeology "with or for the public rather than just by and for professionals." Shackel and Chambers (2004) provide excellent case studies, many that include CBPR principles.
Civic engagement archaeology	Archaeologists work with communities, but projects are not necessarily community-driven. It intersects in multiple points with goals and principles of CBPR, but the focus is on using archaeology to increase civic awareness and engagement.	Little and Shackel (2007) and Little and Amdur-Clark (2008) provide examples of archaeology's role in social justice and building civil responsibility. See Putnum (2000) for foundation—need for increased civic engagement.
Service-learning archaeology	Involves community at all levels, emphasizes benefits to community. Focus is on training students and building civic engagement.	Nassaney and Levine (2009) provide excellent examples and theoretical discussion to support engaged teaching in the twenty-first century.

conducted a form of community-based research without knowing there was a name for it or a literature dedicated to studying it (Keene and Colligan [2004] and Nassaney [2008] make this point for community service learning). However, archaeologists should link community-based research with broader theoretical and methodological understandings to achieve its full potential. Such linking improves practice, while also raising the profile of the work within the academy, which often undervalues community-based research, sometimes labels it as "service," or discounts it all together.

My goal has been to take the important step of connecting archaeology with the wider intellectual conversation about knowledge production and research methodologies, particularly dialogues focused on decolonizing the research process. There are a number of excellent case studies about archaeological collaboration. But what I want to demonstrate in this book is how on-the-ground CBPR projects also inform and should be informed by theories for creating and mobilizing new knowledge and the power dynamics involved in processes of making and moving archaeological knowledge. There is an direct connection here to public archaeology or "outreach," as it is often termed, because CBPR is explicitly concerned with moving knowledge. However, it does so as part of a broader framework of engagement, research partnerships, and power sharing.

Public and community archaeology are important and useful, but they are different from CBPR in several ways. Neither is (or claims to be) fundamentally community-driven or gives substantive control and decision-making authority to communities. Although both focus on engagement with various "publics"—another complex concept that requires unpacking (McManamon 1991)—they have tended to do so primary through fieldwork or in K–12 educational settings. Furthermore, CBPR has an explicit political and action focus that most public and community archaeology projects do not. Reaching out to communities with the results of archaeological research, developing excellent community programming, and working with teachers to develop educational materials are all significant activities for archaeologists to carry out. Community-based archaeology contributes to those efforts in that it requires a fundamental shift in the way research is conducted, and it necessitates a redistribution of power to disrupt and redirect the way knowledge flows.

KNOWLEDGE MOBILIZATION
AND KNOWLEDGE FLOWS

There is a well-developed and extensive theoretical literature on CBPR, knowledge production, knowledge mobilization and flows, and Indigenous knowledge systems. Scholars working in this area have thought long and hard about how new knowledge is created, how it is mobilized, and how it is effectively moved to reach people in their daily lives. My goal has been to draw from such theoretical and practice-based discussions, and apply the lessons learned to archaeology.

We have done an exemplary job as a discipline in creating a literature of case studies about archaeological collaboration. What we need at this juncture is further effort toward compiling information gleaned from individual collaborative projects to create new knowledge; first, by drawing out common themes at the meta-level that can inform theoretical conversations about community-based research. This process reflects what others have termed *collaborative inquiry*—outlined by Bray et al. (2000) and utilized by Colwell-Chanthaphonh and Ferguson (2008b, 10) to conduct "collaborative archaeology." Extending the work of John Dewey, scholars using collaborative inquiry explain that "knowledge is derived from experience reflected upon." We then need to mobilize that knowledge, and ensure it flows to the communities of practice where it is needed—including, but not limited to, the community of archaeologists and other scholars who helped to create it.

As I hope my research demonstrates, archaeologists have much to learn about collaborative approaches to making and moving knowledge. Useful models and information can be found in the work of scholars in other disciplines who are well versed in CBPR, and also from practitioners in communities that have acquired important information about how to produce and move knowledge. Certainly, we need ethnographies focused on knowledge mobilization and flows so that we can understand how information from archaeological research is used to create knowledge, and how that, in turn, reaches and influences policy makers, governments, communities, and individuals. Archaeologists and anthropologists have already made notable progress in this regard through ethnographic analysis of archaeological projects (Mortensen and Hollowell 2009; Castañeda and Matthews 2008). Scholars from other disciplines who are involved in CBPR have also turned a keen eye to these concerns (Lutz and Neis 2008). Are we dealing with a trickle-down economy of archaeological knowledge? Is there an "upward" flow? Or is knowledge blocked along the route to policy and government decision makers? The flow of knowledge and crossing of boundaries between researchers and communities is one critical part of moving archaeology forward, and that is what I am working to achieve with community-based archaeology.

I am attempting here to cross some of the scholarly boundaries that exist in social sciences, humanities, and medical research, and also the boundaries that exist between communities and researchers; between lay knowledge, traditional knowledge, and scientific knowledge; and between theoretical and applied knowledge (Ommer, Coward, and Parrish 2008). Archaeologists can learn a great deal from such exchanges, but I also think we have a lot to offer those conversations. My framing of community-based archaeology is explicitly broad because it is meant to bring archaeology into global, interdisciplinary, cross-community (in academic, government, tribal, and policy communities) conversations taking place about how we make and move knowledge and how Indigenous knowledge systems contribute to greater understandings that solve contemporary problems.

A PARADIGM SHIFT?

Community-based participatory research is a growing practice, taking hold in multiple fields. It is increasingly utilized in public health, natural resource and forestry management, education, and literature. Is this a paradigm shift in the social sciences and humanities? Will it have a long-term impact on the way research is done, shifting toward a more humanistic approach that involves nonacademics in creating knowledge? That remains to be seen. Certainly, in the study of Indigenous people, the shift toward community-based participatory research is well underway.

In 2002, for example, the Social Science and Humanities Research Council of Canada (SSHRC)—the primary research funding agency of that country—funded a dialogue on aboriginal research to discuss research practices that affect Indigenous peoples. The report explains how the initiative for the dialogue came from an unsolicited brief written by the Saskatchewan Indian Federated College (SIFC, now the First Nations University of Canada). The brief stressed the need for the SSHRC to recognize the paradigm shift underway in what they term *aboriginal research*. To support this, the brief cites comments from the Royal Commission Report on Aboriginal Peoples about the need to shift research toward a paradigm in which Indigenous people conduct research and initiate solutions. The SIFC brief lists seven characteristics of research within the new paradigm. These include ensuring that aboriginal communities benefit from the research, respecting Indigenous knowledge traditions, and placing research on aboriginal people in the care and custody of aboriginal people themselves (McNaughton and Rock 2003, 5).

With the comments from the SIFC brief in mind, the SSHRC solicited comments from other First Nations communities in Canada and relied on those to inform their report. The fifty response briefs gathered by the SSHRC (including input from a cross-section of First Nations communities and organizations) repeatedly named a paradigm shift in Indigenous research. The report states, "The Dialogue on Research and Aboriginal Peoples consistently confirmed that a paradigm shift is well underway in the way Aboriginal research is understood" (p. 15). For those within Indigenous communities, CBPR is the norm. They now expect a robust participatory process from archaeologists and other scholars who wish to study Native American topics.

In terms of paradigms within archaeology, David Hurst Thomas considers the substantive changes that collaboration and conducting archaeology in partnership with communities have brought to the discipline:

> Paradigms guide our path of inquiry, influencing not only the nature of questions we ask but also conditioning our view of acceptable data for answering questions. Those of us who share the same paradigm develop a sense of community and an ability to converse with one another. So viewed, then, the shift toward collaborative archaeology can be seen as a paradigm shift from exclusivity toward inclusivity.
>
> (THOMAS 2008, XI)

This movement toward inclusivity brought us to the exciting point where we are today in archaeology. We now have the opportunity to "problematize the future," as Paulo Freire (Couto 1995) called us to do three decades ago. Developing partnerships affects both archaeologists and communities, each in different ways. Bringing these groups together through a CBPR process creates new, interesting, and often complex points of intersection. As methodologies and guidelines for effective collaboration have developed, archaeologists have learned that collaborative projects must include communities in substantive and meaningful ways to be successful.

To understand how to apply CBPR to archaeology, we must first understand what CBPR is: its history, how it has been effectively used in other fields, the challenges it poses to both researchers and communities, the critiques waged against it, and, of course, the possibilities it can open for everyone involved. This is the subject of the next chapter.

Community-based participatory research (CBPR) is best understood by examining the principles that guide the practice. The primary principle is collaboration with community members. Wondolleck and Yaffee (2000, xiii) discuss what is meant by a "collaborative relationship." They rely on collaboration scholar Barbara Grey's defining criteria, which includes three points: "(1) pooling of appreciations and/or tangible resources, e.g., information, money, labor, etc., (2) by two or more stakeholders, (3) to solve a set of problems which neither can solve individually." As Chapter 2 explained, not all collaborations use a CBPR framework; many do not. CBPR involves a specific type of collaborative relationship. Grey's definition is intended to define collaboration broadly. As such, it is a useful point of departure for examining the principles that guide collaborative relationships while doing CBPR, because it sets the stage for elaborating on two critical points.

The first comes from Grey's first criteria and relates to pooling resources. In a CBPR collaboration, those involved acknowledge that *each* group—academic scholars and their community partners—contributes something valuable to the research process. Although each side has different skills and knowledge, a successful CBPR project combines these differing assets to produce rigorous results. Pooling resources is not simply about money or labor; it involves community *knowledge* and the recognition that such input is valuable and necessary for an effective research process.

The second critical point comes from Grey's observation that neither of the collaborators can solve the problem(s) at hand on their own. Each side needs the others in substantive, authentic ways. Within a CBPR framework, community input is not considered a friendly "add-on" or something done to appease community partners. CBPR is not an "add community and stir" approach, to borrow a well-known phrase from feminist scholars. Rather, community engagement is a necessary component of the research process. The knowledge derived weaves together critical strands from each to arrive at a complete solution to the problems posed.

This does not mean that all research should follow a CBPR paradigm. The approach may not be suitable in some situations (Murphree 2008, xxi). Fortmann (2008a, 2), who has extensive experience in participatory natural resource management, explains: "I have come to understand that scientists can answer some questions, people with other kinds of knowledge answer other equally important questions, and that some questions are best answered in collaboration." We know that research can certainly be done without community engagement. Those following a CBPR approach, however, realize that research does not exist in a vacuum; it cannot be separated from its use in the contemporary world. Remaining mindful of the connection of research to contemporary society is particularly important in archaeology, because the field deals with the heritages of living people.

CBPR's collaborative approach is persistently grounded in communities; it involves community members directly in all aspects of the research process. Gaventa (1988, 19) explains that, "participatory research attempts to break down the distinction between the researcher and the researched, the subjects and objects of knowledge production by the participation of the people-for-themselves in the process of gaining and creating knowledge." Because it is community-based, CBPR aims to address community-identified concerns or problems, and it does so by working within a framework of a community's core values. The participatory process can be used to build capacity in any number of key areas. What's critical is that community members define the areas of focus.

POWER AND SYSTEMS OF KNOWLEDGE PRODUCTION

What is the nature of knowledge? This is a key point raised in the theoretical CBPR literature. Gaventa (1993) details the political economy of knowledge in our contemporary society. He notes that the world we live in is an information society. Knowledge is powerful capital, and those who produce it gain power. In this social, economic, and political process, experts have not been held accountable to those affected by the knowledge they produce.

Wilmsen's (2008, 13) analysis of CBPR pushes the issue of power and knowledge production further when he identifies "science" as a "social activity." He notes that CBPR differs from conventional science: "researchers who adopt a participatory approach explicitly acknowledge that the knowledge science produces is negotiated. Moreover, they seek to expand the pool of people involved in that negotiation." Community partners in CBPR projects are directly involved with or impacted by the research topic. Their involvement in a CBPR project helps in two ways: The participatory process produces better understandings of the topic under study, and it shifts the relationships of power inherent in scholar-driven approaches to research.

Gaventa discusses the power imbalances in scholar-driven research: "Underlying all of these elements of the power of expertise is the expert's lack of any accountability to the nonexperts affected by his or her knowledge. Knowledge production, then, is accountable not to the public interest, not to the needs of the powerless who may be affected by it, but to an ideology which serves to justify the superiority of the expert—the ideology of science and objectivity" (Gaventa 1993, 29). This is precisely the point that Indigenous people have raised about archaeologists in relation to being disenfranchised from the locations, materials, and bodies of their ancestors. Within the United States, Native American communities have vehemently voiced their dissatisfaction when archaeologists claimed stewardship over these items, devalued their knowledge, and ignored their Indigenous understandings.

Gaventa's work also details the kinds of responses that people have to such attempts to control knowledge production. He outlines three basic responses. The first is to reject the dominant knowledge system in a form of anti-intellectualism that denounces any type of knowledge from the dominant system. This response raises relevant issues for Native Americans: What is the exact nature of their protests against archaeological practices? Native people have often been accused of taking this stance—of opposing science and being anti-intellectual. Some Native people may, in fact, reject science, but what seems to be much more accurate is that Indigenous people refuse to accept how science has been conducted. They reject any ideology that equates knowledge exclusively with Western science. They oppose such ideologies when the approach fails to recognize the value in other, non-Western forms of knowledge, or when the approach does not acknowledge that Native forms of science are embedded within Indigenous systems of knowledge. Furthermore, as ample evidence suggests, many Indigenous people value the knowledge produced by Western science and respect those who devote time to carrying out research.

The second response Gaventa identifies stands at the opposite end of the spectrum. Rather than rejecting scientists and other "experts" outright, those dealing with experts who try to control knowledge may develop an extreme faith in the experts to solve problems and produce knowledge. In such scenarios, communities may hire and rely on outside experts to conduct and control research. Many communities around the globe—both Indigenous and not—have taken this strategy and hired experts to conduct research for them.

While often "a tactical necessity" (Gaventa 1993), this response has limitations. It tends to make a group dependent on a researcher and does not address the power imbalances that can arise. Advocates of decolonizing and critical Indigenous research methodologies highlight these imbalances and explain why they cause negative outcomes not only for Indigenous people but also for the research itself (Smith 1999; Denzin, Lincoln, and Smith 2008).

If one wishes to change the system of knowledge, Gaventa argues, the most important response is to change the *process* of how knowledge is produced. He states, "to the extent that these struggles attempt to change the content of knowledge, without altering the process *for whom* and *by whom* it is produced, they are inevitably limited. The mere substitution of one set of social diagnoses and prescriptions for another does not make them more democratic, or more accountable to those who remain the objects of another's theory" (1993, 31, emphasis added).

This is where CBPR enters the picture. It calls for conducting research with, by, and for a community in ways that build community members' skills and capacities. Gaventa is careful to point out that this involves working together and developing a division of labor that relies on each partner's strengths. It does *not* require practitioners to "clone the expert in every person" (1993, 39). Instead, community members engage directly—based on what they already know—throughout the decision making, planning, and conducting of research.

Traditionally, debates about how to involve nonexperts in archaeology have come up around public archaeology or community outreach projects. Archaeologists have made substantial efforts to share archaeological knowledge with a range of public audiences. As I explained in Chapter 2, professional associations, such as the Society for American Archaeology and the Archaeological Institute of America, have created and supported highly successful public education programs. Their websites include excellent activities. Both organizations have active and useful committees that work on public education issues, and they produce great literature for schoolteachers, children, and a range of other audiences.

These efforts play an important role in sharing knowledge with the public, but it is knowledge that *archaeologists* produce. The programs do little to democratize how archaeological knowledge is produced. Public education *is* a critical component of CBPR, but it is not the primary goal: "It is not enough simply to democratize access to existing information. Rather, fundamental questions must be raised about what knowledge is produced, by whom, for whose interests, and toward what ends. Such arguments begin to demand the creation of a new paradigm and organization of science—one that is not only for the people, but is created with them and by them as well" (Gaventa 1993, 40).

HOW CBPR DEVELOPED ITS METHODS AND TERMINOLOGY

Tracing a precise history of CBPR and its related practices is difficult. CBPR responds to a natural impulse in humans to be included in processes that affect us. Not surprisingly, then, movements toward being more inclusive about generating knowledge can be found all over the world and have a complex history. For the purposes of this book, exploring all these currents is unnecessary, and beyond the scope of my research. Even so, a summary of its more immediate historical roots might be useful for archaeologists who want to understand the intellectual and practical context in which the approach evolved.

A democratic paradigm for generating knowledge first emerged in the United States during the popular education movements of the late 1800s to early 1930s. It gained momentum in the 1960s, when a number of scholars from different fields began experimenting with producing knowledge in new ways. Hall (1993, 2005) attributes the first use of the term *participatory research* to work coming out of Tanzania in the early 1970s. However, different disciplines and fields in various parts of the world trace the history differently (Strand et al. 2003).

Theoretically speaking, Fals-Borda views the roots of CBPR within a Marxist context. He describes it as an attempt to build a "popular science." Linking science to both class struggle and political power, he emphasizes the social context of knowledge creation that Kuhn outlined (1970, 23, 181–87). Fals-Borda writes, "It occurs that at certain historical conjunctures, various constellations of knowledge, data, facts, and factors become articulate according to the interests of social classes entering into struggle over social, political, or economic power." Although Fals-Borda does not trace the roots of CBPR to Russia or China (nor does he use the term *CBPR*), he does draw lessons from both the *proletkult* in Russia and the Cultural Revolution

TABLE 2   Influences Leading to Community-Based Research (based on discussion in Strand et al. 2003)

Influencing Model	Characteristics	Key Projects or References
Popular education: emphasis on people self-educating for social change	Learning occurs through investigation; research, education, and plans for sustainable, community-controlled social change projects.	Hull House, 1889; Jane Addams and Ellen Gates Starr (Polikoff 1999), Highlander Folk School 1933; Myles Horton (Horton 1990; Horton and Jacobs 2003); Iowa Fox Indian Project (Tax 1958); Paulo Freire adult literacy (1970)
Action research: academics in conjunction with social institutions	Focuses on workplace management, with less emphasis on active community participation; combined theory and practice.	Kurt Lewin (1948); William Foote Whyte (1991) later reworked it as "participatory action research" or PAR
Participatory research: emphasis on people doing their own research for social change	Examines purpose of research, limits of objectivity, relations between researcher and researched, ethics of data collection, knowledge ownership, and intellectual property issues. Reliance on local knowledge for solving problems.	Sclove et al. (1998); Hall (1975, 1977); Park 1993; Park et al. 1993; Fortmann 2008b. These studies outline many examples globally.

in China. In fact, he observes how the revolutionary practices of both negatively impacted the ability to develop a "people's science" (Fals-Borda 1980, 28–33).

Strand et al. (2003) place the start of CBPR solidly within the social sciences and professional fields. They discuss the critical roles played by those working both within and outside the academic world. They identify three basic influences that led to community-based research, which I summarize in Table 2. The popular education model is best known from the work of Myles Horton (1990; Horton and Jacobs 2003) at the Highlander School, and Paulo Freire's (1970) adult literacy projects in Brazil. The "action research" of Lewin (1948) and later Whyte (1991) developed from a more pragmatic focus on workplace issues. Their work is heavily based on John Dewey's philosophy that knowledge cannot be separated from action. Participatory research places a strong emphasis on involving communities in the research process (for example, Fortmann 2008b).

The multidisciplinary history of CBPR has introduced both a range of terms that now identify it and variations in approaches and practices. Terms include *popular education, participatory action research, action research, community-based research,* and *empowerment research.* Wilmsen (2008) and Strand et al. (2003, 4–8) discuss each term, noting that the different terms and historical distinctions are less apparent in how CBPR is now practiced.

Using the broader term *community-based research,* Strand et al. (2003) examine the principles and practices being used in contemporary higher education settings. They define CBPR as "the systematic creation of knowledge that is done with and for the community for the purpose of addressing a community-identified need." They put forward three central principles—core tenets of community-based research: collaborating; valuing multiple sources of knowledge; and achieving social justice through social action. Orlando Fals-Borda's early community-based research in Columbia laid out much of the theoretical argument for the approach. He has since put forward fundamental principles central to his conception of CBPR. He describes an approach of "systematic restitution," which parallels Strand et al.'s concept of community-based research.

FALS-BORDA'S RULES

Fals-Borda notes four primary "rules" for systematic restitution, which, for him, means bringing new knowledge "from the masses to the masses." He calls the first rule, "communication differential." It advocates delivering research results to communities in accessible ways. Fals-Borda describes several methods he has used to do this, including comic strips; audiovisual aids, such as films, slides, and recordings; and even musical and drama performances by local groups.

His second rule, "simplicity of communication," calls for plain language in delivering results. The third rule, "self investigation and control," refers to the community-based aspect of the research. Here, Fals-Borda aligns with Strand et al.'s more contemporary concept of CBPR. Fals-Borda notes, "No intellectual or researcher determined by himself what was to be investigated, but arrived at a decision after consultation with popular bases and their cadres, and taking into account the needs and priorities of peasant struggle" (1980, 24). Like his approach in general, this comment reflects the strong Marxist orientation that

Fals-Borda and others (compare to Erasmie, Vries, and Dubell 1980) bring to community-based research.

Fals-Borda's fourth rule is "technical popularization." Here, he describes the participatory aspects of CBPR—how community members are directly involved in the process of creating new knowledge. This participatory aspect contributes to community capacity building. This has long-term benefit for communities, because members can use these skills in other settings.

Fals-Borda's theoretical outline of "participatory research" bears much in common with Strand et al.'s overview of "community-based research." Both highlight several primary building blocks for effective CBPR practice that the wider, multidisciplinary literature also identifies. First, both refer to the important contribution of different forms of knowledge. Fals-Borda's discussion of community or "popular" knowledge overlaps with Strand et al.'s second principle/tenet of community-based research, which acknowledges the value of multiple knowledge systems. And second, both view *action* as a critical component within the CBPR paradigm. Strand et al.'s third core tenet—social action for social justice—calls for knowledge creation for the direct purpose of acting and making change. Fals-Borda focuses on what he calls the "action-reflection rhythm" and the dialogical techniques that accompany it (1980, 26–27).

For Fals-Borda, creating knowledge and acting on it go together in a two-step rhythm. These processes spur further reflection, creating an ongoing, generative process that he maps through what he calls "dialogical techniques." He describes this process from his own experiences with CBPR: "Knowledge moved on like a continuous spiral in which we would go from the simplest to the most complex tasks, from the known to the unknown, all in permanent contact with the bases. From these the data were received, we acted with them; information was digested at a first level, and reflection took place at a more general level . . . and so on indefinitely, but within prudent terms determined by the struggle itself and by its needs" (1980, 27).

The spiraling movement that Fals-Borda first described has remained a critical aspect of the CBPR process, and more contemporary practitioners also highlight it. McIntyre (2008) describes how, "The initial questions that framed the projects led to other questions that emerged as the research processes evolved. Those questions then became points of entry into further reflection and dialogue that again led to new and different ways of perceiving the issues that were generated." McIntyre notes the recursive nature of this process and the "spiral of adaptable steps" involved. He describes it as a "braided process" that involves "exploration, reflection, and action" (2008, 5–7).

FIVE PRINCIPLES FOR
ARCHAEOLOGICAL CBPR

The concepts highlighted by these and other researchers help to define CBPR, laying the theoretical and methodological groundwork for its practice. However, as Jackson, Conchelos, and Vigoda point out, "the dynamics of participatory research are infinitely complex and entirely unsuitable to reductionist analyses" (1980, 41). Therefore, trying to define an exact process for conducting a CBPR project is not as productive as putting forward some foundational principles and examples of how they have been applied in specific contexts (Wilmsen 2008)—in this case, in archaeology.

Based on my own experiences with planning and conducting five CBPR projects as well as with analyzing the collaborative and community-based archaeological research of others, I have identified five principles that archaeological CBPR projects have in common: (1) They utilize a community-based, partnership process; (2) they aspire to be participatory in all aspects; (3) they build community capacity; (4) they engage a spirit of reciprocity; and (5) they recognize the contributions of multiple knowledge systems. In practice, these five principles interrelate and overlap in varying degrees, yet each is distinct and plays an important role in making an archaeological CBPR project successful.

COMMUNITY-BASED PARTNERSHIPS

Chapter 2 traced the development of collaboration in archaeology, particularly within the practice of Indigenous and community archaeologies. I discussed how archaeological practices are shifting from doing research "on" or "about" Indigenous people, and their related sites and materials to conducting research "with, by, and for" them. The community-based partnership process of CBPR aligns with this shift, because it involves working with communities as equal partners in the research process. Murphree (2008, xix) describes this as a "shift in power to the local: the power to define the research problem, the power to set the research agenda, and the power to interpret the results."

Community members are, therefore, involved in all aspects of the research: planning, developing research questions, funding, collecting and analyzing data, interpreting data, disseminating results, and then curating the data. This "community-centered control" (Wulfhorst et al. 2008) locates the ability to define a research problem within the community. Communities then receive both short-term and long-term benefits from the research. Moreover, community members develop a shared sense of ownership of the research. In this context, ownership implies that community members are familiar with the way the research is carried out and the results obtained. They are comfortable utilizing the data and interpretations themselves (Wilmsen 2008).

Sharing authority is central here. And, as Strand et al. (2003, 10) point out, both partners experience benefits: "Everyone in the group is regarded as both a researcher and a learner. In this way, the research process itself become a means of change and growth for everyone involved." The shared understanding is that each partner brings something valuable to the collaboration. Writing about participatory natural resource and forestry management, Fortmann (2008a) underscores the importance of forming partnerships between "conventional scientists" (those who work as academics and make a living as researchers) and "civil scientists" (members of local communities who have knowledge-producing practices of their own that they use to solve problems). For Fortmann, this means treating "civil scientists" as equals in learning.

This shift in power balance in a community-based partnership does not mean that academic training and expertise become unnecessary or irrelevant. Many CBPR practitioners demonstrate that academic expertise continues to have a place and value. Archaeologists generally bring to CBPR partnerships a wide range of knowledge and experiences: case studies, methodological and theoretical training, diverse research experiences, and knowledge of field methods. Community members may lack these skills, but they contribute to the partnership in areas where the archaeologists lack knowledge, experience, and training.

A community-based partnership does not involve a "download and learn" approach to public education or community outreach. The model is not that of experts who teach what they know to a community. Nor is it a paternalistic endeavor in which archaeologists claim to be "learners" in order to collect ethnographic information or community data, while affirming a power structure in which the archaeologists are in charge. Conducting archaeological research from a partnership perspective demands a substantive shift in control—real power sharing. This may take time and substantial effort. For example, as in some of the cases that follow, a community may automatically concede decision-making power to an outsider they perceive to be more knowledgeable. CBPR practitioners will acknowledge this dynamic, rather than deny it, and work to offset it. They aim to be self-reflective in how decisions are made and the ways this power differential plays out in daily research practices. Their goal is to develop equal, power-balanced relations with communities, because they understand that this is the most effective as well as most ethically responsible way to do research.

In cases where power roles have been entrenched, a fully equitable research partnership is particularly challenging to develop. Rebalancing power requires effort for both researchers and community members to view themselves and each other differently. According to Murphree, the transition may require "a degree of epistemological ecumenicism for which professional scientists are ill prepared" (2008, xix–xx).

REWARDS OF ARCHAEOLOGICAL CBPR

Along with the challenges of CBPR, scholars who make the shift and forge equal partnerships reap substantial benefits: "Accepting a relationship in which their presence is invited rather than imposed, their focus is directed rather than directive, and their function is facilitative rather than manipulative, they find that the barriers of suspicion that mask local realities fall away, that their data take on added dimensions and that their skills are welcomed rather than rejected."

Archaeologists are now reporting similar experiences. Those who have conducted community-based research in partnership with communities describe clear benefits from the approach. For example, Mills et al. (2008) note that collaborative relationships in one area may improve relations that are troubled or have a problematic past. They describe, for example, how their collaborative field school with the White Mountain Apache gave them an opportunity to rebuild a strained relationship between the University of Arizona and the tribe. The unresolved tensions arose years before from the university's use of an Apache sacred mountain as an observatory. Archaeologists have also pointed out that community-based research contributes to civic engagement (Little and Amdur-Clark 2008; Little and Shackel 2007). Little and Shackel's (2007) edited volume provides well-researched case studies to illustrate this point for both urban and rural settings.

Researchers who utilize a CBPR approach benefit by having their research move in exciting new directions. Just as engagements at the intersection of multiple fields create new perspectives and innovative solutions, I found that conducting research in partnership with communities generated fresh lines of inquiry. Partnering with Indigenous communities has led archaeology toward new and renewed harmonious areas of intersection with cultural anthropology and Native American and Indigenous studies. Archaeologists conducting research with, by, and for Indigenous communities have also found broader theoretical and methodological intersections with scholars in religious studies, comparative ethics, and even philosophy of science.

On the more personal level, I found it extremely rewarding to be involved with research that has a real and visible impact on the world around me. Our work as scholars, educators, and field archaeologists often takes us away from time with our families and communities. I need to feel that time away has been well spent, in a way that benefits future generations. Conducting community-based archaeology provides me with a sense of lasting accomplishment that was lacking in non-CBPR work. It also provides me the opportunity to teach and model for my students and children important cultural ethics, values, and teachings.

The Anishinabek have a set of principles for living life in a good way. We refer to these as the Seven Grandfather Teachings (Benton-Benai 1979: nibwaakaawin (wisdom), zaagi'idiwin (love), minaadendamowin (respect), aakode'ewin (bravery), gwayakwaadiziwin (honesty), dabaadendiziwin (humility), and debwewin (truth). These teachings, together with the prophecies given by the Seven Grandfathers, guide Anishinabe people on their path in life. As I describe in the preface of this book, my own work in archaeological CBPR was inspired by these teachings and one of the Anishinabe prophecies.

CBPR allows communities to identify core tribal values and use them as scaffolding for building new knowledge. The Seven Grandfather Teachings have a prominent place within Ziibiwing's permanent exhibit (Lonetree 2012), and they are visible throughout the Ziibiwing Center in the form of words (Ojibwe and English) and artwork (see Figure 2). For the three Ziibiwing projects that were foundational for this book, these seven teachings guided the research process. As Ziibiwing's curator William Johnson noted during a planning meeting for the Flint Stone Street Ancestral Recovery Project, "Here at Ziibiwing, we view every opinion as a gift to the community." The spirit of respect and humility carried in that statement drove the entire research and planning process. Reflecting on research ethics within a framework of Anishinabe tribal values was both personally and professionally rewarding.

PARTICIPATORY

What does "participatory" mean in research? In CBPR, it means community members engage directly in conducting research. People take part not only in decision making but also in the day-to-day activities of gathering data, analyzing it, and disseminating the results. Community member *involvement* is not the same as research that is *participatory*; in participatory research, community members are active in conceptualizing a project, its daily practice, and how it is "brought to bear on the life-world" (McTaggart 1997, 28). Participatory involvement challenges the idea that *only* professional researchers are capable of doing the intellectual labor

FIGURE 2.
Ziibiwing's Director, Shannon Martin, working with Indiana
University graduate student, Terri Miles, on a community report
for the Flint Stone Street Ancestral Recovery Project. The Seven
Grandfather Teachings are visible on the wall behind them.

that research requires; community members are also capable of producing and analyzing knowledge (Kassam 1980).

The approach to participation varies from project to project and field to field.
However, for archaeology, it's important to draw a clear distinction between ethnoarchaeological research and community-based projects that are participatory.
In the ethnoarchaeology community members provide ethnographic data or other
sources of information. Ethnoarchaeology, experimental archaeology, and conducting ethnographic interviews *of* community members do "involve" those who
agree to participate as research subjects. But this is not participatory in the ways
that are implied in a CBPR methodology, and such research methods should not be
labeled as community-based or participatory.

Archaeologists now have extensive examples of substantive community
participation in excavation and survey fieldwork. Several edited volumes

FIGURE 3.
Sullivan County American Indian Council President, Reg
Petoskey, discusses the depth of a surface scraping on the
Waapaahsiki Siipiiwi mound with Sonya Atalay.

(Colwell-Chanthaphonh and Ferguson 2006; Nicholas and Andrews 1997; Swidler
1997; Marshall 2002; Derry and Mallory 2003; Kerber 2006; Silliman 2008a;
Phillips and Allen 2010) present many cases of including and training community
members successfully in data collection and, to a more limited extent, data analysis.

Members of the Sullivan County American Indian Council (SCAIC) were
directly involved in decision making during all aspects of the project. In some
situations, SCAIC members asked for my input or would ask me to make an
informed choice about the project. In other cases, particularly on sensitive issues
that involved ancestral remains or sharing data publically, SCAIC members were
the sole decision makers. For example, they made all decisions regarding the depth
of surface scrapings on the Waapaahsiki Siipiiwi mound itself (see Figure 3). The
rich literature of community participation in archaeology shows the benefits of
training community members in archaeological methods and including them in
fieldwork.

Farmers in a Honduran CBPR agricultural seed experiment (Corea et al. 2008, 63–64) articulate some of the same benefits as they explain the difference between "paternalistic research practices" and participatory ones. They note that, in the end, it is better to be participatory, because local people become involved in the process and learn how to think long-term and care about future resources. The same can be said for archaeology. Community participation can increase local commitment and skills to manage and protect sites.

Fewer archaeological projects have involved community members in the process of research development and design, or in creating and distributing research results and educational materials, although examples from the museum literature that highlight collaborative curatorial and exhibit design practices are plentiful. An important critique of CBPR more broadly is that communities are sometimes excluded from how research results are applied (Simpson 2000). In archaeology, the rising interest in collaborative heritage management (Balenquah 2008; Hays-Gilpin and Gumerman 2008) and archaeological tourism helps to address this critique.

How communities participate in research can unfold in many different ways. It's the *process* that's key (McIntyre 2008). McIntyre's case studies show that community partners and researchers can work together to define for themselves what "participation" entails, so that their ways of collaborating are a choice rather than an imposition. In their recent work, several archaeologists (Silliman 2008b; Silliman and Dring 2008; Mills et al. 2008; Lightfoot 2008; Rossen 2008) emphasize this point, highlighting the importance of "process" in community partnerships.

The participatory aspect of CBPR is not without its challenges and critiques. One concern has to do with who is involved. Is a diverse group of community members participating, or is only the elite or a select few being given the opportunity (Schafft and Greenwood 2003)? Which community partners have the "interest, time or expertise to participate in every phase of the research" (Strand et al. 2003, 11)? This is a challenge I faced working with communities around Çatalhöyük. Agricultural communities are extremely busy in the summer months when most archaeological fieldwork occurs, and, in Çatalhöyük, community members also felt strongly that their limited archaeological knowledge hindered their ability to participate in the research process.

The critical questions in these situations—questions I address throughout this book—are the following: How can we structure the partnership around existing time commitments? And how can we build the community's knowledge base in ways that do not re-create and further increase power inequalities (Cooke and

Kothari 2001; Hickey and Mohan 2005)? Furthermore, defining participation is far easier than implementing it. The process is often slow and time-consuming, and it may lead to challenging time and funding constraints (McIntyre 2008).

Communities may not wish to participate on all parts of the project (Stoecker 1999). Strand et al. (2003, 34) provide reasons why this may occur, noting that community partners may not have expertise in certain areas (for example, sample selection, instrument design, and analysis strategies). In archaeology, these may be things such as survey or excavation sampling strategy, specifics of transect size, number of cores or other samples taken, types of analyses or chemical techniques. Areas of greater community expertise may include determining whether excavation should take place; addressing how to avoid sacred or culturally important areas; and determining whether destructive testing, nondestructive testing, or testing of any kind are appropriate. If community participants are not knowledgeable about the techniques or methods, and when they have an interest in obtaining such skills, training can certainly fill the gap.

A further challenge to participatory processes is that it can be difficult, even impossible, to include all members, or even a large segment of the community. Women (Maguire 1993) or working-class groups (Jackson 1993) may be overlooked or even actively discouraged from participating. Such was the case with Çatalhöyük. In public, women defer to their husbands and elder male children, even though they have very clear ideas and opinions on how to proceed in private.

In Çatalhöyük, for example, it was often a challenge to gain regular input from women in the community. I encountered one situation where I interviewed a woman in her home. She had very clear ideas about the need to educate herself and her children about archaeology and to be involved in the research that was taking place on-site. However, the next day, when I returned to provide her with booklets containing the very information she requested, her husband was home. She said she did not want the information; her children did. I understood her need to do this and asked if there was any further information they would like. She replied that she knew nothing about it and that we should ask her husband. She did bring her family to site visits and attended regular women's meetings. However, as this project continues, it seems unlikely that she will readily offer her voice in making decisions.

One solution at Çatalhöyük has been to involve local female interns in the project. The interns have become on-the-ground researchers from the community. As such, they have a level of trust from local residents that I, as an outsider—even one who has worked in the community for twelve years—does not. This was apparent in one of the women's meetings we organized to gather preliminary ideas for collaborative research questions and projects. Some women spoke freely about their ideas and were very vocal about the interests and needs of their family. Other women were silent. After the meeting, several younger women who had remained silent quickly went to greet the interns. They shared their ideas and concerns with them, asking them to speak for them. I thought this was because the women were shy, but the local interns corrected me. They explained that the young women did not speak up for fear of angering their mothers and elder relatives. The elder women may not like their ideas, or, more likely, the elders may feel that the young girls should not speak their opinions on such matters but should leave the decisions to the men. The local interns increased the input of female youth in the project.

CAPACITY BUILDING

Building community capacity is one of the central principles of CBPR. Involving communities in a participatory way in daily practices, at all levels of the research process, is important for capacity building because it is through such hands-on engagement that community members acquire new skills. These new skills not only contribute to a community's level of "research literacy" but also increase proficiency in other areas, such as public speaking, computer or other technological training, and community organizing. These new skills are then transferable to other contexts.

For example, as I go on to show, my partnering as an archaeologist with the Ziibiwing Center of the Saginaw Chippewa Indian Tribe of Michigan to conduct NAGPRA-related research gave community members the experience and confidence to move forward on other repatriation claims (Shannon Martin, personal communication, 2009). And, in the Flint Stone Street Project that Ziibiwing carried out, partnering with archaeologists increased the community's knowledge of archaeological methods and led them to appreciate its usefulness for the community in other projects (see Figure 4). In Turkey, community participation in grant writing and engaging with site management and planning has led to further community organizing and discussions about a school for girls and a health clinic. These activities opened opportunities for women in these communities. Experience gained from CBPR projects may also increase a community's knowledge of archaeology and its desire to utilize it.

Building a community's capacity can help members create a sense of independence from academics. Capacity-building efforts are particularly useful for Native American communities that are engaged in development on their tribal lands and want to conduct site assessments, or handle inadvertent discoveries of human remains on or off tribal lands. Having trained members of the community who can conduct such research may be far preferable to hiring outside consultants.

FIGURE 4.
Members of the Saginaw Chippewa Indian Tribe screening
backfill to recover ancestral remains during the Flint Stone Street
Ancestral Recovery Project. They were trained to identify historic
and precontact era artifacts, human bone, and faunal remains.

Several Native communities are, in fact, working to develop their own archae-ology departments. The Zuni Archaeology Project and the Navajo Nation archaeology department are probably the best-known examples. Although not planned as a formal archaeology department, Ziibiwing is exploring certification and further training for the tribal field crew who worked on the mitigation in the Flint Stone Street Project. These community members can then serve as a resource for other tribal nations who face challenges relating to inadvertent discoveries of human remains and who want to use culturally sensitive methods of mitigation.

This does not mean that researchers are no longer needed as experts. In fact, research within a CBPR process may have the opposite effect. Communities may want to work with researchers more closely and frequently. This has been the response at the Ziibiwing Center (Shannon Martin, personal communications, 2009). In other cases, communities may develop extensive research skills through CBPR projects, yet choose to use the recognition and prestige that a research partner brings to a project in order to reach their goals (Stoecker 1999). The structure of conventional research permitting and funding often still requires that academically trained professionals be involved as principal investigators, even when communities can demonstrate proficiency in research training. So it is unlikely that researchers will be excluded from research anytime soon as a result of capacity building in CBPR. For some researchers and communities, though, independent research is a stated goal.

RECIPROCITY

Because Native Americans and other Indigenous peoples have critiqued anthropology, archaeology, and research programs in general, they are sometimes portrayed as being anti-intellectual or antiscientific. This generalized characterization is simply not true. Nason (2009) writes: "They [Native Americans] are opposed to bad science and to scientists who would destroy Native American civil and other rights in the name of science." Many Indigenous communities have worked productively with scientists, each having their own aims and goals that converge or overlap. Such partnerships require a give-and-take. In many ways, they parallel collaborations between teams of multidisciplinary specialists or co–principle investigators on archaeological projects. All the participants benefit from the research, but in different ways. Each has distinct primary goals. They agree on a set of practices for achieving these diverse goals by working together. In many cases, they enhance and build on each other, because each brings different knowledge, experience, and skills to the work.

Burnette and DeHose (2008, 88) refer to a type of reciprocity in their research. Both are members of the White Mountain Apache community who partnered with Jonathon Long in a CBPR project that involved youth in examining ecological changes in waterways on tribal land. They adhere to the view that researchers can come to communities and gather data, but they also have to "leave something." Archaeologists (for instance, Silliman and Dring 2008; Kerber 2006) describe mutually beneficial projects as well. Mills et al. (2008) describe the strong commitments to balancing reciprocity and to reaching common goals in the collaborative field school between White Mountain Apache and the University of Arizona. They detail a very useful practice of using "Kane's Rule," which White Mountain Apache elder Raymond Kane put in place to ensure that at least 51 percent of the demonstrated benefits go to the tribe and its people. Although "benefits" can be very difficult to quantify, the rule has proven a helpful guide in considering what is gained and by whom. Such a process ensures critical consideration: Both sides must assess and evaluate who is benefiting and how.

Approaches to CBPR do not require that all benefits of research go to the community, nor do they necessitate a 50/50 (or other predetermined) split of benefits. What I find to be important is to approach the partnership with a *spirit* of reciprocity. What I mean is that it is critical to approach the research with a sense of humility. Proceeding as if communities will be the only or primary beneficiary of the research may foster a sort of employer/employee mentality. Instead, researchers should approach the work by openly acknowledging that they are gaining something valuable from the process as well. This leads not only to critically considering who benefits and how, but often to reevaluating how we frame the concept of "benefits."

Archaeologists and other scholars tend to view the act of doing research from a presumed neutral position. They assume that, with the proper education, training, experience, and permission, it is natural to do research. Research is assumed to be a value in and of itself, and benefits to the researchers are often not a point of consideration. By contrast, the epistemological stance of CBPR asks us to acknowledge more explicitly how we benefit—that conducting archaeology, or other forms of research, benefits us in many ways. For example, we reap intellectual and professional benefits from our research experiences. Our disciplines benefit from the training students receive in planning and conducting fieldwork. And, the mere fact of being given the opportunity to be involved with and to study someone's heritage in any capacity is a clear benefit. However, it is a privilege, not a right.

Viewed from this perspective, the question of archaeologists' benefits are reframed, and the issue of reciprocity becomes less about putting quantitative numbers on benefits and more about entering a place where all parties feel they gain something valuable from the partnership. This framing and the spirit of reciprocity that it fosters ensure that communities benefit through the use of basic principles of CBPR. Using a community-centered approach through practices that are participatory and that aim to build capacity in the community will most likely benefit the community. And, if the community does not experience benefits, they have the power to say so and alter the relationship, or end it, if need be.

It's important to stress that nothing prohibits archaeologists from approaching a project with intellectual curiosity. Archaeologists will naturally develop questions that they hope to answer through the research. CBPR does not put a stop to archaeological contributions to the growth of knowledge for the discipline. However, by establishing clear goals and unambiguous expectations of each partner's interests and what they hope to achieve, and by paying attention to how benefits flow to each participant, practitioners of CBPR strive to protect the integrity of the research—morally, intellectually, politically, socially, and in every other way that matters to those involved.

INDIGENOUS AND LOCAL KNOWLEDGE

CBPR raises questions about who counts as a credible "knower." Fortmann (2008a) observes that credibility is frequently aligned with social power. The powerful are viewed as the "credible knowers," and they set the criteria for what is acceptable and valued. According to Strand et al. (2003, 11), "CBPR answers the question, 'Whose knowledge counts?' in distinctive ways. It places the less powerful members of society at the center of the knowledge creation process. This means that people's daily lives, achievements, and struggles are no longer at the margins of research but are placed firmly at the center."

Epistemological changes within the social sciences and humanities, including those occurring in post-processual archaeologies, led many researchers to acknowledge that we do not have access to the real, knowable world and are never simply objective observers of it (Wilmsen 2008). Rather, we are always viewing the world through a cultural lens—from a "situated" position (Haraway 1988).

This epistemological stance is central to the principles of CBPR, because recognizing that knowledge is always filtered through experience instills respect for other knowledge systems. It also widens who can contribute to and benefit from research. People's experiential and local knowledge become valued as critical in developing better understandings of the world (Wilmsen 2008; Fortmann 2008a). Coming from a "philosophical stance of inclusiveness," in which all people create knowledge, CBPR practitioners strive to integrate multiple knowledge forms and generate an "interdependent science" (Fortmann 2008a, 1).

Natural resource management provides several examples of how interdependent science can be done successfully in practice (Jackson and McKay 1982; Arora-Jonsson 2008; Burnette and DeHose 2008; Wilmsen et al. 2008). In each case, the examples demonstrate that an inclusive approach to knowledge not only is morally and philosophically correct but also enhances our knowledge of the world. Fortmann (2008a), for example, shows how scholars used CBPR because the local knowledge they acquired through a participatory approach provided important answers to the question: "How can we learn what we need to know and understand to create, sustain, and enhance healthy ecosystems and human communities?" (Fortmann 2008a, 7).

Applied to archaeology, local and Indigenous knowledge can help us understand the rich picture of past cultures and to protect and sustain these histories for future generations. The question then becomes: How can we successfully integrate different forms of knowledge in culturally appropriate ways when we do archaeological research?

Archaeologists have been discussing the validity of multiple knowledge systems for at least three decades. Those in post-processual and Indigenous archaeologies in particular have led these debates, because they ask that we consider how Indigenous and local knowledge contribute to how data is gathered and interpreted (Bendremer and Thomas 2008; Lightfoot 2008). For example, some scholars (Lightfoot 2008; Anyon et al. 1997; Ferguson et al. 2000; Nicholas and Andrews 1997; Basso 1996) point to the spiritual significance embedded in many oral traditions and underscore the sensitivity required when outsiders seek to incorporate such knowledge.

Beyond expanding archaeologists' concepts of histories, Indigenous and local knowledge have been combined in substantive ways with archaeological knowledge. These areas include, for example, integrating Indigenous concepts of time (Yellowhorn 2002; Atalay 2010); ethics (Colwell-Chanthaphonh and Ferguson 2004, 2006; Bannister and Barrett 2006); archaeological education (Atalay 2008c; Silliman 2009); and core tribal values (National Congress of American Indians 2009). As I explained in the Preface, I was drawn to explore a CBPR approach in the first place because I wanted to find ways of respecting multiple knowledge systems and of braiding diverse forms of knowledge.

The distance between Indigenous/local knowledge and scientific archaeological knowledge, though challenging to bridge, forms a space for tensions that can be valuable in leading to better archaeological theory (Nicholas 2008). Bringing together multiple forms of knowledge in substantive ways that resist a simple "add local/Indigenous knowledge and stir" approach is a critical part of archaeological CBPR practice. The goal is not to replace scientific archaeological knowledge with local or Indigenous concepts; it is rather to "recombine" these in successful ways. I think here of DNA recombination: It does not follow a preset formula or make a precise 50/50 mix. Rather, the combinations fit the situation and are worked out on a case-by-case basis.

Integrating local knowledge works best when it takes place at every phase of research. The integration is ongoing, not simply an add-on at the later stages of interpretation. This means researchers incorporate Indigenous protocols and concepts into how data is gathered, shared, "owned," curated, and archived. A community's knowledge of its own needs for managing cultural information, sites, and materials pervades each step.

For example, in Çatalhöyük, Turkey, understanding the archaeological site as part of a wider cultural and historic landscape involves examining the way local communities experience the landscape and incorporating their understandings of what is needed for management and development of the site. This was not an either/or proposition. Researchers and community members did not have to choose between conventional forms of scientific knowledge/approaches and traditional/local knowledge. Research within a CBPR paradigm builds two-way paths of learning. Local communities become more fluent in scientific approaches, while also retaining confidence in what they know traditionally. As these communities learn about scientific approaches, they may simultaneously value, seek out, protect, and maintain their own systems of knowledge. And researchers can do the same.

Integrating Indigenous knowledge and local knowledge into archaeological practice is not without its challenges. Scientific discourse and local discourse are quite different. Successfully combining them is time-consuming and takes daily effort (for example, Bendremer and Thomas 2008; Lightfoot 2008; Dowdall and Parrish 2003; Mills et al. 2008). The aim is to truly *integrate* different systems of knowledge, which takes considerable care and sensitivity. Each sphere of discourse must inform and guide the other.

Integrating the two is different from simply presenting them as alternative interpretations, as some multivocal approaches do. A critical analysis of multivocality reveals that it is not necessarily empowering; at times, it can be detrimental. When interpretations of multiple stakeholders are presented side by side, for example, without proper context on the validity of multiple systems of knowledge, one view can have a dismissive effect on the validity of another. The normative view from conventional science is often given priority, whereas Indigenous and local approaches and information are relegated to the realm of quaint folk knowledge (Atalay 2008b). Feminist thought made this point decades ago.

Valuing local and Indigenous knowledge as well as respecting multiple *ways* of knowing involve working out hybrid approaches. Yet the implications go beyond shifting how scholars conduct specific research projects; they call for a shift in the public mind as well. The public needs to be educated about diverse knowledge systems—their validity and value—just as researchers do. Archaeological outreach programs can teach these complexities to K–12 children and then continue through training at the undergraduate and graduate levels. CBPR programs that highlight these complexities to K–12 children are important elements of a larger project of fostering what I refer to as "knowledge multiplicity" in the wider society.

ROLE OF SOCIAL CHANGE AND SOCIAL JUSTICE

Many people have written about the direct connection of CBPR to action, social change, and social justice. They emphasize that these values are not just guiding principles; they permeate the entire practice of CBPR. For example, Kassam (1980, 63–64) includes action and social change in four of the five characteristics he uses to describe participatory research. One particularly important point he makes is that researchers who work with communities in CBPR projects must hold a commitment to that community. "This implies a rejection of the possibility of 'value-neutrality' and of the conception of the social researcher as a tool or technician. The researcher must have a sensitivity and democratic identification with the people." Not everyone who utilizes a CBPR methodology would state this point as strongly, but most agree that knowledge created through a CBPR project is ideally used in an *active* way to effect social change and bring about social justice.

Indeed, social change is a core concept that led to the development of participatory and action forms of research. It can be traced to the early work of Kurt Lewin (1948), who is considered one of the founders of action research, and to Paulo Freire (1970), Myles Horton, and Budd Hall, who each established various forms of popular education and participatory research. The work of these early practitioners and the practices they inspired are parallel in many ways. They all share the goal of democratizing research. However, they developed from different philosophical concepts (Wilmsen 2008). As I explained earlier, Lewin's action research approach was based on a philosophy of pragmatism influenced by the work of John Dewey, whereas Horton, Hall, and Freire's approaches were strongly rooted in Marxist philosophy.

Graduate students in my CBPR methods courses tend to be very interested in how archaeology can bring about social change and how it involves social justice. Most directly, a CBPR methodology promotes social change by engaging descendant and local communities in substantive ways—in studying, planning, and managing their heritage. Repatriation research, land claims projects, and studies that contribute to cultural tourism to build local economies are other ways that a CBPR approach within archaeology and heritage management can contribute to positive social change and social justice initiatives. These projects can be linked to a wider project of decolonization in which research becomes a tool of liberation for those who have experienced oppression or been disenfranchised from their heritage.

CBPR projects also contribute to social change through building capacity in communities. In our archaeological CBPR project in Turkey, for example, rural farming communities had been disenfranchised from engaging in meaningful ways in protecting and managing their heritage because of class and educational inequalities. Through our Çatalhöyük CBPR project, this is changing. Village residents are becoming actively engaged in the research and its ongoing practices. As a result, community involvement is impacting long-standing class and gender inequalities.

This case is not unique. Archaeology is being used elsewhere as a tool to promote literacy, to introduce science education, and to address racism (Rossen 2006, 2008). It can be very successful at bringing youth and elders together (Burnette and DeHose 2008; Lyons 2011; Lyons et al. 2010)—an important goal for many Indigenous communities (Fox 2010). How a project might result in positive social change may not be immediately obvious, but this should not prevent archaeologists from using the approach.

DEMOCRATIZING KNOWLEDGE

Using CBPR to democratize knowledge and its production is closely linked to the topic of social change. De Vries (1980, 86) argues that, "science is a tool used to promote learning of the world." If we agree with him, then CBPR widens the spectrum of who has access to such learning. Rather than a trickle-down model of education in which knowledge is produced by academics and shared with those who have access to higher education and academic literature, CBPR allows non-scientists to actively engage in the process as part of a "grass-roots production of knowledge" (Heany 1993). The concept of knowledge democratization places the university front and center in CBPR discussions. For some, democratizing research through a CBPR approach creates and fosters an important connection between academia and communities, "linking the university to the world it studies" and opening up academia to scrutiny (Arora-Jonsson 2008, 142). A CBPR approach can "shift the perception of the academy as an exclusive space for thinking and theorizing, to a site for collaborative experiences with local, national, and global communities" (McIntyre 2008, 8). Many believe that forming two-way, balanced relations between the academy and communities brings benefits to both.

For others (Heany 1993), democratizing knowledge means keeping CBPR centered in communities. They worry that communities might depend too much on "assumed special knowledge." Heany argues that the grassroots aspect of CBPR makes it such a powerful tool, precisely because it empowers communities and democratizes knowledge, yet "expert knowledge" can have the opposite effect. He cites how the practice of the law in handling disputes alienates a community from the process of producing knowledge: "Clients and communities led by professors are always at risk of losing control, as with the practice of law, where a dispute quickly becomes submerged in the incomprehensible 'legalese' of litigation" (1993, 46). He warns that attempts to legitimize CBPR practices by bringing them into a university can have a similarly alienating effect on communities. Instead of democratizing knowledge production, legitimate knowledge can become limited and circumscribed—"less than."

How can we ensure that a CBPR practice is effective at democratizing knowledge? Certainly, we must heed Heany's warnings. We must critically consider what it means to enter into relationships with large-scale institutions, such as a university. Making CBPR a part of mainstream academic research practices will have pitfalls. Power imbalances cannot be ignored and can be very difficult to offset.

However, we need to have these discussions, and they should not be confined to academic discourse. Community members should have a say, and the large-scale issues should also be discussed on the smaller-scale level of each CBPR project. Community-evaluation procedures at regular intervals help. They ensure that the community is both involved in producing knowledge and shares ownership of the research results. Researchers are bound to ask themselves: What does it mean to democratize knowledge in authentic ways? And, how do we monitor the process to ensure that this is taking place? As important as it is for researchers to wrestle with these questions, they can be addressed authentically only in partnership with the community in which they are working. Having that dialogue gets to the heart of what adhering to a CBPR approach means.

COMMUNITY ENGAGEMENT ON A
NATIONAL LEVEL

Thus far, I have discussed power sharing in archaeology at the level of individual archaeology projects. This is where collaborative research occurs day to day and on the ground. But the principles of community-based research also intersect with the way archaeologists practice their discipline and teach it at the national level. The practices that universities and anthropological and archaeological professional associations support directly affect how Native communities view not just archaeologists but the profession as a whole. Individual archaeologists who are committed to collaboration and community-based research must pay attention, then, not only to how they personally interact with communities, but also to how larger organizations engage communities. If archaeologists aim to take seriously the ideals of meaningful and substantive collaboration and power sharing—ideals that many archaeologists are now embracing—then the practice of these ideals must extend to the way professional associations work with Indigenous and local communities. We need to involve communities in discussions about research partnerships and collaboration at the institutional and national level as well. The daily practice of archaeology will not shift to involve greater power sharing unless those of us within the archaeological community insist on instituting it within our professional organizations. This is an appropriate "problem" for collaboration to address, but so far, the need for a wider collaborative mind-set within archaeological organizations has not been "problematized," as Freire put it. Hence, Indigenous and local communities have not been invited to facilitate collaboration at the national and international level.

Based on my comparative research, I have concluded that the most critical tool for successful collaboration is *will*. We need the will to tie our successes as archaeologists to our willingness to share power and control. We need the will to work together to make policies that affect both archaeologists and Indigenous people. And many individuals and teams of archaeologists are proving that they have this will. On a project-by-project basis, at the level of individual archaeologists, collaboration and power sharing are becoming part of practice.

Yet shifting archaeology from an expert-driven to a community-based endeavor at the national and professional organizational levels has not occurred. Professional archaeological organizations do not have mechanisms in place to involve descendant communities in policy decisions that affect their heritage. As a nationally funded discipline, archaeology has not set the high bar at developing partnerships with descendant communities based on an ethic of partnership and power sharing. For example, sharing power and involving Native people fully in policy decisions, especially about what happens to Native American ancestral remains and other critical issues, have not yet become the norm of national practice. The same holds for non-Indigenous, local communities globally.

Can we be truly collaborative? The power-sharing collaboration I'm referring to leaves critical space for communities to say "no," to stop excavation or the research process altogether, if they choose to do so. It is not a neocolonial collaboration, as feared by Boast (2011) in the context of museums, in which archaeologists still maintain the ability to act (research, excavate, train students) in the same ways, but now doing so with more partners. I believe archaeology can become a truly collaborative endeavor. But perhaps it requires that we ask ourselves another question: Can we be fully successful in creating and mobilizing knowledge about the past in authentic ways if we do not engage, share power, and partner with communities? Framed this way, the challenges of CBPR are challenges we, as archaeologists, must face collectively.

RESEARCH RIGOR

CBPR increases trust between communities and researchers, and provides communities with access to research, as insiders. We have substantial examples of how CBPR can be used to involve Indigenous and local people in creating knowledge, and it affirms their role as knowledge stewards within their communities. The interdisciplinary literature and my own experiences with the five community-based projects I conducted support these claims.

But can CBPR create rigorous results? Some see the action aspect of CBPR as taking away from the objectivity of the work. They fear it reduces the intellectual rigor and trustworthiness of the findings. Hale (2008) raises this concern about "activist scholarship" and calls practitioners to "reclaim methodological rigor." Some CBPR practitioners have raised these issues too, highlighting how complex current notions of intellectual rigor have become.

While CBPR may complicate issues of rigor, it can also enhance rigor when it braids different perspectives and knowledge systems together in skillful ways. For example, in her work on plant harvesters in the Pacific Northwest coast of the United States, Ballard (2008) addressed these concerns and demonstrates the need to balance between rigor and participation. Her research "required negotiations between the accepted level of rigor for ecological research and the principles of participatory research" (p. 111). Ballard concluded that balancing the two values did not lessen the validity of the results. Rather, the compromise "represents a navigation of two sets of standards." In this case, it led to a better experimental design. Ballard concluded that we need to "broaden the bandwidth" on questions of validity. Resource managers and scientists can improve their research findings by expanding how they define useful knowledge, research, and practice.

Other scholars writing from a CBPR framework (Fortmann 2008a; Hale 2008b), including some archaeologists (Atalay 2011; Silliman 2008b; Nicholas 2008), contend that research done in a community-based framework is just as capable of producing rigorous results as work done within a researcher-driven model, "without compromising the essential goals of archaeological inquiry" (Nicholas 2008, 244).

The growing scientific literature produced using a CBPR approach includes academic reports, books, edited volumes, and journal articles. It also includes a wide range of both written and less conventional community reports. I have seen theater performances, comics, online videos, and public exhibits. Clearly, the knowledge being produced through CBPR is not limited to academics but is reaching a wide audience.

In CBPR projects, community reports take many forms, and they may include technical archaeological concepts and data (Atalay 2006, 2007, 2010). While not in the same format or depth of detail as academic reports, they effectively present research results based on data that were rigorously collected and analyzed. Such research products may be more effective than conventional scientific reports, because they reach a greater number of people in a format that tends to be easily accessible and includes knowledge in forms that are familiar.

Scholars have posed other concerns about rigor, objectivity, and responsibility for managing and overseeing research. Newer academics question how university tenure and promotion committees might view community-based work. They voice concerns that their work is often discounted as "advocacy" or "service," as opposed to *real* research that is presumed to be fully objective. Critics with these concerns focus not so much on the rigor of the method or the results achieved, but on the lack of "objectivity," as they see it, when research is done in partnership with communities.

Hale (2008a) has responded to these critiques. He calls scholars to reveal the idea of a removed, neutral, objective, agenda-free researcher as nothing more than a myth. Interestingly, this critique can also be posed in reverse. In my own CBPR work, one colleague asked if I was trying to remove myself from the research and trying to put the entire responsibility for the projects on the communities with whom I partner. Still others question the feasibility of archaeological CBPR for projects that federal or other government agencies, such as the National Park Service, fund. Although federal agencies and funders require professional archaeologists or primary investigators on university-based grants to be accountable for funds, this does not preclude the use of CBPR methodology. Successful examples of community-based archaeology in a federal agency context prove this point (for several excellent examples, see Silliman and Ferguson 2010).

These are some of the complexities involved in doing CBPR. They raise challenges that scholars who want to start a community-based project may face. Undoubtedly, doing community-based archaeology calls scholars to work with communities as well as institutions (federal agencies, granting entities, tenure and promotion committees, and university institutional review boards) in ways that differ substantially from researcher-driven archaeology. However, I have found nothing to indicate that scholars doing CBPR cannot produce rigorous results *and* be supported in doing so. CBPR scholars are integrating community-based practice with government agency projects; they are moving through the "human subjects" review process in a timely manner, and they are gaining tenure.

Furthermore, CBPR is raising complex and interesting questions about the nature of knowledge, how humans produce it, the meaning of "objectivity" and "rigor," and the relationship of the university to/within "the community." For archaeology, community-based research is stimulating the discipline. It is making scholars ask new and very different questions, incorporate different approaches to fieldwork, and be accountable in ways substantially different from before. Archaeology remains a powerful and rigorous tool for creating knowledge about the past and the present. However, the daily is fundamentally different in a CBPR paradigm.

ARCHAEOLOGICAL CBPR

How does a CBPR process compare to a more conventional, researcher-driven archaeological process? A side-by-side comparison gives a snapshot of CBPR principles and how they apply to archaeological research. Both Strand et al. (2003, 9) and Maguire (1987 17–27) provide comparisons of traditional academic and community-based research. I designed the following table (Table 3) with concepts from both sources, but I reworked these to show the differences for archaeology.

CRITIQUES OF CBPR

What this chart makes clear is that CBPR involves a tremendous amount of work, which extends the time frame of doing archaeological research. Without a doubt, conventional researcher-driven archaeology is less complicated and faster. But, if we are striving to move away from a model of research that is "extractive" to one that puts science—in this case, archaeology—at the service of ordinary people, as Wilmsen (2008) and many others call for, then CBPR holds great promise and warrants further exploration.

Archaeologists are not experts in community planning, education, or cultural anthropology. CBPR requires skills in areas for which archaeologists currently do not receive much training. Community-based and participatory approaches to research have been influenced by—and in some cases, grew out of—paradigms for

Aspect of Research Project	Conventional Archaeology Research Process	Community-Based Research Process
Primary goal of research	Advance knowledge within the discipline	Primary goal is to answer/address community problems or questions; contributes to betterment of a community (social change); may also include questions that advance knowledge in the discipline, but balanced with spirit of reciprocity.
Source of problem/question	Locating gaps in existing research	Community-identified need or problem.
Who designs and conducts research?	Archaeologists, sometimes with assistance of graduate students	Archaeologists, students, community members (including broad cross-section of members), working in partnership.
Role of researcher with descendant or local community	Visit local community during field season; act as expert "tour guides" during community visits; observe or interview community members for ethnoarchaeology or experimental archaeology; or no interaction at all	Both a research partner and learner; may still engage in ethno- and experimental archaeology projects, but these are also designed in partnership with community.
Role of descendant or local community in research project	Excavation labor force; research subjects/sources of information (e.g., ethnoarchaeology/experimental archaeology); invited to tour site on "community day"	Both a research partner and learner; active in all phases of research.

(*continued*)

TABLE 3   (continued)

Aspect of Research Project	Conventional Archaeology Research Process	Community-Based Research Process
Relationship of researcher to community members	Short-term (duration of each field season), task-oriented, friendly, or in some cases detached	Long-term, multifaceted partnership that takes on different roles throughout the process. Stoecker (1999) identifies community organizer; animator; and public educator.
Determination of value and validity of research	Peer review determines validity, contributes to knowledge for the discipline and general human knowledge.	Community review is primary, followed by academic peer review for work that is published for academic use. Value is determined by contribution to community and applicability, and also contributes to positive social change.
Development of research design (data collection, artifact handling protocols, treatment of sensitive materials, curation, etc.)	Archaeologists develop design using professional standards, often with the goal of objectivity, and a heavy reliance on quantitative methods.	Archaeologists work with a community to formulate rigorous yet flexible research design, and develop culturally appropriate field/lab/curation protocols. Traditional and experiential knowledge play a key role, and oral tradition is a valued source of data. Quantitative and qualitative data are valued.
Beneficiaries of the research	Archaeologists, academic community; sometimes "general public" receives limited information through public archaeology and popular media formats.	Archaeologists, descendant or local community members, and may also include multiple partnerships. Public audiences also considered.
Primary curation and access to data	Archaeologists, and those with access to a university (most often students, after they receive some training)	Community or joint archaeologist/community. Terms are defined in partnership, and rely on cultural protocols defined by the community.

Aspect of Research Project	Conventional Archaeology Research Process	Community-Based Research Process
Method of presenting and disseminating results	Journal articles, academic books, professional conferences; sometimes also popular media via documentaries, news articles, K-12 education and public presentations	Varies widely—academic forms of reporting, but also shorter, plain language reports; may also involve multiple, creative formats (theater, comics, video, oral tradition, radio, ceremonies, narratives, community meetings, or other local media).
Project funding and permission	Grants written by archaeologist (often to university or public funding agencies); permission from government or government agency. Most universities do not require IRB review.	Varied—community-funded, coauthored grants to university or public funding agencies. Grant writing is part of capacity building for community; requires tribal council/community review. IRB review acknowledges impact of archaeology on human communities.
Stewardship	Archaeologists assume the role of steward for the archaeological record.	Community members become stewards or develop joint stewardship plan; community considers how to protect intellectual property related to traditional knowledge and oral history.

development in non-Western countries. Some of the harshest critiques of participatory models stem from the academic literature on development. For example, Cooke and Kothari (2001) describe how participatory research can become a form of "tyranny". La Salle (2010) voices similar frustrations and critiques from an archaeological perspective.

The primary critiques of CBPR can be summarized in five main areas, which the CBPR literature describes in detail (La Salle 2010; Wilmsen 2008). The first is the misuse or misunderstanding of CBPR basic terms and principles. Projects may use the term *community-based* incorrectly, confusing community involvement with being community-driven and participatory. Archaeologists may co-opt a community to gain support for a project that originates elsewhere or that does not involve the community in planning or applying the research (Wilmsen 2008). Second, even when research is truly participatory and community-based, the projects may be deeply embedded in political and economic relations (internal and external) that both hinder and facilitate the research. Third, CBPR cannot guarantee that power inequalities will be removed or even diminished. Fortmann (2008a, 9) aptly states: "Even with the best will in the world, existing power relations are not easily overcome. Creating and maintaining the conditions for an interdependent, democratized science is a daunting task." Wilmsen (2008) encourages scholars to regularly reflect on their successes and failures in this area as they strive to shift the balance of power in research. A fourth area of concern is that communities are complex entities by nature. Defining them is difficult, and working with multiple stakeholders complicates this further. And, finally, engaging a wide spectrum of community members—not just the elites or the men, the educated, middle class, or those likely to agree with your approach—can be incredibly challenging. What is acceptable as *participatory*? Researchers and community members must ask themselves whether CBPR projects can ever be *fully* participatory. If not, when are they "participatory enough"?

CBPR proponents need to acknowledge these challenges. Such challenges are not only natural and inevitable but also valuable during the growth of a fundamentally new approach. CBPR does, in fact, need more study to find successful methods for putting its ideals and principles into practice. Silliman (2008b, 12) and others warn against a global "cookbook" of collaborative methods. They call instead for a framework, for "elucidating the key contexts that frame when, where, how, and why" collaborative archaeologies work in order to "provide guideposts for future researchers."

Silliman's words articulate what I have attempted to do in the chapters that follow. Based on the five archaeological CBPR projects I have been involved with and a critical analysis of CBPR theory and practice in other disciplines, I have identified the primary critiques of community-based research. I go on to propose key contexts that can serve as frameworks for success in archaeological CBPR. These provide some of the guideposts that those collaborating with communities have aptly called for. With them, we can work toward achieving a productive shift in how research is practiced—an endeavor that Indigenous and local community critics as well as scholars from other disciplines have long advocated.

Because CBPR projects are community-driven and are conceived and designed in partnership with community members, some of the first concerns are the following: How do I initiate a CBPR project? How does the start-up differ from embarking on a conventional, researcher-driven project? In practical terms, how do community and researchers connect with each other to begin a CBPR project? The CBPR literature outlines some successful approaches communities have used to connect with scholars and vice versa (Long 2008; McIntyre 2008; Stoecker 2005). But overall, this topic is poorly covered in the CBPR literature. Archaeologists are equally light on details with regards to how they establish their partnerships.

Archaeologists and communities forge research partnerships much as people in other disciplines do. However, key points specific to archaeology do emerge with regard to: (1) how archaeological CBPR partnerships are initiated; (2) how and why archaeologists and communities are most likely to connect; and (3) some of the sensitive issues that may impact a projects' success. Researchers in successful CBPR partnerships regularly cite certain elements that enhance their ability to develop effective projects. Similarly, communities also cite recurring components as crucial for connecting with academic researchers and scholars in a good way from the start. Community concerns often differ from those of academics, yet both are equally important. Both warrant attention for the partnership to find success and the research to be productive.

Stoecker, Tryon, and Hilgendorf (2009) analyze community/university partnerships in service-learning arrangements. They identify the problems and limitations when researchers put the needs and priorities of the university above those of community partners. Overemphasizing university/student needs at the expense of community concerns can lead to a decline or even a complete breakdown in service-learning arrangements. Their research reinforces what CBPR projects have found: Collaborators must identify and address the needs and concerns of *all* research partners, and the early stages of a project are the best time to start doing so. CBPR partners should establish steps to ensure that projects do not overly burden community partners. They need to build into the research design a regular process of feedback and evaluation. This is important even before problems arise. All participants should assess what they need and can offer in terms of time commitment, supplies, and other tangible and nontangible input.

DEFINING "COMMUNITY"

In CBPR, the concept of "community" is central. Communities form the core of CBPR research designs. As I explained in Chapter 3, working in partnership to solve questions and to address research interests on all sides is the theoretical and methodological basis of the CBPR model. But what exactly is a community, and what types of communities might we expect to identify and partner with as archaeologists? CBPR participants need to define, scrutinize, and complicate what we mean by the term *community*, particularly since critiques of CBPR point to the complex nature of communities and the ways scholars define them (Wilmsen 2008). Two issues come immediately to the forefront: First, how do we define the word *community?* Second, who determines membership and how?

Defining the term is complex. Israel et al. (1998, 178) describe communities as being "characterized by a sense of identification and emotional connection to other members, common symbol systems, shared values and norms, mutual—although not necessarily equal—influence, common interests, and commitment to meeting shared needs." They further unpack the concept of community as it functions in CBPR by considering what they refer to as "communities of identity": "Communities of identity may be centered on a defined geographic neighborhood or a geographically dispersed ethnic group with a sense of common identity and shared fate. In some cases a community is based on geographic or political boundaries, a shared sense of identity, or interactions around shared experience." I use the term to refer to a unit of identity that is reinforced through social interactions and characterized by a degree of common identity, shared experiences, and/or geographic proximity.

In addition to defining communities, CBPR practitioners need to remain mindful of various points about their nature and attributes. First, communities are diverse. Each is different from the next, and they are also not internally homogenous; their membership may be quite diverse. Although we often define communities by similarities among their members, they also include a diversity of experiences, opinions, and views. Schensul, Berg, and Williamson (2008) comment on the challenges this brings to anthropological CBPR, particularly with regard to the complex relations created within communities and between diverse community members and researchers. Second, the boundaries of a community are often fluid and indistinct. Membership within communities is regularly in flux. Bartle (2009) observes that some communities existed before their current members were born and may continue to exist after all current members have left. To further complicate the makeup of communities, smaller communities can exist within larger ones, and people can belong to multiple communities at once. A community may be based on geographic location, or it may be quite mobile. In some cases, members may never have met each other in person—online communities, for example. It can be difficult, even impossible, to see a community in its entirety. For all these reasons, community partnerships almost never entail working with all members of the group.

Communities have various types, each defined by what the group has in common. Strand et al. (2003, 17) outline four of the most common types. Communities tend to form around: (1) geographic locations, (2) positions within an institution or social structure, (3) cultural identities, and (4) group alliances. Table 4 lists these four types and the shared criteria around which they form. I have used Strand's criteria, adding examples that demonstrate how each type relates to archaeology and archaeological CBPR partners.

Although partnerships can form with any of these types of communities, archaeologists tend to partner with communities that share a geographic location or a cultural identity. In most cases, archaeological CBPR projects study a specific place—an archaeological site or landscape—that has an identifiable geographic location in a particular regional surrounding. These archaeological sites are connected with groups of people for various reasons. Local communities currently live near a site and may or may not be descendants of the site's earlier inhabitants. Some communities share ancestors who lived near or built a site. Others may have an interest in a particular site or in archaeology more broadly. Collectors can form communities who are interested in artifacts and other objects of material culture, either to add to their personal collections or to sell.

TABLE 4   Four Types of Community Formation with Archaeology-Related
Examples for Each (adapted from Strand et al. 2003)

Community Formed Around	Formation Criteria	Archaeology-Related Examples
Geographic location	Members reside in the same geographic area.	Local residents living near an archaeology site
Position within an institution or social structure	Members are from the same age group or social class.	Elders from a specific city; poor or working-class individuals who live on/near an archaeological site
Cultural identity or relationship	Members share an ethnic or cultural identity.	Members of a specific Native American nation; Chinese Americans descended from those who lived in a historic archaeology site
Personal group alliances	Members share the same religion or profession; or engage in shared activities or interests.	Goddess groups involved at Çatalhöyük; archaeologists; collectors

Communities involved in archaeological CBPR may also form around a particular profession. Ballard's (2008) research in a natural resource management CBPR project offers an example. She worked with a group of salal harvesters (salal is a leathery-leaved shrub in the heather family—*Ericaceae*—native to western North America) to better understand its ecology. The harvesters had developed specialized knowledge about the plant's life cycle. Salal harvesters defined their community by profession, and Ballard's study included only a core group of harvesters, not a broad cross-section of the entire salal-harvesting community.

Profession-based communities may be particularly useful for archaeologists working in industrial archaeology projects. In one project, for example, an archaeologist partnered with former workers in a historic factory site (Mullins et al., forthcoming). Similarly, archaeologists who excavate and study sites form their own professionally based communities.

COMMUNITIES WITHIN ARCHAEOLOGICAL
CONTEXTS

Multiple and diverse communities may have a connection a particular site or region (Marshall 2002), and, as I said, membership in each can be fluid and overlap. As a result, defining "the community" for an archaeological CBPR project can be a challenge. According to some, this task should be left to communities themselves, *not* to archaeologists.

Anne Pyburn (2011) explores the complexities of defining communities in an archaeological context. Complicating the concept of community along three lines, she calls archaeologists to (1) be aware that individuals may be members of multiple communities; (2) refrain from creating and reifying communities (leave definitions to the communities themselves); and (3) work to understand multiple communities: How do communities interact with and influence each other? How do local and descendant communities interact with powerful groups?

The first point—the diverse, fluid, and multiple nature of community membership—is something researchers easily recognize in their own lives. Yet archaeologists often overlook this point when they engage uncritically with other communities. Unintentionally and unknowingly, they may simplify or romanticize the cultures of others. As to the second point, Pyburn shows what happens when archaeologists create and then rely on what she refers to as "imaginary communities" (2011, 8). Using examples of the Maya in Belize, she provides ample evidence of how homogenizing influences of globalization, pressures to perform their indigenous identity and be viewed as "authentic," the desire for economic development, and the rise of cultural tourism can influence and limit community membership. These influences also affect how communities choose to define themselves and how others categorize, name, and define them.

By complicating archaeologists' definitions of community and critiquing their rights to be the definers, Pyburn calls archaeologists to rely instead on people to determine their *own* community: How do *they* set the boundaries and determine memberships? She suggests that the way to begin identifying a community is to ask community members: How do you define your community(-ies) (2011, 12)?

Pyburn's third point is that the situation is never so simple as to include all members of a single community. Thinking in terms of "the" community is rarely an effective approach, because it is nearly always oversimplified and blurs meaningful differences. Rather, community-based research requires archaeologists to engage regularly with multiple groups that are internally diverse and overlap. Pyburn makes this point when discussing the various publics with whom archaeologists engage: These can "be broken down into multiple audiences with differing interests and expectations" (2011, 15).

Understanding the complex character of communities helps archaeologists partner with communities more sensitively and, hence, effectively. This also helps archaeologists become more skillful about engaging public audiences, through tourism, education, or other outward-focused projects. Pyburn makes a further critical point. She argues that archaeologists must come to know and understand not only the local and descendant communities but also the economically and politically powerful groups who are connected to the sites and regions where we work. Mustafa's (1980) work complicates this issue further. His CBPR project included government officials as participants to demonstrate to them what the local residents were capable of. However, such a decision carries risks. In many projects, if government officials or others who represent power are brought in, their presence may inhibit local participation and undermine the trust that a researcher might otherwise develop with community partners. Hemment's (2007) work provides an excellent example of the complexities a community may encounter as it considers partnering with government agencies.

No community exists in a bubble. It links with and operates within an interconnected network of other groups. Each group impacts and affects the others. For this reason, community-based archaeologists need to do some ethnographic research before starting a CBPR project to understand the often complex webs of connection.

In his guide to action research, Stringer (2007, xvi–xvi) notes that CBPR (what he refers to as "community-based action research") "works from the assumption that all people affected by or having an effect on an issue should be involved in the processes of inquiry." A number of archaeological projects regularly face the complexities of how to define communities. Their work both raises specific challenges and encourages solutions for working with multiple community partners.

For example, Ferguson and Colwell-Chanthaphonh (2006) successfully partnered with multiple communities within one geographic area. They conducted a collaborative archaeology project in the Southwest of the United States that involved members of five Native American nations. Each nation has had a continued historical presence in the region since well before European contact. The San Pedro Ethnohistory Project involved representatives from each of the five communities in the decision-making and planning process of the research. The representatives also engaged directly in fieldwork and report writing. Mills et al. (2008) describes a similar intertribal collaboration with a University of Arizona Field School that included the White Mountain Apache, Hopi, and Zuni communities.

To form a community group called SHARE, Rossen (2008) involved both Indigenous community members of the Cayuga Nation and local, non-Native people who were lifelong residents of the area. The partners worked together to purchase and care for a local orchard—land that they turned over to the Cayuga

Nation. This interaction strengthened relationships between the two communities, and it built a foundation of trust and respect needed to form a research partnership related to archaeology.

ÇATALHÖYÜK'S MULTIPLE COMMUNITIES

Archaeologists may work with all descendant communities, as in the San Pedro Valley and White Mountain Apache projects; they may decide to partner with just a few communities; or they may maintain different levels of partnership with several communities that change over time. In the CBPR project at Çatalhöyük, Turkey, I chose to partner with the residents of Küçükköy. This community has the closest physical proximity to the site and arguably has been most impacted by the site's excavation and development, yet it had experienced a great amount of disenfranchisement from site planning and management decision making. I did not make this decision haphazardly but only after I had conducted extensive interviews with members of nearby villages. All of them felt that Küçükköy, because of its proximity to the Çatalhöyük excavations, was the obvious and rightful partner for researching the site and should be the one involved in its management and development. Residents from other nearby villages, as well as those from the nearby town of Çumra, are actively involved in *some* aspects of the Çatalhöyük CBPR project. However, the primary research partner is the Küçükköy community. Since Çumra is a town—larger than a village—it has more government infrastructure. It also holds a good deal more power and voice in local and regional politics than the surrounding villages. Already, Çumra has participated substantively in planning both tourism-related development and how to manage the Çatalhöyük site in the future.

Other communities could have been included as research partners as well. A number of New Age and "goddess movement" groups based in the United States, Turkey, and other countries, for example, have involved themselves with Çatalhöyük since the 1980s (Bartu 2007). While these groups are diverse, they share the view that Çatalhöyük is central to their spiritual beliefs. They have engaged with Çatalhöyük in a variety of ways: performing rituals and ceremonies on site; visiting the site regularly; organizing women's tours; and participating in discussions with site director, Ian Hodder, about the site's interpretation (Hodder and Louise 1998). Members of a goddess group based in Istanbul, Turkey, purchased a house in Küçükköy with the intent of establishing a women's research center near the site. Another group hopes to fund a "Peace Garden" in the garden space within Çatalhöyük's gated grounds area.

Not everyone in the local village community has welcomed their efforts. After the goddess group purchased the Küçükköy house, for example, unknown arsonists burned it to the ground. Some local residents suspect this was done to keep the goddess community from taking up local residence. Bartu Candan (2005) analyzed the incident in light of the larger regional and local political context. While I did not wish to exclude the goddess community from conversations and engaging with Çatalhöyük, I chose only *local* communities as potential research partners. Their lack of resources and power has limited their involvement so far. The decision to partner with the small village community of Küçükköy was intended to build community capacity in a way that would allow local residents—arguably most impacted by the excavations and development of the site—to engage in substantive ways in regional and national level heritage planning and site management and tourism development considerations.

The Çatalhöyük example shows how a CBPR research partnership can impact the region near a site in different ways. The Çatalhöyük–Küçükköy CBPR partnership clearly has a larger impact on local village residents than on nearby residents from villages that are not active research partners or those who reside in more distant villages, towns, or cities in Turkey. In an arena dominated by regional and national politics and larger social entities, the CBPR project carves out space for local villages to have input.

As with Çatalhöyük, CBPR partnerships often impact segments within a single community differently. Even within a small community that seems relatively homogenous, partnering with an archaeological project can have a substantive impact—economically, politically, and socially—on those who participate and those who do not. Bartu (2007) notes that it is the local village residents from Küçükköy who do not own land that most often view engagement with the Çatalhöyük site as attractive, and they utilize their opportunities to be involved with the site to gain both economic and social benefits.

In some circumstances, partnering with archaeologists through a CBPR project can influence how community members view each other and how people view themselves. Not all of these influences are positive. Some of the young female residents of Küçükköy who are involved in the Çatalhöyük CBPR project have faced criticism from their families and relatives for their participation. Several were pressured to withdraw from a heritage crafting project that they had initiated. The project would have provided them income from crafting items that were to be sold at the on-site museum and at other retail locations.

These concerns are not limited to archaeological CBPR. Corea et al. (2008) cite farmers' accounts of their agricultural CBPR project in Honduras. The local people who did not participate in the research had negative views of those who did, referring to them as "crazy." Women involved in a CBPR writing project in India faced more serious penalties from their family and neighbors for doing so (Nagar and Singh 2010). Many of the women were scolded or reprimanded by their families, and several were killed as a result of their involvement. In these examples, the costs and benefits of a CBPR project and the reactions of community members varied considerably. Negative impacts on individuals are usually minimal, in extreme cases can be life threatening. The CBPR process must include thinking through what participation entails and the possible risks and concerns for everyone involved.

Since no community is homogenous, there will be a range of views about the acceptable types of research that should take place; how it should be carried out; the data and details that should be presented in research products; and whether community members should be engaged in research at all. In archaeology, the range of views on how sites should be managed, protected, developed, and studied is wide as well. Conflicting viewpoints can make developing a CBPR partnership very complex and incredibly time consuming.

Understanding the diversity of views within a community is crucial. The results of collaborative research—as with any decision making that leads to community change—can impact community members in different ways. Those not involved in the research can be and often are highly impacted in unforeseen ways by the actions and decisions of other community members. In turn, this can have detrimental effects on those who do participate in the research. The literature on CBPR does not offer easy solutions to these serious dilemmas. At the least, practitioners should consider how a research partnership might impact the community as a whole, not just its benefits to individuals or a specific segment of the group.

ACHIEVING FULL COMMUNITY PARTICIPATION

Along with the complex business of defining communities and considering whom to partner with, CBPR practitioners must keep in mind issues of participation: Are segments of a community being overlooked or ignored? Maguire (1993, 1987) shows how an "androcentric filter" limited the voices and observations of women participants in one CBPR project. She notes that, "gender was usually rendered indistinguishable by terms such as the *people*, the *campesinos*, the *villagers*, or simply, the *oppressed*" (Maguire 1993, 162, emphasis in original). On further analysis, Maguire found that many CBPR projects involved only male community members.

Jackson (1993) addresses a similar issue in his overview of participatory research among Indigenous communities in Canada, but he emphasizes the differences in involvement along *class* lines. Jackson refers to "the new middle class" of First Nations people who are much more involved and who regularly play leadership roles in CBPR projects. Working-class community members tend to be less involved and rarely held leadership positions. He notes that "the neglect of the Aboriginal working class, or the class question generally, is an almost universal characteristic of Aboriginal groups throughout the [CBPR] movement" (1993, 58).

Jackson emphasizes the need to involve working-class First Nations community members in CBPR projects relating to workers' rights and workplace issues. His point applies equally to archaeologists who conduct CBPR projects in partnership with descendant and local communities. In the early stages of the Çatalhöyük CBPR project, class issues quickly became apparent. One obvious example occurred during an on-site seminar to an audience comprised of nearly 100 archaeologists working at the site. I presented an overview of the Çatalhöyük CBPR project and how it aimed to involve local village residents as partners in developing research that would be of interest to their community and would benefit them. During the discussion that followed, one of the Turkish archaeologists on the Çatalhöyük excavation research team was clearly upset about including the local village residents as partners. She asked, "What if the villagers want a swimming pool? Will you give them that too?" This comment was not only an implied critique of the CBPR project; it also revealed the assumptions of the educated, urban, middle class to maintain power and to exercise exclusive rights to conduct archaeology and to study, control, and manage the national heritage within Turkey. Although this reaction was not widespread, it clearly illustrates how CBPR archaeology partnerships can become entangled in issues of class. Local archaeologists, politicians, and members of the public may object to involving community members from the working class: Are they literate? Are they well educated or sufficiently trained? Do they have experience in making decisions for their community? If not, should they be included in research- or archaeology-related matters? In some cases, governments may be highly suspect of involving Indigenous and local communities for fear of giving them power. Such situations can become complex when archaeologists' permits and funding are threatened.

Gender and class are not the only factors affecting community participation in CBPR (Comstock and Fox 1993). Although widespread community participation is a goal, many other constraints can hamper even the best efforts to attain this ideal. Inequalities between a researcher and community in resources (Moser et al. 2002), expertise (Barndt 1980), and interests (Fals-Borda 1980) can limit community participation. Other factors come into play as well, not all of them are the result of researcher–community disparities. According to Comstock and Fox (1993, 109), some CBPR researchers have seen how "internal power structures of communities and local cultures . . . restrict participation" (for example, see Cain 1977; Mbilinyi et al. 1982; Mduma 1982). In several of the Çatalhöyük CBPR initiatives, for example, local women have consistently been pressured to limit their involvement. Some authors (Hudson 1980; Jackson, Conchelos and Vigoda 1980) show examples of how CBPR can disrupt these "local power hierarchies" (Comstock and Fox 1993, 109) by giving community members opportunities to observe the diverse skills and input that others contribute to the research effort. Other scholars (Humphries et al. 2008) observe that, when CBPR projects do not strive to be widely inclusive, they can increase a power structure of privilege. The "elites" become the ones most involved as CBPR participants, because they have greater opportunity to do so. They also benefit the most by increased power when the projects prove successful.

While many maintain that widespread or even complete participation are worthy goals to strive for, other CBPR researchers and community members argue that limiting involvement to particular segments of a community can also be a good choice. De Wit and Gianotten (1980) note that, when members of a community have distinct differences and hold different opinions, a researcher may decide to work with a particular group. If this means excluding certain groups or factions in favor of others who are more likely to agree with the research approach or give consent for a project, then the choice is problematic, of course. It is not only unethical, but can cause resentments within a community and further divide members.

In an environmental water resource project with White Mountain Apaches, Long (2008) chose to work with smaller groups within the larger community for practical reasons. The smaller groups were more homogenous and had more incentive to keep the project going. Long engaged a few community leaders in the project and then worked with youth, who shared the results with their families and the community at large. But this strategy proved to be problematic. Working with a limited number of individuals caused resentments across the wider community.

Arora-Jonsson's (2008) forestry management CBPR project in rural Sweden was also controversial. She chose to work with women; until then, mostly men handled forestry management. Her decision was informed by Haraway's (1991) "positioned rationality." She made a conscious choice to view local forestry management from a specific position, one that had not often been heard, namely, that of local women.

Indigenous communities have made strong arguments for the need to follow cultural protocols when determining research partners. It is critical, they say, to work with those who are knowledgeable and authorized to speak for the community (McNaughton and Rock 2003).

Many other factors may cause uneven participation in a CBPR project. Women may need to arrange child care, which can be prohibitively expensive (Collins, Cruz, and Smith 2008). Or some segments of a community may be more interested in participating than others. In the Peruvian community where De Wit and Gianotten (1980) conducted CBPR development research, for example, they found that women were simply more interested in the project. Many women saw the possibilities that could come from their participation. Whereas the local men went to cities to look for work, the women were open to local training and to finding internal solutions to community development.

Even when a CBPR project involves a wide spectrum of a community, not *all* people will be engaged in *every* aspect of the research. Community members may be interested in or feel prepared to participate in some aspects of a project more than others (Ballard 2008).

WORKING TOWARD FULL PARTICIPATION AT ÇATALHÖYÜK

To address participation issues, the Çatalhöyük CBPR project provides regular updates not only to the on-site archaeology team but also to the government monitor, who lives on-site during excavation season, and to both the men and the women (separately) in local villages. As the CBPR partnership develops, the updates keep local residents informed about project activity and research results. In community updates, I emphasize the value of the data collected from interviews with local residents. The updates show the level of interest among community members to learn about archaeology and the quality of creative and thoughtful input that their fellow residents have provided.

This approach has not solved all the gender and class conflicts, but sharing the results has challenged perceptions of local village residents and what they are able to contribute to an archaeological research partnership. Village residents can see, for example, the positive role that local women have played in heritage development as research partners. Local people's views of themselves have also changed. At the outset of the CBPR partnership, some local residents doubted that they had anything of value to contribute. More recently, however, both male and female residents have felt comfortable enough to make suggestions and to offer input about the direction of the project. Yet tensions remain, particularly around the leadership roles and independent participation that local women can or should have in the CBPR project and in heritage management and cultural tourism efforts more generally.

CBPR literature and examples of archaeological collaborations demonstrate that there are no easy fixes for addressing complicated community politics, especially around issues of power, privilege, gender, and class. Archaeologists (and researchers more broadly) are certainly not in a position to dictate the leadership within a community, nor would it be appropriate for them to do so, even if they had such influence. Archaeologists are often limited in their ability to choose the individuals or groups from a community with whom they will collaborate. While this complicates the class issues Jackson (1993) and others raised, it does not make a CBPR project impossible or unfeasible. These considerations may seem paralyzing at times, particularly when local politics and power dynamics are complex or difficult to assess.

To address these issues while developing sound CBPR partnerships, archaeologists must be mindful of gender, class, and factional ruptures. Knowledge *can* be democratized over the duration of a project. The more it is, the more the impacts and benefits of the research spread evenly across the community. Those most disenfranchised are often working class, rural poor, and other community members who do not have access to education. They are most likely to be removed from their heritage and to not engage with the archaeological past. As I discussed in Chapter 3, CBPR places priority on empowering those who have been oppressed or disenfranchised. However, putting this into practice is not without its complications. Who is an appropriate community partner? No easy rules determine this. Decisions are never clear-cut, and they have to be made on a case-by-case basis.

CONNECTING COMMUNITY AND RESEARCHER

How do collaborators connect? How do researchers initiate relationships? Students in the graduate CBPR methods courses I teach often wonder about how CBPR practitioners approach potential collaborators. Colleagues have also asked me about this. Although the CBPR literature on the issue is scant, a review of it reveals three primary approaches for connecting with a community: (1) A connection develops from an existing relationship, (2) a community seeks a research partnership, and (3) a researcher seeks a community with whom to collaborate.

Those using a CBPR methodology most often advocate for building research partnerships from those already developed between university partners and communities. Projects such as community education or service learning may be in place and are a good place to start. Strand et al. (2003, 44) observe that, "Working with a community organization that already partners with the college or university in some other capacity . . . contributes to the likelihood that some important requirements for a successful collaboration have already been met." They go on to describe key criteria that may have already been developed from existing community–university partnerships: "These include things such as like-mindedness about goals and strategies, mutual trust and respect, familiarity with the constraints imposed by academic institutions, appreciation for the challenges and opportunities offered by working with students, and experience with modes of effective cross-institutional communication and collaboration." Each of these is important and is reinforced by CBPR experiences in several disciplines.

An existing relationship may offer an avenue for academic and community research partners to find one another. However, if we examine the existing relationships in most university settings, we soon see why archaeologists often find this approach limiting. First, universities most often form ties with local communities, and these ties may not extend to the region where an archaeologist hopes to work. Working outside one's own university to explore community–university partnerships in the region where one wishes to work is certainly possible. However, the practical arrangements may prove challenging, particularly if the university and a community have already established memoranda of understanding or research contracts. Archaeologists working in international contexts will likely have an even more difficult time in finding pre-established links for suitable community–university partnerships.

The second way that Strand et al.'s approach may prove limiting for archaeologists—at least for those who want to work on Native American sites—is that, although increasing, partnerships between Native American communities and universities are still not widespread. Native American communities have experienced a long history of exploitative research relationships. If archaeologists hope to establish partnerships, working through established university channels, such as a service-learning office on campus, is worth pursuing, but without a strong existing relationship in place, this approach is likely to be unproductive.

Once archaeologists have established a successful partnership with a community, a more formal link between one's university and the specific community can be fostered, which may in turn help to facilitate further CBPR in other areas. The CBPR partnerships that developed between myself and the Saginaw Chippewa Indian Tribe of Michigan and the Sullivan County American Indian Council laid the groundwork for Indiana University's Office of Service Learning to establish further partnerships with these communities. Other departments and scholars on campus can now consider how they might form partnerships with these communities as part of service-learning courses or community-based research initiatives. As in this case, an initial partnership develops infrastructure within the university that others, both scholars and community members, can use. This is capacity building for the university community.

Indigenous peoples have a history of negative experiences with archaeologists. Furthermore, in many Indigenous communities, archaeology is a particularly sensitive area of research and raises specific ethical concerns. Archaeologists who want to establish a research partnership with a Native American or other Indigenous community through a campus service-learning office may find communities reluctant. They may be hesitant to explore partnerships with archaeologists with whom they have had no previous relationship or contact. This can be true even for communities that have well-established, successful CBPR partnerships in other areas of research, or even for those with extensive experience conducting or partnering in archaeological research.

This hesitancy does not mean that Native American communities are anti-intellectual, against research broadly, or even against archaeological work specifically. It is often a reaction to the violations that have occurred, and to those that continue and have not been addressed or rectified. Although some relationships have improved, the discipline's legacy of harms against Indigenous peoples continues to play a role in the way Indigenous peoples view archaeology and anthropology. As a result, some communities may be less open than others to connecting with archaeologists through third-party groups, such as a university service-learning office.

Trust and social relationships are critical in CBPR, and, as Lightfoot (2008) notes, these relationships involve both friendship and social obligations. This shapes how archaeologists approach a new community because it takes time for trust and relationships to develop. Patience and restraint are good qualities to bring to a potential partnership. Pushing for a meeting or for decisions to happen quickly can end a project before it begins. Indigenous groups (and others too) may prefer that an archaeologist be introduced to the community in a personal way—face to face by someone who has experience in the community, someone who has established trust and personal connections.

Relationships between Indigenous communities and archaeologists and other researchers are always in flux. Because the character of this relationship has improved over the past two decades, archaeologists need not assume that they or their archaeological research will be rejected out of hand (Silliman 2008a). However, communities and scholars operate in the shadow of complicated and problematic historical legacies, and archaeologists need to be cognizant of them. Approaching a community mindful of its history with researchers—academic and professional—is key to approaching a potential community partner in a good and respectful way.

CONNECTING THROUGH PERSONAL AND PROFESSIONAL RELATIONSHIPS

Other effective approaches exist for utilizing connections to identify and engage with a potential community partner. A rich literature along the collaborative continuum shows that archaeologists are forming many positive connections with Native American, Indigenous, and other descendant and local communities, and these connections can lead to further partnerships. In North America, archaeologists regularly work in fieldwork contexts with Native American community members who serve as site monitors. Archaeologists may also be involved in NAGPRA-related work, land claims research, or in developing museum exhibits (see Murray et al. 2009). Those who have long-standing ties and an established relationship with a community may assist other archaeologists, particularly students, in developing new partnerships.

For example, Long (2008) examined the use of natural resources in the White Mountain Apache community. He was introduced to White Mountain Apache leaders by a professor who had contacts in the community. The same professor arranged an internship in the community for Long so he could complete his CBPR-based dissertation research. Other possibilities for forming new connections include interacting on a more informal basis. A researcher can spend time at an archaeological project being conducted at a site nearby the community or at public community-sponsored events.

Furthermore, an archaeologist may build a research partnership with a community through more personal, familial, or cultural relationships—through birth, family ties, or cultural connections. The CBPR partnership I have with the Ziibiwing Center developed this way. Knowing about my interest in exploring community-based approaches to research, Shannon Martin, a close family friend who was Ziibiwing's cultural educator, arranged for me to meet with Ziibiwing's director, Bonnie Ekdahl, to discuss possible research partnerships.

After our initial meeting, Ms. Ekdahl invited me to give a community presentation about Indigenous archaeology and the use of CBPR. I needed to explain how this approach differs from researcher-driven models and how CBPR changes what an archaeology project can mean for a community. Turnout to the presentation was very good, and community members responded positively to the idea of CBPR. Several meetings followed during which I explained my research skills and experience, and Ms. Ekdahl described the goals that Ziibiwing had established for itself. She detailed several projects where we might have common interest. Our first collaborative project—a repatriation research project—developed from there, and further projects developed over time as trust, respect, and mutual understanding and commitment to similar goals grew.

A cultural relationship also led to a partnership I developed with the Sullivan County American Indian Council. As a new resident to Indiana, I attended a local meeting organized by the Indiana Native American Indian Affairs Commission (now defunct). I wanted to learn about the issues Native Americans in Indiana were facing, and I hoped to establish friendships with other Native people and communities. I was surprised to find that one of the members of the state commission, a spokesperson at the meeting, was Reg Petoskey, also an Ojibwe and a fellow member of the Three Fires Midewiwin Lodge. After the meeting, I introduced myself to Mr. Petoskey and told him about my interest in CBPR. We immediately began discussing ways that we could partner on a number of projects that would benefit the state commission and Native communities in Indiana. As it turns out, Mr. Petoskey was president of another local Native American organization, the Sullivan County American Indian Council (SCAIC), which had just been given a free lease for eight acres of property in Sullivan County that contains a Native American mound site. Mr. Petoskey invited me to a SCAIC meeting, where he introduced me to members of the council. I was able to discuss the principles of CBPR and learn from them what they hoped to achieve through a research partnership at the mound site. Council members were enthusiastic, and soon after I attended my first meeting, we started discussing a CBPR partnership to study, protect, and educate others about the mound.

In these cases, personal and cultural connections were responsible for my initial introduction to the leadership of both organizations. However, building a strong and sustainable CBPR partnership involved a *process* and required a considerable time investment from both partners. I attended SCAIC meetings on weekends, and I made a point to visit Ziibiwing every time I went home for a holiday or community event. In both cases, I made a commitment to communicate regularly with community members and/or the community-based organization that I was planning to partner with.

In some cases, being a member of the community or having previous connections or professional ties can also pose challenges. Having cultural or familial ties to a community carries its own baggage in terms of how people situate and view you. For example, in some Anishinabe communities, my being a midewiwin (traditional carriers of cultural knowledge and teachings) may cause people to view me in a particular way. This may engender increased respect and trust from some, whereas others might have concerns. Close connections to a community can bring with them affiliations with political factions, family divisions, and personal conflicts. Although "insiders" often have special privileges and connections that make CBPR partnerships easier to form initially, coming to a community as an outsider also has its advantages. In many cases, people new to a community may be seen as neutral and free from political entanglements. They can be seen as operating outside of the local sociopolitical webs, at least in the beginning.

A COMMUNITY SOLICITS THE RESEARCH PARTNERSHIP

Sometimes a community seeks out a researcher. In my analysis of CBPR projects, I found this is a less common way for researchers and communities to form a collaborative partnership, but it does happen. Many communities view research as something that only specialists do. Often, this understanding developed from past engagement with researchers. When communities have been involved in research, most often their participation has been as the subjects of study, not as those who conduct, much less initiate, the process. This may explain why communities have not often sought out researchers. However, this is changing. Several well-known cases show that communities can decide to solicit a researcher to conduct community-based research.

In one well-documented example, trade union workers at the Lucas Aerospace factories in the UK, a company involved in arms production, sought help from researchers (Wainwright and Elliott 1982). Concerned about job loss and the military focus of Lucas Aerospace, workers put out a widespread call for researchers to assist them in creating an alternative plan for the company. They wanted to secure their jobs, and they wanted the company to shift production away from military supplies toward building "socially useful products" (1982, 1). Of the 180 organizations and individual researchers contacted, three responded and agreed to collaborate with the union leadership to create the alternative plan, which came to be called "The Lucas Plan." The workers mailed a personal letter to each researcher.

One of the three researchers who participated, Dr. David Elliot, was part of the Social Science Research Council's Open Door Scheme, a program designed to "give industrial, trade-union, and community groups access to academic research facilities" (1982, 2). The organizational infrastructure created by the Open Door Scheme provided the means for the Lucas workers to connect with Dr. Elliot.

In anthropology, T. J. Ferguson's work provides examples of projects in which communities have solicited the assistance of an archaeologist to conduct community-driven research projects. Ferguson is both founder and owner of Anthropological Research, LLC, which works with Native American clients. Its projects include determining traditional cultural properties; historic preservation; researching cultural affiliation for NAGPRA claims; and protecting land and water rights. The projects Ferguson takes on are all fully community-driven and supported. He explains that, "the only projects I won't take on are those that won't provide the funding and research opportunities needed to enable communities to accomplish their goals. None of the tribes I work for have ever asked me not to do a project. Instead they often ask me to assist them with developmental projects that are controversial—pipelines, coal mines, and such—because they want to collect the information needed to manage tribal heritage resources as effectively as possible" (Dominguez 2010).

Community-solicited research partnerships such as these are currently the exception rather than the norm. However, as communities learn about the potential of CBPR—its value, usefulness, and success among a range of communities (for example, Sahota 2010)—we can expect that communities will be more inclined to seek out research partnerships and for a wider range of projects.

PROFESSIONAL ORGANIZATIONS' ROLES
IN ESTABLISHING PARTNERSHIPS

As a discipline, archaeology can nurture and enable this development in several ways. Professional organizations, for example, can assist communities in identifying appropriate research partners whose interests match community needs. A number of international, national, and local archaeological professional societies and organizations have memberships of trained archaeologists, many of whom are involved in archaeological fieldwork and research projects around the globe. Organizations such as the World Archaeological Congress (WAC), the Society for American Archaeology (SAA), and the Archaeological Institute of America (AIA)—as well as many smaller, local archaeology professional societies—maintain databases of their members, and most also keep up-to-date information on members' specialties and areas of research interest. Establishing a means by which interested communities and community-based organizations can make contact with archaeologists through professional archaeology organizations is one avenue worth considering. However, organizational changes would need to be made to facilitate this.

Archaeological professional organizations and societies also host regular conferences that community members are welcome to attend. One drawback is that non-archaeologists usually need to pay conference registration fees and/or organization membership fees, which can be several hundred U.S. dollars for a single meeting. With travel and lodging costs, it can be cost-prohibitive for communities to attend professional archaeological meetings to discuss projects with potential research partners. Professional societies now regularly prepare a digital meeting program that includes the titles of sessions and papers along with authors' names. These are usually available online well before the conferences. Using the conference program as a starting point, community members could begin to locate potential archaeologists. From the papers, they could identify who is working in a specific region or with community groups. They could determine a researcher's areas of interest or those who uses a community-based approach to research.

Communities could then arrange to "interview" potential archaeologists, just as employers conduct interviews of job candidates at annual professional meetings. Professional organizations that wish to support CBPR could provide physical space and advertising to help orchestrate these exchanges. Professional archaeological organizations are not currently prepared to handle community inquiries about collaborative research. However, investing in such efforts would not require new infrastructure. A process for people to find one another is already in place to help employers and job search candidates meet. Archaeological organizations might also consider creating and maintaining a searchable online database of archaeologists who are interested in and have experience with community-based research.

Several archaeological professional associations already have programs to encourage community participation. WAC provides free membership to Indigenous community members. The organization also has a substantial travel grant program that provides funds for Indigenous community members to travel to meetings. The SAA's Committee on Native American Relations (CNAR) has also worked to ensure that organizational membership dues are waived for Native American community members as long as they are not archaeologists. A future goal is to also have its meeting registration fees waived. In 2008, the SAA's CNAR organized and hosted a First Nations-Native American Welcome Reception at the annual meeting in Vancouver, British Columbia. One goal of the reception, now an annual event, was to create opportunities for Native American community members and archaeologists to dialogue and explore mutually beneficial partnerships and projects. The reception continues to be well attended by both archaeologists and Indigenous community members. It is now fully funded by the $4 annual fee paid by members of the Society's Indigenous Populations Interest Group.

Projects such as these are forward thinking and hold great promise for helping communities and archaeologists develop partnerships and conduct CBPR. Yet more of this kind of support is needed. Professional archaeological societies can devise many other CBPR-friendly programs from the national level that would encourage communities to engage directly in the archaeological process.

CHALLENGES COMMUNITIES MAY FACE

For communities, each of the strategies I just described has its complications. To start, most universities, professional associations, and individual archaeologists are not organized around conducting research that is community-driven and participatory. Few archaeologists have experience or training in CBPR methods. The conventional model of research—true not only for archaeology but also for most academic fields—remains strongly researcher-driven. The impetus to develop a research project has been one-way: A researcher comes to a community for a project that has already been planned. CBPR is expressly about changing this model and all the dynamics that go with it. This is precisely an area in which CBPR, once established, may be able to make positive change in the overall way that research is practiced as it encourages communities to consider themselves as research partners, and builds capacity within communities so that members can engage confidently as competent and skilled research partners. At the same time, as partnerships are established, they provide opportunities for training students who are interested in CBPR approaches.

But shifting models is difficult, and not only for the researcher. Strand et al. (2003, 47) note how "daunting" it can be for communities to locate appropriate research partners. They offer several suggestions for communities, one of which is particularly appropriate for archaeology. They suggest that communities and community-based organizations use their websites to list project ideas that they want to pursue. Researchers interested in community-based partnerships would then be able to review these listings to find projects that match their expertise. One drawback to this suggestion is that it requires a great deal of time and effort that communities may not be able to afford.

Alternatively, one way to operationalize this within archaeology would be for the National Association of Tribal Historic Preservation Officers (NATHPO) to provide this service, helping communities connect with archaeological researchers. Tribal historic preservation officers (THPOs) are knowledgeable both about archaeology and about the archaeology-related needs of the communities they serve. Many have extensive training in archaeology and could easily function as the community-based organization that coordinates the research. Working with THPOs is the ideal way for community-based partnerships in archaeology to begin locally. At the national level, NATHPO could serve as an excellent hub for compiling, hosting, and maintaining a list of tribal research needs project ideas.

AN ARCHAEOLOGIST SEEKS THE COMMUNITY

For archaeologists who become involved in CBPR, the early phase of initiating a partnership sometimes seems quite backward relative to how they have been trained. Archaeologists are taught to study a particular topic to determine the state of the field and then to develop a series of questions that need to be addressed. Those using a conventional approach look for knowledge gaps in the literature. They may also turn to advisors and mentors to learn about questions within their discipline that need attention. In the academic world, archaeologists are usually solely responsible for developing a program of study. Typically, scholars continue pursuing the interests and expertise that they acquired in graduate training. Getting started in CBPR changes the dynamics. Scholars must not only seek out a community partner and initiate a process of partnering with them but also work with them collaboratively to develop the research questions. For many, this shift may be challenging or even disorienting.

Maguire (1987) discusses this point directly. In her sociological CBPR project, she partnered with a community of Native American women who had endured physical and emotional abuse. Maguire states, "Making the decision to try participatory research was doing things backward. Standard research textbooks advise the social scientist to first identify a research problem and then select an appropriate method. Instead, I had an approach in search of a problem" (1987, 111). The point Maguire articulated is especially relevant for archaeologists, who excavate the remains of the past and whose research experiences don't traditionally involve working with living communities. For some, this may be compounded by a level of concern or trepidation that the community one wishes to approach may not be interested in a research partnership involving archaeology. No question, archaeologists can face special hurdles when they want to initiate a CBPR project with a community. But there is ample evidence to indicate that these can be overcome, and that positive, effective partnerships can result.

AVOIDING "DRIVE-BY" CBPR

Along with feeling disoriented about the process and apprehensive about how their overtures might be received, those new to CBPR must also reflect critically about other aspects of the research process. Indigenous communities have strongly critiqued conventional researchers as conducting "drive-by research," also called "parachute research" or "helicopter research." Too often, academics "drop in" to communities, collect data, and leave. Or they come to a community with well-intentioned goals of helping. Oftentimes, they do not think about the value of developing long-term relationships, or the impact—positive and negative—that their research may have on the community. CBPR has developed in direct response to such critiques, yet even CBPR practices are not immune to being used in exploitative ways. To avoid replicating the "drive-by" pattern, CBPR practitioners must engage prospective communities in open dialogue about the appropriateness of conducting a CBPR project in the community. They must share with community members their motivations for doing so, and they need to explore together the potential drawbacks of a CBPR approach.

More specifically, the self-reflective process of establishing a CBPR project begins with considering several key points, which lay the foundation for an ethical community-based research practice. The first point is how academics may co-opt the CBPR project. This happens primarily when partnerships form between a university and a community. Imbalances in both power and knowledge put CBPR projects at risk.

Recognized globally for his work on community-based research partnerships, Budd Hall (1993, xviii–xx) states that communities, not universities, need to be at the *center* of CBPR processes. He warns, "Our position has been that the center of the process needed to be in the margins, in the communities, with women, people of color, and so forth. Our experience has been that it is very difficult to achieve this kind of process from a university base. . . ." Hall believes this stems from the way knowledge is utilized within academic settings, observing that knowledge is more than an intellectual issue. For academics, knowledge has both economic and political properties: "[K]nowledge within the academy serves a variety of purposes. It is a commodity by which academics do far more than exchange ideas; it is the very means of exchange for the academic political economy."

Hall himself is affiliated with a university, and he acknowledges that many of the CBPR projects that he has praised involve university researchers. The take-away message from Hall's critique is that university partners should not dominate the CBPR process. The research must be fully grounded in the community. Archaeologists who wish to seek out community partners have to remain continually cognizant of this. They need to set up structures at the outset of the partnership that allow the community to take a leadership role in the process.

A second important point for CBPR archaeologists to consider up front is the level of long-term commitment that they are prepared to form with the involved community. Humphries et al. (2008, 51) found that long-term commitment is critical. In their Honduras bean plant experiments, they demonstrated that both community members and academics must go through a learning process about CBPR and how to support it in a sustainable way. Others provide similar evidence. Researchers need to recognize their long-term responsibilities to a community to be successful, and their commitment must be to both "place and people" (Lightfoot 2008, 214).

The lack of such commitment can serve to reinforce existing power imbalances. Burnette and DeHose (2008, 93) state, "If researchers do not commit themselves to the community, then we, the people in the community, are making them the experts by providing information that they then use for their own purposes." Such an outcome runs directly counter to the goals of CBPR and specifically against the goals of decolonizing the discipline of archaeology. Others (Jackson, Conchelos, and Vigoda 1980, 54) underscore the importance of not "parachuting out" of a project. They note that CBPR practitioners must also consider what is expected of them in terms of continued accountability to a community once the research project has ended.

A third point: CBPR researchers from a range of disciplines emphasize the importance of considering why or why not to take a CBPR approach. Vio Grossi (1980) argues that CBPR is not about including people simply to obtain better research results. Ethical reasons and a priority on solving community concerns should motivate the work, if it is to be authentic. CBPR is also not about setting up one-way community education or diffusing ideas to a community that serve outsiders in some way (Wilmsen 2008; Calhoun 2008). The point, Vio Grossi argues, is to change the way research is conducted. CBPR is not about using the community as a form of "window dressing" to maintain the status quo—a point that some archaeologists (La Salle 2010) echo. CBPR is meant to engender deep change.

It's unlikely that an archaeologist sets out to engage in acts of "window dressing." But to ensure that deeper level of change is reached, archaeologists must engage Indigenous and local people in the decision-making processes around archaeological heritage. Archaeologists interested in starting a CBPR project need to seriously consider their ability to commit long-term to the community as well as to making the substantive shift in power that a community-centered approach to research involves. While the experiences of others with CBPR projects can provide guidance and foundational structure for developing a successful process, each partnership is unique. Communities and archaeologists need to work together to develop approaches and solutions that fit the community and the project, both of which are unique.

Publishing these processes improves the practice of archaeological CBPR and forms an important aspect of the commitment involved in this approach (Kanhare 1980). As Strand et al. (2003, 50) put it, "CBR as a pedagogy is still in its infancy, and there is much we have yet to learn about how to do it well." Training students in these methods and processes means introducing both the positive outcomes along with the more messy, challenging experiences and failed attempts. Good, balanced, honest training—training that is self-reflective and self-critical—is an essential component of pushing the practice further. Later in this book (Chapter 8), I address some of the education and training issues of CBPR for the archaeology curriculum.

COMMUNITY-BASED ORGANIZATIONS

One way to connect with a community is to open dialogue with a community-based organization (CBO). CBOs provide specific services to individuals or segments of the group. These services may include health, educational, or other services. CBOs might also be nonprofits, public agencies, or small grassroots groups. They may be controlled and staffed (fully or in part) by community members. Or, they may link to the community through a governing board made up of community members (Strand et al. 2003). A major benefit to developing a CBPR project in partnership with a CBO is that CBOs are established and already have a relationship of trust with the community. They usually have extensive knowledge of the community as well as experience in working effectively within it. For all these reasons, many researchers have found it significantly easier to get a project *started* by partnering with a CBO.

My CBPR partnership with the Saginaw Chippewa Indian Tribe of Michigan began with a CBO: the Ziibiwing Cultural Center, a community-based organization that provides educational and cultural services to tribal members. My partnership with Ziibiwing is an excellent example of the benefits that a CBO can offer a researcher. Ziibiwing houses an award-winning museum and cultural center. The center's guiding vision is that, "the culture, diversity and spirit of the Saginaw Chippewa Indian Tribe of Michigan and other Great Lakes Anishinabek must be recognized, perpetuated, communicated and supported" (Ziibiwing Center 2011). Ziibiwing has twenty-four people on staff. This includes a director, a curator who also fulfills the tribal historic preservation duties, educational and research staff, and those with administrative responsibilities. The center is nearly fully self-funded, with additional assistance from the Saginaw Chippewa tribe. The facilities include permanent and changing exhibits, a research center, meeting and conference facilities, a gift shop and lounge, and a number of administrative offices.

In our three collaborative projects, Ziibiwing not only initiated the research projects, but also did the heavy lifting needed for the Ziibiwing board and tribal council to review and approve them. The center also provided a range of cost-sharing contributions to the research. These included substantial staff support, a location for research meetings, as well as a home for the project archive and the curation of the materials we derived from the research. Ziibiwing has long-standing relationships with elders and spiritual leaders who have worked with the center to develop museum exhibits and related cultural programs (Lonetree 2012). These community connections and the trust that Ziibiwing has built over decades paved the way for me to develop good relationships with the appropriate tribal historians and spiritual leaders.

How can archaeologists locate CBOs? Those most interested in, knowledgeable of, and familiar with archaeology-related work tend to be associated with a tribal museum, cultural, or educational center. A tribe's designated THPO office, if the tribe has one, can also be a helpful place to begin exploring potential interest in collaborative partnerships. CBOs can be found not only within Native American and Indigenous groups but also in a range of communities around the globe. When contacting and working with a CBO, researchers need to assess the amount of direct involvement community members play in the organization and how much meaningful control they have in directing research development (Maguire 1993; 1987). Real community participation—not tokenism—is the primary concern.

By contrast, CBPR archaeologists should avoid—or be highly wary of—partnering with organizations that conduct research on a community but do not include community members in leadership roles or that do not directly involve, benefit, or report to the community. Such organizations may conduct excellent work and have highly talented and competent staff. But their lack of connection to the community will result in research that is not grounded in the community context. It is neither developed nor carried out with a truly community-based approach.

COMMUNITIES WITHOUT CBOS OR OTHER "STRUCTURED" PARTNERS

Some communities do not have an easily identifiable CBO or other organizational framework in place to help facilitate the partnership. CBPR practitioners from other disciplines have encountered these situations with great regularity, and their work provides examples for assisting community members in organizing to form a board or other form of representative group to act as a research partner (Park 1993a; Maguire 1993, 1987). Strand et al. (2003, 34) note that, in some cases, the community may not be organized enough to participate in a fully collaborative way in the research, particularly in the early stages of the project. In such cases, "an academic with effective community organizing skills may be able to bring together community members so that they can participate and take charge of the next stages of the project."

Stoecker (1999) argues for three approaches that academics might adopt toward participatory research. In his view, academics in CBPR projects vacillate between being initiators, consultants, and collaborators. The role they take on depends upon what best fits the situation, and on the skills and the level of organization within a community. Even within one project, academics typically move back and forth between these roles. If a community is well organized, a researcher may successfully take a consultant role: The community commissions the research, and the academic carries it out with community involvement, guidance and supervision.

If a community is poorly organized, however, the CBPR process calls for academics to expand their work to include community-building efforts. To initiate a successful CBPR project in such communities, academics need proficiency in realms well beyond traditional research skills. They must be prepared to act as community organizer and as a popular educator who successfully "facilitates the learning process." Furthermore, they may be required to do work in the initial stages of a project as "an animator" (Stoecker 1999)—someone who translates, facilitates, builds self-esteem, and helps a community recognize that its concerns and knowledge are important.

The animator role was critical in the Çatalhöyük CBPR project. The community had very limited organizational structures in place, particularly relating to archaeology or heritage issues (Atalay 2007, 2010). During the early stages of the project, I had to play an active role as "an animator" and popular educator, and an extensive amount of my time went to community organizing. These efforts stretched over several years. They involved hosting community meetings; creating a series of educational programs that included children's comics; producing a regular newsletter; developing a local internship program and community theater program; and hosting an annual archaeology festival. Making these activities happen contributed to developing a local heritage committee that could serve as a research partner.

Organizing within a community involves a detailed process (Brydon-Miller 1993). It is time-consuming (see Maguire 1993, 1987, in relation to CBPR dissertation projects), and it requires a particular skill set (Stoecker, Tryon, and Hilgendorf 2009) that not all archaeologists have and that many may not care to invest the time and effort to develop. Above all, community organizing must be carried out in a culturally appropriate way and conducted through established community leadership. At Çatalhöyük, this meant that every aspect of the community organizing work was done after discussing potential actions with the town manager, Muhtar Ali Barutcu. He assisted in arranging for the project's first local interns, supported both financially and organizationally in planning the annual festival, regularly provided space and support for community meetings, and became the first official member of the village heritage committee.

One of the critiques of CBPR is that it requires those who utilize the approach to do much more than pure research. The five archaeological CBPR projects I am involved with prove that to be so. Following Stoecker's (1999) observations of what is needed, I advise archaeologists to carefully assess both their skills and their willingness to move beyond the activities of archaeological fieldwork when considering establishing a CBPR project. Not every researcher will be proficient in the required skills. Lacking the necessary skills does not mean that a CBPR partnership is impossible, but it does require identifying and collaborating with other researchers who can fulfill the roles necessary to conduct a successful project.

COMPLEX COMMUNITIES: LARGE, DISPERSED GROUPS AND MULTIPLE STAKEHOLDERS

Communities that are large and cases that involve a number of diverse stakeholders present their own set of challenges to archaeologists who want to establish a CBPR project. Locating CBOs to work with can be helpful, particularly if they have established ties with a wide range of community members or members of various stakeholder groups. In some cases, a primary partnership develops with only one community or a segment of the community, while other groups engage in the project in less extensive ways.

An excellent example of working with a CBO and multiple communities comes from the Madame C. J. Walker project in Indianapolis, Indiana. This historical archaeology project aimed to understand the social impact of Madame Walker, the first self-made female millionaire in the United States (Mullins et al., forthcoming). The project, directed by Dr. Paul Mullins of Indiana University-Purdue University, Indianapolis, involved working with multiple "stakeholders": the Madame Walker Foundation (a CBO); the residents in the urban Indianapolis area; local schoolchildren; Madame Walker's descendants; and the wider African American community. Although the project has been largely researcher-driven and limited in its participatory aspects, it has involved multiple communities to help guide the research process. It also involved aspects of reciprocity for community members, including access to university resources for members of the CBO. Working with the Madame Walker Foundation provided a central means for bringing members from multiple communities together. While the foundation exists to care for the estate of Ms. Walker, foundation staff listened to the needs of other stakeholders and members of the local communities. They incorporated their concerns when the foundation made decisions about the community's role in the research and how to best utilize the project's results.

Engaging multiple communities is a significant issue in CBPR and an important one in archaeology as well. A common perspective among professional archaeologists is that archaeological sites and landscapes belong to no one, but rather everyone has a right to such places as part of a shared cultural heritage. Similar concerns exist in natural resource management, where shared access and the rights of all stakeholders to engage with the resources are critical points of consideration. On this issue, I agree with Jack Rossen, who has conducted collaborative archaeological research in the politically complex region of central New York. For Rossen (2008, 112), "The inclusion of all stakeholders is a gradual, long-term effort and learning process for an archaeologist." While I adhere to the ideal of involving all stakeholders in archaeological research, I do not take this to mean that every community must be engaged in the archaeological process in identical ways or at the same time. Nor must all affected and interested groups be research partners in the same archaeological CBPR project at the same time.

In some cases, multiple stakeholders may be actively engaged with a site and may have substantial opportunities to provide input on a site's management, planning, and program of research. Others in the same community may have had their voices silenced or been otherwise disenfranchised. In other situations—as Rossen observed in New York—several stakeholders are openly hostile to each other. This makes it impractical or even dangerous for them to engage in the project together and equally. In the central New York case, Rossen feels—and I agree—that all affected and interested communities, even those archaeologists do not like or with whom they do not agree, have a legitimate right to engage with the local archaeology.

In all of these situations, the question is not *if* archaeologists should engage with all communities, but *how* to do so *productively*. For some, educational workshops or programs are appropriate first steps. In other cases, involving different communities in fieldwork may be most productive. Even in cases where the majority or even all of the stakeholders are involved, researchers might choose to work in partnership with one or more communities for some aspects of the project, while they develop and build relationships with others. These are complex and rarely straightforward decisions that each archaeologist must make. Conversations about this should include the various communities involved, in an open and transparent process.

CBPR provides no easy answers or clear criteria for dilemmas involving multiple stakeholders, and practitioners from other disciplines have adopted a variety of strategies to deal with them. Since one of the primary principles of CBPR is to work with those who have been oppressed, and social justice is an important goal of the practice, many CBPR researchers have chosen to develop CBPR partnerships exclusively with oppressed communities. However, this choice does not get us out of murky ground or provide clear-cut guidance either. It raises further questions, such as: What does it mean to be oppressed? Who makes such determinations?

Some will argue that it is not the archaeologist's role to determine who is (most) oppressed and who is privileged. In considering what it means to work for the oppressed, it should be noted that oppression need not be monetary. The CBPR partnerships with the Saginaw Chippewa Indian Tribe of Michigan illustrate the point. As a gaming tribe, enrolled tribal citizens have some degree of economic security. Yet as a community, they have been disenfranchised from their own history and heritage in many ways. They still fight for the basic human right to bury their ancestors, for example, thousands of whom remain at the center of NAGPRA-related battles. Their oppression also occurs around knowledge production and their rights to maintain their oral history traditions, particularly with regard to repatriation struggles. Strand et al. (2003) guide CBPR practitioners to partner with the powerless. Yet even this can become complicated. Sometimes "the powerless" includes groups with whom a researcher does not share a sense of like-mindedness.

In some cases, as with the Madame Walker project, some stakeholders must be included as research partners, or at least in some decision-making aspects of the work, because they hold certain legal responsibilities as land or estate owners. In other situations, an archaeologist may choose to partner with a particular community(-ies). For example, in the Çatalhöyük CBPR project, I chose to partner with the local village communities around Çatalhöyük. As I said earlier, they are the most impacted by the excavations but have arguably been the most disenfranchised from higher, governmental-level decision-making and planning processes. While the Çatalhöyük CBPR project did not exclude or ignore other stakeholders, the main energies and resources of the collaborative partnership have focused on residents in local villages. The New Age or "goddess" communities involved with Çatalhöyük are certainly legitimate stakeholders, but I did not choose them as my primary research partners (although I remain optimistic about partnering with them in the future). Largely middle-class, they have the economic stability and educational opportunities that allow them to actively engage with the site and access the knowledge produced there on their own.

When archaeologists approach a new site, they need to learn whether the communities involved recognize a *primary* stakeholder. In the Çatalhöyük example, I started by collaborating broadly, working with a wide number of nearby villages as well as with Çumra, the nearest town (see Map 3 in Chapter 1). After interviewing community members in each of these places, I found those in Küçükköy clearly felt a close relationship to the site and a strong sense of "ownership" about the right to work collaboratively and to be involved in the site's planning and management. In contrast, those from villages outside of Küçükköy did not articulate a strong connection to Çatalhöyük, and they overwhelmingly expressed that Küçükköy or Çumra held "the rights" to the site. Çumra, a town and therefore larger in population and government-supported infrastructure than any of the local villages, also felt a strong association with Çatalhöyük and enjoyed the support of the regional and national governments in the project.

I chose Küçükköy residents as my primary research partners, but not with the intent to disenfranchise residents of Çumra or the other villages. As with the goddess groups, Çumra's leadership already enjoyed a great deal of input and engagement in Çatalhöyük's planning and management. My intent was to align with those who were closest to the site but whose voices were not being heard. Rossen (2006, 105–06) made a similar choice when he chose to collaborate with the Cayuga

Native American community. A primary motivation for him was to "counteract politically motivated historical revisions." An anti–land claim group made up of local (non–Native American) citizens had organized to keep the Cayuga from gaining land, and they were using false data and negative statements about Cayuga history and culture to block Cayuga land claim efforts.

These issues become even more complicated when archaeologists do not agree with the views or practices of a community. Something I refer to as "the Nazi scenario" illustrates this point. Should CBPR researchers partner with neo-Nazis to produce research on Nazi sites that meets their community's needs? Or is it acceptable to partner only with those who were victimized or members of local communities where such sites are located? This is an extreme case, but it illustrates the complexities that researchers could face when they choose community partners.

CONTEXT, CULTURAL COMPETENCY, AND CONSEQUENCES

Understanding local and regional politics is central for recognizing a project's potential impact, both positive and negative: Who is likely to benefit? Who might be marginalized, exploited, or otherwise negatively impacted as a result of a research partnership? Conducting oneself appropriately and demonstrating a basic understanding and respect for cultural practices and local protocols are fundamental to good anthropological practice. They are also critical for successful CBPR. Cultural competence takes on even greater importance in an archaeological CBPR project, starting with the first connections researchers make with a community partner. As potential partners begin developing questions and a comprehensive research design for a project, these considerations gather greater importance. In the next chapter (Chapter 5), I address the need to understand local sociopolitics and to educate oneself in appropriate cultural protocols. I raise these issues briefly here, though, because they can set the tone for one's initial meeting with a potential community partner.

CHOICES HAVE CONSEQUENCES

In the Çatalhöyük case, a house purchased in Küçükköy by members of the goddess community was burned down reportedly because local people (many suspect the men of the village) did not approve of the women's empowerment ideology implied in the goddess movement. It would be helpful for any outside researcher to know about the arson and why it happened if thinking about choosing the goddess community as a partner. At best, the researcher may face anger, and local community members may refuse to participate. But the repercussions for those in the community, especially local women, of collaborating in a project that also partners with the goddess groups could be much more dire. At worst, CBPR partnerships may have life-threatening consequences for community members. In the case of the Sangtin Writers collective (Nagar and Sangtin Writers 2006), a woman was killed by her family for choosing to write about oppression, exploitation, and other aspects of her life in rural India. The archaeology CBPR projects I'm involved with have not resulted in violence of any kind. Yet, it is important to look at the case of the Sangtin Writers and others like it to develop a real sense of caution when entering and conducting CBPR projects. Archaeology is embedded in political and social dynamics that people care deeply about. Violence can happen for reasons that outsiders may not grasp. Even in relatively straightforward CBPR partnerships, the work involves challenges and decisions that have real-life implications.

The CBPR literature underscores the need to be up front about one's choices and the reasons behind them. I have been very straightforward with the Küçükköy community about my choice to work with them and not to develop similar partnerships at this time with the goddess community. But this choice has not been without its challenges. I had to conduct initial research to get the "big picture" of the community's social, political, cultural, and spiritual context, yet I also had to avoid using that knowledge as a tool to "define the reality of their situation" (Stringer 2007, 52–54). As with all communities, men and women from Küçükköy have their own understandings of gender roles and cultural practices. Although I found it challenging at times, I knew that, as a researcher, I could not impose my own views and sensibilities on a community partner.

SOCIOPOLITICAL CONTEXTS

Before approaching a community about a research partnership and well before any research and planning begins, archaeologists must understand the social and political landscape and factor it into their decision making. Otherwise, they can unwittingly create or contribute to local or regional tensions. This is particularly true when multiple stakeholders hold animosities toward one another. For example, to understand the realities of those who are oppressed and/or who have very limited control, researchers need to do at least some preliminary analysis of powerful entities as well (Pyburn 2011). Politics, community divisions, and factions can be multilayered and complex, and they can heavily impact a CBPR project. Investigating a community's political context and that of the surrounding region is, therefore, critical to initiating a new community-based project (Rossen 2006, 2008; Nicholas 2008). Nor should the investigation of the sociopolitical context be limited to "out there" and "them." Archaeologists must also look inward—at themselves, their profession and discipline, and the historical practice of archaeology—to understand "the legacies of past research practices" (Long 2008). How has archaeology been conducted within a particular community? How do members feel about that history in the present historical moment? Like it or not, these legacies impact our ability to work productively today. As Stringer (2007, 51) aptly highlights, "Past events sometimes leave legacies of deep hurts and antagonisms that severely limit prospects for successful projects unless they are handled judiciously."

Silliman (2008a, 9–10) considers this critical reflection an important part of working collaboratively with communities. In his words, this "means also coming to terms with the social, political, historical, cultural, and personal milieus that help to make possible the final product." I argue that "coming to terms" is, in fact, essential for decolonizing the discipline of archaeology. Sociopolitical issues impact archaeological CBPR projects at every phase, and researchers must keep them constantly in mind. Getting key issues right at the formative stages of a CBPR partnership creates a solid foundation for a project. Knowing the context in time, space, and culture also helps researchers ensure that benefits are reciprocal and flow to all the research partners.

INCREASING CULTURAL COMPETENCY

As I have said, CBPR researchers must make every effort to be aware of the expected behaviors and cultural practices of the community they are approaching. Raising their cultural competency and their understanding of the community's cultural values are central to the work (Nicholas 2008). For archaeologists, this involves learning culturally appropriate ways to behave at archaeological landscapes, sites, and sacred places as well as how to respect and care for them. Nicholas (2008) shows further that what archaeologists learn about Indigenous stewardship can prove useful for archaeological practices in the long term, not just at the outset of a project.

Burnette and DeHose (2008), two White Mountain Apache tribal members, discuss how cultural education is a two-way process—one that continues throughout the research. Tribal members taught scientists the traditional ways to care for important cultural and sacred places through prayers and songs. They, in turn, learned how scientists work to preserve and protect those locations. Their collaborative process meant working on the landscape together as they visited important

FIGURE 5.
Sage burns in an abalone shell after smudging the equipment and
site during the Flint Stone Street Ancestral Recovery Project.

cultural places. The community archaeology literature offers other examples of
processes used to raise cultural competency. For example, Silliman and Dring
(2008, 82–83) arranged for students to visit the Pequot Elders Council and attend
an orientation from tribal members. Cultural education has had a central role to
play in each of the community-based projects I'm involved with. For example,
students and local community volunteers at the Flint Stone Street Project learned
about the importance of smudging at the start of each workday and, and they
received instruction on appropriately handling ancestral remains (see Figure 5).
And students in the community-based research graduate methods course I teach
learned about the importance of acknowledging the time and respect of elders and
community partners with tobacco (see Figure 6).

Every community has important norms, protocols, and practices. These can
relate to daily practices of dress and eating, or can be of a spiritual or social nature.
I address the importance of recognizing and learning Indigenous cultural protocols at length in Chapter 6. For now, I raise the issue briefly simply to note how

FIGURE 6.
Juan Berumen, one of the PhD students in the CBPR service-
learning course I teach is following cultural protocol, handing
a tobacco gift, to Reg Petoskey during our initial community-
student meeting.

important it is to be mindful of these issues during background research and at the
early stages of a community partnership.

PRESENTING YOURSELF

One final point: How do researchers present *themselves* to communities? This personal aspect of CBPR practice is discussed extensively in the CBPR literature.
Before going to Turkey for an extended period of fieldwork while I was a graduate student, my dissertation committee chair advised me that I could not expect
people to want to work with me based on charm or other endearing qualities; she
noted that the relationships would be driven by intellectual concerns. This was
certainly true. In the academic world, working well with others is a bonus, but
what counts most is one's knowledge and command of the discipline. In conducting research with communities, however, the balance shifts and personal qualities can become critical for success. This is overwhelmingly the case with CBPR.

When it comes to working with communities, personal connections matter, and they matter a great deal.

Successful CBPR depends on one's willingness and ability to present *yourself* to a community and to articulate your research interests, goals, and motivations clearly and honestly. Transparency is key, as is jargon-free communication on a regular basis. In presenting myself to communities in Native North America and in rural Turkey, I invited local residents to attend a community meeting where I explained the ideas that inspired my commitment to CBPR. Before our research partnerships were even discussed, I gave a community talk at the Ziibiwing Center about the need to decolonize archaeology, and shared my personal views and commitment to that effort. And at Çatalhöyük, I hosted a series of community meetings for both women and men. I spoke openly about mistakes archaeologists had made previously in excluding communities from the archaeological process. In both cases, these critiques of archaeology helped to "frame" me as a person by clarifying my motivations and the nature of my own investment in a potential partnership. The meetings also established an initial sense of understanding about what community members might expect from me.

Others have found that similar personal connections are what inspire community members to become involved in a CBPR project. I suspect that the success of these meetings and the interest they created in a potential research partnership went beyond the community's appreciation of the critical view I presented of archaeology. They were responding equally to my willingness to make a personal connection, to be humble, and to admit that we, as scholars, do not have all the answers (Bergelin et al. 2008).

In some cases, stating one's position on major issues that concern the community can be important. Rossen (2006) notes that his willingness to state up front that there would be no excavation of human remains helped build trust between himself and the Cayuga community. When you introduce yourself to a potential community partner, showing respect, humility, and a readiness to listen are important beyond words (Bergelin et al. 2008). The farmers (Corea et al. 2008) involved in a CBPR seed project in Honduras made it clear that the researchers coming in needed to be genuinely humble. The farmers believed it was important that they feel respected by the scientists who wanted to work with them. Listening was also a critical value for them, since, as they observe, those who always speak fail to listen.

Strand et al. (2003, 48) note that academics should be prepared to be tested by members of a community: What is their true level of commitment? Do they really desire to work in partnership? Randy Stoecker (1999) was asked to clean a storeroom when he first approached a community organization with an offer to conduct research in partnership with them. His willingness to comply showed his commitment, built trust, and led to a long-term research partnership that has lasted more than twenty years. Archaeologists who work closely with communities recount all kinds of tasks they have been asked to do, from eating unusual pieces of a porcupine (Stephen Loring, personal communication, 2010) to shoveling snow (George Nicholas, personal communication, 2010). Either the community wanted to see their level of commitment, or the tasks were simply what the community needed help with at the time.

Bryceson and Mustafa (1982) address issues of personal interaction and how a researcher approaches a community from other perspectives. When clear class differences exist between the researcher and the community partner, they argue convincingly that it is "false and patronizing" to act as if the two are operating equally on a level playing field. Others (for example, Vio Grossi 1980) discuss class-difference realities in terms of authenticity. They argue that academics should act like researchers, not as laborers or as people other than who they are. Furthermore, researchers should recognize that they have specialized skills and valuable access to resources that can benefit a community in terms of grants and other opportunities (Humphries et al. 2008). Some (Jackson, Conchelos, and Vigoda 1980; Comstock and Fox 1993, 110) see this as a "convergent relationship." The researcher and the community partners move through a process of change as the CBPR project proceeds. The effect is that the sense of inequality between them begins to break down.

In establishing connections with research partners in the past, I have chosen not to present myself as an "expert" on community-based research. This was not an inauthentic attempt to establish camaraderie. When these relationships were first established, CBPR was new to me, and I wanted to make that clear to my potential partners. The tone from the start was one of partnership. We each had skills that we could bring to the research we were doing together. I made my goals clear from the outset: I hoped to use my research skills to work in partnership with them to address the archaeology and heritage management issues they had identified in their own community. I was also clear that our work together would form the basis for a book about archaeological CBPR.

Now that I have much more knowledge about archaeological CBPR—what makes it work well and where problems commonly arise—I also humbly share those experiences with community members. When I do, I always emphasize that each member of the community has expertise and valuable experience that will benefit our partnership. I also make a point to limit my explanations, so that I can encourage discussion as I listen. I want to make sure that community members have the time and space to engage with ideas and concepts in ways that have meaning for them. In short, I have found that a continual and consistent demonstration of a commitment to the principles of CBPR and the ideology behind it is the most powerful tool available to someone hoping to develop a long-lasting and productive research relationship with a community.

FIVE · Building a Strong Foundation

The CBPR process hinges on successful working relationships between researchers and their community partners. The better the relationships are, the more effective and productive the project, and the more detailed the results. Practitioners of community-based research consistently emphasize how important it is to build a strong foundation right from the start. Practices established at the outset of the collaboration set the tone for the rest of the project and often affect how the work goes in future projects. Early practices have an impact on the long-term success of a partnership, either enhancing or narrowing the potentials for collaboration. Some elements of a successful research partnership, such as trust between partners, must develop over time. However, other qualities and values play a role in bringing communities together early on. I mentioned humility, respect, and forthrightness about intentions, for example. These qualities sustain good relationships throughout the life of the project and even over the course of several projects.

Within the CBPR literature, scholars and community practitioners identify key factors for success. Some are case-specific, but many others provide more generalizable insights that CBPR practitioners can use as guideposts to inform their projects at the early stages. One point consistently cited is that researchers must demonstrate a commitment to the core philosophy of community-based research. In developing a partnership with a community, the specifics of the research topic, the field methods, and projected outcomes or products actually play a minimal role. What matters most is a shared ideology of mutual respect and a commitment to partnering in equitable, authentic ways. This spirit brings partners together and provides the common ground on which to build strong researcher-community relationships.

Specifically, those engaged in various forms of community-based research consistently identify two interrelated principles of CBPR practice that must guide researchers from the start, if they want to build strong foundations for their collaborative endeavors. Being committed to the *ideology* of producing knowledge in partnership is the first principle of practice. The second is acknowledging that community knowledge and involvement has value and contributes to scientific understanding.

What does this mean for archaeology? Archaeologists will experience more success in community research partnerships when they, first, acknowledge that descendant and local communities have the right to be involved in researching and managing archaeological locations and cultural heritage; and second, operate from the premise that communities have something worthy to contribute to archaeological understandings. This is what I have experienced in my CBPR projects in Native North America and in Turkey, and other archaeological collaborations have reported similar outcomes.

RESEARCH REVIEW AND APPROVAL

Gaining permission to collaborate and carry out research with a community is an important practical step in the CBPR process, one that involves multiple entities at both the university level and within the communities involved. Various publications address the history of and need for ethics committees and the role of university-level institutional review boards (IRBs) to protect "human subjects" in anthropology research (for example, see Fluehr-Lobban 2003; Bendremer and Richman 2006). Archaeologists in the United States often lack experience with protocols for projects that involve human subjects, because they rarely go through the IRB process. This is because some archaeologists do not consider deceased humans who are excavated to fall within the category of human subjects. And, although this is changing, many do not link the deceased to the living communities who are affected by archaeological research. Bendremer and Richman (2006) have demonstrated, however, that archaeological research *does* include human subjects and, they argue, it should fall under the purview of University Human Subjects Review committees.

For community-based archaeology, this is particularly so. This is because working with communities is a central part of the process of any community-based project. Community input is required to develop and carry out the research, and to share the results locally, in academic circles, and with lawmakers, policy makers, and government entities.

COMMUNITY REVIEW

Gaining the appropriate approval for carrying out archaeological research with a community is a complex process—as it should be. It is part of initiating the research process on the right foot by building good relationships. Even projects that are fully community-based and participatory still require review and authorization from the appropriate community leadership before work can begin. Some communities have been inundated with researchers who want to study them. Too often, the researchers used methodologies or conducted research projects in ways that were exploitative. In response, many Indigenous communities now have formal processes that researchers must follow to obtain permission to conduct any form of research, community-based or otherwise. These processes are sometimes referred to as tribal IRBs or community advisory boards (Sahota 2009; McDonald, Peterson, and Betts 2005). Even communities that do not have formal review boards often have a process to review and approve research.

Nicholas (2008) notes that many tribes have their own permitting systems in place. They have also developed cultural protocols that researchers must follow when they handle human remains or other cultural or intellectual materials. Many more tribes are in the process of developing such protocols. Communities may also develop less direct ways of controlling research and access to certain forms of data. Mills et al. (2008) describe how the White Mountain Apache community decided *not* to use the state site recording system to enter sites found on their reservation. Not making the information public allowed them to maintain greater control over who would be researching this data. Their decision functioned as an informal permitting system, since researchers had to go through the tribe's approval process to obtain access to the site location data. Researchers should expect both the university-level IRB and any tribal IRB or other community authorization or permitting process to review their projects before they can proceed.

GOVERNING COUNCILS

Not all communities have a review and permission-granting process in place, and the expectations and requirements of those that are in place vary tremendously. Some involve a lengthy review process, whereas others can be as straightforward as obtaining verbal permission from appropriate elders or nongovernmental leaders.

Increasingly, Indigenous communities are developing their own community advisory boards or governing councils, which are charged with reviewing and granting permission for proposed research projects (Bendremer and Richman 2006).

Native American communities routinely require researchers to present their proposals to the tribal council or other governing body for approval. Kerber (2008) provides an example of a Native American community whose governing body is not a tribal council. He submits his annual proposals for a youth summer workshop to the Oneida Indian Nation's Men's Council and Clan Mothers, which is the governing body within that community. In some cases, projects need to meet specific requirements before being approved. When they went before the tribal council, Mills et al. (2008) were required to detail the benefits that their proposed collaborative field school would have for the White Mountain Apache community. They explained the "51 percent rule" (also known as "Kane's rule") that the White Mountain Apache tribal council uses as a guiding principle when considering whether to participate in a collaborative project. The rule requires that "the majority of the benefits—economic, managerial, and educational—must accrue to the tribe and its members" (Mills et al. 2008, 44). Whatever the requirements and whichever the appropriate authorizing group, no research should take place without first acquiring permission through the appropriate protocol.

MULTILEVEL REVIEWS

In some cases, a project needs several layers of approval. CBOs may have advisory boards, political leadership, governing councils, and elders and spiritual leaders who need to review and approve a project. In working with Ziibiwing, the Saginaw Chippewa Indian Tribe of Michigan required Ziibiwing's director to submit a description of each of our proposed projects for the tribal council to review and approve. However, the projects first needed to be vetted and approved by Ziibiwing's board of directors. A similar dual process of review and approval is common for CBOs, particularly those that report to a governing board. When I partnered with the Sullivan County American Indian Council, for example, the council president, Reg Petoskey, was able to approve our research partnership only after consulting with council officers. The council is a relatively small community and does not have a formal review process for research projects. The approval and permission process was more informal, involving only face-to-face discussions and email conversations.

Other projects require multiple layers of agreement from officials at different levels of government—national, regional, and local. For example, in the

Çatalhöyük CBPR project in Turkey, the project first needed to undergo review and approval as part of the larger Çatalhöyük excavation project at the national level by the Turkish Ministry of Culture. It then went through a much more informal process of review at the local level. Before visiting local villages and talking with residents, I visited the village manager (*muhtar*) to discuss the possibility of working in partnership with community members. I talked about what such a project would involve for local residents. Although I was not required officially to get formal permission from the village manager to conduct research in local villages in Turkey, I was expected to keep him informed as the project progressed and to provide him with periodic updates.

WHO SPEAKS FOR THE COMMUNITY?

In Chapter 3, I discussed how those working in CBPR define the term *community*. I provided examples of different types of communities that archaeologists might partner with. This brings us to a complex and important question that relates directly to the previous discussion on obtaining community authorization to conduct research: Who speaks for the community? Clearly, those in a position to authorize research on behalf of the community have themselves been authorized by the community to speak for them to some degree. But in Indigenous communities, the issue of representation can be more complex. Traditional knowledge is involved in many projects, and this raises the question of who has rights and stewardship responsibilities over cultural knowledge. Does a thumbs-up from one elder or family mean that the research has been community sanctioned? How do we define "community consent"?

These considerations usually arise most often when an archaeologist seeks out a community partnership, because researchers new to a community do not yet know who the appropriate knowledge stewards are. To take the first step, archaeologists need to identify the appropriate people who can give such permission before they consider working in a community. In fact, what constitutes consent from a community and who can give it are questions that persist even when communities and researchers have an established relationship.

Identifying who rightfully "speaks for" the community or provides "consent" for doing research can be exceedingly complex. The official, state-sanctioned leadership may be different from those the community recognizes as responsible for making decisions about research, particularly when traditional knowledge is involved. McNaughton and Rock (2003) highlight this point in their report entitled, "Opportunities in Aboriginal Research: Results of SSHRC's Dialogue on Research and Aboriginal Peoples." Their report was funded by the Social Science and Humanities Research Council (SSHRC), the Canadian equivalent of major U.S. funding agencies, such as the National Science Foundation and National Endowment for the Humanities. McNaughton and Rock aimed to inform the funding agency about how to develop an aboriginal research agenda.

Their report addresses many issues that researchers must keep in mind when they conduct research related to Indigenous peoples, in Canada and elsewhere. For example, McNaughton and Rock (2003, 12) point out that permission protocols for doing research vary by community. They cite Ryan Heavy Head, who explained that, among the Blackfoot, certain *individuals* are responsible for granting permission for conducting research; among other communities, similar responsibilities are given to particular *families*. Wiynjorroc et al.'s (2005) work supports Heavy Head's point. They outline the proper protocols for requesting permission to conduct archaeological research in Australian Aboriginal communities. The process involves talking with traditional keepers of particular land regions. Having these rules and expectations published is not common, though. More likely, researchers have to invest time visiting with local residents to find out who has the right to speak for a community, whether it be appropriate individuals, groups, or both.

Although many of the examples on collaborative archaeology here and in the literature involve Indigenous people, the issue of research protocols, permissions, and consent also relate to local descendant and nondescendant communities. Leadership roles within a community can span a spectrum, including political, spiritual, and local governmental leaders, as well as others. All these representatives may need to be involved in the consent process, but they may not all see eye to eye. Furthermore, individuals and/or groups may have disagreements and/or conflicts among them already. Though these tensions have nothing to do with the CBPR project, they *will* directly impact it.

LEARNING THE PERMISSION GRANTING PROCESS

Learning the local permission processes for partnering with a community is a critical part of one's preliminary research. It has to take place well before the project begins. Judging from the timelines of other CBPR projects, researchers should allow at least one field season just to clarify and sort out the process and protocols. This can pose practical challenges, because it affects the timing of grants as well as the start of research activities.

As with conventional approaches to conducting research, starting a CBPR project involves obtaining state and/or federal government permissions. However, unlike a traditional researcher-driven paradigm, CBPR does not entail going into a community to get the required approvals with a full-blown research design already in hand and then making the appropriate connections to obtain required approvals. Following established and accepted cultural protocols requires obtaining approval and consent to work in the community from legitimate and recognized leaders. Researchers do not enter a community and begin asking around for permission until they find someone who will agree to the partnership. Obtaining community consent often may involve a less formal process, yet it is critical for it to be done appropriately if the CBPR project is to be a success. Making connections, discussing shared research goals, and educating the community to some degree about the principles and practices of CBPR are appropriate ways to begin the process, because they align the relationship with a CBPR approach from the start.

THE PACE OF GETTING STARTED

In some cases, the transition to an archaeological CBPR project happens quickly. The initial interviews or community meetings move directly into planning a project and developing focused questions, followed by a detailed research design. In other situations, establishing a project can be a prolonged process. Archaeologists committed to doing community-based archaeology may assume that the community will be equally enthusiastic about the partnership. In reality, that is not always so. Some communities may not feel comfortable delving immediately into a community-based archaeology project. The transition period can be lengthy, and can even take months or years.

One scenario that can be surprisingly challenging is when an archaeologist who has been conducting long-term, conventional archaeological fieldwork in a region decides to initiate a community-based archaeology project. The archaeologist may have already developed personal friendships and connections with members of the local community. Perhaps the archaeologist has given public tours or talks, hosted a community day or children's activities on-site, or even developed public education materials about the site. The challenge lies in shifting the way of working. In the researcher-driven model, the archaeologist engages with the local community primarily as a work force or an interested public. How can the archaeologist switch to a model that engages the community members as coresearchers?

One approach is to rely on established community contacts to gain entry into the larger community. This can be productive in some cases, but it can also present challenges. The existing connections may associate the researcher with a particular group, faction, or family within the community. Such perceptions can be difficult to overcome.

Another approach is to connect with a local community organization or group that is involved with heritage, history, or a related area of interest. This can provide a relatively easy entry into a community on a more official level, and it presents the archaeologist to the wider community in a more neutral way. CBOs already have a general understanding of the community's interests. They may also be able to advise on appropriate cultural protocols and provide contact information for those who are recognized authorities on community traditional knowledge. As I experienced in my work with the Ziibiwing Center, archaeologists who develop a collaborative relationship with the CBO can benefit from the trust that the CBO has already established within the community.

An archaeologist might also choose to make the transition to CBPR without working through a CBO. Even when one has a long history of working in the community, shifting from the standard, researcher-driven archaeological paradigm to a collaborative, community-based model can be difficult. Whatever choices a researcher makes along the way, the transition is likely to be time-consuming and will pose challenges.

TRANSITIONING TO CBPR: THE EXAMPLE
OF ÇATALHÖYÜK

I went through a transition process firsthand in the CBPR project I conducted in Turkey. The Çatalhöyük community partnership meant building a CBPR component within the context of a large, previously established archaeological project. This example demonstrates that successfully developing a community-based archaeology project requires a substantial investment of time, and may involve a process of transition for *both* the archaeologist and the community.

Archaeologists have worked at Çatalhöyük since its "discovery" by archaeologist James Mellaart in 1961. Mellaart carried out extensive excavation at the 9,000-year-old site (Mellaart 1967). He employed men from the nearest village of Küçükköy as laborers during four productive field seasons. However, due to rumors that he was illicitly trafficking in antiquities (Pearson and Connor 1968), Mellaart's excavation permit was not renewed. Archaeological research at the site halted until an international team led by Ian Hodder was given permission in 1995 to renew excavations at the site. Hodder's project also employs members of the local Küçükköy community as labor. Local men work screens and run the flotation machine. Women sort heavy residue materials, and a crew from Küçükköy and the nearby town of Çumra work as kitchen and housekeeping staff for the excavation project.

During the renewed excavations, local residents have been invited to engage with the site in more substantive ways as well. Women from Küçükköy were invited to contribute to an on-site visitor center exhibit about local plant use (Bartu Candan 2005), and local residents have also participated in several ethnoarchaeological projects, as paid participants who provide ethnographic data that enhance archaeological understandings and interpretations of the site (Hodder 2005).

Like other archaeologists working at Çatalhöyük, through these experiences, I came to know some of the residents from Küçükköy and Çumra fairly well. Over the years, the archaeology team developed positive working relationships and friendships with those in the local communities. The challenge of starting a CBPR project in this context was not about identifying a community partner or making initial contacts. It was a matter of organizing the community to create an entity that could function as a research partner.

Cultural anthropologists (Bartu 1999, 2000, 2007; Bartu Candan 2005) have provided insight into the community and the history of the research there. They have documented some of the impacts of the Çatalhöyük excavation on residents' lives. It is clear that the residents of Küçükköy had been quite disenfranchised from engaging with their own history. Turkish law stipulates that cultural resources are the shared patrimony of the Turkish people. However, local communities such as Küçükköy had been involved in only a very minimal, cursory way in discussions about the archaeological research occurring in their own backyards. Arguably, they were the most impacted by the excavation research and resulting heritage-based economic development going on at Çatalhöyük. Yet their decision-making power about the management of the site and the tourist development was minimal. Often a handful of residents were invited to discussions about the site's development, but they frequently left frustrated because they had no substantive influence or real decision-making power. I was concerned with how a CBPR project could be developed in this scenario. The local community was not organized around issues of archaeology and heritage, and members had no structures in place with whom an archaeologist could partner and collaborate. My primary question became: How does one go about organizing within a community, so that a genuine research partnership can emerge?

COMMUNITY ORGANIZING AT ÇATALHÖYÜK

The first step was to determine if the local communities around Çatalhöyük were interested in archaeology. What level of commitment to a research partnership might they have? As with my Ziibiwing experience, I had to do some up-front education to define CBPR and demonstrate how this approach is different. The critical difference to highlight in such discussions is the collaborative nature of CBPR and how this changes the one-way role community members previously had as excavation laborers or ethnographic informants.

At Çatalhöyük, I conducted a series of in-home interviews with Küçükköy families to discuss community-based archaeology and CBPR concepts. Interviews began by discussing ethnographic topics and questions that archaeologists working on the site had previously asked the community. These were familiar topics asked in a comfortable setting that was familiar to many residents because they had engaged with the archaeologists in this way before. I then moved the discussion to CBPR and described it as a way to involve the local community in the research about Çatalhöyük. Using this approach, I was able to effectively utilize the ethnoarchaeological model of questioning as a contrast to the CBPR approach to demonstrate how CBPR is different.

Starting with an ethnographic framework helped to put people at ease, because it allowed them to demonstrate the valuable knowledge they have to contribute. Interviews began with the familiar framework of questioning local residents about their daily lives and practices (for example, how much barley they stored annually to feed a family of four, and how much meat they dried and processed at a time)—things they were experts in and felt comfortable discussing. I then shifted toward discussing principles of CBPR and the value it places on local knowledge and collaborative partnerships. I was hoping to model the transition from a researcher–ethnographic informant relationship to one of research partner–research partner. Such a partnership recognizes that we both contribute specialized skills and knowledge. In some ways, I found this strategy to be very effective, because it highlighted the valuable knowledge and perspectives that local residents have. Yet, contrary to what I was hoping to achieve, I was still playing the role of expert because of the level of knowledge I had about CBPR.

COMING TO TERMS WITH "EXPERTISE"

This contradiction can discourage archaeologists who hope to engage in a collaborative and participatory fashion. Despite my efforts to interact as equal partners, the feeling that I was an expert remained. I spent some time in this uncomfortable space before I resolved this for myself. I came to understand that being equal partners does not mean that we have similar knowledge. The strength and beauty of a CBPR partnership comes in the acknowledgment that both sides bring valuable knowledge to the table. Assuming that I had all the knowledge because I understood CBPR reinforced the idea that the community had nothing to offer. Once I recognized this point, I relaxed and felt free to show my willingness to establish a different sort of relationship with those I was interviewing. I was introducing CBPR in a way that was consistent with CBPR principles and philosophy. My self-reflection also allowed me to articulate for myself—and later to the local residents of Küçükköy as well—the trepidation I had been feeling. Through this process, the dynamics shifted. Respect based on recognizing how our different knowledge could work in complementary ways became much clearer, and future interviews reflected this shift.

WORKING BEYOND POWER IMBALANCES

Prior to developing a CBPR project at Çatalhöyük, I conducted ethnoarchaeological research in Küçükköy, and I always approached community members as equals who had valuable knowledge. I was aware of the power dynamics involved in researcher–subject relationships. Indeed, this awareness was what initially led me to investigate alternative methodologies for archaeological research. But what I realized through these first steps toward CBPR in Küçükköy was how critical it is for archaeologists to be self-reflective and self-critical about what we are doing. We need to recognize and name the ways that uneven power relations play out in our daily engagements with community partners. We also need to develop solutions for addressing these power imbalances, so that both partners feel that their power and voice, though different, can come together in balance. Part of this process of transition involved me realizing that the way community members perceived and experienced these imbalances mattered just as much as my own perceptions of the situation. At times, I felt certain that the balance was off while my community partners felt a sense of equilibrium. The reverse was also true, at times.

Transitioning from a traditional archaeological model to a CBPR model involves a *process*. It takes time for both the community partner(s) and the archaeologist, and adjusting to the transition may happen at a different pace for each. I found it was critical to keep from worrying about being "collaborative or participatory enough." Instead, I focused on how we could make decisions in a collaborative fashion.

I found it helpful to read about others doing collaborative research, especially when they talked about the challenges of being fully collaborative. Ballard (2008), for example, openly discusses the ways that the CBPR project she initiated with immigrant workers who held harvesting jobs in the United States was not fully collaborative and how they could improve. She points to the need to use a participatory process at each step. From there, the partners can work together to increase community involvement as they initiate and design the research for a project.

Silliman (2008a, 9) also talks about collaborative research. He explains that collaborative archaeology is not about the end point or what is produced, although conducting rigorous research and producing new knowledge is clearly important in CBPR. Rather, what is important is the process involved in designing and implementing the research.

This reiterates Freire's point that ideology comes before methodology in community-based research. Community-based archaeology is not measured by the specifics of how CBPR is done or even whether a project achieves full participation in all aspects. Rather, it is a way of working and a mind-set that starts from and is rooted in a place of power sharing and reciprocity.

PRESENTING CBPR PRINCIPLES

One of the first steps in establishing a CBPR project is explaining CBPR's principles and practices and how these differ from traditional approaches to research. As with my experience at the Ziibiwing Center, this step can be straightforward and can lead directly into discussing possible research questions and project partnerships. However, when an archaeologist needs to help organize a community partner and has to offset a community's long history with a more traditional research methodology, presenting CBPR to a community may take longer and require more effort. This was the case with the Çatalhöyük project. CBPR principles and the concept of working as research partners was not immediately recognized or understood by the local residents. I prepared what I felt were straightforward ways of explaining CBPR and how it differed from traditional research. The basic principles and concepts of CBPR were well received, but I frequently encountered unexpected reactions once community members understood the partnership approach. In several cases, community members voiced displeasure with not having been involved as research partners earlier. Although they had never mentioned this before, many of them said they had felt excluded or overlooked in the past. In other cases, only after explaining key concepts such as "research partnership" and the goal of "building community capacity" several times was I able to relay the principles clearly.

TRANSLATING CBPR AT ÇATALHÖYÜK

One family who had long-standing ties with the Çatalhöyük project had much to say about how archaeologists had treated their local community. The male patriarch of the family was the oldest living person in Küçükköy who had worked at the Çatalhöyük site during the 1960s excavations. In my initial visits to his home and in my early interviews with him, he shared stories of how unhappy the villagers had been about their interactions with James Mellaart (the site's first excavation director) and his team. They were happy to have employment at Çatalhöyük, but they felt the Mellaart team had not respected them.

In one of the most illustrative examples, the village had invited Mellaart's team for a large festival feast. The archaeologists reportedly accepted the invitation, but by 11 p.m., after waiting hours for the archaeologists to arrive, village residents gave up and started the feast without the honored guests. Mellaart's team never arrived, and residents have never forgotten the event. It is not clear why the archaeologists did not attend. Events such as this demonstrated to Küçükköy residents that their relationship with the archaeologists was one of labor to boss. These events fueled a feeling of distrust while at the same time establishing the model of how archaeologists and Küçükköy residents would interact with one another. The man who described these events had never been back to the site after James Mellaart was forced to halt excavation in the mid-1960s.

The Cambridge-Stanford excavations had been in full swing for ten years at the time of my initial interview with his family. In all this time, the elder had never come to the site for community feast nights or to view the excavation areas and latest findings. I found it very interesting and not at all surprising that he had difficulty digesting the principles of CBPR. When I interviewed his family in the early stages of organizing the community to develop a CBPR partnership, he and his relatives asked me repeatedly, "What questions do you have for us?" They wanted me to ask the "usual" questions—the ones they knew how to answer—about storage practices or building mud-brick houses. Despite my efforts to explain that I wanted to work as partners and to explore ways to create and answer questions of mutual interest, the family gave the same response.

A similar example came from another family that included several members who were employed by the Çatalhöyük project. The elder male insisted throughout the interview about CBPR that the type of community-based project we were proposing would never work in Küçükköy. His main reason was that the people in the village did not care about archaeology or places like Çatalhöyük, no matter how important or famous they were. He insisted that the local people were not educated and thus had no interest in their own heritage. When I tried to explain how much interest I had already received from villagers in developing a CBPR partnership and in examining ways to collaborate on archaeology research related to Çatalhöyük, he just denied it and said it simply was not possible. He came across as quite negative about both the process and the possibilities.

However, when I asked him how he felt about the ideals and principles of CBPR in general (rather than CBPR being practiced in his village), he expressed his full support. In fact, he insisted that he had been advocating for such a process at Çatalhöyük all along. Ironically, throughout the interview, his grandchildren were utterly engrossed with our conversation about archaeology. They had been reading a set of archaeology comics about the Çatalhöyük site that we had developed and distributed in the village. Unnoticed by the grandfather, the comics had captured the children's imagination and got them thinking and talking about archaeology.

LOCALLY APPROPRIATE TERMINOLOGY
AND EXPLANATIONS

These examples demonstrate how research can become entrenched in one paradigm of practice. In the conventional academic model, researchers are often uncritically viewed as the ones who have useful knowledge (and all the decision-making, economic, and social power), while descendant and local communities are viewed as informants. Archaeologists engage with communities either to obtain ethnographic information or to report excavation results through public outreach. It can be a real challenge to move beyond these patterns, disrupting the power dynamic and engaging a new research paradigm. Even when the new practice involves benefits to the community, local people who have been on the receiving end of conventional, researcher-driven archaeology can respond with confusion, mistrust, and pessimism.

These examples also demonstrate the need to find creative ways for presenting CBPR principles to community members. Without purposeful thought about what is most appropriate for the local circumstances, a community's initial response can be frustration. This should not be interpreted as lack of interest, though. Presenting CBPR principles is not always a simple, straightforward process. It requires preparation and an understanding of the history and social context of the community (-ies) involved.

As these examples suggest, developing an appropriate way to present CBPR to the communities with whom you hope to partner takes time. This not only involves having a clear understanding of key CBPR principles, but also having the appropriate language and terminology to explain them. Terminology is particularly relevant in situations where an archaeologist will be communicating in a foreign language. Terms such as *participatory* and *collaboration* may not have direct translations. I faced terminology problems repeatedly when I talked about CBPR in Turkish. I often needed an entire phrase or several sentences to describe a word or key concept of CBPR. Direct translation was not possible, because Turkish lacks terms for many of the concepts. Plus, community members in rural villages used different phrases from those used by the city-born Turkish archaeology students who were working with me and helping to find useful ways of describing CBPR concepts. Developing a shared language about CBPR became part of the initial collaborative work for us. Eventually, we were able to develop a shared language to describe CBPR work. But these phrases may not be equally useful for communicating CBPR ideas to those outside the region.

ASSESSING COMMITMENT, AND ESTABLISHING TRUST

Critically important in any early exchange is the sense of trust that is established and an understanding of both partners' commitment to the project. CBPR researchers often observe that community partners will quickly begin to assess a researcher's long-term commitment to the community.

Corea et al. (2008) call attention to the need for long-term commitment and the importance of trust in CBPR projects. They describe how trust has been pivotal to success for their agricultural research project in Honduras, which involved collaboration among agronomists, plant breeders, and more than 500 farmers over the past ten years. They found that trust grows at an uneven rate in CBPR partnerships: slow at the beginning and then more quickly, rather like the S-curve that typifies growth processes. Vio Grossi (1980) stresses the importance of trust as well in his analysis of multiple CBPR projects throughout Asia and Africa. He found that the barriers that existed between a researcher and community members at the outset of a project slowly broke down. Long (2008) observed that in his partnership with the White Mountain Apache tracing ecological changes and understanding natural resource management strategies, the importance of building and sustaining relationships has been key to the project's success. He refers to the "reservoir of trust" (Long 2008, 80) among community members and himself. It had started very slowly, but it developed over time.

Building trust can be particularly challenging for community-based archaeology because of the timing and flow of the fieldwork. Archaeologists tend to work in a community for several months each summer, but then they return home to conduct analysis and/or teach. This can present challenges, particularly at the start of a CBPR project when developing trust is so critical. Ballard (2008) discusses her experiences around this issue with salal harvesters in the Pacific Northwest of the United States. She describes the challenges she had to overcome because of her distance from the community. Not only is Ballard from a different class and economic background from the community members with whom she partnered, but she also had long segments of time away from the community (during the academic school year) and needed to continually reestablish trust and the partnership when she returned to do fieldwork each season.

Community partners have described the challenges they face in establishing trust with community members. Bergelin et al. (2008) describe a case that involves another common trust issue. Community members from villages in Sweden were research partners in a CBPR project that examined forestry management from a village level. Several community members initially distrusted Seema Arora-Jonsson, a researcher from the Swedish University of Agricultural Sciences. Arora-Jonsson visited villages in Sweden hoping to initiate a CBPR project with local women. The women could not understand why a researcher would be interested in working with them, and thus had a significant amount of initial distrust because of the status differences between themselves and Arora-Jonsson (Bergelin et al. 2008).

"LIKE-MINDEDNESS" AND THE VALUE OF COMMUNITY KNOWLEDGE

One of the coinvestigators in the Ziibiwing CBPR projects, Ziibiwing's director Shannon Martin, emphasized the importance of like-mindedness in establishing trust. I interviewed Martin about the factors that build a strong foundation for a partnership in community-based archaeological research. I was particularly interested in understanding if my being an "insider" as an Ojibwe person trained in archaeology was key or if other factors held primacy. This is a critical issue for the discipline and its potential for shifting to CBPR. The vast majority of archaeologists working with Native American communities are non-Native. Around the globe as well, archaeologists are rarely "insiders" or members of the community with whom they are developing a research partnership. I asked Martin, "Did you feel my being Ojibwe played a central role for the Ziibiwing staff in your decision to collaborate with me on our initial NAGPRA CBPR project?" She replied:

> You were approached because you are Ojibwe . . . but if I had learned, or if Bonnie [the Cultural Center's previous director] had known, of your scholarship and your research and your willingness and priority to focus on collaborative archaeology and decolonizing archaeology, it wouldn't matter what race you were or what ethnicity you were. But sharing in that like-mindedness for Indigenous groups to regain control of their own history and to rewrite their own history, in many instances, from their own perspectives is what matters.

Finding more individuals who are willing to work with tribes and, you know, creating that network for Indigenous peoples to build a trust . . . that is so important.

(MARTIN, *Personal Communication*, September 1, 2009)

In the Ziibiwing partnership, the ideology and community-based approach were clearly the most significant factors. The role of "like-mindedness" that Martin described for the Ziibiwing case is not specific to that project. Many archaeologists cite it as a necessary criterion for success in their CBPR projects. Martin's comments show how critical being of a similar mind can be, especially at the outset of a project, because it creates a solid base from which further trust can grow.

Martin also identified a second key factor for developing community–archaeologist partnerships: respect for and appreciation of multiple forms of knowledge. Communities have the right to engage in producing knowledge about the past. And their contributions make archaeological endeavors successful in ways the projects could not otherwise be. Recognizing the rights that communities have to be engaged in producing knowledge about the past and the value their contributions make to the endeavor are concepts emphasized throughout the literature on collaborative archaeology.

These two key points—building on like-mindedness and respecting community knowledge—are essential. However, this should not be understood to imply that archaeologists and community partners will, or even should, agree on all issues. Disagreements will occur, both while establishing a partnership and throughout the course of the project(s). Yet coming together around these two points lays a foundation in a shared understanding of CBPR principles and a shared commitment to practicing them. Partners can at least agree to approach the research as equitable partners, both of whom have important skills and knowledge to contribute during the process.

ESTABLISHING LIKE-MINDEDNESS WITH ZIIBIWING AND AT ÇATALHÖYÜK

Building "like-mindedness" between community participants and myself has been fundamental to the success of each of the community-based research endeavors with which I have personally been involved. It ensured our ability to work productively toward common goals. The NAGPRA-related research on the cultural affiliation of human remains was my first partnership with Ziibiwing. We agreed at the outset that Anishinabe oral traditions needed to be a central part of the data gathered and that it should form the basis for any claims. According to NAGPRA, oral history is one of the nine categories of data that can be used to determine cultural affiliation. But, more importantly for our partnership, this agreement demonstrated my intellectual, professional, and personal stance that Anishinabe oral tradition is a valid and valued source of knowledge that is as important to understand as "scientific" or archaeological data. Respect for oral tradition matters a great deal to Native American and other Indigenous communities, but other issues matter too.

Building like-mindedness and acknowledging the rights of local communities to engage in archaeological research have proven equally critical in the Çatalhöyük CBPR project. The cultural values and priorities of rural communities in Turkey are different from Native North American communities. Oral tradition, for example, does not carry the same weight with Turkish communities. Their culture largely relies on written histories, even though a substantial portion of the aging population has limited literacy skills and has limited access to written narratives. Furthermore, unlike many Native American and Indigenous communities, local residents in the Çatalhöyük CBPR project did not feel they had any knowledge to contribute to archaeology in the region.

But alongside substantial differences, similarities exist between these projects as well. One similarity is the conviction that communities have a right to take a substantive role in managing archaeological sites. In over 70 percent of the interviews I conducted over a four-year period in the Çatalhöyük CBPR project, local residents from Küçükköy repeatedly raised issues about their rights and their ability to take part in the site's management and tourist development. One major concern, raised more often than any other, was that Çatalhöyük had been sold to Çumra, the nearest town.

RESEARCHING THE SALE OF LOCAL RIGHTS
TO ÇATALHÖYÜK

Many Küçükköy residents told me that the previous village manager had made a self-serving deal with the mayor and municipality of Çumra. They explained that the outcome was that all the rights to develop and profit from Çatalhöyük in commercial or tourism-related ways were sold to Çumra. According to Turkish law, archaeological sites are the property of the Turkish Republic, and all citizens have equal right to them. This legal definition of access and rights was not the way local communities understood and engaged with Çatalhöyük. Discussing the legalities with community members quickly proved to be a moot point. As the CBPR project took form, I realized that selling Çatalhöyük to Çumra was a core issue for the CBPR project. It would play a crucial role in developing a sense of like-mindedness with community partners in Küçükköy.

To address this issue, I had to investigate the sale. Working with the community interns, our CBPR research team conducted further interviews throughout Küçükköy and Çumra to gather information about the sale. We spoke with the family of the former village manager who had supposedly made the sale (who was quite ill and unable to meet with us), the current village manager, and the mayor of Çumra. Our research determined that, at least officially, there was never any sale of Çatalhöyük. Further investigation revealed that Küçükköy residents felt it was not "the site" of Çatalhöyük that was allegedly sold, but the rights to use the name, to be associated with the site, and to benefit from it.

Currently, both Çumra and Küçükköy use the Çatalhöyük name. It is on everything from the village school (Küçükköy-Çatalhöyük Primary School), to the Çatalhöyük Electric shop located en route from Küçükköy to Çumra. The annual agricultural festival even bears the name of Çatalhöyük (Çumra-Çatalhöyük Melon Festival). The extent to which Çumra has associated itself with Çatalhöyük was apparent from the town flag, which includes an image of the famous Çatalhöyük "mother goddess" and lists the founding date of the town as 7,000 BC (the estimated habitation date of Çatalhöyük). Associations with Çatalhöyük and the use of the name were evident in both the town and the village.

We found no evidence that any sale of the mound itself or the "rights of use" ever took place. Our research indicates that any exchange, monetary or otherwise, that may have taken place was done off the books and is not legally binding. I spoke with Çumra's mayor, Mr. Yusuf Erdem, to learn about the details of the agreement and the specific terms of the exchange.

Mayor Erdem provided one possible explanation of what may have caused this widespread belief among the residents of Küçükköy. He explained that, in 1996, when the excavations at Çatalhöyük were gearing up, it became clear that, with so many people living on the site, they would need help with basic city services—of primary importance was garbage pickup at Çatalhöyük. Normally, Çumra only provides this service for those within its town boundaries, and garbage pickup is not available in the nearby villages. Residents in Küçükköy store their garbage outside in open courtyards and periodically burn it, sprinkling the ashes on their fields. According to Mayor Erdem, Çumra agreed to redraw its boundaries for garbage pickup service to include the mound of Çatalhöyük, thirteen kilometers outside the Çumra town boundary. It was unclear why Çumra decided to take on this additional cost. Perhaps the unwritten agreement was that the rights to the name and associations of connection to Çatalhöyük from that time forward would be given to Çumra. However, Mayor Erdem assured our team that there was no contract or agreement related to this. Poor communication during this redistricting process led to many misunderstandings, and the mayor attributed the village rumor mill for the widespread misunderstanding.

Sorting out the facts with members of the Küçükköy community clarified several points. First, it reiterated that Küçükköy residents have a legal right to engage with Çatalhöyük and to take part in its future planning, care, and management. Second, it helped to establish a critical sense of like-mindedness between the residents of Küçükköy and myself by demonstrating my commitment to addressing community concerns. The experience also gave proof of my claims that local knowledge and participation have value.

Vio Grossi's (1980, 75) analysis of CBPR projects in Africa, Asia, and Latin America shows that communities assess researchers' reliability and what they are able to contribute to a partnership. My willingness to investigate the Çatalhöyük ownership issue with seriousness and determination, combined with my willingness to stand up for the village against a more powerful government entity, demonstrated to Küçükköy's community members that we were on the same page. These examples from Ziibiwing and Küçükköy point to a shared concern that each community has about its rights to research and manage archaeological sites and materials. However, these examples also demonstrate the locally specific nature of "like-mindedness": how the common concern about rights plays out differently place to place, community to community.

IDENTIFYING AREAS OF SENSITIVITY

As in these cases, ethnographic research early on builds a baseline knowledge about a community. This research can help archaeologists identify sensitive areas or critical points that may impact the partnership. For some communities, such as in Native North America, areas of dispute are well known, such as genetic testing, reburial/repatriation issues, or the validity of oral tradition. However, considering the enormous diversity of Native communities and other Indigenous groups, it is problematic to assume what the most relevant issues will be. A literature review that includes research-based knowledge of a community but also takes account of local information sources, such as community newspapers or tribal websites, is an important initial step of the CBPR process and needs to be conducted prior to entering a community. Other important early steps are further investigation through interviews, surveys, focus groups, or informal conversations with community members to understand local views on archaeology as well as their level of interest in, and concerns with, developing a potential research partnership.

Household interviews formed a critical part of the ethnographic process in the Çatalhöyük CBPR project (Atalay 2007, 2010). They provided valuable knowledge that continues to prove beneficial. In other CBPR projects, living in and working with a community brought substantial benefits in building a strong and lasting partnership. Humphries et al. (2008) detail how a trust relationship between agronomists and farmers developed over time. Because the agronomists lived and worked with farmers, they began to see the wider context of the farmers' concerns and struggles, and they stopped thinking of their agricultural problems as a mere lack of technology. Engaged with the community to this extent, the researchers were able to see the links between socioeconomics and the farmers' disenfranchisement. This understanding greatly improved the scientific quality of their research. They explain that friendship, trust, and respect are key ingredients for building a successful partnership (2008, 40), which in turn is key for producing reliable, accurate knowledge.

Background research through qualitative methods and sharing time with a community partner help researchers raise cultural competency and understand a community in greater depth. CBPR practitioners highlight that the process of understanding and learning in a successful CBPR project is never unidirectional. Community members also need to learn about researchers as individuals, the culture of academia, and other issues that affect their partnership and work together. Community members need to know where a researcher stands on key issues, so that both partners can assess their fit as collaborators. As potential research partners communicate openly, community members learn about the archaeologist's views and approaches and the expectations that the archaeologist has for the partnership.

RESEARCHING THE COMMUNITY SOCIOPOLITICAL CONTEXT

In Chapter 4, I discussed the need to develop a basic understanding of both the sociopolitical context and the culturally appropriate protocols and practices of a community, even at the very early stage of meeting a potential community research partner. These issues become even more important once the partnership is established. Both researcher and community members must do their part to develop a productive working relationship. Successfully navigating complex issues of archaeological CBPR involving multiple stakeholders, appropriate cultural protocols (which can vary widely, depending on the cultural context), political alliances, community factions, and any number of potentially explosive situations requires that archaeologists research the context of the community and region where they hope to establish collaborative relationships. And the importance of understanding the local political and social context is a central part of community-based archaeology, regardless of how archaeologists establish a connection to the community and no matter if they plan to partner with a CBO or with multiple community groups. Researching political, social, and economic dynamics is a critical step, and one that is best started well in advance of any fieldwork.

Those who have conducted CBPR projects with communities from diverse locations around the globe emphasize how important it is to obtain a clear understanding of community contexts (de Wit and Gianotten 1980; Jackson, Conchelos, and Vigoda 1980). Maguire writes frankly about her experiences as an individual researcher attempting to establish a CBPR project. She characterizes the important first step as "Entering, Experiencing, Establishing Relationships" (Maguire 1987, 113). She relates the importance of understanding community context, stating:

> As I organized a tentative model for conducting participatory research, I envisioned the steps in the process set within an historical and material context. The context can be explored from both a quantitative and qualitative perspective. The quantitative perspective includes understanding aspects such as socio-economic, demographic, geographical, and political data. . . . The qualitative perspective includes beginning to understand the meaning people give to their experience of that reality.

For archaeologists, this means not only having a grasp of the archaeological data that has been produced in the region and on sites with which the community has a cultural affiliation and/or interest, but it also involves gaining awareness of the level of knowledge and interest local people have in archaeology broadly, and in engaging in community-based archaeological research. This involves conducting background research into the ways community members have been disenfranchised from creating knowledge about their cultural heritage, and also how they have been successfully included in that process.

ETHNOGRAPHIES OF ÇATALHÖYÜK

Over seven years of archaeological excavations at Çatalhöyük, I developed a solid understanding of the social and political context of the region. But I lacked an accurate picture of the "qualitative perspective" Maguire describes. I did not yet understand how people felt about archaeology or their level of knowledge and interest in the archaeological research that was taking place at Çatalhöyük and elsewhere. I also did not know the heritage management issues that might concern them once cultural tourism efforts were put into place. Coming to understand these contexts turned out to be a lengthy and laborious process (Atalay 2007), and it took much longer than I had anticipated. But it produced interesting results, many of which were equally unanticipated. The process was greatly aided by the work of two cultural anthropologists who had worked in the area.

When the excavation at Çatalhöyük was in its early stages, two cultural anthropologists studied both the archaeologists working there and the site's impact on local communities (Bartu 1999, 2000; Shankland 1996, 1999). Bartu's research is particularly informative. She argued for a CBPR-like model of archaeology to be used in the region. Although she did not call it CBPR or have a name for it, Bartu made the case for expanding the archaeological "site" to include the nearby village of Küçükköy (Bartu 2000). As an archaeologist wishing to conduct CBPR in Küçükköy and with other local village communities, having the luxury of cultural anthropologists studying these issues was immensely valuable. Bartu's work laid the foundation for what developed into the Çatalhöyük CBPR project. However, this is a luxury that archaeologists rarely have. More often, researching the broader social context of a community before embarking on a CBPR project is something archaeologists must do themselves.

ETHNOGRAPHIC TRAINING

Pyburn (2009) argues that ethnographic training is very important for conducting community archaeology. She describes the damage that archaeologists have done to communities when they had poor or inappropriate training but attempted to do ethnography. Pyburn states, "Appropriate ethnography for archaeologists is not about learning about other people or about teaching other people, but about *sharing* with other people. Attempts to 'help,' 'teach,' or 'evaluate' other people without this effort, especially when the engagement is between wealthy, educated, government supported 'scientists' and people without such advantages, is every bit as hegemonic and colonialist as field programs that make no attempt to engage non-specialists; perhaps more so" (2009, 165). As Pyburn accurately points out, the problematic aspect of this approach is that it pursues an ideal of "helping": Archaeologists engage in abstract development without appropriate training and often without careful consideration of the effects on real people—their lives, families, and daily needs as basic as food, housing, and safety.

This directly relates to CBPR principles and how they create benefits. Solutions and actions are formulated directly in partnership with descendant and local groups who are most acutely aware of their own needs and what kind of approach suits their community situation. Archaeologists are not ethnographers, nor do we need to be. I agree with Pyburn (2009, 168) when she states that, "What archaeologists need to learn to do is not full-fledged academic ethnography that amounts to a second career, but something a bit more strategic and humble." Pyburn advocates that we use participatory research methods, and like Maguire, she also stresses the need to understand the meaning people give to their lived experiences. My research supports these points. I've found that good, effective community-based archaeology depends on understanding both the social and material context of a community, and no one knows this context as well as the community members themselves.

My comparative research on CBPR also demonstrates that archaeological and heritage research is most effective and least likely to do harm when it is participatory. A community-based methodology provides a productive way forward for archaeologists, precisely because it relies on community members to identify priorities and solutions for themselves. They can take leadership roles in projects, such as cultural tourism or other archaeology and heritage-related economic development plans, that address needs that they themselves have identified as priorities.

I also agree with Pyburn that archaeologists who plan to engage with a community as a CBPR partner cannot do so successfully without understanding the community's political, social, and economic environment. Long-term success in collaborative archaeology requires that archaeologists know the proper cultural protocols and who provides the most appropriate leadership. Both require a sophisticated cultural understanding of prospective community partners. It will be very difficult, if not impossible, to develop a productive partnership without such an understanding, in part because building the solid foundation that allows for long-term success in community-based archaeology begins with following proper cultural protocols and engaging with the most appropriate community leadership—both require a sophisticated cultural understanding of the communities in question.

I am not advocating that archaeologists conduct a full ethnographic study of a region. However, community-based archaeology does require a solid and accurate understanding of the social context within which a potential community partner operates. As most archaeologists now realize, it is not wise to show up in a community, arrange a meeting with the local political leadership, and then start knocking on doors and conducting surveys and interviews to assess community problems. It is equally untenable to select one family as a community research partner. As the evidence indicates, success in a CBPR project requires that archaeologists spend not only time and research effort but also funding dollars to raise one's level of knowledge about a community. This awareness must extend not only to social, political, and economic structures but also to how these vary within and between communities.

ETHNOGRAPHIES OF POWER

In this context, I want to elaborate on a point I touched on earlier. Pyburn (2011) argues that the ethnographic understandings that archaeologists need to have under their belts should not be limited to the local or descendant communities. They must also understand the more economically and politically powerful groups. Pyburn comments, "Often the communities that we really need to understand anthropologically are those that wield the most political and economic power, such as government officials, school boards, multinational hotel chains, USAID missions, and archaeologists themselves" (2011, 12). I would add nongovernmental organizations (NGOs) to that list. All of these powerful groups have cultures and practices that need to be understood, if our community-based partnerships are to be successful.

Analyzing the workings of these groups and the ways they intersect with local and descendant communities is not a static action that happens once and is complete, nor should it only involve the archaeologist. This activity should continue throughout the partnership with the community, and community members should be given opportunities to take part in this aspect of the research (Brydon-Miller 1993; Comstock and Fox 1993; Wainwright and Elliot 1982). In many communities, members are disenfranchised from larger political and economic processes. Their opportunities to gain access to the workings of these powerful groups may be limited or nonexistent. Producing ethnographies of power thus becomes part of a larger capacity-building process that can be utilized and applied to address other areas of community concern.

A critical next step in the Çatalhöyük community-based archaeology project is for me to complete one such ethnography of power. I think it is essential for us to understand the articulation of powerful international heritage organizations (such as International Council on Monuments and Sites [ICOMOS] and United Nations Educational, Scientific and Cultural Organization [UNESCO]) with Turkish national, city, and local governments who oversee archaeology, tourism, and heritage endeavors. We must see the direction and character of the knowledge flows between these entities. I suspect it will be helpful to frame the intersection of local communities with these more powerful entities as "contact zones," being mindful of the critical gaze that scholars such as Boast (2011) have voiced about the woeful inequalities that remain within these spaces.

In my work in Turkey, I was fortunate to have a firsthand account describing some of the community interactions with Çatalhöyük in a book written by a site guard (Dural and Hodder 2007). Adding to that, as I mentioned previously, is the work of two cultural anthropologists who studied the local residents' interactions with Çatalhöyük, recording some of their views on archaeology. David Shankland lived in Küçükköy for several years, and he recorded very useful data about local perspectives on Çatalhöyük. Some of the data he produced helped me understand potential concerns that might arise during a collaborative archaeology project.

For example, Shankland wrote about a local woman who was buried in recent times at the top of the Çatalhöyük mound. Shankland's informants explained that she was buried on the mound because she was a prostitute and was denied burial in the town's cemetery, following the usual custom. According to village rumor, the woman had several gold teeth. And it was said that "thieves" had tried to dig up her grave to remove the teeth but were frightened off by "spirits." Tales of ghosts—cinler in Turkish—near the mound are common in the village.

Understanding this context was extremely helpful when I started the community-based archaeology project in Küçükköy. Realizing that spirits were a real concern for local people, I understood their sensitivity for the mound as a spirit dwelling—a place where spirits of both ancient and recently deceased individuals might be found. In my own interviews, I tried to identify the types of research that community members might like to pursue collaboratively and which areas they wanted to avoid altogether. How the local people managed their concerns about spirits residing on the mound came out during the interviews I conducted at the outset of the CBPR project.

I began inquiring about Shankland's story about the woman buried at Çatalhöyük, and I asked local people who worked on the site if they felt comfortable working there, considering that her spirit (and those of others) were thought to be nearby. I received very interesting responses. One of the local men employed on-site explained that it bothered him to work there because people's graves were being disturbed. Concern for the dead who were being excavated was an important issue for him. He explained that he had gone to the village imam (spiritual leader) to ask if excavating the human remains was a sin. The imam told him it was not a sin, because the people being excavated were not Muslim. Shankland had concluded that the residents of Küçükköy were not concerned about the burials on the site because they felt no connection to those who had occupied the mound 9,000 years earlier.

His work emphasized the local communities' connection to their Islamic past and their utter lack of concern for the Neolithic residents who had been buried below the 9,000-year-old houses in the mound. I was therefore quite surprised that, despite what the imam had told him, this resident was still bothered by the excavations; he felt it made "their bones ache" to be excavated. The same line of inquiry about spirits and how this might affect our collaborative research on-site led another local man with long-term experience as a workman on the site to ask, "Where is the mass grave where you bury the bodies after you have dug them up?"

These interviews showed what little information local community members had about the archaeological work at Çatalhöyük. Even those who had worked many years on the site were unaware of the archaeological analyses and types of research taking place. Their concerns about excavating human remains and their beliefs in the *jins* (spirits) who resided nearby affected their decisions about whether to be involved in archaeological research and explore a CBPR partnership. The desire and economic necessity of some local residents to make an income and support their families had overcome their concern about the dead and the spiritual implications of their work on-site. In planning a community-based archaeology project, it was clear that these issues would need to be addressed if a successful partnership was going to develop between us. As in this example, firsthand accounts, published ethnographic research of the region, and one's own background research provide the critical context—short-term and-long term, early in a CBPR process and throughout its course.

TOOLS FOR UNDERSTANDING COMMUNITY VIEWS ON ARCHAEOLOGY

Archaeologists obviously need to find out early on if community members have an interest in archaeology: What do community members feel can be learned from archaeology? Would they consider working in partnership on a project? Do they feel archaeology can benefit their community and in what ways? To answer these questions, archaeologists must hear from community members directly. CBPR practitioners have used several approaches to assess community interest and develop topics for community-based research. Hemment (2007) describes how community meetings may take the form of a workshop in which action plans are developed or key decisions are made. In his introductory guide to action research, Stringer (2007) provides eight tools for assessing a community's views and inter- ests: interviews, focus groups, participant observation, questionnaires, documents, records and reports, surveys, and research literature. He details each of these and provides practical guidelines for using them.

I agree with Stringer that these eight sources can provide useful information. However, for archaeology, I would argue that the best approach is to talk with community members face-to-face (for example, through interviews, community meetings, focus groups, and so on), after completing a careful review of all written sources (reports, documents, research literature). Some communities, particularly many Indigenous groups, have long and mostly negative historical experiences with archaeology. But even when researchers are not trusted, an archaeologist can still enter a community with humility, a sincere desire to learn about people's experiences, and an openness to the ways community members feel archaeology might benefit them. The community may be willing to give community-based archaeology a chance. When done well, a CBPR approach demonstrates its theory through on-the-ground actions and attitudes. How researchers engage with community members from the start communicates volumes about how they view a partnership. It can convey a powerful and positive message to community members.

Stringer makes valuable suggestions for developing and implementing successful interviews, focus groups, and community meetings. As obvious as some of his most important points seem, they are easily overlooked. Stringer (2007, 69) suggests, for example, that interviews and group meetings take place in a relaxed setting where community members feel at home. This may seem counterintuitive to many archaeologists, who are used to inviting community members to the archaeological site itself. Visiting people in their homes or in local public spaces may feel like an intrusion.

COMMUNITY MEETINGS

I learned the value of meeting local residents in places comfortable and familiar to them during the Çatalhöyük CBPR project. Residents from local villages consistently commented that they enjoyed my coming to visit them in their homes, and they appreciated that I took the time to do so. I found that, in the small villages around Çatalhöyük, some residents enjoyed being visited at their place of work. For example, the man who owns the small grocery and supply store in Abditolu invited our small group to interview him at his store (see Figure 7). Certainly, cultural norms are the best guide for what is appropriate in each case. It may not always be advisable to visit someone's home to conduct an interview. Cultural traditions should inform the approach and how to carry it out. In most rural parts of Turkey, for example, it is not culturally appropriate for men and women to attend public functions together. In Küçükköy, I regularly held two separate community meetings, one for men and another for women and children. These were also held

FIGURE 7.
Interview in the village grocery and supply store in Abditolu,
Turkey.

in different locations. The men felt most comfortable meeting in the local teahouse, a male-only space; and the women and children met in the village school.

The meetings were even announced differently to men and women. Men were invited to the meetings during daily prayer services at the local mosque, attended by both men and women. However, I learned that it was more appropriate to invite women to the meetings through an individual, written invitation. The invitation was considered more formal than a verbal invite. Women are often expected to remain at home during the day, so the written invitation gave them a more formal reason to attend a meeting. Using a written invitation for women surprised me, because there is limited literacy in rural communities in Turkey, particularly among older women. I learned, though, that even if the women could not read the invitation themselves, their male relatives could. Having a written invitation that they could show their husbands demonstrated their need to attend the meeting. For some, their attendance seemed to be more about demonstrating hospitality or curiosity about the archaeologists working at Çatalhöyük. Others clearly had a strong interest in discussing the research on-site, potential community-based projects, and the site's development.

FIGURE 8.
Impromptu community meeting in Abditolu, Turkey. Children
who attended can be seen reading and discussing the Çatalhöyük
comic series produced as part of the CBPR project.

The process for organizing a community meeting was different in each village.
In Abditolu, the village manager agreed to host a community meeting, and followed an impromptu process for organizing it. He told me he would organize and
announce the meeting within the village and asked me to return the next day at a
specific time. When I arrived, he went to the mosque and made an announcement
on the village loudspeaker that someone was in town to talk about Çatalhöyük. He
asked anyone interested to meet at the local elementary school fifteen minutes later.
It was my understanding that the town manager was going to do more to organize
and announce the meeting the day before it occurred. In agricultural villages such
as this one, most people work in the fields during the day. When I realized that he
was only announcing the community meeting fifteen minutes in advance, I was
surprised and disappointed because I assumed there would be very low attendance.
In fact, the turnout was surprisingly good. Older men, children, and even a few
young women attended the meeting (see Figure 8).

FIGURE 9.
Indiana University graduate students Dawn Rutecki and Sarah
Dees talk with a local Sullivan County resident who played on
the mounds as a child.

In working with the Sullivan County American Indian Council (SCAIC), community members requested to host a community meeting at the home of two council members. SCAIC members also invited the chief of the Miami Nation of Indiana and his family, local residents who live near the mound that we were studying, as well as several people who work in local museums. The SCAIC played a key role in organizing the meeting. They rented chairs and tables to accommodate everyone. And they were the point of contact for all attendees, arranging for SCAIC members to bring food and other supplies to the meeting. This meeting provided an opportunity for my students who were part of the research team working with the SCAIC to talk with community members and learn about their experience and interest in the mounds and our collaborative work (see Figure 9).

Stringer (2007, 88) suggests that interviews and group discussions be held in calm settings with minimal interruptions. What he suggests is ideal, but it may be difficult, if not impossible, to achieve at times. The community meetings and home interviews that I conducted in the rural villages surrounding Çatalhöyük were often held in noisy, extremely hot, and crowded conditions. Children and young babies were frequently present, and conversations were regularly interrupted.

This is simply how people interact in the culture, and I had to adjust if I hoped to succeed in talking with people about archaeology and the community-based approach.

I faced another culturally based challenge. Women do not have many opportunities to meet together publically or outside the home, so they viewed the community meetings as occasions to socialize and visit. At times, I had a hard time keeping the discussion focused on archaeology. I slowly learned to accept that community meetings were never going to follow an agenda or schedule. We would never walk into the schoolroom and simply get down to the business of discussing research. In some meetings and interviews, we never got around to the subject at all.

ASSESSMENT AS A RECURSIVE PROCESS

McIntyre (2008, 6–8) describes the exploratory phase of a CBPR project as a "recursive process." The process starts with some initial questions, perhaps in a focus group, interview, or group meeting. Those questions lead to others, and ideas begin to evolve and emerge. McIntyre describes this as a spiral of adaptable steps: questioning, reflecting, dialoguing, and making decisions. The process resists linearity. The same method can be used to develop ideas for research topics. McIntyre describes how the process was used to identify research goals in two participatory action research projects: "The initial questions that framed the projects led to other questions that emerged as the research process evolved. Those questions then became points of entry into further reflection and dialogue that again led to new and different ways of perceiving the issues that were generated in both groups" (McIntyre 2008, 6).

The community-based archaeology projects I have been involved with support McIntyre's approach. In the case of Ziibiwing, our discussions organically led to new ideas of how we could collaborate. As we pursued them, those ideas led to new and different ways of looking at the other projects we had in the works. In Turkey, the recursive process worked somewhat differently. After my initial in-home interviews, I reported the results at community meetings. The discussions in those meetings led us to focus on specific areas of research or work, and I then discussed our progress and asked further questions on how to proceed during further home visits and interviews. Through this ongoing, organic process in both the Ziibiwing cases and in Turkey, questioning led to ideas, then to discussion, feedback, and further discussion. Eventually, we made a decision about how to move forward or how to develop a project.

ADAPTING TO LOCAL CIRCUMSTANCES

Comparative analyses of archaeology case studies that use a community-based approach suggest a turn on a familiar motto: "Think collaboratively, adapt locally." In other words, any general CBPR methodology works best when it is adapted to fit local circumstances. For example, Bryceson, Manicom, and Kassam (1980) provide a theoretical analysis of the "array of methodologies" that can be utilized in CBPR. In his edited volume on collaborative archaeological field schools, Silliman (2008a, 8) warns against expecting a cultural or intellectual unity in collaborative methods. Other archaeologists affirm the value of having a diversity of approaches (Colwell-Chanthaphonh and Ferguson 2008b; Kuwanwisiwma 2008). Nicholas (2008) points out that examining opposing ideas and working through different ways to approach the work are not negative. In fact, the struggles can be productive. They generate an array of possible approaches, from which solutions and best practices can be adapted on a case-by-case basis. The following is the guiding question: What fits the situation locally?

Archaeologists operate this way routinely when they develop a research design for archaeological fieldwork. They work on a site-by-site basis, deciding what fits the local geography and climate. Being sensitive to "the local" hones our ability to discover what will be effective, useful, and will have the most positive impact. This attunement to the local is precisely what gives CBPR such a powerful potential for success.

Humphries et al. (2008, 44) show how this works in agricultural research. They describe how one person, Joe Jimenez, was committed to adjusting the overall principles and practices of a general CBPR approach to the local situation in Honduras. The scholars involved referred to this as the "Jimenization" of the CBPR methodology.

Building trust from the outset and sharing a sense of like-mindedness, for example, are commonly held principles of CBPR, yet how we put them into practice must fit the local context. There is not one correct way or best practice for establishing trust with community partners in archaeology. Yes, basic guidelines frame the process. What emerges as being most important with CBPR—and this applies to nearly all aspects of community-based research practices—is not the specific methods. What counts are the ideology, the philosophy, and the collaborative spirit that inform the work.

IDEOLOGY DETERMINES METHODOLOGY

Paulo Freire (1971) made this point emphatically when he discussed participatory research and adult education: "First of all I must underline the point that the central question that I think that we have to discuss here is not the methodological one. In my point of view . . . it is necessary to perceive in a very clear way the ideological background which determines the very methodology. . . . In social science it is easy to see that the ideology determines the methodology (of searching) or of knowing."

Luis Alonso Meza, a community partner and farmer working on a CBPR project in Honduras, echoes Freire's point. Referring to the agronomics project he was involved with and the CBPR process, Meza said, "Perhaps it is not the methodology or path that is worth fighting for, but instead, the mentality with which it was implemented. [This project] makes people feel valued and when they feel valued, they defend their rights. However, when a person feels devalued, as with paternalistic projects of the past, anything said makes that person feel instantly humiliated" (Corea et al., 2008, 55).

From Meza's words, examples of my own work, and the experiences of others in CBPR, one thing is clear: At the outset of a CBPR project, we need to establish not a specific method but a way of working with communities. The specific details and approach for each project will change. How shall we integrate *this* local knowledge and *this* scholarly research? Or, what is the best way for *this* archaeologist and *this* community partner to connect initially? What remains constant is the commitment to the ideology of working in partnership. Partners remain committed to asking, for example, what benefits and strengths will the partnership bring to producing knowledge and addressing concerns on all sides?

FLEXIBLE AND LOCALLY SPECIFIC METHODS

The ethnographic research that archaeologists conduct early on to build their cultural competency and understand a community context can guide them in choosing a method of approach. Community meetings may work very well in one scenario, whereas surveys or one-on-one interviews may work better in other cases. If the community has had no previous contact with archaeologists, or if their experiences with archaeologists or other researchers have been mostly negative, a community meeting is not likely to be well attended. Individual interviews may be a more successful way to start.

When I worked with the Ziibiwing Center in Michigan, our research partnership developed from several brief, informal conversations with Ziibiwing's director and staff. I talked about community-based forms of research and my efforts to incorporate these into the field of archaeology. Based on these conversations, Ziibiwing's director invited me to give a public lecture about contemporary archaeological practices to the wider community. In the talk, I emphasized an approach to archaeology that involves a community-driven process and a partnership approach.

I shared examples of how archaeology could be conducted following a community-based model. The talk was both well attended and well received. My presentation sparked an extended dialogue with community members about archaeology and how other Indigenous groups were engaging in aspects of archaeological research.

Soon after, Ziibiwing's director, Bonnie Ekdahl, approached me to explore possible collaborations. Ekdahl and the staff at Ziibiwing had clear ideas of the types of collaborative archaeology they hoped to carry out. Their research agenda was based on the long-term goals of the center: caring for ancestral human remains and preserving important cultural places. Working with a CBO whose goals intersect with those of archaeologists and who has authority within the community to carry out the project made interviews with community members, focus groups, or community meetings unnecessary. I could develop research questions by working directly with Ziibiwing's leadership.

In Turkey, however, I had no CBO with whom to partner, and I had no idea about the level of interest that people had in archaeology either. In that local context, I had to use interviews and community meetings to discern the community's interest and potential areas of partnership. Turkish culture prides itself on hospitality to guests and places great cultural value on spending time visiting people in their homes. So I decided to begin by interviewing community residents in their homes. I had planned to interview one or two individuals at a time, but the sessions turned into family group interviews. Often, all the extended family members who were at home when I visited came to greet me and wanted to join in the interview process.

CLARIFYING EXPECTATIONS
AND TIMELINES

The decision to develop a formal research agreement or contract between a researcher and community partner is another point to consider during the process of obtaining community authorization to conduct research. Some communities insist on this. Others prefer to use a verbal agreement or to leave things in a more flexible state. The best approach is to work this out through direct conversation, so that all the research partners agree. With or without a formal research contract, partners need to know each other's expectations, goals, plans, and timelines, even if the format is verbal.

Establishing a regular review process is another useful CBPR practice. The review may simply involve reiterating a commitment to the goals, expectations, and timelines already set down. Strand et al. (2003, 48–49) offer a set of questions that each potential research partner can consider when embarking on a partnership project. These questions were developed by the University of Michigan's Center for Community Service and Learning. They include general questions that apply to virtually any community-based project, such as the following: Where will the data that are collected be housed? Who owns the data? And how will conflicts about the research be addressed or resolved? These questions provide a useful starting point, but researchers will likely need to expand on these to cover issues specific to every project, the local situation, and the subject and nature of the research being considered.

In some cases, communities are not concerned about developing a *general* research agreement or contract, but they may have specific concerns about one particular area. For example, Mills et al. (2008) explain that the White Mountain Apache wanted all archaeological field school students to sign a nondisclosure agreement. The agreement established the tribe's ownership of data (both informational and material), and ensured that tribal members had control over the publication of all data and images. Chilton and Hart (2009) describe the agreements they developed with descendent communities in Massachusetts about the storage of materials and the need to limit press coverage of their fieldwork. Many of the items addressed in research contracts concern intellectual property: the ownership and long-term care and curation of cultural knowledge and materials. The projects I am involved with have not used research contracts. The community partners and I decided to make decisions on an informal and situational basis. Whatever form partners use—contracts, verbal agreements, or ongoing dialogue—what matters is that all partners understand the expectations on all sides and that discussing issues becomes an established practice early on.

ONGOING PROCESS OF REVIEW

Obtaining a community's authorization for community-based research is best thought of as an ongoing endeavor rather than a one-time requirement. Approval is rarely extended for the "life" of a project. More likely, agreements are formed on an annual basis or on some other regular schedule—sometimes at the start of each phase of the research project (fieldwork, data analysis, interpretation, and so on)—or when community leadership changes. Regular reviews provide opportunities for partners to reevaluate the goals of their collaboration and to assess the progress toward accomplishing these goals. Chilton and Hart (2009) conducted reviews during fieldwork. They describe the regular process of "on-site peer review" with communities involved in their collaborative work.

Doing research is a primary focus of an archaeologist's professional life and plays a central role on a daily basis. However, a community's attention and commitment extend to many other areas: economic, educational, political, and social concerns. A research project is most likely not a daily focus for community partners, even among those who are strongly committed to a project. As a result, community goals and priorities can shift, sometimes quite quickly and unexpectedly. A collaborative project can be affected. Progress might slow for a time or, in some cases, projects may be forced to end abruptly.

When community leadership changes, for example, researchers can expect *some* degree of adjustment and change. New leadership brings new goals and priorities. The impact on community-based research projects and community-researcher partnerships can be substantial. Transitions to new leadership may require renewed approval, or it may bring delays for research requests that were already in progress. Projects can be stalled or even discontinued if the new leadership feels that community goals and/or priorities have changed.

For example, Rossen (2008) discusses how the installment of two new chiefs within the Cayuga Nation might significantly change, even end, their community-based archaeology research. He recognizes that, for some, the decision to conduct archaeology, even when it is done in a fully community-based and participatory way, can be complex and involve a serious risk–benefit analysis. For the Cayuga, "they must decide anew if these benefits are worth the spiritual risks of excavating" (2008, 119).

Rossen has also made a clear decision about what he will do if the Cayuga choose not to continue their research partnership: "Should they decide against further archaeological research, I am prepared to discontinue my academic work on the Cayuga." Community-based archaeologists must ask themselves what they would do in such a case. Most who follow an ideology of power sharing and who are committed to the CBPR process will make the choice to discontinue the research rather than work without the community partner. Most would likely agree with Rossen when he says that, "Ultimately, I believe that archaeologists must be prepared to walk away when native people view the archaeology as more dangerous and harmful than interesting and useful" (2008, 119).

WHEN COMMUNITY LEADERSHIP CHANGES

The CBPR literature documents many examples of how leadership changes can negatively impact a project. However, such changes can also have a positive effect and may sometimes even move a CBPR partnership in exciting, new directions. For example, the Ziibiwing Center's leadership changed as it welcomed a new director in 2008, and the tribal council membership has changed several times since the start of our first CBPR project in 2004. Fortunately, neither of these changes had negative effects on our research, although they could have. Instead, our research together has increased, and we began exploring other areas where we could work together. Ziibiwing is now involved, for example, as a community partner in the service-learning graduate CBPR methods courses that I teach.

Similarly, in Turkey, when local elections in early 2009 led to changes in the majority of all village managers in the Çatalhöyük region, I was initially quite concerned. I feared that the plans we had developed for fieldwork that summer might be delayed. The previous village manager had always approved of our community-based research, and I was hopeful that the newly elected manager would continue to support the work. As it turned out, Küçükköy's new manager was even more enthusiastic than the previous one had been. He quickly became a great source of assistance. He not only approved of the project but also became an active participant. He even took the lead in involving other members of the community who previously had not shown much interest in participating. His assistance was instrumental and led to a number of successful new programs: a local internship program, a community heritage committee, an annual Çatalhöyük community festival, and a local archaeology-based theater group (Atalay 2010).

WHEN PROJECTS ARE NOT RENEWED

No question, community-based research carries special risks. It can be daunting for a researcher who is not used to sharing decision-making authority to consider that a CBPR project may not be (re-)approved, that it may come to an end earlier than planned, or that plans for further collaborative work on other projects will not be realized. However, one of the strengths of CBPR (and an argument for doing research in this way) is the community "buy-in" at the outset. Because the research is designed from the ground up with community needs and benefits in mind, communities recognize the benefits of the work and can become more strongly committed to achieving the goals than with a conventional research approach.

Certainly, CBPR projects are not immune to the effects of local politics or changes in community leadership. But are conventionally structured projects immune either? What if the new leadership in a community opposes what a conventionally trained archaeologist is doing in the community, especially if the archaeologist's approach has offended some community members? What if communities decide to sabotage the research in creative and effective ways? The local residents in Turkey were prepared to burn down a house to block a project. Moreover, how reliable will the findings be if the community rejects what the archaeologist is doing and refuses to participate in any way? Archaeologists must weigh these risks as well.

When a project is not renewed or approved or when further research projects do not develop, one should not assume the research partnership was a failure or that the working relationship has come to an end. As Kerber (2006) rightly notes, the duration of a project or partnership is not the measure of its success.

If community members choose to discontinue an archaeology project, it does not mean they will not want to partner again in the near or distant future. Community decisions stem from multiple factors, not the least of which are limited time and resources. Such decisions may involve complexities wholly unrelated to the research project. To make sure that projects are meeting expectations, researchers are wise to solicit regular feedback and to set up a regular assessment program. This involves building a regular process of evaluation and assessment into the research design and ensuring it becomes part of any research contract or agreement that is developed. Community members' comments about the project over its course provide a record that is valuable when it comes time to decide whether to continue or to stop.

In all cases, archaeological CBPR partnerships strive to achieve a reciprocal balance, so that the research interests of both community partners and archaeologist are met. In my own research and in analyzing the practices of others, I have found that success depends on building a strong foundation. This begins with establishing a sense of like-mindedness; requires understanding the sociopolitical context of the communities involved; and involves doing ethnographic research to determine community interest level and archaeological topics of potential interest. Laying a good foundation also requires that archaeologists learn who has the right to speak for the community, and that archaeologists develop competency in cultural practices and proper local protocols.

The pace of CBPR can be slow as things get started, and CBPR can involve a lengthy transition to a fully community-based and participatory process. Archaeologists who want to engage in community-based research may need to develop and utilize skills beyond those required in conventional research. Certainly their training as educators will help. But they may also need to develop skills as community organizers and exercise a wider range of interpersonal skills than would be required for conventional archaeological research. These are the building blocks of community-based archaeology, and regular communication provides the glue that binds this foundation together and makes it strong.

SIX · Identifying Research Questions
and Developing a Research
Design

Making the initial connection between archaeologist and community, and putting in the necessary time and effort to build a solid foundation for the research partnership can be time-consuming and present complex challenges, in part because archaeologists have limited experience and less familiarity in these areas than they do with initiating a conventional research project. Once a research partnership is established, though, the steps that follow put archaeologists on more familiar ground. Just as with other archaeological research, conducting a community-based research project involves developing research questions; defining methods to answer those questions; planning the project, which includes a plan for interpreting data; carrying out the work; and deciding how to disseminate results. All of these steps are articulated in a research design, which goes to potential funders in hopes of securing financial support for the project. In a conventional approach to archaeology, an individual or team of archaeologists carries out these activities. In a CBPR project, archaeologists and community members work together to formulate these steps. So, while the steps in the research process remain the same, how they are carried out changes substantially.

SHARED DECISION MAKING

Strand et al. (2003) outline four important aspects of CBPR that I have found helpful at this stage of a community-based archaeological project: (1) sharing power, (2) communicating clearly and listening carefully, (3) understanding and empathizing with one another's circumstances, and (4) remaining flexible. These principles have been central in the projects I have conducted, and the researchers engaged in the projects I have studied also emphasize them. Perhaps in all disciplines, but certainly in community-based archaeology, these must be viewed through the ever-present lens of power, and each requires cultivating effective strategies for shared decision making. Strand et al. (2003, 34) link such shared authority with the social justice goals of CBPR: "When community members are afforded less authority than their academic colleagues, the research is likely to be of far less value to the community than otherwise would be true. Moreover, CBPR partnerships that mirror conventional notions of academic expertise and authority end up perpetuating the sort of inequitable power structures that they ultimately seek to challenge and change."

In the projects I have conducted, developing a research design with these four aspects of CBPR at the forefront did require substantially more time and effort. However, the shared decision making did not in itself create further complexity. Rather, it revealed the underlying complexities and layers of power that exist in the real world. These layers are silenced when a single archaeologist holds power and makes the decisions.

Collaborative practices are on the rise in archaeology, but they do not all necessarily constitute authentic CBPR. For example, sharing a predesigned research plan with a community, encouraging site visits, or involving community members in a researcher-driven project are fundamental to doing good archaeology. But, as critics (La Salle 2010) point out, they do not constitute community-based research. Similarly, inviting community members to play the roles that an archaeologist determines and controls is only partial power sharing and falls short of what CBPR practitioners consider "shared authority." Multivocality approaches involve communities in archaeological interpretations that engage a range of stakeholders. This, too, is an important component of archaeological practice (see examples in Habu, Fawcett, and Matsunaga 2008), but it is distinctly different from power sharing in CBPR. Involving communities in interpreting findings should not be confused with community-based research or the shared decision-making authority that participatory methodologies put into practice. The power sharing that CBPR practitioners discuss involves substantive community involvement: The archaeologist and the community partner(s) engage shoulder-to-shoulder in planning the research project and in its daily operations.

Shared decision making has been central to the planning and research design stages of the Ezhibiigaadek asin—Sanilac Petroglyph Intellectual Property (IP) project. Working as partners, the Ziibiwing Center members and I outlined the research questions and concerns that each of us had in relation to the intellectual property issues at the Sanilac site. Holding extensive in-person meetings, followed by phone conversations, we developed a verbal agreement to share the responsibilities of preparing the grant proposal and moving it through the tribal and university IRB approval processes. My job was to draft the grant proposal, using extensive notes from our conversations. I then shared the proposal with Ziibiwing's director and staff for feedback and comment. As questions arose, I immediately addressed them by phone or email with Ziibiwing's director, Shannon Martin. Ziibiwing's staff developed the budget and guided the proposal through the tribal review and approval process. We met in person to jointly develop the IRB protocol documents for the two universities involved. Simon Fraser University administered the intellectual property grant, of which this case study was to be part. Indiana University administered the funds for our Sanilac IP case study.

What is significant about this project is that developing the research design moved quite quickly because we had worked in partnership before on two other community-based archaeology projects. A process of shared decision making that involved frequent, open communication was already in place. It's also worth noting that we have not used a research contract in any of the projects we have conducted together. Relying on verbal agreements has helped us maintain a degree of flexibility and has strengthened the trust between us.

This is not to say that disagreements do not arise; they do. One example from the Sanilac IP project illustrates well how we have handled these differences. At the planning stage of the project, both Ziibiwing's staff and I agreed that a fictional children's book about the Sanilac site would be a useful product of this research. However, after the grant proposal was submitted, Ziibiwing's director and curator shared their concerns that a booklet would be too costly and time-consuming. They feared it might take away funds from the primary goal of developing a tribal site management plan. The plan included protecting the intellectual property and cultural images related to the petroglyph teachings at the site. We discussed this concern and decided to remove the booklet project from this grant. However, soon after, Ziibiwing's staff developed a proposal to fund the children's booklet through another granting opportunity. I was willing to compromise on the booklet, and

Ziibiwing staff demonstrated their commitment by finding funds independently to make the booklet happen.

Such compromises have made our projects stronger and more sustainable over the long term. Ziibiwing's staff has a clear view of what their priorities are and where to focus their time and resources in productive ways. We share the decision making, and we also work on a case-by-case basis to decide who will take the lead on which aspects of a project. This shared decision making extends to deciding how to administer grant funds. The granting agency that funded the Sanilac project required that funds be administered through a university. Therefore, my home department (anthropology) at Indiana University administers the grant funds. However, Ziibiwing's staff has full control over determining how the project is carried out: which students will be involved (tribal members and university graduate students); how the data will be gathered, archived, and curated; and how results will be shared with community and academic audiences.

Over the course of our community-based projects, we have developed a working process for presenting research results to academic audiences. We discuss conference opportunities, settle on how to present the project, and determine who among us shall attend and present the research. When community partners from Ziibiwing cannot attend, I share written and PowerPoint presentations with them beforehand. They provide feedback and assist me in editing the material. They also provide guidance on culturally sensitive materials that should *not* be included in public presentations. For example, the first time I was scheduled to present our project in an academic setting, I asked Ziibiwing's director to advise me on the use of photographs of the petroglyph images. She replied that, according to spiritual leaders who had been consulted about the care of these images and the teachings they carry, the images of the petroglyphs should not be replicated exactly. They could be used, however, if we modified them for the presentation.

In working with Ziibiwing, I have found that the communal decision-making power is relatively easy and straightforward. Ziibiwing is an organized CBO with a clear decision-making structure already in place. They have a clear process established for approving projects: Ziibiwing's director first takes all requests for research to the board of directors. If a request is approved, she then sends the material to the tribal council for review and approval. The director has the authority to make smaller day-to-day decisions. This allows us to act nimbly and make quick decisions on some issues, particularly at the planning stages of a research project before funds and resources are committed.

However, working out how to handle communal decision making is not always so simple. It can be complicated or seem nebulous and unresolved. This is especially true when an archaeologist works with a community that is not organized around archaeology and heritage management issues, or one that does not have a clearly established protocol for making decisions about research.

DIALOGUE AND COMMUNICATION

One of the most basic areas where daily research practices change in a CBPR process is in the area of dialogue and communication. Who an archaeologist talks with on a regular basis, and the form of that communication is often quite different than in conventional research. In CBPR processes, archaeologists communicate with community partners on both large and small issues to make informed decisions. Partners may develop a standard process for making decisions, or they may set up meetings to discuss issues as they arise. Whatever the process, I suggest that partners establish a regular practice of communicating and sharing in decision making, rather than waiting until they face a conflict or a complicated issue. Some communities and researchers may choose to allow the process to develop organically. As partners work together, they develop a feel for each other's communication style and pace. Researchers need to be cognizant of the schedule and method of communication that community members find comfortable, but they must also reflect on their own practices and preferences. The process has to be authentic on both sides for it to work.

The specific forms of communication will depend on several factors: What does the community have access to? What is most efficient and suitable for both partners? And, what do both partners feel comfortable with? Some community members may prefer to talk by phone or in person, whereas others may prefer email correspondence. Similarly, the frequency of communication will vary. For some projects, daily or weekly communication makes sense; in other cases, months may lapse between correspondences. Phone calls and email are common in the academic world, but these may not work for community members, whose access to phones and email can be limited or nonexistent. In some communities, face-to-face engagement is most culturally appropriate: It demonstrates commitment and helps to build trust.

Researchers cannot assume which methods community members might prefer. Texting, instant messaging, and social networking via services such as Facebook and Twitter are all forms of communication that communities globally now use, even in rural and impoverished areas. I have regular Facebook conversations about research issues with Ziibiwing's director. She uses Facebook to post updates about grant proposals and share information on what the center is doing in the Saginaw Chippewa Indian Tribal Community. The president and treasurer of the Sullivan County American Indian Council text me on a regular basis to keep me informed about our community-based work to develop an interpretive trail at the Waapaahsiiki Siipiiwi mound site.

These forms of communication offer quick responses that can help the pace of CBPR, which tends to move in fits and starts—slow going to rapid change. Archaeologists need to explore the communication options and discuss them with their community partners. Along with affecting the *pace* of the work, the method of communication may also pose challenges for researchers. In some cases, the communication may not be as fast as researchers would like or are accustomed to with academic colleagues. In others, community partners might pressure a researcher to make decisions more quickly than academic institutions or funding agencies—both of which can be slow-moving—allow.

While developing a research design for a researcher-driven archaeological project, archaeologists commonly work alone or with a small number of academic collaborators. Decision making can move at a fast pace in this setting, because the chain of decision makers is short. Plus, academics often share a "communication culture": They do much of the day-to-day project design work by sharing drafts of a research proposal over email. When multiple community members join the decision-making process, the timeline and process for making even simple decisions can become much longer. Different communication methods—phone, email, faxes, snail mail, and face-to-face meetings—may be utilized. The pace of the work can slow dramatically.

The opposite can also happen. Communities can push for results much faster than academics can manage. Faculty members have multiple commitments to teaching, university responsibilities, talks, conferences, and other professional commitments. To make things even more challenging, slower/faster paces can happen simultaneously: One community member may not respond to requests for input or feedback for weeks or months, whereas others are urging the researcher to pick up the pace and make decisions more quickly. I have experienced all of these scenarios in community-based archaeology projects. The situation often changes—even quickly—over the course of one project. This can be challenging, demanding, and downright frustrating at times. One cannot always foresee when a CBPR project might require major attention on short notice.

In one case, I waited months for community representatives to review a document and provide feedback on a research design and funding proposal. At the same time, I was getting phone calls from other community members who were frustrated that the proposal was not yet complete. In working with Ziibiwing on the Sanilac IP project, Ziibiwing staff and I each faced time constraints that kept us from planning and carrying out our research within the time frame that we first envisioned. When Ziibiwing staff was able to work on the research design, I was facing a publishing deadline to finish this book; when I was ready to move forward, Ziibiwing staff was working to complete several other grants on a tight deadline. When multiple communities are involved, the challenges can multiply and become even further complicated.

Much of the communication I do on several CBPR projects happens over the phone and outside of "regular" working hours. Managing who is able to talk to whom and when can be a tricky piece of the CBPR process. Those who are employed by CBOs or who hold official community leadership positions often have designated work times, and they prefer communicating or working on projects within those hours. But community members often hold down jobs unrelated to the research project that make it hard for them to communicate during standard work hours. Archaeologists also have times when they are more available than others, and not being able to confine communication to regular "office hours" can be a difficult adjustment for academics. Talking about this up front can alleviate some of the challenges. More likely than not, CBPR will require compromises and changes in the way researchers are used to operating. Researchers will have to be flexible in how and when they work. Setting up initial guidelines may help, especially as part of informal conversations rather than holding procedural meetings to establish rules and formally solidify these issues.

Forms of communication may change over the course of a single project, and can vary according to the person one works with. When CBO directors or political leadership change, communication practices may change as well. Phone calls and emails are standard for academics, but some communities prefer written correspondence. It produces records that they can archive in their local governments. Instant messaging and Facebook conversations are hard to archive and harder to maintain as an official record of correspondence. If keeping a record of communication and decision making about the project is important, these are not workable options. In some cases, informal conversations via these methods can be written out more formally later, shared with both partners, and then added to the record.

As a CBPR partnership progresses, researchers should anticipate facing a (sometimes seemingly overwhelming) number of practical points. Many of the practical bumps stem from differences in communication practices between two or more cultures—the academy and multiple communities. Communication issues are not insurmountable or even substantial; they just have to be addressed with sensitivity, flexibility, forethought, and planning. As simple and basic as communication issues are, they need to be considered as the project progresses. They can have a surprising impact on the planning and ultimate success of a community-based project.

COMMUNICATION IN THE ÇATALHÖYÜK PROJECT

In the small village of Küçükköy, local community members use mobile phones regularly, but it is cost-prohibitive for them to make or accept international mobile phone calls. Email is not possible because the village lacks Internet service. Furthermore, poor connections and language difficulties can create barriers to these forms of communication. When I am on-site during the field season, I use my local mobile phone for regular communications with community members. During the academic year, however, I am not in Turkey, and my local Turkish mobile phone is not in operation. I have worked around this by using email to send messages to a Turkish graduate student who assists on the CBPR project and also serves as a translator. She phones the local partners in Küçükköy to relay critical information and to get updates. The process is time-consuming, to be sure, and it is not overly effective at developing the individual working relationships that I would like to have with key community leaders. But this is the best method I can devise at the present time.

International collaborative projects that rely on phone communication have to consider the costs for both partners. Telephone costs need to be included in the project-planning budget. The Internet can help with some of the practical sides of communication. For example, Internet chat is free, and voice-over Internet protocol (VoIP) phones provide affordable international rates, but both require Internet on one or both ends. The critical point here is to consider the means of communicating on a regular basis and how to facilitate trouble-free communication.

Adding to the communication challenges, I am in Turkey for only several weeks or months each year during summer fieldwork. Summer months are the busiest time for local community members, because their work schedules require them to be in the fields for long hours during growing season. Community members have consistently voiced interest in working together to brainstorm on ideas for research projects and to develop a research design, but they can only commit real time and effort to this endeavor outside of the summer months. I addressed the problem by incorporating some aspects of our project into the fall and winter. For example, much of the community-based archaeological education takes place then. The comic series and newsletters we have developed are planned for fall, winter, and spring distribution. The community theater project has taken place in the summer and throughout the academic school year, while children were in their classrooms. Naturally, this meant working closely with local teachers (Atalay 2010).

APPROACHES TO DEVELOPING
RESEARCH QUESTIONS

As I explained in Chapter 5, conducting focus groups, interviews, and community meetings are important skills in CBPR practitioners' toolkits. CBPR depends on community input. At the start, these tools can help identify a community's level of interest in archaeology. As a project progresses, they help partners explore areas for research as well as specific topics and questions. The concerns and research questions of Indigenous and local community members may differ substantially from those of archaeologists; however, they often overlap in fruitful areas as well. Identifying areas of mutual interest is critical.

No matter how well one knows a community, researchers should not presume to know where a community's priorities might lie. Similarly, presuming to have better insight or understanding of community needs than the community members themselves is equally unwise. As Pyburn (2011) notes, the best way to understand the views of community members is to talk to them directly. This is the point at which the dialogue tools come in.

In the Çatalhöyük CBPR project, I gathered information during individual and family interviews and during men's and women's community meetings to gauge interest and identify gaps in archaeological knowledge. These processes also served to identify potential research projects and areas of reciprocal interest. Face-to-face meetings of this sort can be effectively combined with written or online surveys to identify community concerns regarding archaeology and cultural heritage, and to define preliminary approaches for culturally appropriate research to address those concerns.

Once I started engaging with Çatalhöyük's local residents through interviews and community meetings, research ideas began to emerge organically. Community members generated a wide range of ideas for educational projects, including a children's comic series (see Figures 10 and 11), archaeological community theater, a newsletter to be distributed at local teahouses, slide shows and displays in nearby parks, and an annual Çatalhöyük festival hosted jointly by the archaeology team

FIGURE 10.

One of a series of comics about the archaeology process, cultural tourism, and heritage management at Çatalhöyük. The subject of this issue is the potential impact of Çatalhöyük's bid for inclusion on the UNESCO World Heritage List.

and the Küçükköy community (Atalay 2007, 2010). Later, the ideas moved beyond archaeological education. Projects focused on cultural tourism, development, and heritage management began to emerge.

FROM PROBLEM IDENTIFICATION TO RESEARCH QUESTIONS

Based on her research partnership with abused women in a Native American community, Patricia Maguire describes another way to assess a community's research

FIGURE 11.
Reverse side of comic. The idea for the comic series stemmed
directly from village residents.

needs and interests. She used the Freirian problem-posing format to establish initial dialogue. Her goal was to "dialogue with them about problems they faced in their daily lives, about problems they thought other such women faced, why the problems existed, and what could be done about them" (1993, 165). While this method brought out the women's concerns, Maguire notes that it never led them to focus on specific research questions. Those not accustomed to doing research may not feel comfortable developing a research design, she observes. They may feel more comfortable talking about their experiences or the ways they have been disenfranchised. In this case, the dialogue did not move from identifying problems to developing solutions through research, as valuable as it might have been to do so.

Although research questions and a formal project never developed, Maguire's problem-posing method was nonetheless productive. The women experienced the approach, even though it was not pushed to its full potential. The same methodology could have moved the women from naming community concerns to developing research-oriented solutions. Maguire herself recognizes this point and discusses why the transition did not take place. She was hesitant to push a research agenda at the time. Reflecting back, she comments that, if she had connected with the local women's shelter rather than with individual community members, a more formal research agenda might have gelled.

From her work with abused women, Maguire concluded that the idea of "research" can seem daunting to some communities. Stoecker (2005) discusses this at length in his guide to community-based research. He describes how community members may feel unprepared to do something so "big" as research. He suggests one way around this: Develop community discussions and give people a chance to pose questions. Through such a method, research topics can emerge in a natural way without labeling the process as "research."

ACADEMICS AS "ANIMATORS" AND "ORGANIZERS"

Each CBPR partnership is unique, and research questions will develop differently for each project. The researcher's role and how community members participate in generating topics will vary as well. Stoecker (1999) links this variability to the goals of CBPR itself. Participatory research is only one aspect of CBPR; the broader goals include action and building community capacity toward self-sufficiency. Stoecker (1999, 845–46) argues that to achieve these goals, someone must fulfill four basic roles: (1) an animator who "helps people develop a sense that they and their issues are important"; (2) a community organizer who acts as a catalyst for the research and can help identify problems and effective solutions; (3) a popular educator, who facilitates the learning process by "helping people identify what they already know and create new knowledge"; and (4) a participatory researcher who facilitates the research process itself.

When a community is well organized, community members may do all or part of the work involved with each of these roles. In other cases, the researcher may take on more of the responsibilities. The roles can also change over the course of working with a community partner, even within the scope of one project. Sometimes the researcher will take on an "animator" and/or "organizer" role to help launch a project and develop research questions; other times, community members fulfill these tasks themselves.

Rossen (2008, 107) discusses how roles change due to politically complex situations and in communities where archaeologists have a dubious history, such as where he works with the Cayuga of New York. Archaeologists can take on an "expanded identity" and become advocates or community activists for contemporary issues that go well beyond archaeology. Given Cayuga history and current struggles, Rossen talks about the roles he has played that involve other collaborative projects in the community. He details how important it is for him to work alongside the Cayuga as a community organizer.

In all cases, the community's views are central to identifying archaeological research questions and areas of potential interest for community-based projects. But this does not mean that archaeologists cannot serve as a resource to communities in making these decisions. Indeed, archaeologists should rally their full knowledge and experience to help communities define fruitful areas of focus or develop specific questions for a research design. They should feel comfortable offering a range of suggestions and providing guidance. As professional researchers, archaeologists have mastered skills for developing and carrying out research, and we should make these skills available to communities. If a discussion about research questions seems unproductive, for example, we might offer an overview of comparable projects and their outcomes. We might prepare a community presentation or a slide show that highlights other case studies and shows how they turned out. This knowledge can stimulate the discussion. Sharing our knowledge also helps to balance the power, since decisions can be made from a wider pool of knowledge and experiences.

Anne Pyburn's work with members of the Kyrgyz community provides an interesting example of this approach. Pyburn organized and then wrote a grant to fund a visit from a delegation of community members and scholars from Kyrgyzstan. The community members were interested in archaeology and heritage management, and they wanted to visit the United States to view firsthand several heritage management projects/sites (Pyburn 2009). Some CBPR practitioners may critique such an approach: It was not internally generated, and external influences would likely have a great impact on community members; their exposure to other practices might narrow their opportunities for developing their own ideas.

I would argue that Pyburn's approach not only brings great benefits to potential projects, but also can prove highly successful in many cases. Researchers exercise enormous privilege in their access to knowledge and global experiences as they conduct research and think critically about its production. It seems arrogant for them to deny community partners access to the same base of knowledge and experience. Developing research designs in partnership with communities does not mean that we must restrict their ability to benefit from our experiences as professional researchers. Nor does it mean that we should prohibit their access to knowledge that we ourselves take for granted.

On the other hand, CBPR is not about convincing communities to take on projects that are "led, designed, and managed" by researchers (Cornwall and Jewkes 1995). "Co-opting" community support for projects that originate elsewhere is obviously not CBPR (Wilmsen 2008). Responsible CBPR researchers do not impose their own research questions on a community, but neither should they withhold help or suggestions at the research development phase or any other. The CBPR process depends on a mutual trust that the partners contribute to the joint endeavor honestly, openly, and to the best of their abilities. One side does not withhold relevant information to manipulate the other or to predetermine the outcome.

When researchers present communities with options and ideas for archaeological projects and research questions, they can assume that community members are not lacking in all knowledge (that is, not unintelligent) and so will not assent to being led blindly. Communities most often have a clear and complex understanding of how the world works and what is best—as well as what is not at all good—for their own communities. In many cases, communities have been quite successful at adapting project ideas to their own local situations.

DEVELOPING A RESEARCH DESIGN FOR ARCHAEOLOGICAL CBPR

Some archaeological CBPR projects take a long time to develop a set of research questions and an appropriate research design to pursue them; other projects move more quickly. The process is more complex in community-based projects than in a conventional research model because it involves a greater number of people. Plus, partners often lack a common "language" to discuss archaeological and cultural heritage issues, and sometimes they come with very different priorities and timelines.

In my experience, each project has followed its own path toward a research design. In the Ziibiwing repatriation project, the research goals and approach were defined quickly and were driven primarily by the Ziibiwing staff as they drafted a NAGPRA repatriation research repatriation grant. The Waapaahsiiki Siipiiwi Mound project with the Sullivan County American Indian Council in southern

Indiana took longer. The general goal of protecting the nearby mound site under control of the council was clear from the start. But more specific long-term goals for protection and management of the site took longer to assess and clarify and involved an extended process. The long-term goals and a research design aimed at studying, protecting, and managing the Waapaahsiiki Siipiiwi mound site through development of an interpretive trail was drafted by a team of Indiana University graduate students as part of a community-based research graduate methods course that I developed.

During the same course, another team of students worked in partnership with Ziibiwing's staff to develop a research design that included drafting a management plan for the Flint Stone Street Ancestral Recovery Project. Archaeologist Dr. Beverly Smith developed the initial field aspect of the project. The tribe chose her to oversee the fieldwork for two reasons. First, as a faculty member at the University of Michigan (UM)—Flint, she had an office within walking distance of the site. Second, Frank Raslich, a tribal member and PhD graduate student in anthropology, suggested her as someone who would be sensitive to cultural protocols and practices. Dr. Smith was Raslich's undergraduate professor at UM—Flint.

For the Flint Stone Street Project, the Ziibiwing Center identified different stakeholders and priorities for each phase of the project. The recovery of ancestral remains required a protocol to gather and care for the remains and artifacts that were inadvertently removed from the ground along with 76,000 cubic feet of soil during a construction project. Tribal elders and spiritual leaders were involved in developing an appropriate research design and spiritual protocol of field practice for recovering, housing, and reburying the remains. The plan for managing and protecting the site as a memorial and space for cultural education involves many more people: Anishinabe elders and spiritual leaders, Saginaw Chippewa tribal members, nonnative members of the local community in Flint; educators from the tribe and the Flint community; and other interested stakeholders.

For both the ancestral recovery aspect of the Flint Stone Street Project and in the UM NAGPRA repatriation research project, the Ziibiwing staff was clear about the topics of interest, the questions to be investigated, and the approach to developing a research design. In Turkey, by contrast, members of local villages undervalued their own knowledge. They felt they had nothing to contribute to a community-based research partnership. It took more than four years of interviews, community-based educational programs, and community meetings for our partnership to identify research themes and potential projects. These very different experiences offer many lessons about the research design phase of a CBPR archaeology project. What stands out most for me is that projects are locally specific. They require flexibility in timelines, communication methods, and expectations, as each project progresses through different stages of research.

COMMUNICATING ABOUT TIMELINES AND EXPECTATIONS

Communities and archaeologists often have different timelines for developing a research design. The lives of academics tend to run by time segments that fit a university semester or quarter calendar. Furthermore, academics must deal with tenure and publication requirements that communities do not face and aren't likely to be familiar with. And, communities have schedules too. Their pace can be slower, faster, or in sync with an academic researcher's. The more open and honest partners can be about their timelines, motives, expectations, limitations, and needs, the more successful the research design work is likely to be. Frank discussions can minimize misunderstandings and stress. If tenure or publication requirements put demands or limitations on what an archaeologist can accomplish, then a straightforward and honest discussion about these limitations should happen at the early stages of planning, when project concepts and expectations are forming.

The research design phase is the time for partners to clarify what they can each offer and what they each hope to gain from the research. It is also a good time for researchers to consider and discuss what they are *not* willing or capable of doing, topics that are *not* appropriate for research, or methods that are *not* acceptable. If researchers lack expertise in some areas, then they should make this clear at the research design stage as well.

This was a situation I faced at the start of the Ziibiwing repatriation project. Prior to that first community-based partnership, I had not conducted NAGPRA research and had little experience with repatriation laws and procedures. When Ziibiwing's director, Bonnie Ekdahl, suggested we partner to conduct research for repatriation claims, I suggested that Ziibiwing find someone who was more knowledgeable and experienced than I was to work on those aspects of the project. Ziibiwing acknowledged my concerns, and then reassured me that they were sure about their choice to work with me to carry out the research. Because of the sensitive nature of the repatriation work, the trust they had in me as an individual took priority over their desire to have a more experienced researcher. One of the unexpected benefits of our CBPR partnership is that I have learned a great deal in the process, and Ziibiwing's staff has learned from the research partnership as well. They now regularly submit successful NAGPRA claims and have repatriated over 600 ancestors.

At this stage, the community or the researcher may want to clarify the terms of the agreement in a formal document, such as a memorandum of understanding (MOU). In some cases, though, a formal agreement can seem too contractual, limiting, or legalistic. It may alter the relationship between the researcher and the community in undesirable ways. Bonnie Newsom, the Tribal Historic Preservation Officer for the Penobscot Tribe of Maine described the shift as turning a partnership of trust into a business exchange (personal communication, October 2010).

CULTURAL PROTOCOLS

The expectations of behavior in a community setting can be very different from those that archaeologists follow in academic settings or conventional fieldwork projects. In Chapter 4, I discussed these cultural differences briefly in relation to understanding a community's social context and the need for researchers to build cultural competency. I also pointed out how cultural practices need to inform the way archaeologists present themselves to a community. Respecting cultural protocols is important throughout a CBPR project, but it is especially critical at the stage of developing a research design (Lightfoot et al. 2001; Rossen 2008).

Lightfoot (2008) emphasizes that researchers need to be both formal and flexible. He calls for formality in developing an outline—verbal or written—of basic parameters and cultural protocols during the research design phase of a project. He describes a fluidity that involves regular discussion about project outcomes and expectations; being flexible and fluid keeps the door open to solving problems more creatively and to generating unforeseen options. Archaeologists may ask, for example, what are the possibilities for publishing? What restrictions do we need to follow during fieldwork? Are there any off-limit places or prohibitions?

Lightfoot et al.'s work (2001) and the work of those who follow a similar model (Gonzalez et al. 2006; Dowdall and Parrish 2003) provide excellent examples of how to define and implement cultural protocols in fieldwork. They detail their work with the Kashaya Pomo community members and how they honor the Kashaya Pomo's cultural menstruation taboos for women during an archaeological field school. Implementing these cultural protocols was complicated. This involved nonnative field school participants having restrictions, some of which had potential legal implications in Western law. Yet Lightfoot explains that the team was quickly able to devise a system for respecting Kashaya beliefs without major disruption to the archaeological fieldwork. Dowdall and Parrish (2003), who also worked with the Kashaya Pomo, provide further examples of incorporating cultural protocols into fieldwork. They detail how, following the guidance of Kashaya Pomo elders, they started excavation with a prayer ceremony and ended with a feast. And, as with Lightfoot's field school, Dowdall and Parrish also asked that all participants in the excavation observe rules related to women's reproductive cycles and that they abstain from alcohol.

FLEXIBILITY

In writing about their experiences, CBPR practitioners drive home the need to be flexible when partners work together on developing CBPR research designs. Community partners in a community-based harvesting project in the northwest coast of the United States, for example, explain that the ideas of the scientists working with them were "too lofty" at first. Fortunately, the researchers realized they needed to adjust the research plan and adapted accordingly (Collins, Cruz, and Smith 2008).

Archaeologists have also pointed out the importance of flexibility. Silliman (2008a) found it useful to apply Hodder's reflexive methodology to doing collaborative archaeology "at the trowel's edge." Lightfoot (2008) discusses how to be flexible about research designs in some detail. He advocates rethinking both their content and structure to "make them more applicable to contemporary collaborative archaeology (2008, 216)." He points out that few discussions in the archaeology literature of the past twenty years have grappled with research design processes.

Flexibility is also critical in when carrying out community-based archaeological fieldwork. For example, Dowdall and Parrish (2003) describe how Kashaya tribal members initially wore gloves during fieldwork so that they could engage in the archaeology without breaking tribal traditions of not touching archaeological materials with their hands. After tribal member scholars and trainees developed a rash on their hands, elders instructed them to stop working on artifact screening. For the rest of the project, they were told to focus instead on traditional Kashaya activities, which included learning tribal history from elders. The Kashaya used the fieldwork opportunity to sing traditional songs, collect materials, and weave baskets, and the fieldwork directors accepted this. Indeed, the fieldwork plan included time for archaeology students to learn traditional teachings and tribal history from elders who were on-site regularly.

CULTURAL PROTOCOLS IN ZIIBIWING'S PROJECTS

In Ziibiwing's Stone Street Ancestral Recovery Project, Ziibiwing's director and curator worked with Dr. Beverly Smith, the project's principle investigator who directed the majority of fieldwork, to develop a set of daily spiritual practices to be used when those working at the site recovered ancestral human remains. I had firsthand experience with these practices, as I worked on the site during the first season of the recovery fieldwork. The process involved smudging the site with sage at the opening of each fieldwork day. We stored recovered ancestral remains in cedar boxes in close proximity to any cultural materials immediately after they were recovered. We tracked the locations where remains and artifacts were recovered, so that they could be reburied as close as possible to where they were found. All human remains and pre-contact period artifacts were reburied at the end of each season—without being analyzed, drawn, or studied. The historic-period artifacts were bagged and stored separately. With the Tribal Council's permission, Dr. Smith used them for a teaching collection in her lab at UM–Flint.

Cultural protocols established at the outset set the parameters for talking about the project with the press. Ziibiwing staff decided who was able to speak about the recovery to ensure that the remains were treated with respect. Tribal members, students, and all other volunteers who worked on-site were required to sign a legal agreement. It predominantly related to safety and liability, but it also contained a section in which anyone working on-site agreed that only designated representatives would speak to the press about the details of the project.

In some cases, the cultural protocols that are put forward set personal limitations for who can participate in the research process at certain times. While working with Ziibiwing on the UM repatriation research project, I was pregnant. Spiritual leaders instructed that I could not be part of aspects of the work that put me near the ancestors' physical remains. They also instructed that I wear a face mask and gloves while handling any associated funerary objects. Because I am Anishinabe, I understood the reasons behind this and didn't find it problematic. The practices coincide with my own spiritual beliefs as a midewiwin. However, such restrictions might be an issue for other women, who may view them as curtailing their employment rights (compare to Dowdall and Parrish 2003).

PROCESS FOR DEVELOPING PROTOCOLS

Archaeologists will need to educate themselves about cultural protocols that should be followed during research, lab analysis, and fieldwork. For Indigenous communities, protocols are rarely written; they are communicated through discussion.

Nicholas refers to these cultural protocols as "community values." He points out that it may take time—months, even years—to know what these are (2008, 238–41). He suggests that researchers conduct interviews and focus groups to help them learn these practices and develop guidelines for them. Community members may not always feel comfortable initiating discussions about cultural protocols.

During my twelve years of doing conventional archaeological fieldwork at Çatalhöyük, for example, I never realized that local community members who work on-site might want short breaks during the several times each day that the call to prayer occurs. Only when I conducted in-home community interviews did I realize this. When I took a break during the call to prayer so that family members could pray, several people noticed and commented. They said they understood if I preferred to keep working through the call to prayer, because they were used to not being able to pray when they were working at Çatalhöyük. For our CBPR project at Çatalhöyük, we've now made it clear that we respect and will follow traditional cultural practices and will break for prayer. To avoid confusion and to ensure sensitivity to cultural practices, archaeologists should not expect community members to raise these issues. The researchers must open the conversation.

ARCHAEOLOGICAL TRAINING AND EDUCATION

COMMUNITY CONCERNS REGARDING LACK OF ARCHAEOLOGICAL KNOWLEDGE

One of the major obstacles I faced in the Çatalhöyük CBPR project was that local residents felt they did not know enough to participate in a community-based archaeological partnership. Turkish archaeologists, most of whom came from middle-class, urban families, also thought that the local community members' lack of archaeological knowledge posed a problem. Several were convinced that Küçükköy residents did not have the skills and training needed to act as competent research partners. Such suggestions were based, at least in part, on class perceptions. Yet whatever the basis, the residents of Küçükköy themselves struggled with the issue.

When I asked village residents about the archaeological questions they had and the research topics we might address together, it became clear that a CBPR partnership could not be developed until local community members felt comfortable with their level of knowledge about Çatalhöyük. Local residents had a positive response to the idea of CBPR and to creating a research partnership. They were especially interested in topics around heritage management and cultural tourism. But their enthusiasm for the concept was peppered with hesitation. Community members did not feel they knew enough to engage in such research. In over 90 percent of the initial interviews I conducted while I was attempting to organize and develop the partnership, community members stated that they could not be effective research partners. They knew too little about archaeology in general and Çatalhöyük in particular.

This example illustrates a concern that other archaeologists are likely to encounter when establishing community-based archaeology projects. A primary principle of CBPR is respect for multiple knowledge systems and recognition of the value that each partner can bring to the table. The Çatalhöyük case demonstrates that for a community to be an effective partner, they must feel confident in their ability to contribute to the research process in the ways they see fit. In the case of Çatalhöyük and the residents of Küçükköy, I felt it was important to honor community member requests to learn more not only about archaeology but also about the site in their own backyards. It seemed both extremely shortsighted and condescending to tell residents that they only needed their "local knowledge" of their village and their employment-based experiences. They clearly wanted access to the specialized archaeological knowledge being created around them.

Moving forward with a community-based archaeology project without taking the time necessary to explore and carry out education efforts would have gone against the spirit of CBPR. It would have been particularly problematic because, through their ongoing labor at the site, Küçükköy residents helped create the archaeological knowledge we hold about Çatalhöyük. I was thus in a position of trying to share knowledge about the site, as requested by the community members, while still attempting to overcome the traditional model of archaeological "experts" downloading information to "passive", "uninformed" community members. The solution I settled on—and what I advocate here—is a community-based process of archaeological education.

COMMUNITY-BASED ARCHAEOLOGICAL EDUCATION

Archaeologists regularly provide educational opportunities for local and descendant communities to increase their archaeological knowledge. Community-based archaeology projects do so as well. Within a CBPR model, though, community members are not mere recipients of educational activities; they are active participants in them. They develop a plan for community education, and they assist in implementing it.

In all five of the CBPR projects I have conducted, our community partners have been interested in learning more about archaeology. Yet I did not approach these communities with the goal of convincing them of the importance of archaeology or the benefits it would bring them. That would be contradictory to the goals and principles of CBPR. Rather, I led with curiosity about what each community might like to learn and how I might facilitate their educational goals.

In the United States, early discussions aimed at improving relations between Native Americans and archaeologists were laden with assumptions. Nonnative academics assumed that if Native Americans were given chances to learn about archaeology, and if they realized all the information it could provide, then tensions would decrease, and Native Americans' resistance to archaeologists and archaeological research would decrease as well. On these assumptions, educational programs designed for Native Americans, and the funding to support Native American involvement in archaeological training programs, increased. But this approach has problems. It is based on the false belief that Indigenous communities resist archaeological research because they do not understand the benefits it offers. This is problematic for two reasons.

First, from the perspective of many Indigenous communities, the questions that archaeologists ask and the knowledge they produce have had clear benefits to archaeologists and museums. But the projects were not designed to even consider research benefits from the perspective of Native Americans.

Second, even when archaeology could provide information that had positive benefits for Indigenous communities, those within the community often faced a hard challenge. To what extent did these community benefits go against their cultural traditions or spiritual beliefs? What toll did they take on their responsibilities to protect sacred sites, knowledge, and landscapes in culturally appropriate ways, not to mention the basic human rights of their ancestors? Rather than lessening tensions and increasing understanding, the programs can create even greater resentment and distrust on the part of Native Americans toward archaeologists. Top-down educational programs do not grow organically from communities. Too often, researchers or specialists develop them *for* a community rather than *with* them. Communities are posited as objects to be educated. They do not function as participants in education. The top-down approach reproduces the same power-over dynamic that Indigenous people have critiqued for decades.

It seems so obvious, and yet it bears saying: Public outreach and education projects that communities collaborate in developing have a greater chance of success.

If communities are to benefit, then they must have a say in what they experience as beneficial. Yet many well-intentioned efforts toward increasing knowledge and literacy of a particular discipline are designed with a top-down approach. Researchers make assumptions about what the intended audience knows, where they lack knowledge, what they are interested in and want to learn, and how they would like to gain information. They fail to include communities in developing the program.

Archaeological education programs within a CBPR approach start from a place of *asking* rather than a mind-set of knowing. No matter how well intentioned we are about sharing knowledge with a community or pouring energy into archaeological educational efforts, our efforts can backfire. The wiser approach is to start with humility, a willingness to listen and learn, and an attitude that acknowledges the gaps in our own knowledge. Certainly, experience and formal education can give archaeologists specialized knowledge about sites, regions, artifacts, and lifeways of the past. But this does not provide archaeologists with insights into what descendant and local communities want to learn about archaeology, nor does it make them expert educators.

The first step in a community-based archaeology education project is to find out what sorts of things community members want to learn about archaeology. The next step is to work with them to identify effective and culturally appropriate ways to convey such information to a diverse population. What topics interest community members? Where do they feel they have gaps in their knowledge, and how might the research partnership address these?

Community members may be highly educated and informed about archaeological data from a site; they may have knowledge gaps or outdated or inaccurate information; or they may know little to nothing about archaeology. Those within a community who are well informed about a particular site may not know much about the process of archaeological research, how archaeologists gather data, or how they construct their arguments. Community members' knowledge and exposure to archaeology are bound to be diverse.

But whatever the range of archaeological knowledge, the process of developing a community-based archaeological education program follows a common pattern. First, assess what is and is not known and the topics about which people want to learn more. Second, explore with community members the best ways to approach education, so that the information can be shared in ways that will make it easiest to receive. Third, partner with community members to develop and carry out community education projects.

In some situations, developing a community-based education program may go on simultaneously with developing a community-based research project. A community may be interested in partnering on a research project, but members may feel unprepared and want to increase their archaeological knowledge before proceeding. Or, an archaeologist who is not familiar with CBPR may want to begin developing a partnership with a particular community(-ies) by integrating a community-based archaeology education project into their research design. Heckenberger (2009) provides an example of how including community members as fieldwork participants was a "middle ground" that eventually led to fully community-based projects in which power sharing in decision making existed. This may also be an ideal area of research for graduate students who want to incorporate CBPR into their dissertation project. Students may be leery of conducting a large-scale community-based archaeology fieldwork project because of the long timelines required to work in partnership and the need to complete a dissertation on an academic schedule. In such cases, a community-based educational program can build the foundation for a collaborative relationship and more extensive research partnership.

Archaeological education, sometimes referred to as "outreach" or "public archaeology," receives a lot of attention from the professional archaeological community. Archaeological professional societies and organizations, such as the Society for American Archaeology (SAA) and the Archaeological Institute of America (AIA), have active committees that work on education. Resources abound in this area—everything from teaching modules and lesson plans to traveling kits, archaeology camps, and websites. The audiences for these materials include teachers, K–12 students, local community groups, and the general public.

In community-based archaeology, these materials can provide community members with useful examples of how to teach archaeology. Community partners may wish to browse the materials and may even choose to use or adapt them for local schools and in community education programs. However, presenting such resources to community members as a first step can also have a stifling effect. I have had greater success with giving community members an opportunity to develop their own ideas for how to teach archaeology within their communities.

EDUCATIONAL APPROACHES AT ÇATALHÖYÜK

Several engaging and excellent educational activities are regularly offered for local residents near the Çatalhöyük site: children's summer workshops (Sert 2010), K–12 curriculum materials (Doughty 2003), and an on-site visitor center display and illustrated informational panels geared toward adult visitors. Local site guards also lead tours. These projects are well done and help educate visiting audiences about Çatalhöyük. Using a CBPR approach, I wanted to develop further programs for local community members by partnering with them in designing and carrying them out.

My research during the Çatalhöyük CBPR project demonstrates that communities can be quite creative in developing ideas for educational materials without being given models of what others have produced. Community members suggested and participated in developing several innovative approaches to archaeological education. Their ideas diverged from the more standard educational approaches set up on-site for adults and children. Responding to a community-based process that involved family interviews and a series of community meetings, local residents shared in detail the kind of archaeological information they wanted to learn more about and the methods they felt would work for education. During interviews and community meetings, residents regularly discussed methods that they felt would be effective for teaching archaeological information to children and to their fellow adult residents. CBPR was extremely useful and effective in this effort. It gave community members a voice in the educational materials they wanted and a role in producing them.

What the community suggested surprised me. They wanted a comic series for their children, a regular newsletter for distribution at local teahouses, kiosks at outdoor parks and community garden areas, and a community theater program focused on Çatalhöyük (Atalay 2007, 2010). Although the residents said the comic series was for their children, rural areas such as this have a limited rate of literacy. Adults could also use the comic series (see Figure 12) as an educational tool.

Both comics and archaeological cartoons hold great promise for reaching adults and youth in rural Turkey. Comics and cartoons with familiar local characters that display the qualities taught in Islam are being used for education and to provide positive role models throughout the Middle East (including Turkey), as evidenced in Naif Al-Mutawa's popular comic *The 99*. The comic, produced by the Kuwaiti-based Teshkeel Media Group, produced its first comic book in 2008, and has rapidly grown into an animated television series, a host of merchandise based on the comic's characters, and even a major theme park (Gustines 2011). Considering *The 99*'s rapid growth and extreme popularity, it is not surprising that community members expressed a desire for comic-based archaeological educational material several years before the first issue of *The 99* was released.

FIGURE 12.

Front page of the first Çatalhöyük comic.

Illustrated by John Swogger for the Çatalhöyük Research Project.

Community-based theater (Kidd and Byram 1978; Williams et al. 2009; Mosavel and Thomas 2009) has equally powerful potential. Augusto Boal (1979, 1998) has done some wonderful pioneering work in community theater, and his approach has been successfully applied in rural Turkey (*Gökdağ* 2002). Based on the experience of the Çatalhöyük CBPR project, archaeological community-based theater has tremendous potential as an educational tool, and perhaps also as a form of economic development.

The idea for an archaeology community theater program originated with Mehmet Ali Selçuk, a teacher at the Küçükköy-Çatalhöyük Primary School.

FIGURE 13.
Küçükköy children prepare to perform the first archaeology
community theater program, "Spirits of Çatalhöyük" during the
4th Annual Çatalhöyük-Küçükköy Festival.

Children, adults, and other teachers from Küçükköy worked with London-based
theater producer, Serdar Bilis, to develop the first archaeology-based performance
entitled "Spirits of Çatalhöyük" in 2009 at the 4th Annual Çatalhöyük-Küçükköy
Festival (see Figure 13). The story line, which the children assisted in developing, focuses on the future care and management of the site. A central premise is
that Çatalhöyük's ancient inhabitants (the "spirits of Çatalhöyük") pay a visit to
local schoolchildren and voice their desires for current generations to take on the
responsibility of site stewardship.

   This initial production led teachers from the school to initiate a partnership
with the Çatalhöyük CBPR project to apply for a collaborative European Union
grant that would fund a traveling archaeology community theater program. The
aim is for the troupe to tour Turkey and the European Union, giving community-
developed plays focused on Çatalhöyük and other famous or endangered
archaeology sites in Turkey.

I suspect that if I had provided models of previously developed educational materials, the community would very likely have chosen to replicate those, adapting them to present the local data from Çatalhöyük. However, without such examples to follow, community residents easily generated creative approaches to teaching about local archaeology and heritage management, and they used methods that were most appropriate to the local culture.

Once community members put these ideas forward, local residents joined in to further develop and carry them out. The village manager provided ideas and further support; the principal from the local school contributed time and effort; and children, their parents, and their grandparents all offered suggestions for how to develop the educational materials.

Community-based archaeology educational efforts play an important role throughout the life of a CBPR project. They can be a good practical starting point for a community-based archaeology project that is just getting off the ground. Furthermore, community-based archaeology projects should include a thorough knowledge mobilization plan that is developed with community partners as part of the research design.

Funding agencies, such as Canada's Social Science and Humanities Research Council (SSHRC), recognize the importance of having a detailed plan for mobilizing the knowledge that is created through research. For example, SSHRC (2011) now requires that a detailed knowledge mobilization plan be submitted with grant proposals. They define knowledge mobilization as "the specific activities and tools that facilitate the multidirectional flow and exchange of research knowledge. Effective knowledge mobilization is seen as facilitating and enabling the benefit and impact of research on and beyond the campus." Community-based archaeology projects should use a grassroots approach to develop and carry out the knowledge mobilization plan and include it as part of the research design process.

Community members and archaeologists can together identify key places where knowledge from their work should flow. Community members and academic audiences are obviously important targets, but NGOs, government agencies at all levels, and policy makers are also critical audiences. Reaching those with decision-making power with results of archaeological, heritage management, and cultural tourism and development data generated as part of a CBPR process can have important positive impacts on communities. The change that can be fostered through an effective knowledge mobilization plan can assist CBPR partners in reaching their goals of bringing about positive change.

Ongoing communication, dialogue, and feedback with community partners make community-based archaeology education programs successful. One of the most critical components in this educational process is time. Interviewing community members about their educational needs and turning those ideas into usable education "products" involve a substantial time investment. Two entire field seasons at Çatalhöyük focused solely on this process. Today, in the community-based archaeology project at Çatalhöyük, educational efforts continue, even though our partnership now focuses on developing research projects that do not center solely on education.

SEVEN · Gathering Data and Sharing
Results

As detailed in Chapter 6, scholars and communities can work effectively to develop research designs that are relevant for both groups. But how do they move from planning a project to putting CBPR principles into practice for data collection and analysis? And what happens when analysis is complete and the task turns to interpreting information and presenting results? What is most important at this stage is that archaeologists not impose a set of standard field practices on community members, but that they provide communities with tools and training to make informed decisions. This process can be lengthy and may present ethical dilemmas for archaeologists as well as other complexities in daily practice.

DATA COLLECTION AND ANALYSIS

Gathering data, conducting analysis, and producing interpretations are central research tasks in any discipline. Because of the interdisciplinary nature of archaeology, and the range of research projects archaeologists conduct, many forms of data can be gathered in any one project, and these can differ substantially project by project. The approach to data collection and analysis is dependent upon the type of project and its goals. These points are also true for community-based archaeology projects, with the primary difference being that community members and archaeologists work together to determine which data are appropriate to address the questions being examined, and which methods are to be used in obtaining that data.

Of primary importance is that these aspects of the research should be both community-based and participatory. These principles of CBPR result in practices that are interrelated and often overlap, with one being dependent on, or closely related to, the activities of the other. Jackson, Conchelos, and Vigoda (1980, 46–52) demonstrate that there is not one correct participatory method to utilize for gathering and analyzing data. In their overview of CBPR, they call attention to research projects that involved at least ten different methods, including local research committees or teams, group interviews, community meetings, and popular theater. They also note that one CBPR project will typically make use of several of these methods throughout the course of the project. As with research designs, it is the ideology—being community-based and participatory—that drives the process.

COMMUNITY RESEARCH TEAMS

In community-based projects, community members are involved in a fundamental way in planning and carrying out both data collection and data analysis. The process of involving community members varies from project to project, but often entails the community putting forward members who will serve as decision makers and participate in fieldwork and lab activities. Decision making at this stage often does not involve the entire community, but more often chosen representatives, or a community-developed or defined research team. A number of excellent examples in the CBPR literature highlight successful use of community research committees or teams (Mduma 1982; Gaventa 1980; Levin 1980; Barndt 1980; and Jackson and McKay 1982). Some archaeological examples provide details of how a community research team functions and the roles they might play (Murray et al. 2009). The San Pedro Valley Ethnohistory (SPVE) Project provides one excellent archaeological example. In the SPVE Project, each of four tribes living in the region used its own process to define a research team for a collaborative project that included site and museum visits, interviews, and artifact analysis.

Although community research teams can rarely represent the views and feelings of everyone in the community, it's critical that they are representatives *chosen* by the community and that they are appropriate knowledge holders of cultural and/or sacred information (Murray et al. 2009). Such teams often provide a bridging function (Burnette and DeHose 2008; Long 2008). They share information about data collection procedures and progress with community members (and, when culturally required or appropriate, also with political decision makers and/or spiritual leaders), while also providing input and feedback to researchers from the wider community.

Prior to the start of any research, community representatives work with the archaeologist to determine the types of relevant data to be collected, the method to be used in its collection, and how the data will be analyzed. The methods used must be task-, context-, and culturally appropriate (Jackson, Conchelos, and Vigoda 1980), and archaeologists can work directly with community members to determine what the appropriate methods of data collection are (Lightfoot 2008). Rather than the archaeologist determining *a priori* the types of data collection and forms of analysis that are appropriate, the community becomes directly involved in the decision-making process. These decisions can be straightforward, but they can also be very complex. Gaventa (1980) describes the choices that the community he worked with needed to make about the types of data on which they were going to focus. They had to choose between an emphasis on collecting scientific varieties of information or data based on community knowledge. Others (Murrray et al. 2009) explain why it is central to include "Native knowledge," and describe how it both adds new information that complements scientific data and provides alternative views about the data being collected.

In some areas of research, methods of data collection are flexible and can be adapted to local circumstances. For example, Jackson, Conchelos, and Vigoda (1980) suggest that field notes may be recorded using video, sound, and/or written notes. Other examples highlight that some methods of data collection are more difficult within a participatory approach than others (Jackson, Conchelos, and Vigoda 1980; Gaventa 1980). There are added complexities involved in data collection and analysis in archaeology because of the ethical concerns involved in excavating sites. Archaeologists are ethically obligated to collect certain minimal amounts of data because excavation is not replicable and essentially destroys a site. This can be an issue in cases where community views differ substantially from those of archaeologists with regard to what material should be photographed, illustrated, collected, and/or disturbed. Decisions of this nature become even more challenging when we consider, as Chilton and Hart (2009) note, the number and diverse nature of the groups (landowners, museums, historical preservation and government entities, and even avocational archaeologists) with an interest in archaeological locations and the management of the data that comes from excavation.

In cases where the community has limited or no previous involvement with archaeology, the data collection and analysis stages of a CBPR project will involve a learning process, as communities become educated on the types of data that can be collected, the knowledge each provides, and the methods and procedures involved in each. To be effective decision makers, community members should be provided with options about the range of data collection methods and types of analysis that are possible. Education at this stage is not one-way. It also involves learning on the part of the archaeologist, who will need to become familiar with what community members hope to accomplish, and the types of analysis they do *not* want or will not allow.

In communities where members are familiar with archaeological research and methods of data collection, as well as those in which they are new to the process, community representatives should be actively involved in planning and decision making. Some community members may have interest in one aspect of data collection, while others may be interested in another part of the process. It sometimes makes sense for communities to turn over control of portions of the research to their academic partner (Stoecker 1999). Communities may choose to have the archaeologist formulate portions of the research design while they oversee the process and maintain a level of review over how data is gathered or how the analysis is being conducted.

This is not meant to allow communities to censure what is found. But it can be particularly important for Indigenous communities who wish to maintain decision-making control over ancestral remains, sacred and ceremonial objects, and the types of analyses that will be conducted on these materials. What is important is that communities work in partnership with researchers to determine which aspects of the project they want to be actively involved with, and in which parts they are comfortable playing a less active role.

In Native American settings, communities may be more interested in identifying the types of analyses they do *not* want. This can be particularly true with regard to data collection and analysis of ancestral remains or other biological material. Community-based archaeology projects often include a form of "veto power" that allows research partners the option of refusing some forms of analysis. Community partners and researchers should discuss "veto power" and agree upon a plan for implementing it. Some communities, such as the Navajo Nation, have strict regulations regarding study of biological materials of any sort. So the approval, or disapproval, of these types of data collection and analysis may not occur at the level of community representatives, an appointed community research team, or a community-based organization. Instead, it may require decision making directly from a community's political leadership. In the case of the Navajo Nation (and among other tribes), these and all other decisions about research must go through the process of tribal IRB.

The Flint Stone Street Ancestral Recovery Project provides one illustrative example involving determinations about the type of data to be collected, the process involved, and the methods of analysis to be employed. In this case, Ziibiwing leadership developed a policy regarding which artifacts and materials were to be collected, how these were to be categorized and stored, and how the items would be curated and analyzed. The policies were developed to be flexible and became further refined as ancestral remains and other materials were uncovered. A simple walk across the site and examination of the up-heaved dirt piles on the Flint Stone Street site yielded visible human bone and artifacts. The majority of the artifacts appeared to be modern garbage, construction material, and glass bottles. From the initial inadvertent discovery, we expected to recover further Native American ancestral remains and anticipated there would also be associated funerary objects. The history of the land's use, which was provided by the landowners at the time of the inadvertent discovery, revealed that houses had been built on this location in the early 1900s. These were later abandoned, condemned, and torn down. Although the majority of the house debris had been hauled away, we anticipated finding further debris from the initial construction, as well historic period artifacts associated with the early occupation of the houses.

Ziibiwing staff worked with the project principal investigator, Dr. Beverly Smith, and two field assistants (Frank Raslich and Nicole Raslich) to develop a preliminary plan for the materials collection process. Ziibiwing staff determined that any historic artifacts, animal bone, and precontact artifactual materials were to be collected. Modern garbage was discarded.

This project was designed by Ziibiwing as a recovery and mitigation effort. As such, the focus was not on analyzing artifacts, but rather on recovering ancestral remains, and any associated funerary materials—all of which were to be reburied. Ziibiwing staff worked with myself and Dr. Smith to determine what to collect and how to categorize the material. All historic material (including faunal remains of domestic species) was bagged together, while all precontact ancestral remains, artifacts, and indigenous animal species were stored on-site, separately, in prepared cedar boxes.

Attempts were made to teach local volunteers (including tribal members and neighborhood residents) to identify modern animal bone from what was likely to be human or precontact animal bone (see Figure 14). Dr. Smith checked finds in the field to distinguish human ancestral remains from animal bone. Any modern faunal

FIGURE 14.
Ziibiwing's curator (William Johnson) and research assistant
(Anita Heard) work with Saginaw Chippewa Tribal Member,
Mark Spencer, to screen soil in an effort to recover ancestral
remains and burial items.

material that was clearly from the historic period (determined either by saw cut marks or because it was an animal present after contact) was categorized and stored with the historic material. More importantly, any faunal material from indigenous species was placed together with prehistoric artifacts. Human bone was bagged separately, but stored together with wild animal remains and precontact artifacts.

The rationale for these protocols came directly from Ziibiwing staff. They decided to store human remains with artifacts and animal bone because the ancestors buried in this place may have had these objects (bone and artifacts) buried with them, as part of their "traveling bundle" for passage to the spirit world. Furthermore, because of Anishinabe beliefs about clan relationships, people may have been buried with particular animals, in whole or part, that represent their clan. In such cases, the animals would not have been thought of as separate from individuals—they were relatives and ancestors. Thus, the categorization of animal and human were not discrete in the same way as they are for archaeologists;

and the treatment of the faunal remains during excavation and the reburial that followed reflected community categorizations. We followed appropriate cultural protocols for handling, storing, and reburying these materials also, as described in the following.

These decisions were made, to the greatest extent possible, during the planning phase of the ancestral recovery project. But we could not foresee all of the issues that might arise. Once the fieldwork aspect of the project started, there was regular communication and feedback (sometimes involving multiple phone calls daily) between the archaeologists working on-site and Ziibiwing's director. Ziibiwing staff were sometimes on-site, but often needed to remain in the Ziibiwing Center office, 2½ hours away in Mt. Pleasant, Michigan. From the outset, it was clear that the ancestral remains would be reburied and no further analysis would be done on the remains prior to reburial.

As the first season of the recovery project came to a close, and Ziibiwing prepared to rebury the recovered materials, the issue of recording and studying the recovered precontact artifacts was raised again. Dr. Smith requested that the postcontact European material be stored in her laboratory at the University of Michigan–Flint, and that the material be analyzed and used for teaching—a request that Ziibiwing staff supported and that was approved by the Saginaw Chippewa Indian Tribe of Michigan's Tribal Council. Dr. Smith also offered to carry out a basic demographic analysis of the ancestral remains to determine the number of individuals, their age, and sex. This request was also approved. Lastly, Dr. Smith inquired about drawing and photographing the precontact artifact materials.

In the early weeks of the recovery project, precontact artifacts had been drawn and photographed until Ziibiwing staff instructed that these items not be recorded. Before the items were reburied, Ziibiwing staff carefully considered Dr. Smith's request to draw and/or photograph them. After deliberation, Ziibiwing staff denied the request. Their decision was based on the cultural beliefs that inform Anishinabe burial practices. Ziibiwing's director, Shannon Martin, described the decision in this way:

> For Anishinabe people those items are buried with an individual for a reason. Their intention was for them to be covered and to remain unseen. Since the burials at the Flint Stone Street site were part of an inadvertent discovery that was accidentally uncovered, we felt we needed to remain true to the initial intent of those who buried their loved ones at this location. We decided that those items should not be photographed or drawn because they were never meant to be seen again. And we also explained to the students and volunteers working on the project that the items were not meant to be passed around or viewed.

The purpose of this project was the respectful recovery and reburial of these ancestral remains—it was not meant to be a field school that teaches how to study or analyze materials. It was meant to give students experience in working with a tribe to respectfully mitigate a site in these sorts of unfortunate circumstances.

(SHANNON MARTIN PHONE INTERVIEW, March 15, 2011)

Although Ziibiwing started with a stated policy related to data collection with regards to photographs and illustrations of artifactual material, the flexibility of the project's data recovery and analysis practices allowed for Ziibiwing to consider requests and develop appropriate policies as the project progressed.

The field and lab process was fully community-based, and the decision-making power was in the hands of the tribe at all times. It is important to note that, in this case, the tribe funded this recovery project, which was on private land, and thus the tribe was able to maintain all decision-making authority. Similar community-based data collection and analyses are possible in other publically or university-funded research projects, but they can pose substantial challenges and ethical dilemmas for some archaeologists. The Flint Stone Street site was not excavated using archaeological methods. It was a construction site that had turned up massive amounts of soil using large machinery. The project was designed to recover and rebury human remains and associated material, but was not designed to study them.

For archaeologists using federal funds to excavate a site, the process of reburying artifacts without photographing or otherwise studying them may pose ethical concerns. Federal and state agencies that are charged with protecting archaeological "resources" require detailed archaeological plans for how artifacts will be recorded, studied, curated, and protected. It's unlikely that a plan such as the one from the Stone Street Ancestral Recovery Project would be approved by a state or federal agency. However, archaeologists are able to work in partnership with communities to develop field and lab methods that are culturally appropriate and also fit within required federal and state guidelines.

SHARED DECISION MAKING IN ARCHAEOLOGICAL
FIELD AND LAB METHODS

Other archaeological projects provide examples of community-based data collection and analysis practices. The San Pedro Valley Ethnohistory Project (Ferguson and Colwell-Chanthaphonh 2006) was developed by T. J. Ferguson and Chip Colwell-Chanthaphonh, and carried out in collaboration with representatives from four local tribal nations who have long-term cultural connections to what is today the San Pedro Valley of Arizona. The project was funded by a grant from the National Endowment for the Humanities and is one of the best archaeological models of how a major archaeological research project can follow CBPR guiding principles of being community-based and participatory. Notably, this project did not simply include tribal representatives as ethnographic informants or seek their approval for a predesigned project—it was a partnership from the outset. Officials of the Tohono O'odham, Hopi, Zuni, and San Carlos Apache played an instrumental and substantive role in developing the project methodology (2006, 12). They also determined "its administrative structure"—that is, they defined community contacts and the research team that was to carry out the work, and developed a list of community interviewees. Each of the four teams of tribal community partners had already been involved in archaeological or cultural heritage projects in some capacity, so they were knowledgeable about what was involved in data collection and interpretation. Silliman and Dring (2008) provide further examples of shared decision making in lab analysis procedures with the Eastern Pequot tribal council. They agreed that noncultural materials (including rocks and flotation soil), rather than being discarded, were returned to reservation land. Silliman also worked out a compromise with the tribal council to allow artifacts to be temporarily removed from the reservation for analysis in his campus lab. This agreement required daily monitoring and accounting of finds bags.

Each of these projects involved power sharing and joint decision making. Achieving positive results required a commitment to sharing authority and a willingness to compromise. These examples also demonstrate that creative solutions result from sustained and open communication between research partners. Also significant is that students and community members involved in these projects were made aware of the decision-making *process* itself; they were also educated about the importance and complexities involved in sharing authority and the cultural reasons that prompted changes in conventional field and lab practices. These are critical points for incorporating CBPR into archaeological training and curriculum.

COLLECTING AND UTILIZING QUALITATIVE DATA

Increasingly, archaeologists are utilizing ethnography (Castañeda and Matthews 2008; Meskell 2005; Pyburn and Wilk 1995) and other qualitative research methods to inform archaeological and heritage management projects. Meetings, focus groups, surveys, and interviews with community members can be employed to develop community-based research designs, to plan archaeological education programs, and to understand the types of data collection and analysis methods communities wish to utilize. Often, archaeologists are required to gather other forms of data, such as tourism statistics, qualitative data related to developments' impacts, ethnohistorical or oral history data, and comparative heritage and cultural tourism development data from published secondary sources.

For example, the ethnohistorical, place-name, and qualitative observational data of artifacts that Ferguson, Colwell-Chanthaphonh, and their colleagues from four tribal communities (Ferguson and Colwell-Chanthaphonh 2006) gathered during site visits formed a central part of their ethnohistory project in the San Pedro Valley. In the Sanilac Petroglyph Intellectual Property project I am conducting in partnership with the Ziibiwing Center, we developed a two-pronged approach that includes community-wide surveys and meetings of traditional spiritual leaders to determine how the petroglyph site should be managed; what traditional knowledge about the site should be shared with non-Ojibwe audiences; and culturally appropriate methods of preserving the site. We are coupling the qualitative data from the surveys with information gathered during meetings with spiritual leaders to determine if the petroglyphs should be re-etched. These data are also informing us on how the continued use of the petroglyphs fits with Anishinabe concepts of preservation. We are also gathering data from secondary literature in heritage management to assist us in developing a tribal site management plan. These data-collection methods will provide our joint research team with an understanding of tribal members' cultural views toward the care, management, and interpretation of the Sanilac Petroglyph site. They also help us ensure that the Sanilac IP project includes a wide array of community input and is as inclusive as possible.

The Ziibiwing NAGPRA repatriation research project also involved collecting qualitative data. Ziibiwing staff determined that developing a strong repatriation claim to demonstrate cultural affiliation with ancestral remains held by the University of Michigan Museum of Anthropology (UMMA) required two things: (1) documenting the cultural affiliation of the ancestral remains from the Anishinabe perspective, and (2) combining those data with archaeological data to support the claim. The traditional Anishinabe kinship system and oral traditions clearly demonstrate that the remains are the ancestors of the tribes who reside in the state of Michigan. However, Ziibiwing staff had not gathered and analyzed the archaeological data that would corroborate and strengthen a claim for the remains under

NAGPRA. And they had not yet documented the oral tradition data required to support their claim.

The types of acceptable data used to support a NAGPRA affiliation claim are clearly set forth in the law: archaeological, historical, linguistic, oral tradition, ethnohistorical, kinship, anthropological, and expert witness data. Ziibiwing staff needed to make a determination about which forms of data were relevant, and the process for how they would collect and present the data in a NAGPRA claim.

Ziibiwing's director at the time, Bonnie Ekdahl, determined that the best way to approach the research was for me to conduct archaeological research and share it with Ziibiwing staff, community elders, and tribal representatives from all other federally and state-recognized tribes in Michigan, tribal historians, and spiritual leaders. Ziibiwing's staff determined this would be done through a series of community-hosted meetings that were held at the Ziibiwing Center in which I and the spiritual leaders would each provide teachings. I shared the archaeological data I had researched about the sites from the scientific perspective. Spiritual leaders and tribal historians presented the traditional knowledge that they were charged with protecting.

This process was a means whereby both partners developed an increased understanding of the relationship of the remains to the contemporary tribal communities in Michigan. Using both types of knowledge, Ziibiwing staff and I worked together to develop a statement about the cultural affiliation of the remains. The decision of how to present the NAGPRA claim, the data to include and how to organize it, and which forms of data deserved priority (and which would not be included in the claim at all) were all determined by community representatives. As the archaeological research partner, I provided professional advice and offered input, in addition to the archaeological data. I drafted reports and provided detailed community presentations to educate all participants about the archaeological data. I was not simply an archaeologist in this project or a consultant paid to produce research. I was also a student, and in this capacity I learned a great deal about traditional Anishinabe tribal histories, the kinship system, and cultural protocols relevant to burial practices and our responsibilities as Anishinabe people to care for the dead.

At the direction of Ziibiwing staff, I worked with tribal historians and spiritual leaders to develop the written NAGPRA claim that was submitted to the UMMA. At every step, the community determined which data was to be collected and included in the claim, how it should be presented, and the weight and priority that should be given to various forms of data.

Because NAGPRA law requires repatriation claims to come from tribes, this sort of community-based approach is not uncommon in NAGPRA research. Archaeologists are often hired as consultants to work for tribes in preparing NAGPRA claims. I present this case not because it is unique, but because I think these sorts of partnerships provide an obvious positive model for how other, non–NAGPRA-related archaeological CBPR projects can be carried out. In this example, community members actively determined which lines of evidence were most relevant; which elements of their traditional teachings are too sensitive to be included; and what forms of data should be emphasized or highlighted. Ziibiwing staff, community members, elders, spiritual and traditional leaders, and I all learned something new. We worked together to find ways to "braid together" the forms of knowledge we each shared to present a multifaceted view of the past.

The San Pedro Valley Ethnohistory (SPVE) Project that I mentioned earlier in this chapter followed a similar process, working with multiple communities in the southwestern United States. The project was based in the community, valued multiple forms of data, and worked with community members to determine how to integrate and interpret the data. As in the Ziibiwing NAGPRA project, research partners in the SPVE Project worked together to created a final "product"—one that utilized multiple data sources that they wove together to create a rich, multi-faceted, and situated picture of the past.

Susan Dion (2009) uses the term *braiding histories* to communicate Indigenous experiences in new ways in educational settings. I reworked Dion's term because I think it accurately reflects the potential for knowledge to be valued, reworked, and combined in community-based archaeology projects. Rather than a multivocal model in which a cacophony of voices can emanate from numerous, unspecified locations, and focused in no specific direction, a model of "braiding knowledge" brings distinct forms of knowledge together. Research partners engage in situated weaving to create complex histories that are grounded in specific locations.

While effective in many ways for portraying a CBPR process of collecting, analyzing, and interpreting data, what this model is not as effective at describing are the challenges that can arise when different forms of knowledge are brought together. CBPR offers no easy solutions for situations when Indigenous or local data conflicts with or overtly contradicts archaeological or other forms of knowledge.

Lightfoot (2008, 223–25) provides some guidelines for handling contradictions between community knowledge and archaeology results, and he warns against assumptions that these will merge into a "single homogenous version of history." Potential solutions are likely to be found in careful reflection on some of the resulting tensions, but we currently have too few examples of attempts, successes, and failures of braiding knowledge in community-based approaches to offer any definitive model forward. This is an area where further work in community-based archaeology (and CBPR approaches more generally) is badly needed.

BEING PARTICIPATORY AND BUILDING CAPACITY

In addition to working with community partners to develop approaches to data collection, analysis, and interpretations, CBPR projects are also participatory in conducting these phases of research. The first step in the participatory process of data collection and analysis involves determining the role and level of involvement that local people want to play, identifying the skills required to do so, and pursuing ways of cultivating those skills, if they don't already exist. Technical training plays a sizable role here, and much of the archaeological training comes from involving community members in field schools.

FIELD SCHOOLS

In the Flint Stone Street Ancestral Recovery Project, Ziibiwing staff decided to offer a nontraditional field school to help mitigate the problem created by the inadvertent discovery of the site during construction for a housing project. The Saginaw Chippewa Indian Tribe funded the large-scale recovery of human remains and associated materials at the Flint Stone Street site. Ziibiwing staff hired me and two other archaeologists as PIs to supervise and train local residents and tribal members to recover human remains and associated historic and precontact materials. Three field supervisors—Frank Raslich, a tribal member; his wife, Nicole Raslich (both of whom are archaeology graduate students); and a tribal elder, Ruby Meshaboose—also participated in the recovery project. One of the principal investigators and a supervisor were on-site at all times, training community members to screen soil, and to identify and sort artifacts and ancestral remains. All volunteers also received training in cultural protocols for handling and storing ancestral remains and the necessary spiritual protocols involved in smudging the site. And all were also invited to attend the reburial ceremonies that took place on-site at the end of each field season. As a result of this field training, Ruby Meshaboose, who served as a field supervisor, decided to further her archaeological training and enrolled in Dr. Smith's lab methods course at UM—Flint.

The CBPR literature is ripe with excellent examples of field schools and innovative approaches to community training. Humphries et al. (2008) and Corea et al. (2008) both discuss a method used in their partnership in Honduras in which local residents are elected by the community to attend a field school in order to learn to set up field trials using controlled experiments, and then receive training evaluating and analyzing the results. Field school participants then share the results broadly with the community. This method, developed by Jacqueline Ashby et al. (2000), was also successfully used by others (Braun Thiele, and Fernández 2000). The method is not without its challenges. For example, although secret ballots were used for the election, community members voted overwhelmingly for established leaders, which excluded the most marginalized members of the community. Field school attendees were not paid, as they had been in other projects, which created resentment. Furthermore, some attendees tried to use the position for personal gain—the crop yields were held privately, and did not contribute to public good. Upon reflection, the researchers and community partners realized these problems and worked to provide positive solutions—they worked to include all members of the community and invited all residents to a community meeting, which substantially increased participation in the program. These improvements particularly increased the participation of women in the training program and created new roles for them in the community.

There are other positive examples of how field schools and training programs help "demystify research" (Arora-Jonsson 2008, 131) and how they positively impact women. Bergelin et al. (2008) also describes how involving women in training programs had the positive effect of increasing their status and allowed them to assert themselves in other situations. The women also describe the insights they gained into rural development and how they could apply their skills in other work for their villages. These benefits go far beyond training in forestry management (the focus of their CBPR project). It allowed them to claim space and stand up for their opinions, to "dare to talk." The women from the community explained it this way. They said: "I mean something—I am worth listening to." There are increasingly positive examples of the impact that archaeological field schools have for enhancing community capacity for archaeological preservation (Mills et al. 2008) and research (Bendremer and Thomas 2008; Kerber 2008; Rossen 2008); and how they help to "set the context for community members to take over their own heritage management and research in the future" (Silliman and Dring 2008, 74).

Some programs provide training specifically designed for youth. In Burnette and DeHose's (2008) water management program in their home community on the White Mountain Apache reservation, high school and college students measure water quality, test soils, and also gain cultural knowledge through interviewing tribal elders. This project was aimed at making Keith Basso's well-known work discussed in *Wisdom Sits in Places* useful for the next generation. Basso's research was "sitting on the shelf" in the schools and was rarely used by community members. This project and youth training program breathed new life into Basso's research. Those involved in developing training programs for Indigenous youth also describe some of the challenges involved, such as getting tribal youth involved in the programs (Mills et al. 2008), and creating programs that appeal to Indigenous youth (Bendremer and Thomas 2008). The same is true for local communities, such as the youth I worked with in Turkey. It is important to develop training programs that provide youth with marketable skills, not just in archaeological field methods that they may never use once the excavation has ended, but to also incorporate skills such as English language classes, grant-writing experience, interviewing skills, illustration for community reports, and community organizing skills. Kerber (2008) echoes this concern. He details the approach he took in developing a summer workshop in archaeology for youth in the Oneida Indian Nation. The workshop included excavation techniques but also involved other practical research skills.

COMMUNITY INTERNS

Another highly effective method of being participatory and providing community training is to include community members in the research process as interns. At Çatalhöyük, the first two community interns on the community-based archaeology project had a college education (which is unusual for rural Turkey, and particularly so for women), but they had no experience conducting interviews, developing surveys, organizing community meetings and presentations, or conducting archaeological fieldwork. The Çatalhöyük excavation team had trained a local workforce from the village to conduct certain aspects of archaeological fieldwork as laborers. However, the CBPR internships involve archaeological education and heritage management research, and they aim to provide qualitative methods training that can be applied in other community-led efforts. The training is hands-on, as interns engage on a daily basis with the day-to-day operations of the community-based archaeology project at Çatalhöyük.

In some situations, particularly where youth or young professionals are involved, an internship approach can prove useful beyond the training it provides. The more formal nature of an internship (rather than a volunteer position) can provide younger interns with a level of respect in the community. This was an important element in the community-based archaeology project at Çatalhöyük, where younger members of the community were very interested in the project, and their leadership and involvement was critical for long-term success. There are sometimes tensions in the Çatalhöyük setting between younger residents and older community members. Older community members often don't view the younger residents as being particularly capable, and independence from one's family before marriage is not common. This affects both men and women, but presents particular challenges for women in the community, who are subject to even greater pressures to stay within the traditional realm of the household and not venture into public affairs.

Contributing to this is the fact that volunteering is not a common practice or concept in Turkey, particularly not in village contexts where residents are often financially burdened and struggling themselves. The Çatalhöyük community-based archaeology project faced the challenge of involving members of the younger generation, who were clearly familiar with, interested in, and knowledgeable about tourism and issues of heritage management but who were not familiar with or amenable to volunteering time for a research project. The issue of money was another point of consideration. Ray (2009) notes that consideration needs to be given to how community members who participate in collaborative projects are compensated for time and expertise. Sema Bağcı, a Turkish archaeology graduate student who is a valuable research assistant for the Çatalhöyük community archaeology project, was the first to call attention to these issues at Çatalhöyük. Together we considered how to involve younger community residents in the research process in a way that was culturally appropriate and acceptable to them and to their families. Through our discussions, we developed the idea of a paid archaeological CBPR internship program.

The program was initiated with the help of Ali Barutcu, the very efficient and enthusiastic newly elected *muhtar* (village manager) of Küçükköy (the village nearest to the Çatalhöyük site). After discussion about the participatory nature of the community-based archaeology project and our aim to increase participation and training through a paid internship program, Barutcu suggested two residents from Küçükköy as the project's first interns: Rahime Salur and Nesrin Salur. These two women have a number of impressive accomplishments to note, one being that they are the first residents from their village to graduate from college (both received teaching degrees). Despite their college education, both were unemployed and waiting for a government teaching assignment.

The pay for the internship is quite modest, as the position is understood to be about training rather than employment. And very importantly for the interns, it provides them with a title and gives them a level of respect and standing within the community—both critical elements for future cultural development and regional-level planning. The interns assist with every aspect of the community-based archaeology project. Their assistance was particularly critical during our initial women's meeting in Küçükköy. During the meeting, both interns presented information about the community-based archaeology project to the seventy-five meeting attendees, and they took charge in gathering feedback from local women on their ideas for future research partnerships with the Çatalhöyük project. It was immediately clear that local women from Küçükköy felt more comfortable talking with the interns than with either myself or Sema Bağcı, the project's graduate student research assistant (who is Turkish, but lives in the capital city of Ankara, and is not a local resident of Küçükköy).

Directly following that meeting, several women came to the interns with suggestions for community-based research projects. One idea was to create a space on-site for a group of women from the village to learn about the Çatalhöyük iconography and produce handcrafts featuring it. The women hoped to display and sell the items in nearby urban areas. We acted on this idea, and a small handcraft project was developed using the Çatalhöyük site visitors' center as a base. Figure 15 shows two of the first handcrafted items produced as part of this program.

Through the intern program and the handcraft project, women are gaining knowledge about Çatalhöyük while also gaining experience in the realm of cultural tourism. Next steps include us working together to research other models of heritage crafting and their impacts on local economies and community life. Other project ideas were also generated from the women's meeting with the assistance of the interns, including utilizing the dig house buildings as a school that girls can attend and hosting a regular health clinic on-site in the off-season. Both programs are in the works, and are part of a grant to be written collaboratively with the interns, local teachers, and other community members. These projects require research into the heritage laws and practices within Turkey, and community residents who choose to participate will actively partner with the interns, myself, and hopefully other archaeologists on-site to research the laws, regulations, and protocols involved.

FIGURE 15.
Two handcrafted decorative wall hangings that young
women from Küçükköy produced as part of a tourism-related
merchandising effort.

Since community-coauthored grants, presentations, and publications to fund
and inform about this collaborative work are the goals of the community-based
archaeology project at Çatalhöyük, a central part of the internship program
involves becoming knowledgeable and experienced in qualitative research methods and grant writing. The hope is that interns will then be able to utilize and apply
these skills to address other community concerns. Because of the success and community interest, the internship program has steadily increased and now offers four
internships annually to local residents from Küçükköy. The program is building
community capacity so that younger members of the village are knowledgeable
about the research on and management of Çatalhöyük and can actively and confidently participate in the future planning, protection, and tourism endeavors at the
site.

Currently, there is limited participation at the village level during government meetings and planning. At one men's meeting hosted by the community-
based archaeology project, a suggestion was offered by a young man to utilize

the internships to create a local, village-level heritage committee (*kurul*) similar to those in larger cities. Those in the committee would participate in higher, regional-level meetings about local cultural tourism planning. Future plans for the interns include working in partnership to research heritage management strategies and become knowledgeable about the approach others have taken worldwide.

The Çatalhöyük community-based archaeology internship program is building a cohort of local residents who are knowledgeable about heritage management issues, cultural tourism and its challenges, and grant writing practices. And it provides the community with informed representation who have a better chance of being taken seriously in future higher-level government dialogues about site development and planning.

ADULT EDUCATION PROGRAMS

CBPR practitioners have developed adult education programs in a range of contexts (de Wit and Gianotten 1980; Merrifield 1993). Some, such as Levin's (1980) work with trade unions, provide a model for teaching research methods, in this case to factory workers, during community meetings. Involving community members directly in data analysis and interpretation can be particularly challenging. Ballard's (2008) approach in a CBPR plant ecology project provides one possible model: She hosted a dinner and placed bar graphs on the tables that community members learned to read and interpret. Other examples (Jackson 1978; Mduma 1982) demonstrate the usefulness of "collective self-education" (Comstock and Fox 1993, 109), where members of the same community come together with one another or with members of other communities to share knowledge and skills and provide peer training. If Barndt (1980) is correct, and collective knowledge production leads to collective action for social change, then these sorts of horizontal adult education efforts hold great potential.

Ziibiwing Center, the CBO I partner with in Michigan, is considering developing a peer-training program for archaeology. In the CBPR graduate methods course I teach, a graduate student research team partnered with Ziibiwing Center to develop a tribal protection and management plan for the Flint Stone Street site. One component of the research proposed by Ziibiwing staff was a community certification for archaeology mitigation. Ziibiwing requested that the student team conduct research to assist in developing guidelines for this certification. Ziibiwing's plan is that tribal members would be able to receive certification for the work and training they conducted through the mitigation and ancestral recovery efforts at the Flint Stone Street site. Those certified could then act as a consulting team for other Native nations who face similar challenges in mitigating large- and small-scale inadvertent discovery challenges in their home communities.

Particularly inspiring examples of adult education can be found in the work of Myles Horton (Horton 1990; Adams and Horton 1975) and Paulo Freire (1970). Horton worked in the Appalachian region of the United States, where he founded the Highlander School in 1932. The school, devoted to popular education and citizen-based participatory research was instrumental in the labor movements of the 1930s and the civil rights movements of the 1940s and 1960s. Well-known community activists attended classes at the Highlander, including Rosa Parks (weeks before she "sat on the bus") and Martin Luther King Jr. Like Horton, Freire's well-known work in adult literacy programs in Brazil forms a critical theoretical basis for popular education and adult training programs.

Developing adult education programs in archaeology should include training in conventional field methods and data analysis (as many field schools currently do), but should also include instruction in CBPR methods that will build community capacity for conducting research in a participatory and community-driven way. Although research conducted within a CBPR model benefits communities, this does not mean that community members have inherent skills in conducting research in a collaborative way, or that they will be comfortable, skilled, or even familiar with engaging with fellow community members as part of a research team.

Likewise, researchers should not assume they will be skilled at teaching in an adult education setting. As Nicholas (2008) points out, it's important to develop a teaching philosophy that includes adult education (as well as that of children), which requires approaching education differently and gaining a new set of pedagogical skills. An important part of developing a teaching philosophy for adult education requires that archaeologists consider the intention behind these educational endeavors. For Nicholas, archaeology is a tool that can be used however people choose to. His teaching philosophy is to "teach indigenous people to do archaeology without expecting them to do my kind of archaeology" (2008, 236). Lightfoot takes a different approach to training community members. He feels that archaeology is best as a "collaborative effort" that involves archaeologists and community members working together in the process. An adult training program aimed at providing community members with the skills needed to do archaeology independently will likely need to be structured quite differently from one in which students learn to work collaboratively with an archaeologist to conduct fieldwork. Whatever format archaeological adult education programs take, the goals and aims of the community should be central. What do community members hope to accomplish and how to they hope to utilize their training? The answers to these questions should guide the training process.

TRAINING PROGRAMS AT THE NATIONAL LEVEL

Training efforts in which community members learn methods of archaeological data collection and analysis can take place in the field, as with Çatalhöyük, the Stone Street Ancestral Recovery Project, and a range of other field schools (Silliman 2008b), but can also take place outside the field season. In the United States, numerous community education programs now provide specialized training in archaeology. Many are geared toward Native Americans, and aim to raise archaeological research capacity in Native communities.

Archaeologists who want to conduct a community-based archaeology project might consider discussing such training options with their community partner, and consider providing support for community members to attend. Communities that want to conduct community-based archaeology projects might consider identifying potential students within their group and providing funding for them to attend such trainings. The National Association of Tribal Historic Preservation Officers (NATHPO) provides multiple trainings annually for tribal historic preservation officers to learn about archaeology and heritage management and preservation-related research. Likewise, the national NAGPRA office provides free training for tribal communities and other interested parties, including webinars and video programs, that inform participants on the detailed processes of NAGPRA-related research.

Scholarships are available through the Society for American Archaeology for Native American students to attend archaeological field schools. Further programs like this are needed. National-level programs should be developed to support adult training for community members who wish to increase their skills and knowledge about conducting community-based archaeological research. Adult education of this sort would benefit greatly by working with those experienced in developing successful popular education and citizen training programs and facilities, such as the Highlander.

Adult education programs are important for building future community-based archaeological research. They lay the groundwork for community partnerships through capacity building that helps members to develop and/or evaluate data collection and analysis practices. Community training programs in research design would also be useful for facilitating community capacity skills in project planning, funding, and development. Such training need not be expensive or time-consuming, but can take place online, through live webinars or downloadable training packets.

The National Congress of American Indians has developed and published an excellent set of online curricular materials aimed at training tribal members in community-based research methods (National Congress of American Indians 2009). The materials were developed in collaboration with Native American community members and advocates to assist them in using CBPR to do research based on core tribal values. Archaeological professional associations could work with community members to develop such adult education training materials for a wide range of archaeological and heritage management topics.

BENEFITS TO ARCHAEOLOGY

Developing participatory aspects of data collection and interpretation can result in programs that provide benefits to the community, but that can also provide reciprocal benefits for archaeologists. They increase public knowledge about archaeological technical processes and practices, and also allow for residents to become familiar with how archaeologists think, what motivates them, and what is behind their decision making. The Çatalhöyük community-based archaeology project demonstrates the relevance of this in places where, like in Turkey, "subsistence looting" and the illegal sale of antiquities has a long and complicated history, and remains a very real and widespread concern.

Interviews with local village residents in Küçükköy provided interesting insights into looting issues. Several community members mentioned that they believed the archaeologists were using the flotation machine to recover gold from the mound. Our local interns were able to assure them this was not the case, and, more importantly, the interns explained what the flotation machines were used for and why archaeologists have such an interest in decayed plant materials that have no monetary value. These sorts of questions may not have even been raised if we had not involved trusted members of the local community in the CBPR process. Clearly, it means something very different when community members hear this sort of explanation from a family member, friend, or neighbor—someone they know and trust—rather than from an archaeologist. Today, archaeologists in Turkey are sometimes still viewed with suspicion by local residents, who often see them as wealthy, powerful, and holding a great deal of prestige. Speculation about the source of that wealth links directly with people's fears that archaeologists are individually profiting by selling the artifacts they excavate.

This is an issue of particular sensitivity in Turkey, where uneasiness over Heinrich Schliemann's removal of the treasure of "Troy" to Germany in the late 1800s is commonly mentioned. The topic of foreign archaeologists removing, even smuggling, artifacts out of the country for profit is a subject closely linked to Çatalhöyük, where the archaeologist who conducted the first excavations on the site, James Mellaart, had his permit revoked due to rumors of smuggling (Pearson and Connor 1967).

Çatalhöyük provides another example of the benefits archaeologists gain by using a participatory process of data collection and analysis. In Chapter 5, I discussed how interviews with Küçükköy residents revealed that local men who had worked on-site for over fifteen years had no idea of the way the human remains and other excavated materials were studied and curated. It was shocking for me to find out that local community members thought archaeologists were simply digging up bodies and dumping them in a mass grave. For one thing, it confirmed that local people had a fundamental misunderstanding about why archaeologists devote time and money on excavations. From their point of view, archaeologists were excavating to find gold and other materials with a high monetary value, and were unconcerned with things such as human remains, which have little economic worth. What was most disconcerting was that the man who asked this question had been part of the daily process of excavation for years, yet was still completely unaware of what happened to the human remains after they were excavated.

This is a situation where participatory data analysis could play an important role in helping local community members experience firsthand the work bioarchaeologists are doing on-site. For projects like Çatalhöyük that have a long-standing excavation component and are slowly incorporating a community-based archaeology aspect into the project, local residents are best involved in substantive ways in both data collection (excavation) and analysis (laboratory) processes. This provides local residents with the opportunity to gain a clear understanding of the ongoing research in the ground and in the lab, and can help resolve questions or any feelings of discomfort they may have about the research process.

This does not mean that local residents will necessarily be comfortable with what they see once they have a more complete understanding of the analysis and curation processes. But, being sincere in one's efforts to engage with communities as partners means being as open and forthright as possible about the methods involved. It also means being willing to engage local community members at every level of the research and curation process to help them make informed decisions.

This example from Çatalhöyük demonstrates that sharing knowledge about the site and archaeological processes requires more than hiring local people to work on the excavation team. Developing methods of participatory data *analysis* is equally important because it not only engages the community in recovering the materials from excavation, but it also provides them with insight into the processes used to analyze the data, the questions archaeologists are interested in asking, the answers they produce, and how they arrive at those answers. With knowledge of these methods and processes, communities are then increasingly skilled at developing, evaluating, and participating in all aspects of archaeological research.

SHARED MOTIVATION FOR ARCHAEOLOGY

This is not to say that archaeologists' motivations for involving communities in a participatory way should be to convince community members of the benefits of archaeology. Community-based archaeology is not meant to be a paternalistic methodology that uses a participatory approach to convince community members to value and use archaeology in the same ways that researchers do. Such a view is problematic in that it naïvely presumes that lack of knowledge inspires some communities to reject archaeology or choose to limit its scope. This view is particularly prevalent in situations where archaeologists develop or support programs to educate Native Americans about the value of archaeology without realizing that human rights concerns and spiritual beliefs, not lack of knowledge about the benefits of archaeology, are often key factors that inform decision making with regards to the excavation and study of human remains or the treatment of sacred sites and landscapes.

The situation from Çatalhöyük demonstrates that although the local workers on the excavation were uncomfortable with what they thought was happening, they were willing to continue working for the project despite their questioning. The employment offered them financial benefits that they very much needed. Certainly it can be uncomfortable for archaeologists to think that local community members might be opposed to the research they are conducting, and this may make some leery of inviting community participation in data collection and analysis. Making these activities participatory allows for any differences in approach or difficult conversations to come to the foreground, rather than being left unstated or unexamined.

The process of being participatory doesn't create new problems; it simply uncovers existing tensions. Ethically, the imperative is for us, as researchers, to be transparent in the research being done, whether or not in a community-based archaeology project. But the issue of transparency takes on an even greater role in CBPR projects because they are community-driven and are developed with community values, desires, and needs at the core. The only way to develop a CBPR project in situations where there has previously been mistrust, differences in perspective, or even outright hostility and conflict is to bring those issues to light, and to openly and collectively consider how they might be resolved. Providing communities with opportunities for participating in data collection and analysis can help in this endeavor.

At Çatalhöyük, local people's concerns about human remains were resolved by explaining the process of how human remains are studied and curated after excavation. While the village resident who raised the concerns about excavating burials felt reassured by knowing that the remains were not tossed into a mass grave, he still felt uneasy about uncovering the dead, even though his spiritual advisor told him that these were not his ancestors. However, the uneasiness he felt was something he and others were willing to endure for the benefits provided by employment at Çatalhöyük.

In the interviews our community-based archaeology team conducted, many residents reported that the knowledge uncovered at Çatalhöyük was important and useful for the entire world. They also felt that it helped to put their small village "on the map." The possible economic benefits from tourism were clearly of central importance to all Küçükköy residents I interviewed, and they held much higher priority than the concerns voiced by a minority of community members about the "aching bones" of the site's former inhabitants.

In this case, the values of archaeologists were not the same as those of many in the local community who feel that disturbing the remains may be a sin or harmful in some ways to the individuals being excavated. However, the result was not conflict because both archaeologists and community members shared a common desire to continue excavations, albeit for very different reasons. In a community-based archaeology project, motivations of community members and archaeologists do not always need to match. Both may follow very different reasoning yet come to agreement on the same plan of action. It's the shared decision making that is important.

FURTHER BENEFITS OF PARTICIPATORY FIELD AND LAB WORK

The desires and needs of archaeologists and communities will not always correspond, and their differing views may not sufficiently overlap to bring them to a point of agreement. Conflicts are not always easily resolved. Anyone who engages in a community-based archaeology project should anticipate this and must approach the project with flexibility. The CBPR process can also provide an effective way for community members to demonstrate their own practices and values to archaeologists.

At the Flint Stone Street Ancestral Recovery Project, participatory fieldwork had an impact on both community members and archaeologists. Tribal members who were involved in the recovery of human remains were able to experience for themselves how archaeology could be conducted in a respectful way that was not in conflict with either their spiritual beliefs and practices or the human rights of their ancestors. Additionally, tribal members could trust that field methods were appropriate because they were involved in the day-to-day work themselves. They did not have to simply take the archaeologist's word, or wonder if a site monitor might be missing something, because they were involved in the process from the site's opening each morning to closing smudge ceremony at the end of each day.

Mills et al. (2008) note that community-based archaeology projects may help to improve relationships that are troubled or have a problematic past in another way. Their collaborative University of Arizona field school with the White Mountain Apache provided an opportunity to rebuild a strained relationship between the university and the tribe that was the result of the university's use of an Apache sacred mountain as an observatory.

Participatory lab and field practices built trust and understanding while they also increased community knowledge about the processes of archaeology, the way research is conducted, and what can be learned from even very small pieces of material. The project also served to educate the archaeologists involved. They experienced the ways that local residents interact with the past and the values they place on it—all valuable knowledge that is critical for archaeologists to understand if they hope to effect long-term, successful, and sustainable management of a site.

Although the Çatalhöyük community-based archaeology project currently focuses on heritage management and cultural tourism research (rather than "dirt archaeology" questions), taking a proactive approach to involve local residents in a substantive way in field and lab methods builds local capacity that may allow the community-based project to expand and eventually include excavation-based research questions. Humphries et al. (2008, 44) found this to be the case with their CBPR agricultural project with Honduran farmers. The participatory aspects of their fieldwork "yielded the organizational backbone to support longer term natural resource management." Furthermore, the type and degree of community participation in data collection and analysis may change over time, as residents become more aware of the research taking place on-site. Initially, community members may not have defined research questions, but as they become more involved, their interests may expand. Community members may start out with "dirt archaeology" interests, and then later develop ideas for other community-based archaeology projects, some of which may involve site management and maintenance, heritage tourism, or development.

Buruchara (2008) found in her agricultural research with farmers in Rwanda that CBPR was helpful because it allowed her to see what aspects farmers would utilize and which solutions they simply would not adopt. Other CBPR studies indicate that participatory field and lab practices benefit local management and protection strategies, primarily because community members see the impacts firsthand, and if they are involved in analyzing and developing protection and management policies, they are more likely to endorse them (Ballard 2008; Collins Cruz, and Smith 2008; Ticktin and Johns 2002; Endress et al. 2004). Archaeologists have experienced similar results. Participatory practices have resulted in similar benefits with regard to heritage management (Mills et al. 2008), and particularly with regard to protecting sacred sites (Rossen 2008).

PRESENTING RESEARCH RESULTS

All research is produced with particular audiences in mind, and the results are often shared with multiple audiences. For archaeological research, those audiences usually include archaeologists within the academic community, professional archaeologists with ties to cultural resource management, and various community and public audiences. None of these are monolithic; each has a degree of internal diversity and each engages with archaeological knowledge in different ways. In community-based archaeology projects, community partners are not simply one of many possible public audiences, but rather are a *primary* audience for the research. Merrifield (1993) rightly notes that communities often don't have access to scientific journals, and scholarly research is often jargon-filled and not written in an accessible way for nonspecialists. He further notes that scientists are sometimes apprehensive of working closely with communities and presenting results in accessible language because they fear it will be viewed as nonobjective.

Regardless of those concerns, community-based archaeology projects involve producing more than a standard archaeological report, scholarly publication, or conference paper, and often require sharing results and knowledge in engaging and accessible ways. Merrifield is highly critical of the way scientists use language and share research results with communities. He cautions against "fake science." As he explains it, fake science is "when the high status accorded to experts and notion of science as objective, disinterested, and pure are used to assure ordinary people of their own ignorance, in contrast to the power holders' ability to capture expertise for their own side" (1993, 74). Merrifield details how "fake science" can be used by the powerful to "delay and defuse," "impress and bemuse," and "gloss and confuse," and he puts forth a strong argument for CBPR as part of a new science that is accountable and responsible to the needs of ordinary people. This involves producing research results in a format that is both accessible and useful.

This is not to say that CBPR projects are not concerned with producing and sharing knowledge in a scholarly way—they are and do so quite effectively. Community-based research is *reciprocal* in nature, and as such, produces results that are of interest to archaeological audiences. And the action component of CBPR may require reports or materials that are geared toward state or federal government entities, courts, NGOs and international organizations such as UNESCO, or other public communities that have an interest in the research. All of these audiences—community members, tribal councils, archaeology professionals, state, federal, and international agencies and organizations, and wider publics— are diverse and have multiple components.

Those engaging in CBPR projects have provided many excellent models for sharing knowledge effectively with these audiences. Some have explored combining traditional education methods with contemporary practices and community-led seminars (Mustafa 1980), working with a community to produce an official report (Levin 1980), and even more informal approaches such as "coffee gatherings" (Bobiwash and Malloch 1980). Jackson and McKay (1982) take a multipronged approach that includes Indigenous language reports, sharing results through local research committees and community seminars, and community study trips. Descriptions of coauthored reports written by both community members and researchers are well documented—one of the most interesting is reported by Long (2008), who coauthored chapters of his dissertation with White Mountain Apache community members to report on the results of their partnership in a water restoration project.

The CBPR literature is rich with useful, practical advice. Bergelin et al. (2008) provide advice for community partners as they detail the process they took to produce a research report. The five women who authored the report came together in one location, were interviewed by their academic partner, and then listened, talked, and wrote with a facilitator. The academic partner (Arora-Jonsson) translated the chapter to English. All participants commented on and edited the text prior to translation. Although the process they describe was used to author a report for a scholarly audience, the women also describe the importance of constantly sharing updates and results with the wider community, even those *not* participating in the research. It was important for their project to keep local residents informed so they did not become jealous of the women's participation or create scenarios about the research that were not true. Burnette and DeHose (2008) also speak from the perspective of community research partners, and they provide advice to researchers.

They highlight the need to be sensitive to the different learning styles of community members, relating this to the boarding school experiences they and other White Mountain Apache elders experienced in which they were hit and punished for not getting a point quickly enough. This is an important reminder for archaeologists about the need to identify proper pedagogy for training community members and for sharing research results more broadly.

COMMUNITY REPORTS

As with other aspects of CBPR, the process of disseminating research results should be both community-driven and participatory. Archaeologists likely have their own ideas and experiences for effectively reaching nonarchaeological audiences. But communities can also provide very useful input on how to most effectively reach other members of the community. They can provide useful insights on approaches that are both culturally relevant and appropriate.

The Ziibiwing community-based repatriation research project demonstrates what I feel is a very effective approach for reporting research results to community members. Ziibiwing's director, Shannon Martin, reported on our research process and the results publically at a community gathering. Four times each year, members of the Three Fires Midewiwin Lodge meet to carry out traditional ceremonies. The grand chief of the Three Fires Lodge is Eddie Benton-Banaise. He is one of the spiritual leaders who worked with us to put together a NAGPRA claim for ancestral remains held at the University of Michigan. Martin, herself a member of the Three Fires Lodge, requested time within the ceremonies to provide a verbal report on the research that we conducted. Elders and youth alike listened and provided verbal encouragement and feedback about the project, both during and after Martin's report.

This community report was part of an *Ogitchidaw* or Warrior Ceremony. For Anishinabe people, those doing the work of repatriation research are warriors, and they are honored as such publically, alongside those who have served in more traditional battlefields and wars.

In her community report, Martin noted the difficult nature of the work from a cultural perspective, particularly the challenges of reading about and seeing the way our Anishinabe relatives—including grandmothers, grandfathers, their children, and newborn babies—had been uncovered from their resting places, stored, and studied. I will not report on the details of the ceremony, but do wish to highlight here the way a community was able to effectively share the results of our community-based archaeological research in a culturally appropriate method. Martin's community report effectively communicated information, reached the desired audience, and had an impact. This type of community report is not something that can be initiated by an archaeologist, but it is important to mention here to call attention to traditional methods that communities may have for sharing knowledge. These methods are equally if not more important as a method of sharing research results, although they may occur in ways that seem very informal.

Further methods of community research reports can be found in both archaeological literature and in reports on CBPR from other disciplines. Again, the San Pedro Valley Ethnohistory Project conducted with multiple Native American communities in the southwestern United States (Ferguson and Colwell-Chanthaphonh 2006, 13) provides an excellent archaeological example. In this project, where four Native nations (Hopi, Zuni, Western Apache, and Tohono O'odham) worked in partnership with a team of archaeologists, each research partner chose to handle community reporting in a different way. In the case of the Tohono O'odham, the archaeologists were asked to provide oral reports to the community cultural committee and to a full tribal council. With the Hopi, community review followed a slightly different process that did not involve the tribal council, but did include regular feedback and discussion with a Cultural Resources Advisory Task Team, charged by the community political leadership with advising on and carrying out the research. For the Pueblo of Zuni, community reports were less formal, being carried out during fieldwork and interviews with tribal members who served on the community-developed research team (2006, 14). In addition, the archaeologists produced a final written report (Ferguson and Colwell-Chanthaphonh 2006) about the overall project, and 1,000 copies were provided to each community for distribution.

As with the SPVE research, the community-based archaeology project at Çatalhöyük also included a combination of verbal and written community reports. Verbal reports were given during household visits with the aim of updating

Küçükköy residents about how the community-based project was proceeding. House visits were carried out by community interns, a graduate research assistant (Sema Bağcı, a Turkish anthropology PhD student), and myself. We visited all houses in Küçükköy where we had conducted interviews, and also provided regular progress reports to the local city manager. At first we were apprehensive about knocking on doors to offer a report. But the community interns working with us, both of whom were local village residents, assured us this was not at all rude and that visits would be welcomed by Küçükköy residents. Our community interns were correct.

Local residents were extremely enthusiastic about our visits, and in several cases were quite surprised that we had taken time to report back to them with results. In one case, which was both enlightening and frustrating, we spent an extensive amount of time explaining repeatedly to our hosts that we had come to *report* results to them. Elders of the household, both male and female, continually questioned, "So, what are you here to ask us?" We explained once again that we were not here to *ask* anything, but came to report back to them. Their response was telling: "Yes, but what *questions* do you want us to answer this time?" I want to stress that this was not the result of a language barrier—all conversation took place in Turkish. Even our local interns were misunderstood when they explained that we came to report results, not gather data or ask more questions.

It is interesting to consider the reasons for this, and I believe it speaks directly to the pattern of engagement that local residents have come to expect from archaeologists—the practice of involving the community as ethnographic informants who provide data and information that does not flow back into their community in visible and meaningful ways. These encounters also provided me with a way to monitor the effectiveness with which our community-based archaeology project is shaping and changing the community's views of research and their role in producing it. As the project further evolves and expands, I anticipate fewer and fewer of these encounters, and I hope they will be replaced by a greater number of residents asking for and expecting feedback.

In addition to house visits, I also provided regular reports to the community through a series of public meetings. Following local cultural practice, meetings were held separately for men and women. The village manager announced (and thus endorsed) all meetings on the mosque loudspeaker. The village manager arranged for the men's meetings to be held in the coffeehouse directly across from the mosque after the well-attended Friday prayers. Women's meetings were held in the local schoolhouse and were also arranged by the village manager. Meetings were well attended, and people not only listened to the reports (some of which used PowerPoint slides), but also intermittently asked questions and held discussions about the CBPR planning and projects as we presented the results we had reached to that point, and discussed ideas for future plans.

The interns played an important role in the community meetings, as they were able to speak firsthand about the participatory nature of the research project, and the ways they hoped to apply what they were learning to other nonarchaeology projects. The other benefit to involving interns directly in presenting results back to the wider community was that it both instilled pride in the local women to see that one of their own was involved and highly respected in the research taking place at Çatalhöyük. Interns also established a direct link of community-community engagement on these issues. Both of these aspects are critical for the future, long-term sustainability of the Çatalhöyük community-based archaeology project and, more importantly, for the capacity building that will benefit local communities in ways unrelated to archaeology and heritage management.

The Çatalhöyük community-based archaeology project also produces written community reports for residents from all five villages that surround Çatalhöyük. Written reports include a community newsletter aimed at literate adults, and a series of comics aimed at children and the adults with limited reading skills. The comic series and newsletters cover a range of topics, including updates on the excavation as well as information about cultural tourism and site management. But they also include feedback about the progress of the community-based archaeology project. For example, one of the recent comics (see Figures 10 and 11 in Chapter 6) presents two of the young heroes of the series (Rahime and Mustafa—based on two children from the village and used with the permission of their families) learning about the possible futures of Çatalhöyük and how they can be involved. Rahime explains to Mustafa that her aunt went to a women's meeting in the village where they discussed ways to work in partnership with the archaeologists on a project that will help the community. The comic goes on to report ideas that village residents have suggested for collaborative projects—including development of a local Çatalhöyük-themed hotel in which the rooms are Neolithic houses as part of an experimental archaeology project; a school on the Çatalhöyük grounds for village girls; and a village health clinic supported through archaeological tourism.

The idea for the comic and the newsletter came directly from community members. In initial interviews, I asked Küçükköy residents what sorts of methods would be most effective in reporting information about the excavation results and our community-based research—Küçükköy residents suggested both the comic and the newsletters. Allowing community members to determine the format for presenting research enhances the probability that the results will effectively reach the intended audience.

In all three of the community-based archaeology projects with Ziibiwing (repatriation, intellectual property at the Sanilac petroglyph site, and the Flint Stone Street Recovery Project), Ziibiwing staff arranged for brief community reports to run in the local tribal newspaper (the *Tribal Observer*). In one case, I was asked by Ziibiwing's director to write a short report for the *Tribal Observer,* but in other cases, Ziibiwing's director and staff were interviewed or wrote informational reports about the research.

Students in my CBPR graduate methods course prepared a community report on our community-based work at the Waapaahsiki Siipiiwi mound in southern Indiana. Inspired by the Çatalhöyük comic series, two graduate students worked with a community member from the Sullivan County American Indian Council to produce a seven-page "graphic novel" aimed at informing Native and nonnative public audiences about our research together (see Figures 16 and 17). They developed the community report to reach two primary audiences: Sullivan County American Indian Council members who were not directly involved with the project and nonnative residents in the county where the mound is located.

In addition to presenting updates or results to community members broadly, one may also be expected to report more officially to leadership or governing bodies within the community or to community youth. In the case of CBOs, this may include reporting to the governing board of the organization, or to its members. In Native American communities, it is common practice to report research results to the tribal council or other political leadership.

In my partnership with Ziibiwing, the responsibility for preparing such reports was assumed by Ziibiwing, whose director provided regular written reports to both the Saginaw Chippewa Tribal Council, and to the Ziibiwing Board of Directors. The expected content, preferred format, and frequency of such reports will vary from community to community, and it is the responsibility of the archaeologist to make herself aware of these expectations. It may be that, as was the case for me with Ziibiwing, a CBO partner will prefer to organize and present the research results.

Archaeologists have developed stellar community reports and have done well at sharing archaeology with K–12 community audiences. For example, Brownlee and Syms (1999) created replicas of artifacts for display in local First Nations schools in Canada, and Mills et al. (2008) developed materials for the K–12 curriculum and

FIGURE 16.
A page from the comic-based "graphic novel" that Indiana University students (Nicholas Ramirez and Sarah Dees) and Sullivan County American Indian Council member (Cookie Barnard) produced to help educate local Indiana residents about the Waapaahsiki Siipiiwi mound project.

a poster explaining the tribal partner's cultural heritage program. Countless other examples exist.

Even in cases where there is no requirement for reporting research progress or results, it is still beneficial to provide either a written or verbal report to the political and/or organizational leadership, both as a way to keep people up-to-date on a project's progress and as a means to build a lasting relationship for future collaborations. Although we were not required to do so, I provided the village manager in Küçükköy with reports on the results from the Çatalhöyük community-based

FIGURE 17.
A page from the "graphic novel" produced as part of a
community report for the Waapaahsiki Siipiiwi mound project.

research, and I also gave him regular informal verbal updates as the project progressed. He is a busy man with multiple responsibilities, and although he remains quite interested in the community-based archaeology project, it was also clear that he was not able to commit a large amount of time to hearing research updates. This is particularly the case in the summer, when the activity and workload in the community are very heavy. Seasonality can be an issue for many rural communities, which are extremely busy in the warmer months and have a greater amount of flexibility in cooler months. Offering to provide written reports, or to do any planning and correspondence during cooler months (often the time when archaeologists are not in the field) may be an important component to success. Whatever the situation, community reports should be provided in a method, and following the timing, that is convenient for and determined by the community.

CBPR projects are increasingly using the Internet to report research activities and results to community members and other audiences. Social networking sites (such as Facebook and Twitter) and video sharing sites (such as YouTube) are now common tools. In one archaeological example from a project I've worked on, Ziibiwing staff created a Facebook page to recruit community volunteers for the Flint Stone Street Ancestral Recovery Project and to keep volunteers informed of the progress of the work. A Saginaw Chippewa tribal member (Chuck Butzer) created and posted a short informational video on YouTube (http://www.youtube .com/watch?v=LM5l-2-BnI4), aimed at informing both the public and Saginaw Chippewa tribal members about the project. The video has also been used to garner local support in the larger Flint community for developing a memorial and green space at the location of the ancestral recovery.

Long (2008) describes producing a bilingual video to share research findings with both the tribal council and staff from other tribal government offices. Community-based organizations have also found great success using video (and the Internet) to share results of CBPR projects. The Health Planning Council of Northeast Florida has posted several YouTube videos about its "New Town Health Project." The most recent of these reports (http://www.youtube.com/ watch?v=V_JwvChWohA) is in the form of a research video diary, and is meant to inform both community partners and the project's funders.

CBPR practitioners have developed a variety of creative and effective ways to present information. As these examples demonstrate, effective methods for distributing results of research to communities and other nonacademic audiences abound. The critical points to note are that sharing research results will be most effective when the method used is developed directly with the communities involved in the research. Communities may appreciate and be interested in the ideas that archaeologists contribute, but communities must play a central role in developing and writing reports, and also in reviewing and approving them prior to distribution.

One final note about community reports: The process works best when it is not thought of as an *endpoint*. Jackson, Conchelos, and Vigoda (1980) argue that analysis and action operate cyclically, as one leads to the other, and vice versa. The same is true for reporting updates and results to community partners. It should be viewed as part of the process of determining further action, and reports to a community should be used as a time for gaining feedback and input from community members on the research progress, the process followed, and next steps. Considering next steps requires particular attention in a CBPR project because the results of research are meant to be utilized in facilitating positive change within the community.

For archaeologists, the process of reporting research results for academic or cultural resource management (CRM) audiences, usually in academic journals, CRM reports, or at professional conferences, will already be a familiar part of professional training and practice. Reporting results for professional archaeologists in community-based archaeology projects is similar, but the approach to writing, the authorship, and sometimes even the types of data included can be quite different. A foundational point in any discussion about presenting research results has been highlighted by Jackson, Conchelos, and Vigoda (1980, 55) and others: Establishing ownership of data and knowledge and discussing how it will/should be presented is critical so that conferences, academic publications, and other scholarship are not exploiting knowledge or research results. Indeed there are excellent examples to demonstrate that these important intellectual property issues should be discussed from the earliest planning of a research project, and should continue throughout the course of the research.

These are not static conversations that call for a one-time decision to be made conferring permission from community members to archaeologists. The Waanyii women's project (Smith, Morgan, and van der Meer 2003) is an ideal example of how agreements between archaeologists and their community partners regarding curation of knowledge and protection of intellectual property can be determined even before any research begins. The Waanyii women, members of an Australian Aboriginal community, felt it was imperative to keep the data and results of their research private, available only to their community members. In fact, it was agreed that not even all community members should have access to the highly sensitive data and results—it was only the women of the community who would be able to use the information. This was because of cultural protocols that call for protecting this knowledge and requiring that only women have access to it.

The Intellectual Property Issues in Cultural Heritage (IPinCH) project directed by George Nicholas of Simon Fraser University is doing important, groundbreaking research on intellectual property concerns as they arise for Indigenous and local communities around the globe. Members of the IPinCH team have published extensively on these issues (Hollowell and Nicholas 2009; Nicholas 2005; Nicholas et al. 2011), and have produced a knowledge base together with a host of informational web-based material (www.sfu.ca/ipinch/). The critical issues IPinCH are addressing are fundamental for community-based archaeology or, indeed, any research project (CBPR or otherwise) that works with Indigenous peoples. I can't possibly summarize the breadth of work that

IPinCH members have done. But, in brief, I will say with regard to IP issues, that community-based archaeology projects are best when they follow a holistic approach so that discussions about the protection of intellectual property are not relegated to a distinct phase of the research. Open discussion should occur regularly and be integrated into every stage of the research process—as the plan for research is being developed, as data is being collected and analyzed, and as research partners work to interpret results.

JOINT AUTHORSHIP

In CBPR projects, researchers sometimes work with their community partners to jointly author academic reports. Joint authorship may involve a researcher and community members each writing different segments of an article or conference presentation, or it may involve both partners working together to outline the primary points to be included and then sharing writing responsibilities for the entire piece. Writing joint reports can provide an important capacity-building opportunity for some community members, if they don't have a great deal of experience in organizing and presenting data. This was one of the primary reasons for including the Çatalhöyük community interns in the process of giving community reports—they gained experience working with PowerPoint and in public speaking. Although the community interns have not yet worked on any academic reports about the project, this is an area that we've discussed (along with involving interns in future grant writing) and hope to incorporate as we further build the internship program.

One example of a jointly authored archaeology publication is the final report of the Lincoln Burial Mounds (Bakken et al. 2006). It was collaboratively written by archaeologists and members of the local Native American community, and takes seriously the concerns of those in the community. The report is somewhat of a "hybrid publication"—it is meant to be read by the local Native American community, but also includes technical archaeological data about the Lincoln Mounds site for academic audiences. As the authors note, it is meant to raise discussion about the way archaeology can be reported. The report states, "This report is intended to go beyond simply reporting the information—it is intended to have meaning and implications. It is intended to generate contemplation among archaeologists regarding the way they do their work and convey their results, and to generate dialogue between American Indians and archaeologists regarding the issues and politics relating to the 'authentication' and preservation of burial mounds in Minnesota" (2006, 3).

Another example, and one that served as a model for the Lincoln Mounds report, is the "*Kayasochi Kikawenow*: Our Mother from Long Ago" report (Brownlee and Syms 1999)—a hybrid publication that was jointly written by community members and archaeologists with a joint audience in mind. The report details not only the archaeological data, analytical results, and interpretations, but also reports on the research *process*, detailing the First Nations protocols that were followed and the resulting archaeological education work to share the results with K–12 students.

CHALLENGES TO JOINT AUTHORSHIP

In some cases, after working with community partners to decide on the primary points to be presented, researchers will prepare the entire article or presentation and then turn it over to community partners for review and editing. This is the approach I have taken in the majority of the community-based archaeology projects with which I am involved. Joint authorship arrangements can present challenges for scholars who practice CBPR in academic settings, where colleagues as well as tenure and promotion committees often have strict guidelines or requirements for what constitutes research, who appropriate coauthors are, and how publications "count" toward tenure and promotion.

For nontenured faculty members, productivity and authorship matter a great deal, and my community partners are aware that I need to publish about our projects as a requirement of gaining tenure. This hasn't presented any conflicts thus far—community representatives and I discuss my publishing and presentation plans, and I share materials for review before submitting for publication or presenting at a conference. In some cases, we've given joint presentations at conferences; at other times, I've presented our research myself at conferences. I've also been interviewed about our research partnership (Sahota 2010), and have published single-authored articles, but all cases included a careful and thorough process of review and comment from community partners.

This has been much more of a challenge for presenting and publishing results of the Çatalhöyük community-based archaeology project, where distance, lack of computer infrastructure, and literacy barriers all make the process much more difficult. In that case, I have discussed the results of our partnership during community meetings but have not yet been involved in joint authoring conference papers or academic publications. The nature of the communities with which I am working also adds significantly to the challenge of joint authorship and/or collaborative review. Unlike in the Ziibiwing project, where I am working with a CBO, or with the Sullivan County Council, where I work with designated community representatives, the Çatalhöyük community-based archaeology project has required that I do a great deal of community organizing. Yet there are still no designated community members or research teams to collaboratively write with or who I can ask to review the work. This is a challenge that I anticipate many archaeologists will experience, particularly those working in more remote locations and in those without substantial technology infrastructure that would allow for sharing written work electronically or holding working meetings (using Skype, for example).

PAIRED CHAPTER APPROACH

Another possibility for publishing results, and one that I find very interesting and worthy of further consideration and exploration in archaeology, is a "paired chapter" approach. Fortmann (2008b) provides an excellent example of how this can be done well. The edited volume presents the process and results of six CBPR projects in the area of natural resources and conservation. "Professional scientists" and their "civil scientist" (Fortmann 2008a) community partners both contributed chapters discussing their project. This approach works well for reporting on the CBPR process because it provides a rarely heard perspective from the view of community members involved, which can be compared with the academic voice of the "professional scientists." It provides a rare glimpse into the very different perspectives that these groups have on the same project, demonstrating clearly the "positioned objectivity" that Hale (2008) discusses in reference to creating better approximations of reality by involving community members in the research process.

While I think this has a lot of potential and needs to be explored further, I have concerns about how it would work for reporting archaeological research results. Would this serve to further divide the type of knowledge that is being produced, resulting in researchers dismissing chapters written by community partners as non-scholarly, and still giving primacy to the reports written by archaeologists? I wonder how many community partners would want to commit the time and energy to an endeavor that primarily benefits archaeological audiences, and would they feel comfortable writing for this audience? And, from an academic perspective, how would this impact the objectivity/relativism debate within archaeology? Would some see this as accepting "anything goes" versions of archaeological research?

CBPR will always raise these sorts of questions, and it is deeply embedded in debates about objectivity and methodological rigor (Hale 2008). This is an area where further work needs to be done to examine these issues more deeply, and, as with other aspects of CBPR, solutions are likely to be locally contingent and case-specific.

CONFERENCE PRESENTATIONS

Archaeologists commonly use conferences to present the results of their research to the scholarly community. Community members are sometimes invited to professional conferences to present results of their collaborative research. Including community members in conference presentations has several benefits. It allows community members to speak for themselves about the research, its results, and the benefits to their community. It may also provide them with experience and a form of professional training that can be utilized in other contexts. But there are also negative aspects for community members who become involved with this aspect of the research process. There can be language barriers that are both frustrating and pose very real limits on what can be presented. This is particularly so in settings where presenters must follow a strict time limit (often fifteen to twenty minutes) in their presentation. Allowing time for translation, presentation time is cut in half.

Funding is another issue. It can be extremely challenging for community members to find funding for travel and lodging at conferences; add to this the cost of registration fees and membership in the relevant professional association (often a requirement for attending the conference) and the cost can be very prohibitive. Professional associations can take steps to make conferences more accessible to community members.

The World Archaeological Congress (WAC) and the Society for American Archaeology (SAA) have both done so. The WAC provides travel and membership scholarships for Indigenous people that help facilitate them in joining the congress and attending conferences. Within the SAA, Native Americans who are not archaeologists are able to apply to have the SAA membership dues waived as well as their conference registration.

One final challenge for community members that attend archaeology conferences is that few presentations are given in a way that is accessible for nonspecialist audiences. The papers are often very technical and jargon-laden, limiting their utility for community members or others (local teachers, for example) who might wish to access the information. Professional associations and archaeologists can take steps to make conferences more accessible to nonspecialists, including hosting sessions that are geared toward community members, teachers, and the public.

I am certainly not advocating that we exclude communities from participating in archaeological conferences, but I do think we need to carefully consider who benefits from having community members involved. While it is undoubtedly beneficial for archaeologists to hear from community members directly, the benefits for community members in attending professional conferences are not as clear. Inviting community members to present and offering them a clear understanding of what the positive and negative aspects of their involvement will be is important. The choice to attend, and the level of involvement they wish to have, is something for community members to decide.

PRESENTING RESULTS TO DIVERSE PUBLIC AUDIENCES

Beyond community partners and archaeological audiences, community-based archaeology projects will also share research results with a number of public audiences. This takes place in much the same formats as with researcher-driven projects: using site tours, public talks or presentations, and mass media venues such as newspapers or television. Community members often choose to be involved as part of the public face of the project. Research partners will need to work together to determine the types of public education, who will develop materials, and how they will be reviewed and implemented. Although these public education elements often take place once a project is established or after research is completed, it needs to be discussed in the early planning phases of the research to establish who has permission to speak on behalf of the project and what the process will be for sharing data and information publically.

In the case of the Flint Stone Street Ancestral Recovery Project, the issue of presenting results to the public was addressed by Ziibiwing staff and the Saginaw Chippewa Tribal Council (SCTC) prior to the start of the project. In liability release forms developed by Ziibiwing staff and reviewed by the SCTC legal department, all those who volunteered for the project (including tribal members, students, and local residents) also signed an agreement not to speak to the press or in public forums about the work being done on-site. This was done because of the sensitive nature of the ancestral remains being recovered. Ziibiwing wanted to protect the site from vandalism and looting, and also wanted to emphasize to the public the importance of the burial ground for the Anishinabe community.

Managing the public presence of the project was particularly critical since there had been a degree of controversy surrounding it. Prior to the inadvertent discovery of ancestral remains in January 2008, the Stone Street area was part of a gentrification project in which developers tore down abandoned housing and were starting construction on eight new houses. Once the ancestral remains were unearthed, and the extent of the archaeological site was understood, the housing development project came to a halt. Ziibiwing staff worked with the landowners to recover and rebury the remains, and plans are currently being developed (as part of my CBPR graduate methods course) to protect and manage the site, perhaps as a city green space, or an educational museum/visitor center that will teach about the early history of the area.

Because of the strong support for economic development in this very economically depressed area, it was important for Ziibiwing staff to relate the importance of protecting the burial places of their ancestors, and to explain why preserving this site had limited further development. Ziibiwing staff also wanted to ensure that those speaking publically about the ancestors being unearthed in the project were paying the proper respect and reverence required for the remains.

Sharing CBPR research updates and results involves more than interacting with members of the press or mass media outlets; it also includes developing public education materials. The Waapaahsiiki Siipiiwi Mounds Project in southern Indiana demonstrates well how community-based archaeology related to heritage tourism features archaeological education for diverse public audiences. In the Waapaahsiiki project, I worked with members of the Sullivan County American Indian Council and a team of graduate and undergraduate students to survey and map a mound site on land leased to the council by the Indiana-Michigan power company.

The fieldwork was developed and carried out as part of a community-based research methods course I developed and teach. Graduate students enrolled in the course gained practical, hands-on experience with community-based archaeology by working with the SCAIC to develop a management and protection plan for the site. SCAIC community members are developing an interpretive trail to present the research results to the wider public.

The interpretive trail will display mapping and survey data as well as information about the long-term Native American presence in the region, the importance of the mound for the Native American community as a traditional cultural property, and the previous looting that took place at the site. The aim is to allow visitors to learn both the history of the place and the way contemporary Native people engage with the location presently. Interpretive trails are increasingly being used to provide the public with an education experience that is combined with recreation. At every step, the SCAIC members have been actively involved as partners in developing the trail itself and the information that will be presented to the public on panels throughout the trail.

The practices involved in sharing CBPR research are time-consuming. Deciding what's appropriate for which audience and the process of community review and approval all add substantial layers that must be addressed. This can be contrasted with researcher-driven approaches that often involve one individual or a small group of scholars who have a shared "academic culture." Any time more than a single researcher is involved in making decisions of this sort, the process will require significant time commitments. In the case of archaeologists working with community research partners, we can expect the process to take even longer. This is because archaeologists and community members often have different views of what is acceptable, and different points or information they hope to highlight through the research.

This is not to say that there will always be conflict or disagreement, but what can be expected is a learning curve on both sides as to what the partners hope to achieve and what is appropriate. As with other issues in community-based archaeology projects, the time it takes to reach a final decision is likely to lessen as partners gain more experience working together. But as Wiynjorroc et al. (2005) point out, regular, ongoing, open communication between archaeologists and community partners is not only a key to success, but it is also a key part of the basic research ethics of working with communities. Even as trust grows, and an archaeologist develops a familiarity with her community partners and builds a solid understanding of their motives, needs, and concerns, nothing should replace the act of ongoing communication, review, and community approval.

EIGHT · Lasting Effects

> The authors of this book also know that participatory
> research is no enchanted magic wand that can be waved
> over the culture of silence, suddenly restoring the
> desperately needed voice that has been forbidden to rise
> and to be heard. They know very well that the silence is
> not a genetically or ontologically determined condition
> of these women and men but the expression of perverted
> social, economic, and political structures, which can be
> transformed. In the participatory research propounded
> here, the silenced are not just incidental to the curios-
> ity of the researcher but are the masters of inquiry into
> the underlying causes of the events in their world. In
> this context research becomes a means of moving them
> beyond silence into a quest to proclaim the world.
>
> PAULO FREIRE (1993, ix–x)

TAKING ACTION: OUTCOMES
AND BENEFITS

Previous chapters focused on the theoretical engagements with CBPR and the methodological practicalities of applying the approach to archaeology. Taking action is an equally important component of conducting community-based participatory research. "Action" can mean many things within the context of community-based archaeology: It includes creating products that are beneficial for communities and created specifically for their use, and usually involves (re)engaging local communities in the planning and management of their cultural heritage. And, in some cases, action from CBPR projects may also have further-reaching impacts by linking archaeology and cultural tourism endeavors to other socially beneficial endeavors, such as educational programs and even health care opportunities for local communities.

ZIIBIWING'S NAGPRA REPATRIATION RESEARCH

The most direct and meaningful action from the CBPR projects with which I am involved have been positive changes in repatriation policy from the NAGPRA-related research being conducting in partnership with the Ziibiwing Center. For

Native Americans, the issue of repatriation is of critical importance because it involves contemporary human rights and a responsibility we have to our ancestors. This research took on a particular importance because these are my own Anishinabe relatives that we are working to rebury. Repatriation and the right to rebury our ancestors hold great importance for Anishinabe people. It is linked to the resurgence of Anishinabe culture and is part of a wider project of decolonization and community efforts for self-determination. This is evidenced by the role that repatriation plays in the Saginaw Chippewa Indian Tribe's community museum at the Ziibiwing Center. The permanent exhibit, "*Diba Jimooyoung*: Telling Our Story," presents those involved in the work of reburial and repatriation as community warriors and links the work to cultural revitalization and sovereignty.

Ziibiwing's award-winning museum display clearly links repatriation with broader issues such as decolonization and self-determination. It is presented as an important aspect of the civil and human rights activism of the last four decades, but also has ongoing importance for the Saginaw Chippewa Indian Tribal community and for other Native American groups in the state and across the nation. From the outset of this community-based archaeology project, Ziibiwing and its partners within the Michigan Anishinaabek Cultural Preservation and Repatriation Alliance (MACPRA) viewed this research as part of a larger project of action in which the tribes in the state are actively working to facilitate the return of Anishinabe ancestors.

Community members are clear about the benefits of this work, and they actively developed and put forward strategies for achieving their repatriation and reburial goals. Although I was actively involved in the research and contributed extensively to the strategic planning on this issue, it was Ziibiwing's staff and their MACPRA partners who put forth the plan we would follow for actively using the research in repatriation claims. My role was thus not an organizer, but someone who supported the tribe's actions by providing data and comparative information from research on other repatriation cases. In this case, the community partner had clear ideas for how to utilize the research from the outset of the project, and our partnership involved an applied action component from the start.

KÜÇÜKKÖY'S CULTURAL TOURISM

Other CBPR projects may not have such a clear action component at the time they are initiated. The community-based archaeology project I am conducting in Turkey is an excellent example of how a project can develop clear action components well after the initial research has begun. In the case of Çatalhöyük, my initial work with local village residents included multiple discussions during community meetings about possible community-based projects; ways the archaeology at Çatalhöyük could be used for the benefit of the community; and what the long-term benefits might be of a research partnership. Asking residents to consider how archaeology could be used for the community's benefit beyond the short-term economics of seasonal employment revealed an important issue that residents of the local village of Küçükköy wanted to address. In nearly all thirty home interviews with Küçükköy residents during the first stage of the project, one issue continued to surface that the community wanted to take action on: It was believed Çatalhöyük had been sold to the nearby town of Çumra by the previous village manager and the village wanted the site back.

Residents repeatedly explained the details of how Mehmet Kuçukavcılar, Küçükköy's village manager from 1997 to 1999, had "sold Çatalhöyük" to the larger nearby town of Çumra. They claimed this was an action that had stripped the residents of Küçükköy of their right to any connection to or benefit from Çatalhöyük. Residents were outraged about this sale, insisting that the former village manager had profited personally and had not shared any benefit with the village residents. They claimed the sale was completed without community approval, and they demanded that the rights to Çatalhöyük be returned to them.

As described in Chapter 5, researching the details of this sale and what could be done to restore the rights of Küçükköy's residents was the first action the Çatalhöyük community-based research project took on. Yusuf Erdem, Çumra's mayor, assured us that Çatalhöyük was never sold but that this was the result of misinformation and misunderstanding. Our community interns were able to explain to the residents of Küçükköy that they did, indeed, have the right to be involved in researching, managing, and planning the future of Çatalhöyük. This was the first successful outcome of our community-based project. We were able to assure Küçükköy residents that they maintained the rights to engage in planning and decision making about Çatalhöyük. We were also able to assure them that they had every legal right to provide input on tourism and management decisions that will impact their community tremendously in the coming decades.

ARCHAEOLOGICAL COMMUNITY THEATER AT ÇATALHÖYÜK

Once the issue of community rights to the site was settled, we were able to shift focus toward planning several of the community-based projects that community members had suggested during home interviews. Most suggestions involved community-based education about the archaeological knowledge being created on-site, but there were also suggestions related to site planning and management as well as local cultural tourism projects. One groundbreaking project that the community suggested and that is currently being carried out (and was described in an earlier chapter) involves development of an archaeological community theater troupe (Atalay 2010).

As detailed in Chapter 6, local residents first proposed developing a community theater program focused around archaeology as a way to help educate the local children about Çatalhöyük. Küçükköy's school principal suggested that Çatalhöyük be the focus of the village's annual 23 Nisan (Children's Day Festival) performance. From conversations with local residents, the idea quickly grew to developing a community archaeology theater group that could travel around Turkey, giving performances about all the major archaeological sites in Turkey.

Several months after the idea was proposed, Serdar Bilis, a Turkish theater producer who lives in London, became involved and started planning community workshops in which children would both develop drama skills and help draft a script about past and contemporary life at Çatalhöyük. The goal of the project is to enable members of the local community to work together with archaeologists to present the archaeological past and contemporary cultural heritage of Çatalhöyük creatively, through drama. Community members constructed scenes that might have taken place at the site 9,000 years ago, and presented scenerios for the site's future that involve preservation and management.

To our knowledge, this is one of the first community-based archaeological theater program ever developed (certainly the first in Turkey). Because it is the first of its kind, we plan to document our process by shooting a "fly on the wall" documentary that charts the story of this community constructing and performing the archaeological theater program. We are currently preparing to post short versions of the film on Youtube, and plan to produce a DVD-length version for distribution in Turkey, the United Kingdom, and the United States.

For the Küçükköy community, the project has significance in terms of connecting local village residents with the archaeological past while simultaneously allowing them to express *their* values, interests, and concerns about the archaeology at Çatalhöyük. The hope is that it will eventually provide residents with the chance to travel, nationally and internationally, and raise both awareness and funds for their community. It also provides a renewable attraction for visiting tourists to learn about the site.

Through this community theater project, as well as through other discussions about the future planning and use of the site, community members began to consider ways they might engage with the Çatalhöyük project to provide the community with much-needed critical services that would improve daily life in their village. These included plans to utilize the Çatalhöyük dig house buildings in the off-season as a school for girls and to house a small health clinic. Community members also discussed conducting research that would facilitate their involvement in Çatalhöyük's tourism planning. They are aware of discussions at the regional and national level for a Çatalhöyük museum to be built locally, but have only been very minimally involved in the discussions. They want to partner in doing comparative research on heritage management and cultural tourism models that will help Küçükköy put forward a convincing plan for building the museum in the village.

Preliminarily, residents are interested in combining the museum with a hotel and community center. Konya, the nearest city, and the nearby town of Çumra also both have reasons for wanting the museum to be built in their vicinity. Although a Küçükköy location makes sense because of the village's close proximity to Çatalhöyük, both Konya and Çumra have more existing facilities and infrastructure to support this sort of tourism and development. The Küçükköy community is not naïve about its situation and the limited power it holds in the arena of economic development, yet residents are motivated to partner in research so that they can increase their knowledge and experience in tourism and planning. They are keenly aware of how this knowledge will translate into respect and thus decision-making power.

These projects demonstrate how archaeological data or knowledge might be effectively applied to address heritage management concerns and broader social issues. All are complicated and involve multiple stakeholders, many of whom exert powerful control over what happens at Çatalhöyük and in the local region. In most of these circumstances, the local community wanted the archaeologists on-site, particularly the site director, Ian Hodder, to become actively involved in advocating for them and their positions. They recognized the power that Dr. Hodder's influence would have in local, regional, and national political decision making, and hoped to use his influence to their advantage to change the social inequalities present. Residents hope this will allow them to engage substantively with the decisions over tourism and heritage planning in their community.

At this point, the efforts of our community-based archaeology project to increase local engagement and decision-making power appear to be effective, to some extent. As a result of the CBPR project at Çatalhöyük, residents have begun forming a local, village-level heritage committee (*kurul*). Larger political entities such as towns and cities have heritage committees, and these have an active voice in decision making for issues related to heritage planning and archaeology. Forming such a committee at the village level and providing research partnership opportunities that will empower local residents with knowledge, data, and experience is one example of the way this community-based archaeology project benefits the community in ways that have long-term impact and are sustainable without further input from archaeologists.

PROTECTING INTELLECTUAL PROPERTY
AT THE SANILAC PETROGLYPHS

Two other community-based archaeology projects with which I am involved benefit the community partner through community-driven development at archaeological sites. One example is the intellectual property project at the *ezhibiigadek asin* site in Sanilac, Michigan. Community benefits in this project involve protecting both the intellectual knowledge associated with the site and the physical stone that contains over 100 petroglyphs. Once completed, this project will produce a tribal management plan that explicitly defines how to protect the knowledge and teachings held in the petroglyphs in culturally appropriate ways. It will lay out what can be shared publically and what must remain private for community and ceremonial use. How to archive the knowledge held in the stones is also being addressed through our research partnership.

The Saginaw Chippewa Indian Tribe will then be able to use this knowledge to guide the Michigan Department of Natural Resources in its curation and care practices. In terms of protecting the physical site, our research will be used to help determine if the petroglyphs are best preserved through continued use. Figures 18 and 19 show Anishinabe elders, tribal members, and local Sanilac residents working together to follow Anishinabe cultural protocols of care at the site. Water is placed with cedar, a sacred plant, and used to cleanse the petroglyphs during a summer solstice ceremony. This "cedar bath" is part of an important cultural protocol that brings the teachings etched in the stone into contact with water. The process is contrary to the archaeological protocols of preservation and care, which instructs that the petroglyphs should be touched as little as possible. The shelter over the site has kept water, an important element of the Anishinabe sacred protocols, out of contact with the petroglyphs.

FIGURE 18.
Ojibwe elder George Martin works with tribal members and youth to prepare a "cedar bath" for the ezhibiigadek asin-Sanilac petroglyph site.

Our community-based archaeology project is helping to address the issue of how these two conflicting systems of care and preservation can be reconciled. It is also addressing other challenging questions: Should the petroglyphs be re-etched? Or should new teachings be added in the form of new petroglyph inscriptions? This project raises the issue of what protecting a site (and the knowledge held within it) means to Anishinabe people. Cultural protocols of this sort have not been documented in the archaeological literature. The project is producing new, valuable knowledge that tribal leaders can utilize in the future management, care, and use of this site and others.

HERITAGE TOURISM AND PUBLIC EDUCATION IN INDIANA

Similarly, the Waapaahsiiki Siipiiwi Mounds Project conducted in partnership with the Sullivan County American Indian Council is providing the Sullivan County Native American community with a site map and survey data that will be utilized

FIGURE 19.
Community members work together to follow a cultural
protocol of cleansing during a summer solstice ceremony at the
ezhibiigadek asin-Sanilac Petroglyph site.

on panels as part of a community-developed interpretive trail project. Once completed, the trail will provide a usable green space that the public can visit to learn
about the history and culture of Native people in the area. Educating the public
about the history and contemporary experiences of Native Americans in Indiana
is a primary part of the council's mission.

The issue of Native invisibility is particularly challenging in Indiana, because
although the state is home to more than 60,000 Native Americans, it has only one
federally recognized tribe within its boundaries, the Pokagon Band of Pottawatomi.
Other tribes had a historical presence in the state, but were removed to other states.
The Miami Nation of Indiana still maintains a presence in the state, and has struggled for years to obtain federal recognition, without success. An important goal of
the Sullivan County American Indian Council is to inform and educate the public about the continued Native presence in the state, and the important and long-
standing history of Indiana's Native people.

The archaeological mapping and survey project at the Waapaahsiiki Siipiiwi mound contributes to this goal by linking the precontact past, the historic period, and contemporary times in an engaging outdoor venue. Through the interpretive trail, the mound itself is being recorded and studied for the first time, and the intertribal Native American community that resides in the county where the mound is located now plays an important role in caring for and managing the site. The Sullivan County American Indian Council is able to simultaneously interpret and protect the site, while they share it with the larger nonnative community. A long-term goal of this CBPR partnership is to create a Native community youth center on the grounds near the Waapaahsiiki Siipiiwi mound site that can be used for ceremonies, language revitalization, and cultural education. This project utilizes archaeology to actively link the Native past with the present and provides the Waapaahsiiki Siipiiwi mound a protected place in the cultural landscape of southern Indiana.

Both the Sanilac Intellectual Property Project and the Waapaahsiiki Siipiiwi Interpretive Trail research provide benefits to others beyond the community partners. Both projects involve sharing research and a cultural heritage location with the wider public. As a result of our work at the Sanilac site, the Ziibiwing Center is developing a long-term tribal management plan to ensure the petroglyphs will be protected and well cared for so that the public can learn more about the teachings presented there. Currently, archaeologists know little about the meaning of the petroglyphs. Once our project is complete, the teachings that are shared publically will be presented through new signage and educational materials.

The Ziibiwing Center has also received grant funding to write and publish a children's bilingual (English/Anishinabemowin) book about the Sanilac site that both Native and nonnative families can enjoy. The local nonnative community has also been invited to join in annual spring solstice ceremonies to learn traditional methods of curation and care of the site from tribal spiritual leaders. Similarly, through the interpretive trails project at Waapaahsiiki Siipiiwi, a range of public audiences will benefit from the research our project produces since it will be presented on the interpretive panels found throughout the trail.

BUILDING CAPACITY

Along with the positive outcomes and action taken to restore the decision-making power of communities in managing and investigating their own past and cultural heritage, these examples of community-based archaeology also positively impacted those involved by building greater community capacity for research, heritage management, and cultural tourism. Community capacity building will be fostered differently in every CBPR project. Some may increase literacy (Freire 1970) or grant writing proficiency (Gaventa 1980; Kerber 2008); in others, community-organizing practices may be learned or strengthened or economically focused development skills may be enhanced. Some of these may seem small or insignificant, but they can have a considerable impact in the long term. Farmers who were community partners in an agricultural project in Honduras (Corea et al. 2008) discuss their initial fear of speaking publically, and explain how their participation as research partners helped them increase capacity to speak in front of others. Seema Arora-Jonsson and the women with whom she partnered on a forestry management CBPR partnership in Sweden, noted that their research together "enabled us to realize that our experiences and learning stretched beyond the time of inquiry. We carry the lessons with us in our work, in the village, in academia, and in everyday life" (Arora-Jonsson 2008, 126).

CBPR can build capacity for the researcher and for her community research partners in a wide spectrum of ways. Here I've touched upon some of the capacity-building effects that communities experienced through our research partnerships. The impacts of community-based archaeology will vary in each project. Every community will have different needs and will develop its own ways of addressing those in a CBPR partnership. And as Arora-Jonsson touched upon in the previous quote, capacity building doesn't only take place for community partners. CBPR builds different sorts of capacity in academic settings.

Many CBPR practitioners describe the skills they learn through conducting research with communities and how this impacts their lives in positive ways. Some learn to engage with and support their own communities better; others gain valuable experience for community organizing. Brydon-Miller (1993), who's engaged in research partnerships with disabled communities, found that her work in CBPR was not only important for her professional life, but that it also had a large impact on her personal life. She argues that CBPR provides a bridge for blending the two, something she believes is important for academics. "We must continue to follow examples set by Paulo Freire, Myles Horton, and others who have explicitly made their professional and political lives one. Political activity must be recognized as an integral part of professional training and practice. We must insist on becoming involved members of our communities, not in addition to our practice as social scientists but as a critical component of that work" (1993, 142). These are also benefits we provide to our students as we introduce them to local social and political activism through their training and experiences in community-based archaeology projects (Rossen 2008).

BENEFITS TO ARCHAEOLOGY

Beyond the benefits that social scientists gain more broadly, community-based archaeology projects bring specific benefits to the archaeological community. Community partnerships can provide knowledge that was previously unknown, from oral histories and other forms of traditional knowledge, as the Sanilac intellectual property project demonstrates so well. CBPR brings a different shape to archaeological research through the development of new and diverse lines of inquiry, framing questions from different standpoints or places of reference. It can also enhance our understanding of shared stewardship and concerns over global and local heritage issues. This can impact the archaeological community in positive ways by pushing the trajectory of research in new directions. This often entails creating projects and investigations that might never have existed otherwise. Such is the case in the Waapaahsiiki Siipiiwi mound project. The mound is on private land, owned by Indiana-Michigan Power. Prior to our community-based archaeology project, the mound had never been recorded, studied, or registered with the State Archaeologist's Office. Through our partnership with the Sullivan County American Indian Council, the archaeological community gained access to this privately owned site that may have otherwise gone unstudied.

The reciprocal nature of CBPR work means that archaeologists are able to also pursue their own research interests while simultaneously working on projects that are based in communities and designed to meet community needs. Both archaeologists and community members can reap benefits from the research; however, any discussion of a proposed research partnership should involve a frank discussion about the benefits of the project during which the researcher and community members discuss how each expect to benefit. Unanticipated benefits are also likely to arise, on both sides, and these should be discussed openly as part of the project's evaluation. Identifying the benefits that partners feel they achieved through the research helps to highlight where each places value and the ways the goals and outcomes can satisfy the needs of researchers and community members simultaneously. This may, in turn, help to generate ideas for further research and an understanding of where the interests of communities and archaeologists overlap.

Beyond the specific benefits of individual projects, CBPR benefits the field of archaeology more broadly. It brings a much-needed decolonizing practice to the discipline that allows the field to grow in new and exciting ways. Growth can be challenging, and sometimes painful, but the resulting changes for the discipline are substantial. Processual archaeology led archaeologists to give greater detail to research design, and it brought an incredible range of interdisciplinary scientific approaches to the discipline. Feminist archaeologists improved the discipline by asking us to give faces to the people of the past, or at least to begin to recognize that our models included only "faceless blobs" that were implicitly male (and presumably heterosexual). The reflexive approach and other postprocessual theories benefited archaeology by demonstrating that our data are theory-laden and our research is affected by the social context within which it is created. Archaeologists now consider the agency of people in the past, and they are searching for better models to understand the symbolism and ritual that influenced people's decisions, even if it is difficult or impossible to fully understand. Each step and new approach benefits our discipline because it brings richer, deeper understandings of the past.

DECOLONIZING ARCHAEOLOGY

Drawing on theoretical arguments and methodologies in Native American and Indigenous studies as well as a history of practice in a range of other disciplines, CBPR benefits archaeology by providing a methodology that moves the discussion of decolonizing archaeology forward. It fills a methodological gap—one that exists within the space of critical discussions about the colonial nature of archaeological practice in the past and the potential of a decolonized practice for the future. CBPR provides a practical methodological solution for archaeology so that the discipline can finally move beyond its historical legacy of colonial practice and into a new era of shared responsibility to cultural heritage. And, as Silliman and Dring (2008) have pointed out, these are benefits that we share with the coming generations of students that we have the responsibility to train. In my view, we have a growing body of evidence to demonstrate that the experiences and skills students learn in the process and methodology of community-based archaeology are critical for their future professional careers as archaeologists. And, as Silliman and Dring (2008) argue quite persuasively, an effective archaeology education requires knowledge in archaeology methods as well as in *methodology*—which "involves examining the decisions behind certain methods and, more important, the implications of using those methods" (2008, 79).

In her work on feminist theory, bell hooks (2004) has argued that both males and females are damaged by patriarchy. While hooks recognizes that males benefit immensely from the power and privilege they garner in a male-dominated society, she also discusses the ways that both males and females suffer as a result of patriarchy, although in markedly different ways. Parallels with hooks's arguments about patriarchy can be drawn with colonization broadly, and the situation in archaeology specifically. Those in a position of power clearly benefit from colonial practices, but colonization has effects that are damaging to all involved. Its impacts are undoubtedly very different for those who have power and those who have lost it through the historical legacy of colonization, but there are damaging aspects of colonial practices that affect all involved.

For over a century, archaeologists have held power and control over research-ing, interpreting, and managing archaeological sites and materials, often disen-franchising indigenous and local communities from having the ability to manage and interpret their own histories and heritage in the process. As hooks argues in her research about changing the power structure to end patriarchy, a primary step forward is to acknowledge the way those who hold power are complicit in main-taining their place of privilege and control. It is also critical that those with power and privilege acknowledge the damaging impact of colonial research practices. In reference to such acknowledgment in relation to ending patriarchy, hooks states, "Clearly we cannot dismantle a system as long as we engage in collective denial about its impact on our lives" (hooks 2004, 24). The same is true in efforts to decolonize archaeology. Recognizing the ways that colonial practices and scientific privilege within archaeology both disenfranchises others from their own heritage and how they negatively impact the richness and completeness of knowledge that can be gained about life in the past is a critical step forward.

Most archaeologists would agree that disenfranchising Indigenous people and local communities from their heritage is not desirable. Yet even with this recogni-tion, it is challenging to identify and acknowledge where our *own* archaeological research practices work to maintain and perpetuate our power and control over the archaeological past at the expense of disenfranchising others. It is a step further yet to recognize the ways this is damaging to our communities and ourselves on a per-sonal level, and to our profession in terms of limiting knowledge and understandings about the past. Community-based archaeology provides a practical methodology through which archaeologists can actively work to decolonize their own research practices. Even when using a CBPR methodology, power imbalances will still exist between archaeologists and Indigenous and local community partners. However, through this approach to research, archaeologists who work with Indigenous and local communities can make a substantive effort to become increasingly aware of those disparities and actively foster greater equity in research, management, and use related to archaeological places and materials.

In such a context, communities can build greater capacity for research while they also take action to become further involved in the management of their heritage. This action is not something archaeologists impose based on what they might feel is best for a community, but on what is internally fueled and structured. Because the research is community-based with buy-in from the start, the results are more likely to have lasting, substantive impact and be sustainable.

CBPR helps create a more sustainable future for archaeology in another way. It lends to a greater change in academic practice as it contributes to producing scholars and students who are engaged citizens, a point alluded to earlier in this chapter. Richard Couto squarely places CBPR as a foundational cornerstone of what he calls a "scholarship of engagement" (2003, xiii). In working to establish a stronger contemporary relevance for archaeology, CBPR has an important contribution to make because it brings a practice of social responsibility into the field of archaeology. Couto also notes that, "We have had to reassert . . . that research on and about members of a community, especially a low-income community and without accountability to the members of that group, may reproduce and legitimate existing social arrangements of injustice and oppression" (2003, xiv).

When applied to archaeology, CBPR provides a mechanism through which archaeology can move beyond disciplinary boundaries and limitations of conventional research methods that can be oppressive for communities. Through my own community-based archaeology projects and the examples I've provided of others' research, I've demonstrated that archaeology can utilize CBPR to move beyond its colonial past to create a practice that produces rigorous research, while at the same time contributing to practices of social justice. Engaging communities—many of whom ultimately fund archaeological research—in the process of archaeological knowledge creation, contributes to the relevance of archaeology and to its sustainability over the long term.

EVALUATION AND MEASURES OF SUCCESS

Having an article published in a peer-reviewed journal, receiving positive book reviews, and receiving tenure are all typical goals and successes of academic researchers. These are legitimate methods of evaluating research, and are important measures of a successful research outcome. In some CBPR partnerships, community goals and measures of success may be directly in line with those of academics, and a community may wish to strive for publications and other objectives that are more traditional markers of success in the scholarly community. But quite often, communities have very different goals and measures of success for an archaeology project than their archaeologist partners. Evaluating a project and measuring its success are important aspects of community-based archaeology projects. This involves a process that begins early and is ongoing.

Wondolleck and Yaffee (2000) who conducted a study of successful collaborative projects in natural resource management clearly lay out their method of determining a successful project. They allowed success to be determined by the partners involved: "We defined success largely in terms of the perceptions of the people involved in these efforts. If an effort was viewed successful by participants from across the spectrum of involved interests, we took their word for it and worked to understand why they perceived it as a success" (2000, xiii). This is a useful guideline to follow in community-based archaeology as well. Each research partner may have very different ideas of success, but the primary goal is for each partner to be satisfied with the outcome and to feel the project was successful.

It is also important to understand what each partner felt made the project a success. Wondolleck and Yaffee's research relates specifically to this point: They wanted to know why a case was deemed successful in the several hundred collaborative projects they studied over a fifteen-year period. The cases they examined were not necessarily community-based or participatory but involved government agencies working collaboratively with groups outside the agency in the area of natural resource management. In many cases, what they found was quite an uncomplicated explanation of what constituted success: It was often simply that "people were working together, and that alone represented a tremendous step forward" (2000, xiii). This may similarly be the case with a great deal of community-based archaeology projects. Having communities directly involved in archaeological research and fostering opportunities for both partners to investigate the past together may be a major step forward for some communities, and that alone may be a positive sign of an effective and successful project.

However, for other communities, particularly those that have previously worked collaboratively to a greater or lesser degree with archaeologists, a CBPR partnership may be an entirely different type of collaboration, and the expectations for what constitutes success might be quite different. Many Native American communities, for example, have a historical relationship of consulting with museums and archaeologists on NAGPRA-related research. Many have a consultative relationship that is mandated by law.

While NAGPRA requires tribes to consult to determine cultural affiliation of human remains, the law does not require that museums or federal agencies follow the suggestions or input of tribes in making their determinations of cultural affiliation or in other aspects of preparing their NAGPRA summaries and inventories. As a result, although Native American groups may have a working relationship with an archaeologist or museum professional, in situations where there is disagreement between tribes and museums or federal agencies, the outcome may be quite disappointing to the community. In such a case, the act of simply "working together," as described by Wondolleck and Yaffee, may not be viewed as a successful outcome from the community's perspective. Success from a community's point of view in a CBPR project is much more likely to be measured by how substantive the power sharing was and whether the community was able to obtain (or regain) their sense of involvement and control in managing and interpreting their own heritage and history.

Two things are fundamental when considering evaluation and measures of success in CBPR projects: The first is that evaluation is not something that is only conducted once the project is *completed*. CBPR projects involve regular review, conversation, and ongoing evaluation between partners about what is working and what is not. Setting up parameters for this at the start of the project is advisable so that partners can expect to regularly evaluate and assess their progress. This can be done through face-to-face meetings, informally over email, or even using a quick evaluation form that partners codevelop at the start of the project. Such ongoing evaluations need not be lengthy or time-consuming, but they should incorporate a means by which partners are encouraged to think critically about what is working and where improvements need to be made.

In the community-based archaeology projects with which I am involved, regular, informal conversations with community partners are central. I regularly ask directly how the partners feel the project is going. When working with Ziibiwing and the Sullivan County American Indian Council, I have asked community members to also provide feedback on how students in my community-based research methods courses have performed as research partners.

Other CBPR practitioners have developed more formal approaches to evaluation. De Wit and Gianotten (1980) conducted evaluations six times per year as part of regular community meetings. Community members (Corea et al. 2008; Collins Cruz, and Smith 2008) have developed evaluation strategies that involve recording a discussion of the project's progress and then having an outside person act as an editor to organize and string together their comments and feedback to create written progress reports.

The second important point in relation to evaluating and measuring success of CBPR projects is that the starting assumption should be that adjustments and improvements *will* need to be made. When the expectation is that regular adjustments to the research design and process will be needed, then the project remains flexible, leaving room for any modifications to be seen in a positive light.

One final and important point to keep in mind when considering what a successful CBPR project will look like involves the length of the research partnership. Certainly relationships with a community grow and strengthen as research partners continue to develop and carry out CBPR projects. However, partnerships do not necessarily need to involve multiple or long-term projects to be considered successful. Some community partnerships will only be short-term. They may include one project or several very short projects, with new possibilities that crop up intermittently. Still, these are successful because both the needs of the community and researcher are met.

This may particularly be the case in projects that have a strong community capacity-building aspect. The end of the partnership in such cases may actually be the best indicator of success because it demonstrates that the community capacity was built to such an extent that the community is prepared to develop and carry out its own research. One example that illustrates this is the repatriation research I conducted in partnership with the Ziibiwing Center. The staff at the center was very involved in all aspects of the research, and has since started researching and preparing NAGPRA claims without the help of an archaeologist or other research consultant.

Another possible scenario is that archaeologists, who have developed community-based archaeology projects with community partners and worked closely with them, may come to think of the research relationship in exclusive terms. They may begin to consider a group as "their" community. Certainly developing a strong professional relationship with the community partner is a positive outcome of CBPR work. However, it is problematic if this develops into a form of exclusivity that limits a community's options for partnering with other researchers.

It can be a positive indicator of success when a community seeks out partnerships with other researchers, either for conducting further archaeology projects or for community-based research in other areas. A community may want to partner on new projects with an archaeologist who has expertise or experience in other areas, or a community may choose to focus its attention and resources on research in another field.

Contributing to the capacity building that allows such research to happen is certainly a mark of a successful project, and not an indication of failure. For some communities, engaging in an ongoing state of research is not desirable. There may be a natural end to their involvement or desire to actively pursue archaeological projects or research of other sorts. Certainly this can come as a disappointment, but it shouldn't be considered an indication that the partnership was not a success. Substantive and ongoing communication between research partners should be enough so that the final stages of a community-based archaeology project allow for a closing process that is acceptable for all partners.

CHALLENGES

As Paulo Freire notes in the quote that opens this chapter, CBPR is "no enchanted magic wand." It is difficult and challenging work to conduct research in this way. There are numerous challenges involved in both being participatory and community-based. Community-based archaeology sits centrally in the midst of the oft-asked question about who owns the past. Of course we know that the deeper, more pertinent questions are about who controls, has access to, builds knowledge about, and has the ability to ask and answer questions about the many pasts that erupt in our present, contemporary world. These issues are complex, and the challenges that surround community-based archaeology are intricate and multifaceted. I'm providing only a limited discussion in this section focused specifically on the challenges of community-based archaeology, but throughout this book I have presented complexities and difficult issues that archaeologists and communities will likely face when they enter into community-based and participatory research partnerships. Certainly, each project will face its own set of unique challenges. Some of these are easily solved, and others will linger without resolution.

Although I cannot anticipate the specifics of all challenges to be faced when conducting community-based archaeology, to move this methodology forward it is critical that challenges—both resolved and unresolved—be included in research reports and publications. Both scholars and community partners may be reticent to call attention to challenges, but they certainly should not be viewed as failures. I am certain that I avoided making disastrous mistakes by learning from the disappointing outcomes and missteps of others, and many of my own mistakes could have likely been avoided had others been more willing to discuss and share the challenges they faced, and their attempts to overcome them.

COMMUNITY BUY-IN, PARTICIPATION

One of the measures of success of a CBPR project is how well the leadership and responsibility for the project become dispersed within the community (de Wit and

Gianotten 1980). Long (2008) addresses this point in his water preservation work with the White Mountain Apache. He discusses the importance of creating research that future generations can build on and follow. For him, it is important not to think of a project as an end in itself, but to think of it as a link in a long process.

This relates to an important concern that must be addressed with CBPR: What factors are important in developing a community-based project to ensure that it will be sustainable? A critical component here is the issue of community "buy-in." Community members who partnered with an environmental scientist on a CBPR project to study plant-harvesting practices in the Pacific Northwest demonstrate repeatedly that they did not have a commitment to the research, which made it diffi-cult for them to care about the results (Collins Cruz, and Smith 2008). Ballard (2008) points out many reasons for this, including that some only participated to make money; others felt pressure from community leaders to participate. The harvesters were not local and had no long-term commitment to the area. The fatal flaw here was that the research was participatory, but it was not community-based. The project did not address the needs of the community in a way that inspired them to engage further.

Nonetheless, even in situations where communities *are* involved in planning the research and they *do* care about the outcomes, significant challenges can remain. CBPR projects sometimes make the mistake of involving just a few individuals. Working with a broad base of individuals will help to keep some members of the community from undermining the project (Long 2008). But in some situations, several that I've documented in previous chapters, factions within communities (Brydon-Miller 1993) or challenges of working with multiple communities can create problems that are difficult to overcome (Schensul, Berg, and Williamson 2009). CBPR researchers have pointed to the ways that women and working-class community members are sometimes excluded from projects. Sometimes, as in my experience with the Çatalhöyük community-based archaeology project, this exclu-sion is intentional and can raise serious ethical dilemmas for a researcher.

Jackson, Conchelos, and Vigoda (1980) point to another issue that may limit community participation—the high price that community members sometimes pay for CBPR projects, in terms of volunteer labor, space provided for meetings, and other costs. In rare cases, members may even pay with their lives for participating in CBPR projects (Nagar and Singh 2010).

TIMING

One of the primary challenges I faced in planning and conducting the five community-based archaeology projects discussed in this book was the issue of timing and the pace of research. This is a common concern for those involved in CBPR. From the point of view of a researcher, CBPR projects take a significantly greater amount of time to carry out than conventional projects. This is partly because multiple people are involved in decision making, but also because of the different schedules community and research partners follow and the multiple commitments and pressures experienced by those in each community.

In the case of Çatalhöyük, timing issues were related to seasonal pressures felt by local community members. Archaeological fieldwork at Çatalhöyük is conducted each summer, which is the busiest time of the year for residents in the rural, farming community of Küçükköy. Attending community meetings to learn about and become involved as partners in a research project was a challenge for community members because their daily commitments during the summer months involve completing critical tasks that must take priority. As a result, community meetings needed to be scheduled around the cow milking so that women could attend. Men and many younger residents often worked in the fields until very late each night; to accommodate this, we had to schedule house visits that often coincided with meal and prayer times. Community members had a great deal more available time in the late fall, winter, and early spring, but I was not able to work in the community during these times because of my teaching and work commitments. For some projects, these timing conflicts can be fatal. Merrifield (1993) notes that communities can become frustrated with university timelines and the slow pace of action, and it may cause them to lose excitement and to feel a lack of ownership over the research.

Timing challenges also involve the pace at which research is carried out. Community-based research generally proceeds at a much slower pace than traditional research. Because multiple partners are involved, it can take a great deal of time to communicate information, receive input, and develop a plan of action. This is particularly true at the outset of a project, during the early planning and development phases.

Once a protocol or operating practice is established, things often occur at a somewhat faster pace. However, CBPR projects rarely maintain a pace comparable to conventional research practices. This is because decision making is not done by a single individual but rather involves multiple people, many of whom have a number of competing priorities. Communities may be very committed to the research project and very diligent and conscientious in their work as research partners, yet they are not full-time researchers and are often faced with many competing claims on their time (Comstock and Fox 1993). The research project may not always remain at the immediate top of their priority list, and decisions or activities relating to the research project may temporarily take a backseat to make room for more immediate needs facing community partners.

Barndt (1980) has also pointed out a difficult reality. People's priorities are often focused on survival and entertainment rather than research or the challenges of social change. Of course, academic researchers also have multiple, competing claims for their time; they may have to slow their pace and activity level related to their research during the academic year, when teaching and service commitments often eat up large amounts of time. In the case of Çatalhöyük, these two circumstances combined in an unfortunate way so that during my busiest times (September through April), the community members had a great deal of free time they could have devoted to aspects of the project. And I was only able to be in their community and commit full-time to developing and conducting our shared research during their busiest times (May through August).

Timing is also a major challenge for students and junior faculty who want to conduct CBPR. Heany discusses how the academic time frame impacts graduate students. He notes, "A doctoral student working on a dissertation cannot afford the luxury of working with a community on the community's timetable and with the possibility that the project will be called off or take on a different set of goals—in effect, become a different project" (Heany 1993, 45). He also notes that doctoral committees often have a quite rigid set of expectations in terms of methods and results that limit the input community members can have.

These concerns are not only for graduate students, but also similarly affect junior faculty who are attempting to obtain tenure. Tenure clocks are built around standard research timelines, and CBPR takes substantially more time to get started and also more time to complete. As an untenured faculty member, I certainly face these pressures and understand firsthand the constraints. My approach was to utilize a postdoctoral fellowship to begin my initial community-based archaeology projects, prior to applying for tenure-track positions that would initiate a tenure clock.

FUNDING AGENCIES

I am very thankful that the National Science Foundation (NSF) was supportive of my proposed community-based archaeology projects. However, not all granting agencies are, and those that are may not be familiar with CBPR methods and the added time, costs, community review procedures, and different obligations to produce products that benefit a community. CBPR requires long-term commitment, but funding is usually short-term and is difficult to sustain (Humphries et al. 2008). This creates real tensions for doing CBPR.

Another related issue in dealing with funding agencies that are unfamiliar with CBPR methods is that they are not accustomed to research questions being developed by partners in a community, most of whom are not trained "experts," and who have different standards for success. Expectations and intention of the granting agency can have a direct effect on how a project is framed and what can be expected from the outcome (Bryceson, Manicom, and Kassam 1980).

One possible solution is to take a two-phased approach to funding. Apply for preliminary funds to work with a community to develop research questions, and once the questions have been developed, the archaeologist and community partners can work together to apply for monies to fund the joint project. Also, granting agencies such as the NSF expect applicants to explain the "broader impacts" of research, and a scholar engaged in CBPR can use this section to explain in further detail the benefits of CBPR to nonacademic audiences.

CHALLENGES FOR TENURE-TRACK FACULTY

An important issue that tenure-stream faculty will face when doing CBPR involves the expectations of the university (which will predominantly take the form of the university tenure review and promotion committees) with regards to the independent nature of scholarly research. Heany (1993, 45) highlights this point, noting that university-based research must "be attributable to an individual (or a small group of individuals)." He states, "Participatory research . . . diffuses responsibility for its outcomes and makes recognition of an individual's contribution difficult and frequently impossible."

In terms of tenure and promotion of faculty who engage in CBPR, a growing number of packets or guidelines is now in circulation that university administrators and CBPR scholars can utilize to help develop and evaluate a tenure case that involves CBPR.

University human-subjects protocols and IRB reviews can also present challenges for CBPR projects, because it is rarely practical to list an entire community as a "research partner." Partners most actively working with a researcher may be required to take several hours of ethics training before any research can begin. This was the situation I faced with the Sanilac Petroglyph project, and the IRB process was held up considerably as a result. This requirement can pose real challenges for some community partners with low levels of literacy, those who don't have computer access, or non-English speakers. In situations where sensitive research topics are being examined, community partners may not want to have their name recorded as a partner on official university documents. On the positive side, ethics review boards may be open to learning about CBPR methods and how community partnerships will impact the IRB review process. Some are aware of community IRBs and support the need for projects to first be vetted there. These are not insurmountable problems, but do require consideration.

In addressing all of these challenges, Freire's words about the need to problemitize the future come to mind. While the system may not currently be adequately organized to address a CBPR method, it does not mean the procedures are not worth altering. Institutions and regulations shift precisely because of changes in practice. CBPR is becoming increasingly utilized and is a recognized part of scholarship within multiple social science, humanities, and medical fields. The fact that a good deal of public health research now takes a CBPR approach certainly helps the methodology to be viewed as legitimate, and that in turn helps scholars who want to conduct CBPR to do so without feeling as if they need to tackle every aspect of the institutional research procedure alone.

Explaining what CBPR *is* in grant applications, and often in IRB requests, will be an important component of any application for funds and in IRB protocols. It is important to rely on previous studies to tell the story of CBPR and demonstrate its legitimacy. Some who review IRB protocols or grant applications may see CBPR as problematic, but it's more likely that they are simply not familiar with it. As a matter of course, it's wise to provide funders with the information they need to assess the benefits of the approach. Providing examples from other projects and other disciplines that successfully utilize the methodology will strengthen a CBPR proposal.

EFFECTIVE COMMUNICATION

Timing difficulties are often compounded by challenges brought about by methods of communication. Of primary concern is the language barrier. While many archaeologists can speak the local language where they work, this is not always the case. The level of language competency needed to conduct a conventional archaeology project may not be particularly high. However, that is not the case with community-based archaeology projects since working in direct and close partnership with community members requires a high proficiency in the local language(s), or the regular use of interpreters. This is an ever-present problem in the community-based archaeology project at Çatalhöyük. My Turkish language skills are strong, but I don't consider myself fluent. And the majority of the 100+-person team of archaeologists working on-site struggle with speaking Turkish—this was something that posed an immediate and lasting problem for developing and sustaining collaborative research projects between the members of the archaeology team and the local community. The success of the Çatalhöyük community-based archaeology project has been due in large part to the excellent language skills of the project's graduate assistant, Sema Bağcı, who is a native Turkish speaker and is fluent in English. She did a great deal of the "heavy lifting" in getting the CBPR partnerships off the ground and in making them work on a daily basis.

Limitations in day-to-day communication in CBPR projects often go beyond language barriers and also involve practical matters related to lack of infrastructure in the community. Not all communities have access to Internet or even regular, reliable telephones. In some cases, such as in Turkey, mobile phones are widely available but are cost-prohibitive, particularly for making or receiving international calls. Without the ability to communicate by phone or email, the regular interaction and shared decision-making activities that form a central part of CBPR partnerships can be greatly hindered, and can even come to a near halt. Depending on written correspondence via postal service may be the only option when working in some communities, and this can dramatically slow the pace of work. Literacy may also be another issue that needs to be addressed for those working in communities in which large portions of the population do not have access to education.

ACCESS TO LITERATURE AND HERITAGE MANAGEMENT MODELS

I have already discussed facing challenges related to technical training of community residents in Chapter 7. However, there is another issue related to community training that I did not yet highlight. When community-based archaeology projects focus on cultural tourism and heritage management research, an important component of the work involves understanding what others have done and gaining exposure to what might be possible in a local community. Scholars are used to gaining this background and comparative knowledge by reading the extensive and ever-growing literature in this area, including comparative research of cases involving global heritage and tourism.

For those partnering with communities that are not English-speaking, being participatory in this aspect of the research presents immediate and obvious challenges. How will community members be able to access the existing literature and utilize it to inform and inspire their efforts? Even for those working with communities that are highly literate and English-speaking, challenges remain because much of the literature in this area is jargon-filled and can be challenging to follow, even for well-trained anthropology and archaeology students. Like many challenges of community-based archaeology, this is not an insurmountable problem, but it is one that will require effort and creativity to overcome.

I have utilized my teaching as a way to involve students in the process of addressing this challenge. As students in my classes read literature related to subjects that may be useful for one of the communities with which I'm working, I ask them to write a summary of the material that highlights the key points in language accessible by a lay audience. These overviews contribute to an ever-growing library of plain-language summaries that I maintain, and I then work with community interns to translate the summaries and create PowerPoint presentations of them. These materials will form a developing resource archive that community members can utilize. I plan to further expand this "community literature library" to include phone and filmed in-person interviews with those involved in heritage tourism efforts at sites globally.

Others have addressed the challenge of providing models and experience for community members in the area of heritage management and cultural tourism by taking a more hands-on approach. Anne Pyburn's (2009) project working with multiple communities from Kyrgyzstan is one excellent example. Pyburn developed a project to fund a delegation of members from Kyrgyz communities to visit several U.S. heritage sites in person, and she arranged for the group to speak directly with Native Americans and others involved in building community heritage sites, including museums. Participants in this project also faced the language barrier challenge and relied on interpreters to facilitate interaction between the groups.

These are only some of the most common challenges that archaeologists will face when conducting a community-based archaeology project. Certainly many others exist, and each project will face its own unique set of challenges. The primary point I hope to highlight is that CBPR projects are never straightforward and very often take a great deal more time, planning, and effort than conventional archaeological research. The reality of these challenges makes community-based archaeology particularly difficult to conduct in some scenarios. Graduate students, in particular, may find it difficult to carry out dissertation research using a CBPR methodology. Untenured scholars who face the pressures of completing a research project and publishing results within the short frame of time before their tenure review may also have difficulty using this methodology. However, one thing my research has clearly demonstrated is that each of these challenges can be overcome, although it often requires thinking outside of the usual box of conventional research methods.

With every new methodology, a learning curve is to be expected. But even beyond that, part of moving to a CBPR methodology involves changing not only the expectations of how research is conducted, but also the types of products that will result and the pace at which new knowledge is created. Freire's words at the start of this chapter point out that the system of knowledge creation that we now follow and maintain is not "natural," but has been created and can be transformed. Scholars in other fields have demonstrated that the challenges researchers and communities face in CBPR can be overcome. Some of the challenges facing archaeologists will be similar to those from other disciplines, whereas others will be unique to archaeology. As CBPR practice expands within archaeological work, so too will our capacity as archaeologists and communities to successfully address these problems and develop useful solutions.

EMBEDDING ETHICS

Within archaeology, the issue of research ethics is central to collaboration and to the CBPR methodology. This is not surprising considering that CBPR came to archaeology in large part through engagements with Indigenous communities, and largely in response to critiques that anthropological research was exploitative and unethical in its treatment of Indigenous people as research subjects. Several Indigenous groups have identified CBPR as being not only part of a decolonizing research methodology, but also as the way to work in an ethical manner with Indigenous peoples. While a concern for research ethics is central to understanding implications and lasting impacts of CBPR, several issues are particularly relevant and important for a discussion of CBPR within archaeology. Three of the most important are about stewardship and the archaeological record, protecting intellectual property rights of community partners, and virtue ethics of trust and respect.

STEWARDSHIP

The first of these involves the view put forth by the Society for American Archaeology in its Principles of Archaeological Ethics. The SAA principles are based on a model that views archaeologists as the primary stewards of the archaeological record. Following a CBPR paradigm, both archaeologists and community members are partners who work together as stewards for the places, knowledge, and materials of the past. Furthermore, using a CBPR methodology, an archaeologist's primary responsibility expands to also include concern for living descendant and local communities who are affected and impacted by archaeological research.

This involves an ethic of research more closely articulated by the American Anthropological Association's ethics principles that call for researchers' first obligation to be to those they study.

This principle of having an obligation to those we study is also implicated in another way in CBPR. As the basic principles of CBPR indicate, recognizing the validity of other knowledge systems is of central concern. For archaeologists, this means respecting community knowledge and the ways our community partners view the past. For Native Americans and other Indigenous communities, this means taking seriously cultural beliefs and knowledge that explain the past as deeply and continually connected with the present and future. Within this system of understanding, the archaeological "record" is directly connected to the people of the present, extending the obligation of archaeologists to include the living communities of today as an important component of archaeological practice.

The community-based aspect of CBPR moves this ethical concern one step further to a point where researchers move beyond an ethic of "doing no harm" toward one of doing some good, in the sense called for by Fluehr-Lobban (2003). In CBPR, it is the community that determines what it means to "do some good." In being directly involved in planning the research and identifying the questions to be investigated, community members are vital partners who are charged with determining the research most needed in their community. The capacity building that emerges through the participatory aspect of a CBPR project is another way of achieving Fluehr-Lobban's ethical model of "doing some good," since communities benefit from these efforts even after the archaeological project is complete.

INTELLECTUAL PROPERTY

Intellectual property issues have an important role to play in the ethics of archaeological CBPR. The projects that are created in these partnerships often involve substantial study and integration of Indigenous or local knowledge. One of the benefits of community-based archaeology is that it strengthens our knowledge of the past by braiding together Indigenous perspectives and knowledge with scientific understandings. Because this process of studying, recording, and integrating Indigenous knowledge will be an integral part of community-based archaeology, protecting intellectual property becomes an important and very central ethical issue.

As I discussed in Chapter 7, the Intellectual Property Issues in Cultural Heritage (IPinCH) project, directed by Dr. George Nicholas, recognizes this important connection. The IPinCH project formed an ethics working group that aims to gather knowledge that will inform future ethical practice involving intellectual property and archaeology. The working group is meant to draw on the experiences that arise out of the multiple collaborative and community-based intellectual property case studies that the IPinCH project funds.

VIRTUE ETHICS

The third ethics-related issue that has an important place in community-based archaeology is the system of thought related to "virtue ethics." Colwell-Chanthaphonh and Ferguson (2006, 118) have written about the application of virtue ethics to archaeology. They state, "[i]nstead of beginning with questions of obligations and oughts, virtue ethics begins with questions of character, focusing on relationships and the subjectives of social interaction." In their examination of virtue ethics in archaeology, Colwell-Chanthaphonh and Ferguson focus closely on trust—a central part of CBPR ethics.

Colwell-Chanthaphonh and Ferguson discuss the link between trust and obligation, and they provide multiple examples of the important role that trust plays in collaborative work between Native people and archaeologists (2006, 121). They also examine the nature of trust in archaeology, and outline categories of trust relationships held by archaeologists, including their trust with other archaeologists, the public, descendant communities, government, and even past and future generations. They explain that "there is a complex web of trust existing between all these different groups that indubitably affects the relationship archaeologists have with others" (2006, 123).

This is certainly true in the case of community-based archaeology, where the partnership between a community and an archaeologist is built upon trust. Much more than in archaeological research that involves communities acting as ethnographic sources, or in projects that involve community members as consultants, an ethic of trust is critical to CBPR projects because there is an effort to move beyond the past legacy of exclusion, uneven balances in power, and exploitation. Archaeologists who are successful at CBPR will find that an ethic of trust, and the obligations entailed within it to include communities as research partners, is a key factor to success.

LOCAL CONTEXTS FOR ETHICS AND CORE
COMMUNITY VALUES

Using a virtue ethics approach, researchers rely, in part, on values to guide ethical practice. Similarly, those working with Indigenous communities highlight the importance of including core tribal values as an integral part of CBPR work.

For example, the University of Victoria's Indigenous Governance Program has developed guidelines for conducting research in Indigenous communities. Their "Protocols and Principles for Conducting Research in an Indigenous Context" (University of Victoria 2003) discusses the importance of incorporating Indigenous values in the research. They state that "[a]n important aspect of the question of ethics is values. Indigenous values must be acknowledged by incorporation within the research design and methodology of a project" (2003, 6).

Other Indigenous groups and communities stress this same point—that Indigenous and local values will guide ethical research practices. Consideration of virtue ethics and the incorporation of community values bring the issue of ethics necessarily to the local level. This is because values and virtues vary from community to community, and any ethical practices or protocols must then be determined with a consideration of the local context. The Social Science and Humanities Research Council of Canada raises this issue in its recent report, "The Opportunities in Aboriginal Research Dialogue" (McNaughton and Rock 2003). They note that "there has been some ambivalence around the need for national ethics guidelines. There has been some sense that the solution may lie in creating effective research protocols at the local level, because such protocols reflect and respect individual differences in protocol among various Aboriginal peoples" (2003, 12).

The Mi'kmaw provide one example of a community that has clearly articulated ethics principles and research protocols. The community has developed a committee to oversee research and has charged them with developing a specific set of principles to guide its ethical practice (see Mi'kmaq Ethics Watch webpage, www.cbu .ca/academics/mikmaq-studies/mikmaw-ethics-watch). The principles put forth by the Mi'kmaq Ethics Watch are as follows:

- Mi'kmaw people are the guardians and interpreters of their culture and knowledge system—past, present, and future.
- Mi'kmaw knowledge, culture, and arts, are inextricably connected with their traditional lands, districts, and territories.
- Mi'kmaw people have the right and obligation to exercise control to protect their cultural and intellectual properties and knowledge.
- Mi'kmaw knowledge is collectively owned, discovered, used, and taught and so also must be collectively guarded by appropriately delegated or appointed collective(s) who will oversee these guidelines and process research proposals.

- Each community shall have knowledge and control over their own community knowledge and shall negotiate locally respecting levels of authority.

These principles are specific to the Mi'kmaw community, but they do draw attention to a point made by others in Indigenous and local communities—the importance of giving consideration and priority to local levels of authority. For those working in partnership with communities, conversations about local values and how those relate to ethical research practices will be an important early step to take and part of a conversation that will be ongoing.

As with any issue related to research ethics, any principles, protocols, or guidelines are not meant to be static, but should be regularly reevaluated. In a community-based archaeology project, these may develop in greater detail over time, as a community and researcher work together. They may be project-dependent, meaning that some practices will be worked out as a new project develops, or as new questions or ethical dilemmas are encountered.

The Mi'kmaw Ethics Watch committee raises another relevant point. They note that, "Mi'kmaw knowledge may have traditional owners involving individuals, families, clans, associations, and societies which must be determined in accordance with these peoples' own customs, laws, and procedures." As this statement points out, within one community, knowledge and the proper way to gather and care for it may differ depending on the family, clan, or other organizing group. The primary point here is that ethical practices within a CBPR paradigm are complex and require communication with community partners. No matter how thorough or detailed a set of ethics principles or protocols might be, they can't be specific enough to provide answers to every ethical quandary that arises, nor are they meant to. Ethics protocols are meant to provide guidance rather than specific answers, and within a CBPR context, any consideration of specific ethical practices will best be addressed through conversation with the communities involved.

COMMUNITY-BASED RESEARCH WITHIN THE ARCHAEOLOGY CURRICULUM

Incorporating new methodologies into the way students are trained and educated requires archaeologists to consider how to best integrate community-based research into the archaeology curriculum. Considering this issue for CBPR within a higher education context, Strand et al. (2003, xxi) link community-based research to service learning and note the way it integrates key factors of academic life. They point out that "[t]he distinctive combination of collaborative inquiry, critical analysis, and social change that community-based research represents—as well as its potential to unite the three traditional academic missions of teaching, research, and service in innovative ways—has led us to believe that CBR is a next important stage of service learning and engaged scholarship."

Hemment (2007) notes that CBPR training provides a valuable educational experience for students interested in public anthropology, and it is very useful for those who are increasingly working in the nonprofit sector (such as for international and local NGOs). Several examples demonstrate how university–community partnerships that are developed within a community-based research model can effectively provide experience and training for students in areas of teaching, research, and service simultaneously.

One archaeological example of community-based archaeology's utility in student training comes from the Waapaahsiiki Siipiiwi mound project, conducted in partnership between myself and the Sullivan County American Indian Council. From its outset, the plan was to involve students directly in developing the research design in order to train them in CBPR methods. Our initial attempts to gain funding for the project (which included mapping a previously undocumented mound site in southwestern Indiana and developing an interpretive trail and education/youth center on the site) were not successful. I and the council recognized this project as a learning tool to help students gain experience in working collaboratively with communities. The challenge we faced was how to find a way to incorporate students into what was essentially a nonfunded project.

Through conversations with the council president, Reg Petoskey, and the group's treasurer, Susan Petoskey, we decided to incorporate the Waapaahsiiki Siipiiwi mound project directly into a CBPR methodology course I teach. As a newly hired faculty member, I was faced with developing a series of courses that would contribute to my department's existing anthropology and archaeology curriculum. The course was initially developed to introduce students to the theoretical aspects of CBPR and to provide them with an understanding of the basic principles and benefits of community-based archaeology.

It became clear quite quickly that for the course to be most effective, it needed to combine the theoretical knowledge and "book knowledge" of CBPR methodology with a practical, hands-on approach to training by providing opportunities for students to actually do CBPR. I expanded the course to a two-semester graduate

FIGURE 20.
Graduate students (Teresa Nichols and Dustin Cantrel) hold
one of their weekly meetings via Skype with Ziibiwing's director
(Shannon Martin) and curator (William Johnson) to develop a
tribal management plan for the Flint Stone Street site.

methods series in which students are introduced to the theoretical aspects of CBPR
and are then able to apply them in a practical way by conducting a community-
based archaeology project in partnership with local community groups.

The two community partners for the class were the council and the Ziibiwing
Center. Over the course of two semesters, students worked with council community
members and Ziibiwing staff to develop and carry out aspects of the Waapaahsiiki
Siipiiwi interpretive trail project and the Flint Stone Street Ancestral Recovery
site management plan (see Figure 20). Through this two-semester course, graduate students gained both practical and theoretical knowledge of community-based
archaeology, while at the same time providing an important service to the local
Native American communities.

As part of the course requirements, students worked with community partners
to develop a research design, draft grant applications, and conduct the archaeological research and fieldwork. Community partners and the students worked

FIGURE 21.

Graduate student (Teresa Nichols) works with Ziibiwing curator
(William Johnson) to develop a grant proposal to fund further
community-based research for the Flint Stone Street Project.

together to draft a National Endowment for the Humanities grant application to
fund the aspects of the projects they had developed (see Figure 21). The students
learned new methodologies themselves while also gaining teaching experience as
they helped to train community members in field and research techniques. They
also gained professional skills such as grant writing, developing an IRB protocol,
and preparing community reports. Simultaneously, students provided an important service to local Native American communities that helped to build substantive
capacity for conducting research and grant writing and they assisted in building and
strengthening partnerships between the university and the broader community.

These community-based research methods courses, which brought the work
of two community-based archaeology projects into the classroom, provide an
example of how CBPR methods can become integrated into the anthropology and
archaeology curriculum on a university level.

In thinking more broadly about how to integrate community-based archaeology methods into the curriculum on the national level, an excellent place to begin

involves the national and international archaeology and anthropology professional associations, such as the Society for American Archaeology, the World Archaeological Congress, and the Archaeological Institute of America.

With large memberships, these associations provide excellent avenues for integrating CBPR practices into the archaeology curriculum. The Society for American Archaeology has a long-standing committee devoted specifically to curriculum issues that is charged with "implementing the principles outlined in Teaching Archaeology in the Twenty-First Century by making recommendations as to how identified needs might be included in undergraduate and graduate curricula in archaeology" (Society for American Archaeology 2011). The experience of this committee in maintaining a high standard for the archaeology curriculum could prove quite valuable for incorporating community-based archaeology into training at the graduate and undergraduate level.

TOOLS FOR TEACHING CIVIC ENGAGEMENT

Bringing CBPR into the archaeology curriculum serves to help educate and train those who will be archaeologists, but it also provides valuable educational experience for undergraduate students that are not archaeology or anthropology majors, and who will never conduct research with communities. Richard Couto makes the argument that community-based research is "about teaching and the cognitive and moral development of students" (Couto 2003, xv). In this view, teaching CBPR in the classroom and involving students in community-based projects becomes a way to engage students in research as a teaching tool, providing them with lifelong learning skills that can be applied to any number of professions, and even outside the workplace. Strand et al. (2003) point out the benefits of teaching CBPR that reach beyond the classroom and work environment. They argue that community-based research provides students the opportunity to prepare for "active civic engagement" (Strand et al. 2003, xx) by providing them with broad-based skills and ways of approaching research on any number of topics that affect their own community and their daily lives.

In other words, it provides them with research skills they can use to take a leadership role in efforts to better their own neighborhood or community. Why shouldn't such skills be part of the curriculum of anthropology departments? And why not utilize archaeology, a subject of broad public appeal, to engage students in such conversations and provide them with useful lifelong research and collaborative skills they can utilize long after the details of chronologies, artifacts types, and anthropological theories fade from memory?

Archaeologists and archaeological research are, like it or not, deeply enmeshed in contemporary life and politics in multiple ways. We are increasingly recognizing the ways in which the past intersects with, even erupts into, the present. This is the case even for archaeologists who do not focus on issues of heritage, tourism, and collaboration. This engagement of the archaeological past with the present provides a rich opportunity for archaeologists to use this intersection and the public fascination that often surrounds archaeology to draw in students, and provide them with training that enriches their deeper learning and gives them skills to be active and engaged citizens. Nassaney and Levine (2009) and Little and Shackel (2007) provide many positive examples of this. I can envision many ways that students might draw on lessons learned during a community-based archaeology course to address problems in their local communities, examine conditions at their place of work, or document the need for and impact of bringing healthier, more sustainable foods to their children's schools. Taking a course on community-based archaeology can build capacity in our community of university students, providing them with tools to make positive change in their lives and their own communities.

LASTING EFFECTS

The literature on community-based participatory research provides a rich and varied wealth of examples demonstrating the possibilities for how CBPR skills can be applied to improve lives through research. I've examined these to try to understand what archaeology can learn from the practices of other disciplines. Through five community-based archaeology projects, and through careful consideration of projects along the "collaborative continuum," I have considered how CBPR principles and practices might best be applied to archaeology. For archaeologists, successful application of CBPR methods involves an understanding of the theoretical aspects of CBPR as well as an understanding of the principles and benefits of the approach. But that theoretical knowledge is strengthened when it is accompanied by practical guidance and examples of how the principles are best applied on the ground in conducting archaeology projects.

When community members become co-researchers, they begin thinking of archaeology in new ways. Rather than seeing archaeology as something that is done to them, community members might see that CBPR projects create a space in which archaeological research has the potential to positively impact their future. As this shift occurs, it will have positive benefits for archaeology on a global scale.

For one thing, we will see the dichotomy between Indigenous peoples and archaeologists lessen dramatically. Debates about who owns or controls the past will lose their relevance as the paradigm shifts; instead, communities can raise questions about which projects they might like to develop and investigate. However, community-based archaeology also presents real challenges to researchers and communities. It is messy, time-consuming, and involves complex ethical and practical dilemmas. Despite the significant challenges, I feel it offers a positive way forward that has the potential to fundamentally shift the way archaeology is practiced. If we are committed to bringing archaeology to a place that is no longer only for archaeologists, but is something that communities have access to and investment in as well, then community-based archaeology is undoubtedly worthy of further attention.

CBPR is still young and it is very new to archaeology. The approach will grow and evolve with each project, as communities become increasingly involved in studying and caring for their own heritage and past. The history of engagement between archaeologists and communities as they "work together" continues to be written. The incorporation of CBPR is not the final point of this process, but it is a meaningful place in archaeology's trajectory. In this model, archaeology begins to operate using a different mode of knowledge production, one that is reciprocal and more egalitarian in nature. The lasting effects it will have on the field of archaeology and the communities who are intimately connected to the pasts that archaeologists work so passionately to understand will be noteworthy. Community-based archaeology has the potential to substantively change the way we view and study the past—not always with perfect outcomes, but certainly in ways that are more inclusive and relevant to the contemporary society in which we live. And hopefully in ways that make archaeology more sustainable and accessible for future generations.

BIBLIOGRAPHY

Adams, E. C. "Archaeology and the Native American: A Case at Hopi." In *Ethics and Values in Archaeology*, edited by E. L. Green, 236–42. Free Press, New York, 1984.

Adams, F., and M. Horton. *Unearthing Seeds of Fire the Idea of Highlander*. John F. Blair, Winston-Salem, NC, 1975.

Allen, H., D. Johns, C. Phillips, K. Day, T. 'O'Brien, and N. Mutunga. "Wāhi Ngaro (the Lost Portion): Strengthening Relationships between People and Wetlands in North Taranaki, New Zealand." *World Archaeology* 34, no. 2 (2002): 315–29.

Anyon, R., T. J. Ferguson, L. Jackson, L. Lane, and P. Vicenti. "Native American Oral Tradition and Archaeology: Issues of Structure, Relevance, and Respect." In *Native Americans and Archaeologists: Stepping Stones to Common Ground*, edited by N. Swidler, K. Dongoske, R. Anyon, and A. Downer, 77–87. AltaMira, Lanham, MD, 1997.

Ardren, T. "Conversations about the Production of Archaeological Knowledge and Community Museums at Chunchucmil and Kochol, Yucatan, Mexico." *World Archaeology* 34, no. 2 (2002): 379–400.

Arnold, B. "The Past as Propaganda: How Hitler's Archaeologists Distorted European Prehistory to Justify Racist and Territorial Goals." In *Archaeology* (July/August 1992): 30–37.

Arora-Jonsson, S. "'Research Sounds so Big . . .': Collaborative Inquiry with Women in Drevdagen, Sweden." In *Participatory Research in Conservation and Rural Livelihoods*, edited by L. Fortmann, 130–45. Wiley-Blackwell, Oxford, 2008.

Ashby, J., A. Braun, T. Gracia, M. P. Guerrero, L. A. Hernández, C. A. Quirós, and J. I. Roa. *Investing in Farmers as Researchers*. Centro Internacional de Agricultura Tropical (CIAT), Cali, Columbia, 2000.

Atalay, S. "Beyond the Walls of Academia: Archaeology for Indigenous Communities." In *Radical Archaeology Theory Symposium*, 8, State University of New York, Binghamton, 2003a.

———. *Domesticating Clay/Engaging with 'They': Anatolian Daily Practice with Clay and Public Archaeology for Indigenous Communities*. PhD dissertation, University of California, 2003b.

———. "Gikinawaabi: Knowledge Production and Social Science Research from an Indigenous Perspective." In *Women's History*. Queens University, Belfast, Ireland, 2003c.

———. *Multiple Voices for Many Ears in Indigenous Archaeological Practice*. Society for American Archaeology. 2004.

———. "Indigenous Archaeology as Decolonizing Practice." *American Indian Quarterly* 30, no. 3–4 (2006): 280–310.

———. "Global Application of Indigenous Archaeology: Community Based Participatory Research in Turkey." *Archaeologies* 3, no. 3 (2007): 249–70.

———. "Light through the Red Curtains: Beyond Archaeological Window Dressing to Substantive Collaboration on Issues that Count." In *Society for American Archaeology 73rd Annual Meeting* (2008a): 1–8, Vancouver, British Columbia.

———. "Multivocality and Indigenous Archaeologies." In *Evaluating Multiple Narratives: Beyond Nationalist, Colonialist, and Imperialist Archaeologies*, edited by J. Habu, C. Fawcett, and J. Matsunaga, 29–44. Springer, New York, 2008b.

———. Pedagogy of Decolonization: Advancing Archaeological Practice through Education." In *Collaborating at the Trowel's Edge: Teaching and Learning in Indigenous Archaeology*, edited by S. Silliman, pp. 123–44. University of Arizona Press, Tucson, 2008c.

———. "We Don't Talk about Çatalhöyük, We Live It": Sustainable Archaeological Practice through Community-Based Participatory Research." *World Archaeology* 43, no. 1 (2010).

———. "Engaging Archaeology: Positivism, Objectivity and Rigor in Activist Archaeology." Session title: On the Edge of (a) Reason: Archaeology, Activism, and the Pursuit of Relevance, Society for American Archaeology Annual Meeting, Sacramento, CA, 2011.

Atalay, S., C. Colwell-Chanthaphonh, E. Jolie, P. Lazrus, J. Levy, D. Lippert, D. McGill, M. Oxley, A. Pyburn, N. Shephard, A. Wylie, and L. Zimmerman. "An Open Letter to the SAA Membership." *SAA Archaeological Record* 9, no. 2 (2009): 4–5.

Bakken, K., O. Elquist, A. Gronhovd, J. Jones, D. Mather, M. O'Brien, M. Regan, D. Ross, T. Ross, and J. Williams. *Mitakuye Owas, All My Relations: Authentication, Recovery and Reburial at the Lincoln Mounds for the Bloomington Central Station Project, Bloomington, Minnesota.* Summit Envirosolutions, Inc., 2006.

Balenquah, L. J. "Beyond Stone and Mortar: A Hopi Perspective on the Preservation of Ruins (and Culture)." *Heritage Management* 1, no. 2 (2008): 145–62.

Ballard, H. "What Makes a Scientist? Studying the Impacts of Harvest in the Pacific Northwest." In *Participatory Research in Conservation and Rural Livelihoods,* edited by L. Fortmann, 98–114. Wiley-Blackwell, Oxford, 2008.

Bannister, K., and K. Barrett. "Harm and Alternatives: Cultures under Siege." In *Precautionary Tools for Reshaping Environmental Policy,* edited by N. J. Myers and C. Raffensperger, 215–39. MIT Press, Cambridge, MA, 2006.

Barndt, D. "Connecting Immigrant Workers: Community Self-Portraits." In *International Forum on Participatory Research.* Ljubljana, Yugoslavia, 1980.

Bartle, P. 2009. "What is Community? A Sociological Perspective." Community Empowerment Collective. www.scn.org/cmp/whatcom.htm.

Bartu, A. "Archaeological Practice as Guerilla Activity in Late Modernity." *Journal of Mediterranean Archaeology* 12, no. 1 (1999): 91–95.

———. "Where is Çatalhöyük? Multiple Sites in the Construction of an Archaeological Site." In *Towards Reflexive Method in Archaeology: The Example at Çatalhöyük,* edited by I. Hodder. McDonald Institute, Ankara, Turkey, 2000.

———. "Remembering a 9,000-year-old site: Presenting Çatalhöyük." In *The Politics of Public Memory in Turkey,* edited by E. Özyürek, 70–94. Syracuse University Press, Syracuse, New York, 2007.

Bartu Candan, A. "Entanglements/Encounters/Engagements with Prehistory: Çatalhöyük and Its Publics." In *Çatalhöyük Perspectives: Themes from the 1995–99 Seasons,* edited by I. Hodder. McDonald Institute of Archaeology, Ankara, Turkey, 2006.

Basso, K. H. *Wisdom Sits in Places: Landscape and Language among the Western Apache.* University of New Mexico Press, Albuquerque, 1996.

Battiste, M. *Reclaiming Indigenous Voice and Vision.* UBC Press, Vancouver, 2000.

Bell, C. E., and V. Napoleon (eds.). *First Nations Cultural Heritage and Law: Case Studies, Voices, and Perspectives.* UBC Press, Vancouver, BC, 2008.

Bell, C. E., and R. K. Paterson (eds.). *Protection of First Nations Cultural Heritage: Laws, Policy, and Reform.* UBC Press, Vancouver, 2009.

Bender, S. J., and G. S. Smith (eds.). *Teaching Archaeology in the Twenty-First Century.* Society for American Archaeology, Washington, DC, 2000.

Bendremer, J., and K. Richman. "Human Subjects Review and Archaeology: A View from Indian Country." In *The Ethics of Archaeology: Philosophical Perspectives on*

Archaeological Practice, edited by G. F. Scarre and C. Scarre, 97–114. Cambridge University Press, Cambridge, 2006.

Bendremer, J., and E. Thomas. "The Tribe and the Trowel: An Indigenous Archaeology and the Mohegan Archaeological Field School." In *Collaborating at the Trowel's Edge: Teaching and Learning in Indigenous Archaeology*, edited by S. Silliman. University of Arizona Press, Tucson, 2008.

Benton-Benai, E. *The Mishomis Book: The Voice of the Ojibway*. Indian Country Press, St. Paul, MN, 1979.

Bergelin, Å., M. Emretsson, A. L. Halvarsson, E. Halvarsson, and A. Ryen. "För oss är naturen en lisa för själen (Where Peace Comes Dropping Slow): The Forests and Nature for Us." In *Participatory Research in Conservation and Rural Livelihoods*, edited by L. Fortmann, 146–61. Wiley-Blackwell, Oxford, 2008.

Bishop, R. "Freeing Ourselves from Neo-Colonial Domination in Research: A Māori Approach to Creating Knowledge." *International Journal of Qualitative Studies in Education* 11, no. 2 (1998): 199–219.

Blakey, M. L. "An Ethical Epistemology of Publicly Engaged Biocultural Research." In *Evaluating Multiple Narratives: Beyond Nationalist, Colonialist, Imperialist Archaeologies*, edited by J. Habu, C. Fawcett and J. M. Matsunaga, pp. 17–28. Springer, New York, 2008.

Boal, A. *Theater of the Oppressed*. Urizen Books, New York, 1979.

———. *Legislative Theatre: Using Performance To Make Politics*. Routledge, London; New York, 1998.

Boast R. "Neocolonial Collaboration: Museum as Contact Zone Revisited." *Museum Anthropology* 34 (2011): 56–70.

Bobiwash, L., and L. Malloch. *A Family Needs Survey of the Native Community in Toronto*. Native Canadian Centre, Toronto, 1980.

Bowechop, J., and P. P. Erikson. "Forging Indigenous Methodologies on Cape Flattery: The Makah Museum as a Center of Collaborative Research." *American Indian Quarterly* 29, no. 1/2 (2005): 263–73.

Brady, L. M. "(Re)Engaging with the (Un)Known: Collaboration, Indigenous Knowledge, and Reaffirming Aboriginal Identity in the Torres Strait Islands, Northeastern Australia." *Collaborative Anthropologies* 2(2009): 33–64.

Braun, A. R., G. Thiele, and M. Fernández. *Farmer Field Schools and Local Agricultural Research Communities: Complementary Platforms for Integrated Decision Making in Sustainable Agriculture*. Overseas Development Institute, London, 2000.

Bray, J. N., J. Lee, L. L. Smith, and L. Yorks. *Collaborative Inquiry in Practice*. Sage Publications, Thousand Oaks, CA, 2000.

Brownlee, K., and E. L. Syms. *Kayasochi Kikawenow, Our Mother From Long Ago: An Early Cree Woman and Her Personal Belongings from Nagami Bay, Southern Indian Lake*. Manitoba Museum of Man and Nature, Manitoba, 1999.

Bryceson, D., L. Manicom, and Y. Kassam. "The Methodology of the Participatory Approach." In *Research for the People, Research by the People: Selected Papers from the International Forum on Participatory Research in Ljubljana, Yugoslavia*, edited by F. Dubell, T. Erasmie, and J. de Vries, 94–109. Netherlands Study and Development Centre for Adult Education, Amersfoort, Holland, 1980.

Bryceson, D., and K. Mustafa. "Participatory Research: Redefining the Relationship between Theory and Practice." In *Participatory Research: An Emerging Alternative Methodology in Social Science Research*, edited by Y. Kassam and K. Mustafa, 110–14. African Adult Education Association, Nairobi, 1982.

Brydon-Miller, M. "Breaking Down Barriers: Accessibility Self-Advocacy in the Disabled Community." In *Voices of Change: Participatory Research in the United States and Canada*, edited by P. Park, M. Brydon-Miller, B. L. Hall, and T. Jackson, 125–44. Bergin and Garvey, Westport, CT, 1993.

Budhwa, R. "An Alternative Model for First Nations Involvement in Resource Management Archaeology." *Canadian Journal of Archaeology* 29, no. 1 (2005): 20–45.

Burnette, B. M., and J. DeHose. "The Land Has Wisdom." In *Participatory Research in Conservation and Rural Livelihoods*, edited by L. Fortmann, 84–97. Wiley-Blackwell, Oxford, 2008.

Buruchara, R. "How Participatory Research Convinced a Sceptic." In *Participatory Research in Conservation and Rural Livelihoods*, edited by L. Fortmann, pp. 18–25. Wiley-Blackwell, Oxford, 2008.

Cain, B. J. *Participatory Research: Research with Historic Consciousness*, edited by C. F. A. Education, vol. A66. Participatory Research Project, Toronto.

Calhoun, C. "Foreword." In *Engaging Contradictions: Theory, Politics, and Methods of Activist Scholarship*, edited by C. R. Hale, xiii–xxvi. University of California Press, Berkeley, 2008.

Cash, P. E. "Medicine Bundles: An Indigenous Approach to Curation." In *The Future of the Past*, edited by T. Bray, 139–48. Garland, London, 2001.

Castañeda, Q. E., and C. N. Matthews. *Ethnographic Archaeologies: Reflections on Stakeholders and Archaeological Practices*. AtlaMira Press, Lanham, MD, 2008.

Chilton, E., and S. Hart "Crafting Collaborative Archaeologies: Two Case Studies from New England." *Collaborative Anthropologies* 2 (2009): 87–107.

Chirikure, S. and G. Pwiti. 2008. "Community Involvement in Archaeology and Community Heritage Management." *Current Anthropology* 49 (3): 467–85.

Clarke, A. "The Ideal and the Real: Cultural and Personal Transformations of Archaeological Research on Groote Eylandt, Northern Australia." *World Archaeology* 34, no. 2 (2002): 249–64.

Collins, D., J. Cruz, and B. Smith. "'She Fell Out of the Sky': Salal Harvesters' Reflections on Participatory Research." In *Participatory Research in Conservation and Rural Livelihoods*, edited by L. Fortmann, 115–29. Wiley-Blackwell, Oxford, 2008.

Colwell-Chanthaphonh, C. *Inheriting the Past: The Making of Arthur C. Parker and Indigenous Archaeology*. University of Arizona Press, Tucson, 2009.

Colwell-Chanthaphonh, C., and T. J. Ferguson. "Virtue Ethics and the Practice of History: Native Americans and Archaeologists along the San Pedro Valley of Arizona." *Journal of Social Archaeology* 4, no. 1 (2004): 5–27.

———. "Trust and Archaeological Practice: Towards a Framework of Virtue Ethics." In *The Ethics of Archaeology: Philosophical Perspectives on Archaeological Practice*, edited by C. Scarre and G. Scarre, 115–30. Cambridge University Press, Cambridge, 2006.

———. *Collaboration in Archaeological Practice: Engaging Descendant Communities*. AltaMira Press, Lanham, MD, 2008a.

———. "Introduction: The Collaborative Continuum." In *Collaboration in Archaeological Practice: Engaging Descendant Communities*, edited by C. Colwell-Chanthaphonh and T. J. Ferguson, 1–32. AltaMira Press, Lanham, MD, 2008b.

Comstock, D., and R. Fox. "Participatory Research as Critical Theory: The North Bonneville, USA, Experience." In *Voices of Change: Participatory Research in the United States and Canada*, edited by P. Park, M. Brydon-Miller, B. L. Hall, and T. Jackson, 103–24. Bergin & Garvey, Westport, CT, 1993.

Cooke, B., and U. Kothari (eds.). *Participation: The New Tyranny?* Zed Books, New York, 2001.

Corea, D., A. R. Estrada, R. Funez, I. Garcia, and C. Gomez, M. Guada, B. Gutiérrez, Á. Hernández, J. Amado Hernández, M. Hernández, N. Hernández, W. Hernández, C. Herrera, G, Herrera, J. S. Herrera, J. P. Herrera, T. Herrera, M. López, D. Matute, H. Mencía, R. Mencía, L. A. Meza, M. Meza, E. Murillo, H. Murillo, A. Núñez, U. Olvera, A. Orellana, D. Pérez and S. Pérez with L. Classen. "Campesinos Cientificos: Farmer Philosophies on Participatory Research." In *Participatory Research in Conservation and Rural Livelihoods*, edited by L. Fortmann, 55–69. Wiley-Blackwell, Oxford, 2008.

Cornwall, A., and R. Jewkes. "What is Participatory Research?" *Social Science and Medicine* 41, no. 12 (1995): 1667–76.

Couto, R. A. "A Conversation with Paulo Freire." *National Society for Experiential Education Quarterly* 20, no. 3 (1995): 24–30.

———. "Foreword." In *Community-Based Research and Higher Education: Principles and Practices*, edited by K. Strand, S. Marullo, N. Cutforth, R. Stoecker, and P. Donohue, xiii–xvi. 1st ed. Jossey-Bass, San Francisco, 2003.

Crosby, A. "Archaeology and Vanua Development in Fiji." *World Archaeology* 34, no. 2 (2002): 363–78.

de Vries, J. "Science as Human Behavior: One the Epistemology of the Participatory Research Approach." In *Research for the People, Research by the People: Selected Papers from the International Forum on Participatory Research in Ljubljana, Yugoslavia*, edited by F. Dubell, T. Erasmie, and J. de Vries, 81–93. Netherlands Study and Development Centre for Adult Education, Amersfoort, Holland, 1980.

De Wit, T., and V. Gianotten. "Rural Training in Traditional Communities of Peru." In *Research for the People, Research by the People: Selected Papers from the International Forum on Participatory Research in Ljubljana, Yugoslavia*, edited by F. Dubell, T. Erasmie, and J. de Vries, 131–42. Netherlands Study and Development Centre for Adult Education, Amersfoort, Holland, 1980.

Deloria, J., Vine. "Custer Died for Your Sins." In *Playboy* 6 (1969): 131–32, 172–175.

———. *Custer Died for Your Sins: An Indian Manifesto*. Macmillian, London, 1969.

Denzin, N. K., Y. S. Lincoln, and L. T. Smith. *Handbook of Critical and Indigenous Methodologies*. Sage, Los Angeles, 2008.

Derry, L., and M. Mallory (eds). *Archaeologists and Local Communities: Partners in Exploring the Past*. Society for American Archaeology, Washington, DC, 2003.

Dion, S. D. *Braiding Histories: Learning from Aboriginal Peoples' Experiences and Perspectives* (including the braiding histories stories cowritten with Michael R. Dion). UBC Press, Vancouver, 2009.

Dominguez, V. R. "Inside the President's Studio: T. J. Ferguson." American Anthropological Association, http://blog.aaanet.org/2010/07/09/inside-the-presidents-studio-t-j-ferguson/.

Dongoske, K. E., M. S. Aldenderfer, and K. Doehner (eds.). *Working Together: Native Americans and Archaeologists*. Society for American Archaeology, Washington, DC, 2000.

Doughty, L. "The 'TEMPER' Project in 2003." In *Catalhoyuk Archive Report*, edited by I. Hodder. www.catalhoyuk.com/archive_reports/2003/ar03_21.html.

Dowdall, K. M., and O. O. Parrish. "A Meaningful Disturbance of the Earth." *Journal of Social Archaeology* 3, no. 1 (2003): 99–133.

Dural, S., and I. Hodder. *Protecting Çatalhöyük: Memoir of an Archaeological Site Guard*. Left Coast Press, Walnut Creek, CA, 2007.

Endress, B. A., D. L. Gorchov, M. B. Peterson, and E. P. Serrano. "Harvest of the Palm Chamaedorea Radicalis, Its Effects on Leaf Production, and Implications for Sustainable Management." *Conservation Biology* 18, no. 3 (2004): 822–30.

Erasmie, T., J. de Vries, and F. Dubell. *Research for the People, Research by the People: Selected Papers from the International Forum on Participatory Research in Ljubljana, Yugoslavia, 1980.* Linköping University S.V.E., The Netherlands Study and Development Centre for Adult Education, Linkœping, Sweden, Amersfoort, Holland, 1980.

Evans, M. R., L. D. Hole, P. Hutchinson, and D. Sookraj. "Common Insights, Differing Methodologies: Towards a Fusion of Indigenous Methodologies, Participatory Action Research, and White Studies in an Urban Aboriginal Research Agenda." *Qualitative Inquiry* 15, no. 5 (2009): 893–910.

Fals-Borda, O. "Science and the Common People." In *Research for the People, Research by the People: Selected Papers from the International Forum on Participatory Research in Ljubljana, Yugoslavia, 1980,* edited by T. E. Folke Dubell, Jan de Vries, 13–40. Netherlands Study and Development Centre for Adult Education, Amersfoort, Holland, 1980.

Ferguson, T. J. "Archaeological Values in a Tribal Cultural Resource Management Program at the Pueblo of Zuni." In *Ethics and Values in Archaeology,* edited by E. Green, 224–35. Free Press, New York, 1984.

Ferguson, T. J., and C. Colwell-Chanthaphonh. *History Is in the Land: Multivocal Tribal Traditions in 'Arizona's San Pedro Valley.* University of Arizona Press, Tucson, 2006.

Ferguson, T. J., K. E. Dongoske, M. Yeatts, and L. J. Kuwanwisiwma. "Hopi Oral History and Archaeology." In *Working Together: Native Americans and Archaeologists,* edited by K. E. Dongoske, M. Aldenderfer, and K. Doehner, 45–60. Society for American Archaeology, Washington, DC, 2000.

Ferguson, T. J., J. Watkins, and G. L. Pullar. "Native Americans and Archaeologists: Commentary and Personal Perspectives." In *Native Americans and Archaeologists: Stepping Stones to Common Ground,* 237. Altamira Press, Lanham, MD, 1997.

Fine-Dare, K. S. *Grave Injustice: The American Indian Repatriation Movement and NAGPRA.* Fourth World Rising series. University of Nebraska Press, Lincoln, 2002.

Fluehr-Lobban, C. (ed.). *Ethics and the Profession of Anthropology: A Dialogue for Ethically Conscious Practice.* 2nd ed. AltaMira, Lanham, MD, 2003.

Fortmann, L. "Introduction: Doing Science Together." In *Participatory Research in Conservation and Rural Livelihoods,* edited by L. Fortmann, 1–17. Wiley-Blackwell, Oxford, 2008a.

———. *Participatory Research in Conservation and Rural Livelihoods*. Wiley-Blackwell, Oxford, 2008b.

Fox, K. "IPinCH Community-Based Heritage Research Workshop." In *Intellectual Property Issues in Cultural Heritage Newsletter* 2 (2010): 6.

Fredericksen, C. "Caring for History: Tiwi and Archaeological Narratives of Fort Dundas/Punata, Melville Island, Australia." *World Archaeology* 34, no. 2 (2002): 288–302.

Freire, P. *Pedagogy of the Oppressed*. Herder and Herder, New York, 1970.

———. "A Talk by Paulo Freire." *Studies in Adult Education* 2 (1971).

———. "Foreword." In *Voices of Change: Participatory Research in the United States and Canada*, edited by P. Park, M. Brydon-Miller, B. L. Hall, and T. Jackson, ix–x. Bergin & Garvey, Westport, CT, 1993.

Friesen, T. M. "Analogues at Iqaluktuuq: The Social Context of Archaeological Inference in Nunavut, Arctic Canada." *World Archaeology* 34, no. 2 (2002): 330–45.

Fritz, J. M., and F. T. Plog. "The Nature of Archaeological Explanation." *American Antiquity* 35, no. 4 (1970): 405–12.

Funari, P. P. A., A. Zarankin, and E. Stovel. *Global Archaeological Theory: Contextual Voices and Contemporary Thoughts*. Kluwer Academic/Plenum Publishers, New York, 2005.

Garcia, J. "Letter of Introduction to National Congress of American Indians Research Policy Center New Curriculum." In *Capacity Building for Tribes Section*. National Congress of American Indians Research Policy Center, 2009. http://ncaiprc.org/search/node/modules.

Gaventa, J. "Land Ownership in Appalachia, USA: A Citizens' Research Project." In *Research for the People, Research by the People: Selected Papers from the International Forum on Participatory Research in Ljubljana, Yugoslavia, 1980*, edited by T. E. Folke Dubell and Jan de Vries, 118–30. Netherlands Study and Development Centre for Adult Education, Amersfoort, Holland, 1980.

———. "Participatory Research in North America." *Convergene* 21, no. 2–3 (1988): 19–28.

———. "The Powerful, the Powerless, and the Experts: Knowledge Struggles in an Information Age." In *Voices of Change: Participatory Research in the United States and Canada*, edited by P. Park, M. Brydon-Miller, B. L. Hall, and T. Jackson, 21–40. Bergin and Garvey, Westport, Connecticut, 1993.

Gazin-Schwartz, A. "Mementos of the Past: Material Culture of Tourism at Stonehenge and Avebury." In *Marketing Heritage: Archaeology and the Consumption of the Past*, edited by Y. Rowan and U. Baram, 93–102. Altamira Press, Lanham, MD, 2004.

Gökdağ, E. *Theatre of the Oppressed and its Application in Turkey*. PhD dissertation, University of Nebraska, 2002.

Gonzalez, S., D. Modzelewski, L. Panich, and T. Schneider. "Archaeology for the Seventh Generation." *American Indian Quarterly* 30, no. 3/4 (2006): 388–415.

Greer, S., R. Harrison, and S. McIntyre-Tamwoy. "Community-Based Archaeology in Australia." *World Archaeology* 34, no. 2 (2002): 265–87.

Gustines, G. G. "Along the Heated Trail of the Man Who Created Muslim Superheroes." In *New York Times*, October 12, 2011.

Habu, J., C. Fawcett, and J. M. Matsunaga. *Evaluating Multiple Narratives Beyond Nationalist, Colonialist, Imperialist Archaeologies*. Springer, New York, NY, 2008.

Hale, C. R. "Introduction." In *Engaging Contradictions: Theory, Politics, and Methods of Activist Scholarship*, edited by C. R. Hale, pp. 1–30. University of California Press, Berkeley, 2008a.

Hale, C. R. (ed.). *Engaging Contradictions: Theory, Politics, and Methods of Activist Scholarship*. University of California Press, Berkeley, 2008b.

Hall, B. L. "Introduction." In *Voices of Change: Participatory Research in the United States and Canada*, edited by P. Park, M. Brydon-Miller, B. L. Hall, and T. Jackson, xiii–xxii. Bergin and Garvey, Westport, Connecticut, 1993.

———. "In from the Cold? Reflections on Participatory Research from 1970–2005." *Convergence* 38, no. 1 (2005): 5–24.

———. "*Creating Knowledge: Breaking the Monopoly; Research Methods, Participation, and Development. Working Paper No. 1.*". Participatory Research Project of the International Council of Adult Education, Toronto. 1977.

———. "Participatory Research: An Approach for Change." *Convergence* 8, no. 2 (1975): 24–32.

Hammil, J., and R. Cruz. "Statement of American Indians against Desecration before the World Archaeological Congress." In *Conflict in the Archaeology of Living Traditions*, edited by R. Layton. Unwin Hyman, London. 1989.

Haraway, D. "Situated Knowledges: The Science Question in Feminism and the Privilege of Partial Perspective." *Feminist Studies* 14, no. 3 (1988): 575–99.

Haraway, D. J. *Simians, Cyborgs, and Women: The Reinvention of Nature*. Free Association, London, 1991.

Harmon, A. "Indian Tribe Wins Fight to Limit Research of its DNA." In *New York Times*, April 21, 2010.

Harrison, B. 2001. *Collaborative Programs in Indigenous Communities: From Fieldwork to Practice*. AltaMira Press, Lanham, MD.

Hays-Gilpin, K., and G. Gumerman IV. "From the Editors." *Heritage Management* 1, no. 2 (2008): 141–44.

Heany, T. "If You Can't Beat 'Em, Join 'Em: The Professionalization of Participatory Research." In *Voices of Change: Participatory Research in the United States and Canada*, edited by P. Park, M. Brydon-Miller, B. L. Hall, and T. Jackson, 41–46. Bergin and Garvey, Westport, CT, 1993.

Heckenberger, M. "Entering the Agora: Archaeology, Conservation, and Indigenous Peoples in the Amazon." In *Collaboration in Archaeological Practice: Engaging Descendant Communities*, edited by C. Colwell-Chanthaphonh and T. J. Ferguson, 243–72. AltaMira Press, Lanham, MD, 2008.

Heckenberger, M. "Mapping Indigenous Histories: Collaboration, Cultural Heritage, and Conservation in the Amazon." *Collaborative Anthropologies* 2(2009): 9–32.

Hemment, J. "Public Anthropology and the Paradoxes of Participation: Participatory Action Research and Critical Ethnography in Provincial Russia." *Human Organization* 66, no. 3 (2007): 301–14.

Hickey, S., and G. Mohan (eds.). *Participation, from Tyranny to Transformation?: Exploring New Approaches to Participation in Development.* Zed Books, New York, 2005.

Hodder, I. *The Archaeological Process: An Introduction.* Blackwell Publishers, Oxford, UK, 1999.

Hodder, I. *Archaeological Theory Today.* Blackwell Publishers, Cambridge, UK, 2001.

Hodder, I. "Introduction." In *Çatalhöyük Perspectives: Themes from the 1995–99 Seasons*, edited by I. Hodder. British Institute of Archaeology at Ankara and McDonald Institute for Archaeological Research, Cambridge, UK, 2005.

Hodder, I., and A. Louise. "Discussions with the Goddess Community." 1998. www.catalhoyuk.com/library/goddess.html.

Hollowell, J., and G. Nicholas. "Using Ethnographic Methods to Articulate Community-Based Conceptions of Cultural Heritage Management." *Public Archaeology* 8, no. 2/3 (2009): 141–60.

Holtorf, C. *Archaeology Is a Brand! The Meaning of Archaeology in Contemporary Popular Culture.* Left Coast Press, Walnut Creek, CA, 2007.

hooks, b. *The Will To Change: Men, Masculinity, and Love.* 1st ed. Atria Books, New York, 2004.

Horton, M. *The Long Haul: An Autobiography.* 1st ed. Doubleday, New York, 1990.

Horton, M., and D. Jacobs. *The Myles Horton Reader: Education for Social Change.* 1st ed. University of Tennessee Press, Knoxville, 2003.

Hudson, G. "Women's Participatory Research in the Kayahna Area." Presented at the International Forum on Participatory Research, Toronto, 1980.

Humphries, S., J. Jimenez, F. Sierra, and O. Gallardo. "Sharing in Innovation: Reflection on a Partnership to Improve Livelihoods and Resource Conservation in the Honduran Hillsides." In *Participatory Research in Conservation and Rural Livelihoods*, edited by L. Fortmann, 36–54. Wiley-Blackwell, Oxford, 2008.

Israel, B. A., A. J. Schulz, E. A. Parker, and A. B. Becker. "Review of Community-Based Research: Assessing Partnership Approaches To Improve Public Health." *Annual Review of Public Health* 19 (1998): 173–202.

Jackson, G., and C. Smith. "Living and Learning on Aboriginal Lands: Decolonising Archaeology in Practice." In *Indigenous Archaeologies: Decolonising Theory and Practice*, edited by C. Smith and H. M. Wobst, 326–49. Routledge, London, 2005.

Jackson, T. "Resisting Pipeline Imperialism: The Struggle for Self-Determination in the Canadian North." *Alternatives* 7, no. 4 (1978): 40–51.

———. "A Way of Working: Participatory Research and the Aboriginal Movement in Canada." In *Voices of Change: Participatory Research in the United States and Canada*, edited by P. Park, M. Brydon-Miller, B. L. Hall, and T. Jackson, 47–64. Bergin and Garvey, Westport, CT, 1993.

Jackson, T., G. Conchelos, and A. Vigoda. "The Dynamics of Participation in Participatory Research." In *Research for the People, Research by the People: Selected Papers from the International Forum on Participatory Research in Ljubljana, Yugoslavia, 1980*, edited by T. E. Folke Dubell and Jan de Vries, 41–60. Netherlands Study and Development Centre for Adult Education, Amersfoort, Holland, 1980.

Jackson, T., and G. McKay. "Sanitation and Water Supply in Big Trout Lake: Participatory Research for Democratic Technical Solutions." *Canadian Journal of Native Studies* 2, no. 1 (1982): 129–45.

Jameson, J. H. *Presenting Archaeology to the Public: Digging for Truths*. Lanham, MD, Walnut Creek, CA, 1997.

Johnson, M. *Archaeological Theory: An Introduction*. 2nd ed. Wiley-Blackwell, Chichester, West Sussex, UK; Malden, MA, 2010.

Josephy, A. M., J. Nagel, and T. R. Johnson. *Red Power: The American Indians' Fight for Freedom*. 2nd ed. University of Nebraska Press, Lincoln, 1999.

Kane, S. (ed.). *The Politics of Archaeology and Identity in a Global Context*. Archaeological Institute of America, Boston, 2003.

Kanhare, V. "The Struggle in Dhulia: A Women's Movement in India." In *Research for the People, Research by the People: Selected Papers from the International Forum* on *Participatory Research in Ljubljana, Yugoslavia*, edited by F. Dubell, T. Erasmie, and J. de Vries, 110–17. Netherlands Study and Development Centre for Adult Education, Amersfoort, Holland, 1980.

Kassam, Y. "The Issue of Methodology in Participatory Research." In *Research for the People, Research by the People: Selected Papers from the International Forum on Participatory Research in Ljubljana, Yugoslavia*, 1980, edited by T. E. Folke Dubell and Jan de Vries, 61–68. Netherlands Study and Development Centre for Adult Education, Amersfoort, Holland, 1980.

Keene, A. S., and S. Colligan. "Service-Learning and Anthropology." *Michigan Journal of Community Service Learning* 10, no. 3(summer 2004): 5–15.

Kerber, J. E. (ed.). *Cross-Cultural Collaboration: Native Peoples and Archaeology in the Northeastern United States*. University of Nebraska Press, Lincoln, 2006.

Kerber, J. E. "Summer Workshops in Indigenous Archaeology: Voluntary Collaboration between Colgate University and the Oneida Indian Nation of New York." In *Collaborating at the Trowel's Edge: Teaching and Learning in Indigenous Archaeology*, edited by S. Silliman, 88–102. Amerind Studies in Archaeology. University of Arizona Press, Tucson, 2008.

Kidd, R., and M. Byram. "The Performing Arts and Community Education in Botswana." *Community Development Journal* 13, no. 3 (1978): 170–78.

Kluth, R., and K. Munnell. "The Integration of Tradition and Scientific Knowledge on the Leech Lake Reservation." In *Native Americans and Archaeologists: Stepping Stones to Common Ground*, edited by N. Swidler, K. Dongoske, R. Anyon, and A. Downer, 112–19. AltaMira, Lanham, MD, 1997.

Kohl, P., and C. Fawcett (eds.). *Nationalism, Politics, and the Practice of Archaeology*. Cambridge University Press, 1996.

Kohl, P. L., M. Kozelsky, and N. Ben-Yehuda (eds.). *Selective Remembrances: Archaeology in the Construction, Commemoration, and Consecration of National Pasts*. University of Chicago Press, Chicago, 2007.

Komar, D. "Patterns of Mortuary Practice Associated with Genocide: Implications for Archaeological Research." *Current Anthropology* 49, no. 1 (2008): 123–33.

Kovach, M. *Indigenous Methodologies: Characteristics, Conversations, and Contexts*. University of Toronto Press, Toronto; Buffalo, 2009.

Kuhn, T. S. *The Structure of Scientific Revolutions*. 2nd ed. University of Chicago Press, Chicago, 1970.

Kuwanwisiwma, L. J. "Collaboration Means Equality, Respect, and Reciprocity: A Conversation about Archaeology and the Hopi Tribe." In *Collaboration in Archaeological Practice: Engaging Descendant Communities*, edited by C. Colwell-Chanthaphonh and T. J. Ferguson, 151–70. AltaMira Press, Lanham, MD, 2008.

La Salle, M. "Community Collaboration and Other Good Intentions." *Archaeologies* 6, no. 3 (2010): 401–22.

LaRoche, C. J., and M. L. Blakey. "Seizing Intellectual Power: The Dialogue at the New York African Burial Ground." *Historical Archaeology* 31, no. 3 (1997): 84–106.

Layton, R. *Conflict in the Archaeology of Living Traditions*. One World Archaeology. U. Hyman, London; Boston, 1989.

Leone, M. P., P. B. Potter, Jr., P. A. Shackel, M. L. Blakey, R. Bradley, B. Durrans, J. M. Gero, G. P. Grigoriev, I. Hodder, J. L. Lanata, T. E. Levy, N. A. Silberman, R. Paynter, M. A. Rivera, and W. Alison. ———. "Toward a Critical Archaeology [and Comments and Reply]." *Current Anthropology* 28, no. 3 (1987): 283–302.

Levin, M. "A Trade Union and the Case of Automation (Norway)." In *Research for the People, Research by the People*, edited by F. Dubell, T. Erasmie, and J. de Vries, 153–68. Netherlands Study and Development Centre for Adult Education, Amersfoort, Holland, 1980.

Lewin, K. *Resolving Social Conflicts*. Harper and Row, New York, 1948.

Liebmann, M., and U. Z. Rizvi. *Archaeology and the Postcolonial Critique*. AltaMira Press, Lanham, MD, 2008.

Lightfoot, K. "Collaborative Research Programs: Implications for the Practice of North American Archaeology." In *Collaborating at the Trowel's Edge: Teaching and Learning in Indigenous Archaeology*, edited by S. W. Silliman, 211–27. University of Arizona Press, Tucson, 2008.

Lightfoot, K., O. Parrish, R. Jewett, and D. Murley. "The Metini Village Project: Collaborative Research in the Fort Ross State Historic Park." *Society for California Archaeology Newsletter* 35, no. 2 (2001).

Little, B. J. *Public Benefits of Archaeology*. University of Florida Press, Gainesville, 2002.

Little, B. J., and N. Amdur-Clark. "Archaeology and Civic Engagement." National Park Service Technical Brief 23, 2008. www.nps.gov/archeology/pubs/techbr/tch23.htm.

Little, B. J., and P. A. Shackel. *Archaeology as a Tool of Civic Engagement*. AltaMira Press, Lanham, MD, 2007.

Lonetree, A. *Displaying Indians: Museum Representations of Native American History and Culture*. PhD dissertation, University of California-Berkeley, 2002.

———. "Missed Opportunities: Reflections on the NMAI." *American Indian Quarterly* 30, no. 3/4 (2006): 632–45.

———. "'Acknowledging the Truth of History': Missed Opportunities at the National Museum of the American Indian." In *The National Museum of the American Indian:*

Critical Conversations, edited by A. Lonetree and A. J. Cobb, 305–27. University of Nebraska Press, Lincoln, 2008.

———. *Decolonizing Museums: Representing Native America in National and Tribal Museums*. University of North Carolina Press, forthcoming 2012.

Long, J. W. "Retracing the Trail to Wisdom: Doing Science Together in Cibecue." In *Participatory Research in Conservation and Rural Livelihoods*, edited by L. Fortmann, 70–83. Wiley-Blackwell, Oxford, 2008.

Lyons, N. "Creating Space for Negotiating the Nature and Outcomes of Collaborative Research Projects with Aboriginal Communities." *Inuit Studies* 35, no. 1–2 (2011).

Lyons, N., P. Dawson, M. Walls, D. Uluadluak, L. Angalik, M. Kalluak, P. Kigusiutuak, L. Kiniks, J. Karetak, and L. Suluk. "Person, Place, Memory, Thing: How Inuit Elders are Informing Archaeological Practice in the Canadian North." *Canadian Journal of Archaeology* 34 (2010): 1–31.

Lutz, J. S., and B. Neis (eds.). *Making and Moving Knowledge: Interdisciplinary and Community-Based Research in a World on the Edge*. McGill-Queen's University Press, Montreal, Canada, 2008.

Maguire, P. "Challenges, Contradictions, and Celebrations: Attempting Participatory Research as a Doctoral Student." In *Voices of Change: Participatory Research in the United States and Canada*, edited by P. Park, M. Brydon-Miller, B. L. Hall, and T. Jackson, 157–76. Bergin and Garvey, Westport, CT, 1993.

———. *Doing Participatory Research: A Feminist Approach*. Center for International Education, School of Education, University of Massachusetts, Amherst, MA, 1987.

Mandala, L. *The Cultural and Heritage Traveler*, 2009 edition. *Touri*sm report conducted by Mandala Research LLC, 2009.

Marek-Martinez, O. "Forum: NAGPRA's Achilles Heel: The Disposition of Culturally Unidentifiable Human Remains." *Heritage Management* 1, no. 2 (2008): 243–60.

Marshall, Y. "What Is Community Archaeology?" *World Archaeology* 34, no. 2 (2002): 211–19.

Martin, C. "To Scotland Then They Came Burning." *British Archaeology* 6 (1995): 12–14.

Mbilinyi, M., U. Vuorela, Y. Kassam, and Y. Masisi. "The Politics of Research Methodology in the Social Sciences." In *Participatory Research: An Emerging Alternative Methodology in Social Science Research*, edited by Y. Kassam and K. Mustafa, 34–63. African Adult Education Association, Nairobi, 1982.

McDavid, C. "Archaeologies that Hurt: Descendants that Matter: A Pragmatic Approach to Collaboration in the Public Interpretation of African-American Archaeology." *World Archaeology* 34, no. 2 (2002): 303–14.

McDonald, D., D. Peterson, and S. Betts. "More Tips: What If a Cooperative Extension Professional Must Work with Native American Institutional Review Boards?" *Journal of Extension* 43, no. 5 (2005). www.joe.org/joe/2005october/tt1.php.

McGuire, R. H. *Archaeology as Political Action*. California series in public anthropology. University of California Press, Berkeley, 2008.

McIntyre, A. *Participatory Action Research*. Sage Publications, Los Angeles, 2008.

McManamon, F. P. "The Many Publics for Archaeology." *American Antiquity* 56, no. 1 (1991): 121–30.

McNaughton, C., and D. Rock. *Opportunities in Aboriginal Research Results of SSHRC's Dialogue on Research and Aboriginal Peoples*. Social Sciences and Humanities Research Council of Canada (SSHRC), 2003.

McNiven, I. J., and L. Russell. *Appropriated Pasts: Indigenous Peoples and the Colonial Culture of Archaeology*. AltaMira Press, Walnut Creek, CA, 2005.

McTaggart, R. *Participatory Action Research: International Contexts and Consequences*. State University of New York Press, Albany, 1997.

Mduma, E. K. "Appropriate Technology for Grain Storage at Bwakira Chini Village." In *Participatory Research: An Emerging Alternative Methodology in Social Science Research*, edited by Y. Kassam and K. Mustafa, 198–213. African Adult Education Association, Nairobi, 1982.

Mellaart, J. *Çatal Höyük: A Neolithic Town in Anatolia*. McGraw-Hill, New York, 1967.

Merrifield, J. "Putting Scientists in Their Place: Participatory Research in Environmental and Occupational Health." In *Voices of Change: Participatory Research in the United States and Canada*, edited by P. Park, M. Brydon-Miller, B. L. Hall, and T. Jackson, 65–84. Bergin and Garvey, Westport, CT, 1993.

Meskell, L. *Archaeology Under Fire: Nationalism, Politics and Heritage in the Eastern Mediterranean and Middle East*. Routledge, London; New York, 1998.

———. "Archaeological Ethnography: Conversations around Kruger National Park." *Archaeologies* 1, no. 1 (2005): 83–102.

Mihesuah, D. A. *Natives and Academics: Researching and Writing about American Indians*. University of Nebraska Press, Lincoln, 1998.

Mihesuah, D. A. (ed.). *Repatriation Reader: Who Owns American Indian Remains*, viii, 335. University of Nebraska Press, Lincoln, 2000.

———. *So You Want To Write about American Indians?: A Guide for Writers, Students, and Scholars*. University of Nebraska Press, Lincoln, 2005.

Mihesuah, D. A., and A. C. Wilson (eds.). *Indigenizing the Academy: Transforming Scholarship and Empowering Communities*. Vol. 1. University of Nebraska Press, Lincoln, 2004.

Miller, S. A. "Native America Writes Back: The Origin of the Indigenous Paradigm in Historiography." *Wicazo Sa Review* 23, no. 2 (2008): 9–28.

———. "Native Historians Write Back: The Indigenous Paradigm in American Indian Historiography." *Wicazo Sa Review* 24, no. 1 (2009): 25–45.

Mills, B., M. Altaha, J. R. Welch, and T. J. Ferguson. "Field Schools without Trowels: Teaching Archaeological Ethics and Heritage Preservation in a Collaborative Context." In *Collaborating at the Trowel's Edge: Teaching and Learning in Indigenous Archaeology*, edited by S. W. Silliman, 25–49. University of Arizona Press, Tucson, 2008.

Mortensen, L., and J. J. Hollowell. *Ethnographies and Archaeologies: Iterations of the Past.* Cultural Heritage Studies. University Press of Florida, Gainesville, FL, 2009.

Mortensen, L., and G. Nicholas. "Riding the Tourism Train? Navigating Intellectual Property, Heritage and Community-Based Approaches to Cultural Tourism." *Anthropology News* 51, no. 8 (2010): 11–12.

Mosavel, M., and T. Thomas. "Project REECH: Using Theatre Arts To Authenticate Local Knowledge." *New Solutions* 19, no. 4 (2009): 407–22.

Moser, S., D. Glazier, J. E. Phillips, L. N. el Nemr, M. S. Mousa, R. N. Aiesh, S. Richardson, A. Conner, and M. Seymour. "Transforming Archaeology through Practice: Strategies for Collaborative Archaeology and the Community Archaeology Project at Quseir, Egypt." *World Archaeology* 34, no. 2 (2002): 220–48.

Mullins, P. "The Invisible Landscape: An Archaeology of Urban Renewal and the Color Line." *SAA Archaeological Record* 4, no. 4 (2004): 25–28.

Mullins, P., W. M. Labode, L. C. Jones, M. E. Essex, A. Kruse, and B. Muncy. "Consuming Lines of Difference: The Politics of Wealth and Poverty along the Color Line." *Historical Archaeology (special issue on archaeologies of poverty)*, in press.

Murphree, M. "Foreword." In *Participatory Research in Conservation and Rural Livelihoods*, edited by L. Fortmann, xvi–xxii. Wiley-Blackwell, Oxford, 2008.

Murray, W. F., N. C. Laluk, B. J. Mills, and T. J. Ferguson. "Archaeological Collaboration with American Indians: Case Studies from the Western United States." *Collaborative Anthropologies* 2(2009): 65–86.

Mustafa, K. "The Role of Culture in Development: Jipemoyo Project, Tanzania." In *Research for the People, Research by the People: Selected Papers from the International Forum on Participatory Research in Ljubljana, Yugoslavia*, edited by F. Dubell, T. Erasmie, and J. de Vries, 143–52. Netherlands Study and Development Centre for Adult Education, Amersfoort, Holland, 1980.

Mutua, K., and B. B. Swadener. *Decolonizing Research in Cross-Cultural Contexts: Critical Personal Narratives.* State University of New York Press, Albany, NY, 2004.

Nagar, R., and Sangtin Writers. *Playing with Fire: Feminist Thought and Activism through Seven Lives in India*. University of Minnesota Press, Minneapolis, MN, 2006.

Nagar, R., and R. Singh. "Churnings of a Movement: *Sangtin's* Diary." *South Asian Popular Culture* 8, no. 1 (2010): 17–30.

Nahanni, P. "The Mapping Project." In *Dene Nation—The Colony Within*, edited by M. Watkins, 21–27. University of Toronto Press, Toronto, 1977.

Nason, J. "Corps Followed the Law in Handling of Jawbone Found on the Columbia River," *Seattle Times*, 2009.

Nassaney, M. S. "Commemorating French Heritage at Fort St. Joseph, an Eighteenth-Century Mission, Garrison, and Trading Post Complex in Niles, Michigan." In *Dreams of the Americas: Overview of New France Archaeology*, edited by Christian Roy and Hélène Côté, pp. 96–111. Archéologiques, Collection Hors Séries 2, 008.

Nassaney, M. S., and M. Levine. *Archaeology and Community Service Learning*. University of Florida Press, Gainesville, FL, 2009.

National Congress of American Indians Policy Research Center. Research for Tribal Communities Curriculum. 2009. http://ncaiprc.org/search/node/modules.

Nicholas, G. P. "Editor's Notes: On mtDNA and Archaeological Ethics." *Canadian Journal of Archaeology* 29 (2005): iii–vi.

———. "Decolonizing the Archaeological Landscape: The Practice and Politics of Archaeology in British Columbia." *American Indian quarterly* 30, no. 3/4 (2006): 350–80.

———. "Native Peoples and Archaeology." In *Encyclopedia of Archaeology*, edited by D. M. Pearsall, vol. 3, 1,660–69. Academic Press, New York, 2008.

Nicholas, G. P., and T. D. Andrews. *At a Crossroads: Archaeology and First Peoples in Canada*. Publication no. 24. Archaeology Press, Burnaby, BC, 1997.

Nicolas, G. P., A. Roberts, D. M. Schaepe, J. Watkins, L. Leader-Elliot, and S. Rowley. "A Consideration of Theory, Principles and Practice in Collaborative Archaeology." *Archaeology Review from Cambridge* 26, no. 2 (2011): 14–58.

Ommer, R. E., H. Coward, and C. C. Parrish. "Knowledge, Uncertainty and Wisdom." In Making and Moving Knowledge: Interdisciplinary and Community-Based Research for a World on the Edge, edited by B. Neis and J. S. Lutz, pp. 20–41. McGill-Queen's University Press, Montreal, 2008.

Park, P., Brydon-Miller, M., Hall, B., and T. Jackson. *Voices of Change: Participatory Research in the United States and Canada*. Bergin & Garvey, Westport, CT, 1993.

Park, P. "What is Participatory Research? A Theoretical and methodological Perspective." In *Voices of change : participatory research in the United States and Canada*, edited by P. Park, M. Brydon-Miller, B. L. Hall, and T. Jackson, pp. 1–20. Bergin & Garvey, Westport, CT, 1993.

Parrish, O., R. J. Murley, and K. Lightfoot. "The Science of Archaeology and the Response from within Native California: The Archaeology and Ethnohistory of Metini Village in the Fort Ross State Historic Park." *Society for California Archaeology Proceedings* 13 (2000): 84–87.

Pearson, K., and P. Connor. *The Dorak Affair*. Atheneum, New York, 1967.

Phillips, C., and H. Allen. *Bridging the Divide: Indigenous Communities and Archaeology in to the 21st Century*. Left Coast Press, Walnut Creek, CA, 2010.

Polikoff, B. *With One Bold Act: The Story of Jane Addams*. Boswell, 1999.

Preucel, R. W., and S. A. Mrozowski. "Part 1: The New Pragmatism." In *Contemporary Archaeology in Theory: The New Pragmatism*, edited by R. W. Preucel and S. A. Mrozowski, 3–49. 2nd ed. Wiley-Blackwell, Chichester, UK, 2010.

Pyburn, A. "Archaeology for a New Millennium: The Rules of Engagement." In *Archaeologists and Local Communities: Partners in Exploring the Past*, edited by L. Derry and M. Molloy, 167–84. Society for American Archaeology, Washington, DC, 2003.

———. "Practicing Archaeology—As If It Really Matters." *Public Archaeology* 8, no. 2–3 (2009): 161–75.

———. "Engaged Archaeology: Whose Community? Which Public?" In *New Perspectives in Global Public Archaeology*, edited by A. Matsuda and K. Okamura. Springer, New York, 2011.

Pyburn, A., and R. R. Wilk. "Responsible Archaeology is Applied Anthropology." In *Ethics in American Archaeology: Challenges for the 1990s*, edited by M. Lynott and A. Wylie, 71–76. Society for American Archaeology, Washington, DC, 1995.

Rains, F. V., J. A. Archibald, and D. Deyhle. "Introduction: Through Our Eyes and in Our Own Words." *International Journal of Qualitative Studies in Education* 13, no. 4 (2000): 337–42.

Ray, C. "Emerging Consensus and Concerns in Collaborative Archaeological Research." *Collaborative Archaeologies* 2(2009): 1–8.

Rizvi, U., and J. Lydon (eds.). *Handbook of Postcolonial Archaeology*. Left Coast Press, Walnut Creek, CA, 2010.

Robinson, M. P. "Shampoo Archaeology: Towards a Participatory Action Research Approach in Civil Society." *The Canadian Journal of Native Studies* XVI, no. 1 (1996): 125–38.

Rossen, J. "New Vision Archaeology in the Cayuga Heartland of Central New York." In *Cross-Cultural Collaboration: Native Peoples and Archaeology in the Northeastern United States*, edited by J. E. Kerber, 250–64. University of Nebraska Press, Lincoln, 2006.

———. "Research and Dialogue: New Vision Archaeology in the Cayuga Homeland of Central New York." In *Collaborating at the Trowel's Edge: Teaching and Learning in Indigenous Archaeology*, edited by S. Silliman, 250–64. University of Arizona, Tucson, 2008.

Sabloff, J. A. *Archaeology Matters: Action Archaeology in the Modern World*. Left Coast Press, Walnut Creek, CA, 2008.

Sahota, P. C. "Research Regulation in American Indian/Alaska Native Communities: Policy and Practice Considerations." In *Policy Research Center Tribal Research Regulation Toolkit*, 1–20. National Congress of American Indians Policy Research Center, 2009. www.ncaiprc.org/research-regulation-papers.

———. "Community-Based Participatory Research in American Indian and Alaska Native Communities." In *Policy Research Center Tribal Research Regulation Toolkit*, 1–27. National Congress of American Indians Policy Research Center, 2010. http://www.ncaiprc.org/research-regulation.

Schafft, K. A., and D. J. Greenwood. "The Promises and Dilemmas of Participation: Action Research, Search Conference Methodology and Community Development. *Journal of the Community Development Society* 34, no. 1 (2003): 18–35.

Schensul, J. J., M. J. Berg, and K. M. Williamson. "Challenging Hegemonies: Advancing Collaboration in Community-Based Participatory Action Research." *Collaborative Anthropologies* 1 (2008): 103–37.

Schmidt, P. R. *Postcolonial Archaeologies in Africa*. 1st ed. School for Advanced Research Press, Santa Fe, NM, 2009.

Sclove, R., M. Scammell, B. Holland, F. Alimohamed, and Loka Institute. *Community-Based Research in the United States: An Introductory Reconnaissance, Including Twelve Organizational Case Studies and Comparison with the Dutch Science Shops and the Mainstream American Research System*. Loka Institute, Amherst, MA, 1998.

Sert, G. "Çatalhöyük Summer School Workshop Report." In *Çatalhöyük Archive Report*, www.catalhoyuk.com/downloads/Archive_Report_2010.pdf.

Shackel, P. A., and E. J. Chambers (eds.). *Places in Mind: Public Archaeology as Applied Anthropology*. Routledge, New York, 2004.

Shackel, P. A., and D. A. Gadsby. "'I Wish for Paradise': Memory and Class in Hampden, Baltimore." In *Collaboration in Archaeological Practice: Engaging Descendant Communities*, edited by C. Colwell-Chanthaphonh and T. J. Ferguson, 225–42. AltaMira Press, Lanham, MD, 2008.

Shankland, D. "The Anthropology of an Archaeological Presence." In *On the Surface: Çatalhöyük 1993–95*, edited by I. Hodder. McDonald Institute Monographs. McDonald Institute for Archaeological Research, Ankara, 1996.

———. "Integrating the Past: Folklore, Mounds and People at Çatalhöyük." In *Archaeology and Folklore*, edited by A. Gazin-Schwartz and C. Holtorf, 139–57. Routledge, London, 1999.

Shanks, M. "Archaeology and Politics." In *A Companion to Archaeology*, edited by J. L. Bintliff, 490–508. Blackwell, Malden, MA, 2004.

Silliman, S. *Collaborating at the Trowel's Edge: Teaching and Learning in Indigenous Archaeology*. Amerind studies in archaeology. University of Arizona Press, Tucson, 2008a.

———. "Collaborative Indigenous Archaeology: Troweling at the Edges, Eyeing the Center." In *Collaborating at the Trowel's Edge: Teaching and Learning in Indigenous Archaeology*, edited by S. W. Silliman, 1–24. University of Arizona Press, Tucson, 2008b.

———. "Blurring for Clarity: Archaeology as Hybrid Practice." In *Decolonizing Archaeology: Archaeology and the Post-Colonial Critique*, edited by P. Bikoulis, D. Lacroix, and M. Peuramaki-Brown, 15–25. Archaeological Association of the University of Calgary, Calgary, 2009.

Silliman, S., and T. J. Ferguson. "Consultation and Collaboration with Descendent Communities." In *Voices in American Archaeology*, edited by W. Ashmore, D. T. Lippert, and B. J. Mills, 48–72. Society for American Archaeology, Washington, DC, 2010.

Silliman, S. W., and K. H. Sebastian Dring. "Working on Pasts for Future: Eastern Pequot Field School Archaeology in Connecticut." In *Collaborating at the Trowel's Edge: Teaching and Learning in Indigenous Archaeology*, edited by S. W. Silliman, 67–87. University of Arizona Press, Tucson, 2008.

Simpson, F. A. *The Values of Community Archaeology: A Comparative Assessment between the UK and US*. BAR international series. Archaeopress, Oxford, 2010.

Simpson, L. "Aboriginal Peoples and Knowledge: Decolonizing Our Processes." *Canadian Journal of Native Studies* XXI, no. 2 (2000): 137–48.

Smardz Frost, K., and S. J. Smith. *The Archaeology Education Handbook: Sharing the Past with Kids*. AltaMira Press, Lanham, MD, 2000.

Smith, C., and G. Jackson. "Decolonizing Indigenous Archaeology: Developments from Down Under." *American Indian Quarterly* 30, no. 3/4 (2006): 311–49.

———. "The Ethics of Collaboration. Whose Culture? Whose Intellectual Property? Who Benefits?" In *Collaboration in Archaeological Practice: Engaging Descendant*

Communities, edited by C. Colwell-Chanthaphonh and T. J. Ferguson, 171–99. AltaMira, Lanham, MD, 2007.

Smith, C., L. Willika, P. Manabaru, and G. Jackson. "Barunga Rock Art." In *Archaeologists and Aborigines Working Together*, edited by I. Davidson, C. Lovell-Jones, and R. Bancroft. University of New England Press, Armidale, New South Wales, 1995.

Smith, C., and H. M. Wobst. *Indigenous Archaeologies: Decolonizing Theory and Practice*. Routledge, New York, 2005.

Smith, L., A. Morgan, and A. van der Meer. "The Waanyi Women's History Project: A Community Partnership Project, Queensland, Australia." In *Archaeologists and Local Communities: Partners in Exploring the Past*, edited by L. Derry and M. Malloy, 147–66. Society for American Archaeology, Washington, DC, 2003.

Smith, L. T. *Decolonizing Methodologies: Research and Indigenous Peoples*. Zed Books-University of Otago Press, New York, 1999.

———. "Kaupapa Maori Research." In *Reclaiming Indigenous Voice and Vision*, edited by M. Battiste, 225–47. UBC Press, Vancouver, 2000.

———. "On Tricky Ground: Researching the Native in the Age of Uncertainty." In *The SAGE Handbook of Qualitative Research*, edited by N. K. Denzin and Y. S. Lincoln, 85–108. 3rd ed. Sage, Thousand Oaks, CA, 2005.

———. "Choosing the Margins: The Role of Research in Indigenous Struggles for Social Justice." In *Qualitative Inquiry and the Conservative Challenge: Confronting Methodological Fundamentalism*, edited by N. K. Denzin and M. D. Giardina, 151–74. Left Coast Press, Walnut Creek, CA, 2006.

Social Science and Humanities Research Council of Canada. 2011. "Insight Grant Guidelines." www.sshrc-crsh.gc.ca/funding-financement/programs-programmes/insight_grants-subventions_savoir-eng.aspx.

Society for American Archaeology. Principles of Archaeological Ethics, 1996, at www.saa.org/AbouttheSociety/PrinciplesofArchaeologicalEthics/tabid/203/Default.aspx (accessed March 12, 2012).

Society for American Archaeology. Archaeology for the Public, 2005, at www.saa.org/publicftp/PUBLIC/home/home.html (accessed March 12, 2012).

Society for American Archaeology. Committee on Curriculum Charge, 2011. https://ecommerce.saa.org/saa/staticcontent/staticpages/adminDir/committeeDisplay.cfm?Committee=COMMITTEE%2FCURC.

Soto, L. D. "Foreword. Decolonizing Research in Cross-Cultural Contexts: Issue of Voice and Power." In *Decolonizing Research in Cross-Cultural Contexts: Critical Personal Narratives*, edited by K. Mutua and B. B. Swadener, ix–xi. State University of New York Press, Albany, NY, 2004.

Spector, J. *What This Awl Means: Feminist Archaeology at a Wahpeton Dakota Village.* Minnesota Historical Society Press, St. Paul, 1993.

Stoecker, R. "Are Academics Irrelevant?: Roles for Scholars in Participatory Research." *American Behavioral Scientist* 42, no. 5 (1999): 840–54.

———. *Creative Tensions in the New Community Based Research.* Keynote address prepared for the Community-Based Research Network Symposium. Carleton University, Ottawa, Canada, 2004.

———. Research Methods for Community Change: A Project-Based Approach. Sage Publishing, Thousand Oaks, CA, 2005.

Stoecker, R., E. A. Tryon, and A. Hilgendorf. *The Unheard Voices: Community Organizations and Service Learning.* Temple University Press, Philadelphia, 2009.

Strand, K., S. Marullo, N. Cutforth, R. Stoecker, and P. Donohue. *Community-Based Research and Higher Education: Principles and Practices.* 1st ed. The Jossey-Bass Higher and Adult Education series. Jossey-Bass, San Francisco, 2003.

Stringer, E. T. *Action Research.* 3rd ed. Sage Publications, Los Angeles, 2007.

Swidler, N., and Society of American Archaeology. *Native Americans and Archaeologists: Stepping Stones to Common Ground.* AltaMira Press, Lanham, MD, 1997.

Tax, S. "The Fox Project." *Human Organization* 17, no. 1 (1958): 17–19.

Tesar, L. "Cooperative Archaeology: The St. Augustine Example." *Florida Anthropologist* 39, no. 4 (1986): 287–92.

Thomas, D. H. *Skull Wars: Kennewick Man, Archaeology, and the Battle for Native American Identity.* 1st ed. Basic Books, New York, 2000.

Thomas, D. H. "Forward." In *Collaboration in Archaeological Practice: Engaging Descendant Communities,*" edited by C. Colwell-Chanthaphonh and T. J. Ferguson, vii–xii. AltaMira Press, Lanham, MD, 2008.

Ticktin, T., and T. Johns. "Chinateco Management of Aechmea Magdalenae: Implications for the Use of TEKand TRM in Management of Plants." *Economic Botany* 56, no. 2 (2002): 177–91.

Trigger, B. G. *A History of Archaeological Thought.* 2nd ed. Cambridge University Press, Cambridge [England]; New York, 2006.

University of Victoria Faculty of Human and Social Development. *Protocols and Principles for Conducting Research in an Indigenous Context,* 2003. http://web.uvic.ca/igov/uploads/pdf/Indigenous%20Research%20Protocols.pdf.

Vio Grossi, F. "The Socio-Political Implications of Participatory Research." In *Research for the People, Research by the People: Selected Papers from the International Forum on Participatory Research in Ljubljana, Yugoslavia*, edited by F. Dubell, T. Erasmie and J. D. Vries, 69–80. Netherlands Study and Development Centre for Adult Education, Amersfoort, Holland, 1980.

Wainwright, H., and D. Elliott. *The Lucas Plan: A New Trade Unionism in the Making?* Allison and Busby, London, 1982.

Watkins, J., and Ferguson, T. J. "Working with and Working for Indigenous Communities." In *Handbook of Archaeological Methods*, vol. 2, edited by D. G. Herbert Maschner and C. Chippendale, pp. 1,372–1,406. AltaMira Press, Walnut Creek, CA, 2005.

Whyte, W. F. *Participatory Action Research*. Sage Publications, Newbury Park, CA, 1991.

Wilcox, M. V. *The Pueblo Revolt and the Mythology of Conquest: An Indigenous Archaeology of Contact*. University of California Press, Berkeley, 2009.

Williams, E. M., J. Anderson, R. Lee, J. White, and D. Hahn-Baker. "Behind the Fence Forum Theater: An Arts Performance Partnership To Address Lupus and Environmental Justice." *New Solutions* 19, no. 4 (2009): 467–79.

Wilmsen, C. "Negotiating Community, Participation, Knowledge and Power in Participatory Research." In *Partnerships for Empowerment: Participatory Research for Community-Based Natural Resource Management*, edited by C. Wilmsen, W. Elmendorf, L. Fisher, J. Ross, B. Sarathy and G. Wells, 1–22. Earthscan, London, 2008.

Wilmsen, C., W. Elmendorf, L. Fisher, J. Ross, B. Sarathy, and G. Wells. *Partnerships for Empowerment: Participatory Research for Community-Based Natural Resource Management*. Earthscan, London; Sterling, VA, 2008.

Wilson, A. C. "Reclaiming our Humanity: Decolonization and the Recovery of Indigenous Knowledge." In *Indigenizing the Academy: Transforming Scholarship and Empowering Communities*, edited by D. A. Mihesuah and A. C. Wilson, 69–87. 1 vols. University of Nebraska Press, Lincoln, 2004.

Wilson, A. C., and M. Yellow Bird (eds.). *For Indigenous Eyes Only: A Decolonization Handbook*. School of American Research, Santa Fe, 2005.

Wilson, S. *Research is Ceremony: Indigenous Research Methods*. Fernwood Pub., Black Point, N.S., 2008.

Wiynjorroc, P., P. Manabaru, N. Brown, and A. Warner. "We Just Have To Show You: Research Ethics Blekbalawei." In *Indigenous Archaeologies: Decolonizing Theory and Practice*, edited by C. Smith and H. M. Wobst, 316–27. Routledge, New York, 2005.

Wondolleck, J. M., and S. L. Yaffee. *Making Collaboration Work: Lessons from Innovation in Natural Resource Management*. Island Press, Washington, DC, 2000.

Wulfhorst, J. D., B. Eisenhauer, S. Gripne, and J. Ward. "Core Criteria and Assessment of Participatory Research." In *Partnerships for Empowerment: Participatory Research for Community-Based Natural Resource Management*, edited by C. Wilmsen, W. Elmendorf, L. Fisher, J. Ross, B. Sarathy, and G. Wells, 23–46. Earthscan, London, 2008.

Wylie, A. "Foreword." In *Working Together: Native Americans and Archaeologists*, edited by K. Dongoske, M. Aldenderfer, and K. Doehner, v–ix. Society for American Archaeology, Washington, DC, 2000.

Yellowhorn, E. *Awakening Internalist Archaeology in the Aboriginal World*, McGill, 2002.

Ziibiwing Center of Anishinabe Culture and Lifeways. Mission Statement. www .sagchip.org/ziibiwing/aboutus/mission.htm, 2011.

Zimmerer, J. "Colonialism and the Holocaust—Towards an Archeology of Genocide." *Development Dialogue* 50 (December 2008): 95–123.

Zimmerman, L. "Made Radical By My Own: An Archaeologist Learns to Understand Reburial." In *Conflict in the Archaeology of Living Traditions*, edited by R. Layton, 60–67. Unwin-Hyman, London, 1989.

———. "A New and Different Archaeology. With a Postscript on the Impact of the Kennewick Dispute." In *Repatriation Reader: Who Owns American Indian Remains?*, edited by D. A. Mihesuah, 294–306. University of Nebraska Press, Lincoln, 2000.

INDEX

Pages followed by *fig* or *map* indicate figures or maps, respectively.

Canada, 46, 53–54

Cantrel, Dustin, 271*fig*

capacity building: with adult education programs, 214–16; advocacy research, 45; benefits of, 249–50; at Çatalhöyük project, 14–15, 71; community interns, 210–14; end of partnership as sign of success, 256–57; field schools for community education, 208–10; joint authorship for, 233; at national level, 216–17; participatory fieldwork to build, 221–22; as principle of CBPR, 71–73; social change through, 79

Çatalhöyük project: animator role in, 115–16; benefits to archaeology, 218–19; benefits to community, 242–45; calls to prayer at, 186; capacity building and, 14–15, 71; class issues with participation, 98; communication issues, 174–75; community interns at, 210–14; community meetings for, 155–59, 156–58*fig*; community reports, 225–30; disenfranchisement of locals with, 6–7; educational efforts about, 14, 186–87, 190–95, 192–93*fig*; establishing like-mindedness for, 145; ethnographic research at, 149–50, 153–54; goddess group and, 95–96, 120–21; inclusion problems with participation in, 70–71; integrating local knowledge, 77; interviews with residents to develop interest, 13–14, 137; joint authorship issues, 234–35; language barriers, 263; leadership changes in region, 165; looting at, 135, 140, 218; methods used for full participation, 100–101; multilevel review process for, 131–32; overview of, 12–15, 13–14*map*; partnership creation in, 95–97, 119; presenting CBPR principles to, 139–42; research design for, 181; researching sale of to Çumra, 145–47, 241–42; research question

development, 175–76, 176–77*fig*; timing issues, 259; transitioning from traditional to CBPR research, 135–37; transparency to increase trust, 220; women's participation in, 70–71, 96–97

Cayuga Native American community, 119–20

CBOs (community-based organizations), 113–15, 135

CBPR. *See* community-based participatory research (CBPR)

cedar baths, 245, 246*fig*

civic engagement archaeology, 50*fig*, 273–74

class, 98, 126

CNAR (Committee on Native American Relations), 108–9

Code of Professional Standards (AIA), 42

collaboration: consultation compared, 38, 47–48, 48*fig*; continuum of, 30, 47–48, 48*fig*; as core of sustainability, 3, 7; definition of, 44, 49*fig*, 55–56; desire dependent on respect and inclusion, 35–36; Indigenous archaeology compared, 39; motivations for, 43–44; shared decision making, 167–71; as success, 254; terminology for, 49–50*fig*; valuing community knowledge, 3–5. *See also* participatory research

collaborative archaeology, definition of, 49*fig*

collaborative inquiry, 51–54

Colwell-Chanthaphonh, Chip, 31–32, 267

comic series, 191, 192*fig*, 227–28, 229–30*fig*

Committee on Native American Relations (CNAR), 108–9

communication: about data release, 237–39; about reciprocal benefits, 250–51; in Çatalhöyük project, 174–75; difficulty with, 262–63; presenting yourself to the

community, 124–27; in research design, 171–75, 182–83
communication differential, 61
communities, 90–95, 92*fig*, 132–34
communities of identity, 90
community archaeology, 48, 49*fig*, 51
community-based consultant model, 46–47, 48*fig*
community-based organizations (CBOs), 113–15, 135
community-based participatory research (CBPR): benefits to archaeology community from, 250–53; for collaborative inquiry, 52; conventional research compared, 85–87*fig*; critiques of, 87–88; foundations in archaeology of, 44–45; global applicability of, 5–7; lasting effects of, 274–75; linking with theory to improve practice, 50; paradigm shift caused by, 53–54; valuing community knowledge, 3–5. *See also* origins of CBPR; principles of CBPR
community-based research, 61, 62
community-based theater, 192–93, 193*fig*
community buy-in, 257–58
community capacity. *See* capacity building
community-evaluation procedures, 80
community interns, 210–14
community knowledge, valuing of, 3–5, 75–77, 143–44, 266
community literature libraries, 264
community meetings, 154–59, 156–58*fig*
community organizer role, 178
community reports, 224–31
complex communities, 116–20
compromise, 169–70
conferences, 109, 236–37
consent for research, 10
consultation: archaeologists hired for, 46–47; collaboration compared, 38, 47–48, 48*fig*; legally required, 34–35; limits on impacts of, 34–37

contracts to formalize agreements, 162–63, 169
conventional archaeological research, CBPR compared, 85–87*fig*
cooperative archaeology, definition of, 49*fig*
Couto, Richard, 253, 273
covenantal archaeology, definition of, 49*fig*
credibility. *See* trust
cultural competence: increasing, 122–24; respecting cultural protocols in research design, 183–86; smudging at Stone Street project, 123, 123*fig*, 185
cultural tourism: access to literature barriers, 263–65; at Çatalhöyük project, 212, 213*fig*, 242–43; heritage management issues with, 5–6; for Waapaahsiiki Siipiiwi mound project, 238
Çumra, 95, 119, 145–47, 241–42
curriculum issues. *See* education (of archaeologists)
Custer Died for Your Sins (Deloria), 31–32
Cutforth, N., 63, 102, 168

data collection: benefits to archaeology of community participation in, 217–19; community reports as part of, 231; community research team involvement in, 197; determining what to collect, 198–99; at Flint Stone Street Ancestral Recovery and Site Management Project, 200–203, 201*fig*; methods for, 198; overview of, 196–97; qualitative data, 204–8; shared motivations for, 219–22. *See also* capacity building
data presentation: to academic audiences, 232–33; community partners as primary audience for, 222–23; community reports, 224–31;

establishing trust and committment, 142–47; expertise as limiting partnership creation, 137–39; identifying sensitive areas, 147–50; leadership changes, 164–66; pace of starting, 134–37; presenting CBPR principles to potential partners, 139–42; research review and approval, 129–32; terminology problems, 141–42; who speaks for community, 132–34. *See also* collaboration; ethnographic research; partnership creation

Freire, Paulo, 2, 160–61, 215, 240

Fritz, J. M., 2

funding: conference presentations, 236; by corporations, 45; data collection rules and, 203; problems with obtaining, 260–61; rigor issues with, 83–84; shared decision making on handling of, 170

Garcia, Joe, 10

Gaventa, J., 57–59

gender, 100, 156. *See also* women

goddess group, in Çatalhöyük project, 95–96, 120–21

governing councils, permissions from, 130–31

graphic novels, 228, 229–30*fig*

Grey, Barbara, 55

Hall, Budd, 111–12

hantavirus outbreak, Navajo knowledge about, 4

Havasupai tribe, blood samples used without permission, 10

health clinic, 244–45

Heany, T., 79–80, 260, 261

Heard, Anita, 201*fig*

"helicopter research," 111–13

heritage management: access to literature barriers for, 263–65; community participation to improve, 69; for cultural tourism, 5–6; local committees for,

245; shifting to local communities, 6. *See also* Çatalhöyük project

Highlander School, 215

history of CBPR. *See* origins of CBPR

Hole, L. D., 40–41

hooks, bell, 251–52

Hopi, 225. *See also* San Pedro Valley Ethnohistory Project (SPVE)

Horton, Myles, 215

host-guest model, 38–39

human subject protection protocols, 22, 129–30

Hutchinson, P., 40–41

ideology, to determine methodology, 160–62

imaginary communities, 93

Indiana, tribes in, 247–48

Indigenous archaeology, 39–42

Indigenous peoples, 8, 53–54. *See also* Native Americans; *specific tribes*

institutional review board (IRB) process, 22–23, 129–30, 261–62

institutions, participatory engagement of, 80–82

intellectual property issues, 266–67. *See also* Ziibiwing Sanilac petroglyph intellectual property project

Intellectual Property Issues in Cultural Heritage (IPinCH) project, 17, 232–33, 266–67

Internet, 174, 231, 263

interns, 210–14

interviews, 13–14, 67, 137

involvement, participation compared, 66–67

IRB (institutional review board) process, 22–23, 129–30, 261–62

Israel, B. A., 90

Johnson, William, 16, 18, 201*fig*, 271–72*fig*

joint authorship, 233–35

Native American Graves Protection and Repatriation Act (NAGPRA), 8, 34, 206, 216

Native Americans: archaeology training programs for, 188–89; capacity building, 71–72; existing relationships with limited, 102–3; hesitation to partner by, 103–4; in Indiana, 247; legislative changes due to activism by, 34–35; paradigm shift in research about, 53–54; power sharing needed with, 8; Red Power movement, 30–34; respect for knowledge of, 37; stewardship by elders, 31; veto power over data collection, 199. *See also* San Pedro Valley Ethnohistory Project (SPVE); *specific tribes*

Navajo Nation, 4, 72

Nicholas, George, 39, 215

Nichols, Teresa, 271*fig*, 272*fig*

NMAI Act (National Museum of the American Indian), 8, 34

"The Opportunities in Aboriginal Research Dialogue," 268

Opportunities in Aboriginal Research: Results of SSHRC's Dialogue on Research and Aboriginal Peoples (McNaughton and Rock), 132–33

oral traditions, 144–45

origins of CBPR: alternative methodologies sought after Native American activism, 35–37; Indigenous archaeology, 39–42; methodology development of, 59–62, 60*fig*; motivations for collaboration, 43–44; partnership approach development, 37–39; public archaeology impact on, 42–43; Red Power movement, 30–34

oshki anishinabe, 34

outreach. *See* education (of community); public archaeology

pacing issues, 258–60

paired chapter approach, 235–36

"parachute research," 111–13

Parker, E. A., 90

participatory research: archaeologists role in, 178; collaboratively defining extent of, 69–70; community-based research compared, 62; definition of, 59; end of partnership as sign of success, 256–57; as influence on CBPR, 60*fig*; involvement compared, 66–67; national engagement for, 80–82; as principle of CBPR, 66–71; tenure issues, 261–62; who participates in, 69–71. *See also* collaboration

partnership creation: animator role for, 115–16; archaeologists seeking of, 110–11; avoiding "drive-by" CBPR, 111–13; beginnings of, 37–39; in Çatalhöyük project, 95–97; challenges in, 109–10; close connections issues, 106; communities solicitation of, 106–9; community-based organizations to help with, 113–15; in complex communities, 116–20; consequences of choices about, 120–21; contracts to formalize agreements, 162–63; cultural competence and, 122–24; existing relationships to connect for, 102–4; expertise as limiting, 137–39; foundations for, 128–29; full community participation, 97–101; needs defined, 90–95; personal and professional relationships to connect for, 104–6; as power sharing, 64–65; presenting CBPR principles to potential partners, 139–42; presenting yourself to the community, 124–27; professional associations' role in, 107–9; as recursive process, 159; sociopolitical contexts effecting, 121–22; values needed for, 38

patriarchy, damage from, 251–52

peer training, 214–15

permissions: community review, 130–31; institutional review board process, 22–23, 129–30; leadership changes and effect on, 164–65; non-renewal of projects, 165–66; process for granting, 133–34; who speaks for community, 132–34

Petoskey, Reg, 68*fig*, 105, 124*fig*

petroglyphs. *See* Ziibiwing Sanilac petroglyph intellectual property project

plain-language summaries of research, 264

Plog, F. T., 2

Pokagon Band of Pottawatomi, 247

Policy Research Center, 11

politics, 121–22, 148–49

popular education. *See* education (of community)

positioned rationality, 99–100

power: ethnographic research on, 152; imbalance of, 57–59, 138–39; involvement of certain segments limited by lack of, 98–99; and knowledge production, 56–59; long-term committment to help balance, 112; mutuality needed for, 64; partnerships as sharing of, 64–65; sharing for decision making, 64–65, 168–71

primary stakeholders, identification of, 119

Principles of Archaeological Ethics, 42–43, 265–66

principles of CBPR: capacity building, 71–73; community-based partnerships, 63–66; Indigenous and local knowledge recognized, 75–77; national engagement for, 80–82; participatory nature of research, 66–71; reciprocity of benefits, 73–75; social change, 78–80; systematic restitution, 61–62. *See also* collaboration

problematization, 2

professional associations: participatory engagement of, 80–82; partnership creation role, 107–9

protests, by Native Americans against excavation of remains, 33

"Protocols and Principles for Conducting Research in an Indigenous Context," 267–68

public archaeology, 42–43, 48*fig*, 50*fig*, 51. *See also* education (of community)

public involvement, 1–3, 43–44

Pyburn, A., 150–51

reciprocity, 37–38, 73–75, 250

recursive process, 159

Red Power movement, 30–34

relevance, increasing, 2–3. *See also* benefits; lasting effects

repatriation, 9, 33–34. *See also* Ziibiwing repatriation research project

research design: in archaeological CBPR, 180–82; communication needs for, 171–75, 182–83; evaluation to inform changes needed to, 255; intellectual property issues and, 232; research question development, 175–80, 176–77*fig*; respecting cultural protocols in, 183–86; shared decision making for, 167–71. *See also* education (of community)

research results, inaccessibility issues, 47

respect: for elders, 123, 124*fig*; importance of, 37; Seven Grandfather Teachings of, 66, 67*fig*

review processes, 22–23, 129–30, 162–64

rigor, 82–84

Robinson, M. P., 45

Rock, D., 132–33

Rossen, J., 164

SAA (Society for American Archaeology): Committee on Native American Relations, 108–9;

curriculum committee, 273; ethical principles of, 42–43, 265–66; funding, 216, 236; partnership creation role, 108–9

Saginaw Chippewa Indian Tribe of Michigan, 15, 16*map*, 113–14, 118–19. *See also* Flint Stone Street Ancestral Recovery and Site Management Project

salal, 92

Salur, Nesrin, 211–13

Salur, Rahime, 211–13

Sangtin Writers collective, 121

Sanilac petroglyph intellectual property project. *See* Ziibiwing Sanilac petroglyph intellectual property project

San Pedro Valley Ethnohistory Project (SPVE): braiding knowledge at, 207; community reports, 225; data collection community participation, 203–4; partnership creation, 94; qualitative data use, 205

Saskatchewan Indian Federated College, 53

SCAIC. *See* Sullivan County American Indian Council (SCAIC)

Schliemann, Heinrich, 218

Schulz, A. J., 90

scientists, conventional versus civil, 64, 235

self-education, 214–15

self investigation and control, 61–62

service-learning archaeology, definition of, 50*fig*

Seven Grandfather Teachings, 66, 67*fig*

"Shampoo Archaeology" (Robinson), 45

Shankland, David, 153

SHARE, 94–95

shared authority, 168. *See also* power

Silliman, S. W., 36, 39, 122

simplicity of communication, 61

skill building. *See* capacity building

Smith, Beverly, 181

Smith, Linda Tuhiwai, 10, 40

smudging, 123, 123*fig*, 185

social change, 78–80

social justice, 78–80

Social Science and Humanities Research Council of Canada (SSHRC), 53, 194, 268

Society for American Archaeology (SAA): Committee on Native American Relations, 108–9; curriculum committee, 273; ethical principles of, 42–43, 265–66; funding, 216, 236; partnership creation role, 108–9

sociopolitical contexts, 121–22, 148–49

Sookraj, D., 40–41

Spencer, Mark, 201*fig*

spiral of knowledge, 62

SPVE. *See* San Pedro Valley Ethnohistory Project (SPVE)

SSHRC (Social Science and Humanities Research Council of Canada), 53, 194, 268

stewardship, 31, 44, 46, 265

Stoecker, R., 63, 102, 168

Stone Street Ancestral Recovery and Site Management Project. *See* Flint Stone Street Ancestral Recovery and Site Management Project

Strand, K., 63, 102, 168, 270

Stringer, E. T., 122

Sullivan County American Indian Council (SCAIC): about, 20; community meetings for, 158; harnessing personal connections to partner with, 105; participation in decision making process, 68, 68*fig*. *See also* Waapaahsiiki Siipiiwi mound project

sustainability, collaboration at core of, 3, 7

systematic restitution, 61–62